James Philip, Alexander Drimmie Murdoch

The Grameid

An Heroic Poem Descriptive of the Campaign of Viscount Dundee in 1689

James Philip, Alexander Drimmie Murdoch

The Grameid

An Heroic Poem Descriptive of the Campaign of Viscount Dundee in 1689

ISBN/EAN: 9783337190781

Printed in Europe, USA, Canada, Australia, Japan

Cover: Foto ©ninafisch / pixelio.de

More available books at **www.hansebooks.com**

THE GRAMEID

AN HEROIC POEM

DESCRIPTIVE OF THE CAMPAIGN

OF VISCOUNT DUNDEE IN 1689

AND OTHER PIECES

By JAMES PHILIP of, Almerieclose
1691

Edited from the Original Manuscript with Translation,
Introduction, and Notes by the Rev.
ALEXANDER D. MURDOCH, F.S.A. Scot.

EDINBURGH
Printed at the University Press by T. and A. Constable
for the Scottish History Society
1888

CONTENTS.

PAGES

PREFACE—

Family of the Philips of Almerieclose—James Philip, the author of the *Grameid*—Manuscripts of the *Grameid*—The Evidence of Authorship—The name 'Panurgus Philo-caballus'—Historical value of the Poem, ... ix-xlviii

APPENDIX TO PREFACE—

Additional Corrections, ... xlix-lvi

THE POEM—

BOOK I.

The purpose of the Poet is stated—He sings of the civil war in Scotland, and its great hero the Graham—The infamy of such a war—Its origin traced to love of revolution and to religious contentions—The Furies unite themselves with zest to the rising commotions, and seek to renew the wars so lately ended—The spirit of revolution and polemical strife traced in their operation, through the civil wars and death of Charles the Martyr, to James, whose change of faith stirred again the slumbering fires, and Bishops, Nobles, Generals, common soldiers, and people, are lashed into fury through the rumours circulated; 'the signifer doli' being the Prince of Orange—The development of the narrative is accompanied with epic adjuncts of numerous portents, and with copious reference to contemporary history—The denunciations of

CONTENTS.

William and Mary being specially violent, and the devotion to the King, the Queen, and the Prince of Wales very marked—The last named is invoked as tutelary patron of the epic on the Graham—At the hoped-for restoration he promises to sing in nobler strain the story of the Prince himself, . . . 1-37

BOOK II.

With short preface on the state of stupor following the flight of the King, the hero is introduced as a Phœnix rising from the ashes of Montrose—His descent, past history and fame; his association with James before his flight; his return to Scotland; action in the Convention, and departure from it; his raising the standard for King James on the Law of Dundee; his parting with his wife; his retreat to the Glen of Ogilvy, are all given in detail—Dundee marches by Kirriemuir, North Water Bridge, and Cairn o' Mount, followed slowly by Mackay to Fettercairn — He proceeds as far as Forres, and returns to the Cairn, returning again by Aboyne, Huntly, Keith, Castle Gordon, Elgin, to Forres, and then on to Inverness, where he finds Keppoch — Deserted by that chief, he passes by Stratherrick to Invergarry and Kilcummin, and thence by Corryarrick to Strathspey, and by Cluny to Presmochora—Here he fixes the day of gathering, and summons the clans—The time before the gathering is filled up with a descent by Claverhouse and his seventy horsemen upon Dunkeld, Perth, and Dundee, whence he returns with spoil and prisoners to the Highlands, reaching Lochaber by Strathtay and Rannoch, after a fearful march, . . 38-78

CONTENTS.

BOOK III.

PAGES

Description of Lochaber—Physical features—Natives, their habits and customs—Fabulous history—The influence of Fergus in their civilisation—Accounting for their loyalty to the Stuarts—Hardships of Dundee and his followers in Glen Roy — The greatness of the hero shown in these adversities— He apostrophises the absent King — Glengarry joins Dundee — Speech of Dundee—Speech of Glengarry—The uprising of Gaels to take solemnly the oath of loyalty to the King and the General— Another address of Dundee—Denis M'Swyne is despatched to Ireland with verbal message to the King—Mackay's movements referred to—Contrasts presented by the two Generals—Spirited comparison, ... 79-117

BOOK IV.

Glengarry sends forth the fiery cross—Rousing of the clans—The districts from which they come—The preparations for war—The gathering at Dalmacommer—Portraits of the chiefs and chieftains, with description of their various forces, dress, equipment, etc.—The host being marshalled is addressed by Dundee, Glengarry leading the van, and Fraser of Foyers bringing up the rear—The march is begun by Glen Roy, and over the hills to Garviemore—Description of the army on the march—Dundee encamps at the Castle of Raitts— Solemnities of the 29th May—Castle of Ruthven summoned, and allowed a truce for three days, the commander Forbes agreeing to surrender if not relieved by Mackay in that time—Keppoch intrusted with the siege—Forbes surrenders, and is allowed to march out, while Keppoch burns the castle—Mackay is discovered encamped at the Kirk of Alvie—Captain Bruce assails him and the dragoons with reproaches, and hastily returns to Dundee, who moves rapidly against Mackay—Mackay flies in the night, and is pursued by Dundee through Rothiemurchus, Abernethy, Cromdale, Balveny, to Edinglassie, . . 118-186

BOOK V.

Consternation in Edinburgh described—Duke of Hamilton's speech in the Convention and its effect—Despatch of General Ramsay, and his failure to penetrate through Athole—The author (wrongly) relates his junction with Mackay at Suy Hill, and his reproaching that general—Dundee holds a council of war at Edinglassie, and resolves to retreat—He is warned by a dragoon from Mackay's force that that general, with increased strength, is now approaching him rapidly—He makes a forced march by Glen Fiddich and Glen Livet to Cromdale, and thence to Abernethy, pursued by Mackay at considerable distance—The affair of Knockbrecht fully described—Dundee retires to Glen Roy, and Mackay goes south to report himself in Edinburgh—Wearily waiting in Lochaber for the promised Irish contingent, Dundee, to a choice circle of chiefs, relations, and friends, gives a long account of the spirit and the doings of the Scotch Presbyter, from the time of Mary Queen of Scots till his own time, and refers to his own experiences of him, ... 187-235

BOOK VI.

PAGES

The scene is moved to Ireland, where James mourns his defeats, and repents of his attitude towards Dundee, abusing the counsellors who have hitherto treacherously held back the merits of the great and successful general—He determines to send him men and arms, and Buchan, Cannon, and Pursell are despatched—They leave the port, and sail for Scotland, and here at the fifty-fifth line the MS. abruptly closes, ... 236-240

POEMATA, . . . 241-248

EPIGRAMMATA, . . . 249-253

EPITAPH BY THE AUTHOR ON WILLIAM AIKMAN, . . 254-255

INDEX, ... 257-268

PREFACE.

BY way of introduction to the hitherto unpublished and almost unknown verses of James Philip, I propose to place before the Scottish History Society the few facts concerning him and his family which I have been able to gather, and to give some account of his curious work. That James Philip (to adopt the modern spelling of the name, which more frequently in the old documents appears as Philp or Philpe, which agrees with the present local pronunciation) was the author of these verses appears never to have been questioned, but lest question should arise, I propose to submit the evidence when I come to speak of the MSS. in which they have come down to us.

The author was the son of James Philp of Almerieclose, a small property in and near Arbroath, composed of several crofts and bits of lands, separately acquired, and gathered round the old Almonry premises of the ruined Abbey. His mother was Margaret Graham, a daughter of the house of Duntrune[1] in Forfarshire, and second cousin of the hero of the *Grameid*, John Graham of Claverhouse. The date of the author's birth is about 1656 or 1657.

It may be well, before going on with the personal history of the bard, to give at this stage some account of the family from which he came, and some view of his immediate surroundings.

The name Philp is an old one, and, according to Stodart, makes its appearance in Fife about the middle of the fifteenth

---

[1] So spelt in Forfarshire.

century, when Stephen Philp was bailie of Newburgh in 1473, and Sir James Philp was curate of Abdie in 1481. John Philp was Abbot of Lindores from 1522 to 1566; he sat in Parliament, and was a Lord of Session. No doubt these positions, at a time like that of the Reformation in Scotland, enabled their holder to secure considerable possessions, and we find the Abbot granting a charter to his cousin, James Philp of Ormiston, near Newburgh. Philp of Ormiston was chief of the name in Scotland. Pont gives for the surname of Philp gules on a chevron argent, between two mullets or, a boar's head, and a mullet of the field. Elizabeth Fleming, wife of Archbishop Burnett of St. Andrews, was maternally descended from the Philps; the arms ascribed to her in a funeral escutcheon seem at first to have been a chevron between three mascles, and to have been altered to a chevron between three talbots' heads, couped, and charged with as many lozenges. Philp was one of the quarterings of the first Countess of Leven, *née* Renton, for her father's mother. We shall find the talbots' heads re-appearing in the arms which the father of our author registered in 1672. The name had a considerable extension in Fife, embracing the families of Kippo, Over Carnbee, Colden, etc. Henry Philp, a scion of one of these families, the great-grandfather of the Poet, was minister of Criech at the close of the sixteenth century, and was transferred to Arbroath in 1601. The authorities of that burgh had, some ten years previously, completed the building of a parish church, aided by a gift of stones from the dormitory of the Abbey, and other extraneous help; and for the stipend of a clergyman they had received a third of the rental of the Lady Chapel, amounting to at least £30 a year. This would seem to have been Philp's stipend, and there is no record of the provision of a house.[1]

---

[1] Hay, writing in 1876, says : 'It may be mentioned that, although an allowance for house-rent had long been paid to the parish minister, it was only during the present incumbency that a manse was acquired, and, as yet, no glebe is attached to the benefice.'—Hay's *History of Arbroath*, p. 198.

The magistrates were the heritors, and kept an account of their outlays. Some of their payments are germane to our subject as occurring during Philp's ministry. We find 18s. for communion bread, 55s. 4d. for candle to the kirk, 2s. for mending of the sand-glass—no doubt that by which the minister measured his sermon,—£3 for a desk to the school. Thomas Ramsay, 'glass wricht,' had a fee of £4 for upholding the kirk windows.[1] The kirk is the same as that now known as the Auld Kirk, but it has been much changed and enlarged since Philp's day. His immediate predecessor in the charge was Andrew Lamb, who was translated to South Leith in 1600, and consecrated as Bishop of Brechin in the chapel of London House on the 21st October 1610. Lamb's predecessor was James Melvill, the well-known Presbyterian, who succeeded the first of the Reformation ministers, Ninian Clement. Clement had been assisted by Thomas Lindsay, formerly a monk of the Abbey, and to whom, at a meeting of the inhabitants of the Eleemosynary, the Commendator of the Abbey committed the collecting and administering of the dues payable on heritages in that part of the burgh for the relief of the poor. It is probable that Lindsay performed his functions in the dwelling and offices of Almerieclose, where Henry Philp afterwards took up his abode on being transferred to Arbroath in 1601. Presbyterianism was at this time established, along with a titular Episcopacy, but the accession of King James to the crown of England in 1603 brought about, in 1610, the filling of the Scotch sees with consecrated bishops. Henry Philp was therefore the transition pastor of Arbroath, and it is clear that the change from Presbyterian to Episcopal polity was what he earnestly desired. We find him a member of Assembly in 1602, and Clerk of the Assembly of 1606, a post to which he was nominated by the Moderator, James Nicolson, afterwards titular Bishop of

---

[1] Hay, pp. 194 and 195.

Dunkeld, much to the distaste of the fanatical party. The following notice in Forbes's *Records touching the Estate of the Kirk* indicates the view taken by the party which he represents of the line which the minister of Arbroath had adopted. Forbes says: 'About the latter end of June 1606 the King sent for some of the ministers to come to him against the 15th day of September next following. The persons sent for were these: Mr. Andrew Melvill, James Melvill, James Balfour, William Scott, William Watson, John Carmichell, Robert Wallace, Adam Colt, and Henry Philipe, of the which the first eight were known to be of the most learned, wise, faithful, and upright in the land, and thus most opposite to all the wickedness of the bishops and commissioners; the last being of another disposition was purposlie (as it was thought) sent through the policie of Mr. James Nicolson, to the end that, being in company with the others, he might be acquainted with their mind, and give intelligence thereof to the King, and to the bishops and commissioners. But this policie being perceived, the danger was prevented by the others refusing to have him in their companie.' Philp was member of the Assemblies of 1608, 1610, 1616, and 1618. In the last named, which promulgated the Articles of Perth, he took a prominent part in support of the Articles, as witnessed by the well-known letter of the Commissioner, Lord Binning, to the King, dated 'St. Johnstone, 27th August, at night, 1618.' Lord Binning twice mentions Henry Philp along with the two Archbishops and Dr. Lindsay of Dundee, and commends the faithful and profitable endeavours of these wise and learned men to the gracious remembrance of his Majesty. There is no evidence of any gracious remembrance on the part of the King of the wise and learned pastor of Aberbrothock after this date, but previous to it, on 20th January 1610, he was presented by King James with the modified stipend, and he was placed in the unenviable position of a member of the Court of High

Commission. The University of St. Andrews had conferred on him the degree of D.D. in 1616, and the Town Council of Arbroath had bestowed on him the somewhat unusual honour for an ecclesiastic, of electing him an extraordinary member of that body. Among other labours for the good of the Church at large, he had taken part in the Conference at Falkland for the healing divisions, and promoting peace and discipline in the Church, 4th May 1609.

Dr. Philp had married Isabel Paterson (spelt in his will Piterson), by whom he had at least three children, James, Marjory, and Isabel. He died in February 1628, and his wife followed him to the grave the next month. He had earned a character for ability and intelligence, and had the complete trust and confidence of his parishioners. His will was registered by his daughter Marjory at St. Andrews, 2d January 1629. He leaves his property to Marjory, with benefit for Isabel, then in minority. There is no mention in the body of the deed of a son, but the decreet of information ends with these words, 'and Maister James Philpe, only sone and air to the defunct, is become caution,' etc. The document gives lists of utensils, buiks, horses brown and white worth £20 apiece, the whole being estimated at £300. There is a long list of debts due to the dead, and a shorter list of debts due by the dead, and the 'Frie geir' is valued at £2401. I suppose that James, the son, had already been put in possession of Almerieclose. He was a bailie of Arbroath, and may have aided in the purchase of the property. The figures of Dr. Henry Philp and his wife, Isabel Paterson, are represented on the monument which stands over their grave in the Abbey Churchyard of Arbroath, a drawing of which illustrates this volume. The figures, I think, were an offering to the memory of their parents by James, Marjory, and Isabel Philp, but were raised, perhaps, from a recumbent attitude to their present position in the more ambitious structure of which they now form a part, by James Philp, the father of the Poet, who, blazoning his arms and those of his wife, Margaret Graham, describes himself as 'the Buielder.' His initials, J. P., and those of his wife, M. G., in association with their arms, and the date 1674, at which time we know they were alive, plainly indicate the erection of the monument by them to the memory of those below. The initials of Henry Philp and Isabel Paterson in connection with the figures identify them. The other initials, I think, are to be thus read: M. is for Marjory, and J. P. below it for James Philp, the J. G. opposite giving the initials of the wife of James Philp, Jane or Isabel Guthrie,[1] of which couple we have now to speak.

James Philp is designed son and heir of Dr. Henry Philp in the testament of his father, and in charters dated 11th March and 21st April 1628. He was a bailie of Arbroath, and considerably increased the little property of Almerieclose by the purchase of various neighbouring crofts. He married Jane Guthrie, daughter of James Guthrie, minister of Arbirlot, and is described at the time as the 'laird of Almerieclose.' James Guthrie belonged to the family of Guthrie of Guthrie, and was brother of John Guthrie, Bishop of Moray, who held out against the Covenant, and garrisoned Spynie Castle in 1639, but was compelled by Monro to surrender, himself being carried prisoner to Edinburgh. He was set at liberty in 1641, and the following notices from Spalding bring him and his family together at Arbroath, where his

---

[1] For authorities see *Booke of Universall Kirk* under dates applicable. Calderwood's *Hist.*, Melvill's *Autobiog.*, Scot's *Narration*, Forbes's *Records*, Hay's *Hist. of Arbroath*, *Test. Reg. St. Andrews*, Jan. 2d, 1629. For other references see Scott's *Fasti Presby.*, *Arbroath*. Napier's *Dundee*, page 731, should be consulted. I think there can be little doubt that Scott has made a mistake in giving a son Thomas to Henry Philp, while he ignores James. He may have misread James as Thomas in the record, or misread his own note of it. His clear hand and wonderful accuracy are against the idea of a mistake in either way, and I would scarcely venture the suggestion, were it not supported by the high authority of Dr. Thomas Dickson, who has kindly found and deciphered the record for me.

niece and her husband, the bailie, would doubtless welcome them at Almerieclose. 'The sum tyme Bischop of Morray is set to libertie out of the Tolbuith of Edinbrugh, vpone cautioun, and he gois to Angouss, quhair, with his brother, Guthrie, minister at Arbirlet, in Guthrie, and Abirbrothok, now and then he quyetlie remanis, and neuer cam back to Spynne agane. . . . Aluaies, the Bischopis wyf leaves Morray, and, convoyit by hir two sons, Mr. Johne Guthrie, persone of Duffus, and Mr. Patrick Guthrie, cam to Old Abirdene vpone the 13th of May 1642, and from that past touardis Angouss, hir husband remaining in Abirbrothok, who had neuer sein vther since hir husband wes takin south.'[1] The brother of the bailie's wife became laird of Auldbar, while another brother succeeded his father in Arbirlot in 1655. It will be seen that the bailie's marriage maintained the royalist and episcopal character of his family.

We have evidence only of the birth of one son, who was named after his father, and had grown to man's estate before his father's death in 1653. Marjory and Isabel, the sisters of the bailie, had continued to reside at Arbroath, and were probably members of the household of Almerieclose, as the utensils, books, etc., of Dr. Henry Philp had been left to the ladies, the younger of whom, Isabel, was in minority at her father's death. Marjory died about the same time as her brother, and this accounts for James Philp, her nephew, being retoured as heir, not only to his father, but also in special to his grandfather. This retour is dated 11th February 1654.

The place of Dr. Philp, as minister of Arbroath, was bestowed upon Simeon Durie, who was translated from Forgan in 1628, and occupied the post throughout the eventful changes of the Church from Episcopacy to the restored Presbytery of 1638, and into the period of the Commonwealth. He would seem to have died about the time of the

---

[1] Spalding's *Trubles*, vol. ii. pp. 86, 142. Quoted by Hay.

death of our bailie and his sister, 1653. His successor, James Fraser, of the family of Philorth, arrived opportunely at Arbroath, a bachelor, needing a wife, when Isabel Philp was losing her home at Almerieclose. James, the young laird, was courting Margaret Graham of Duntrune, and things were coming to a crisis there. Before the laird's marriage took place, James Fraser and Isabel Philp had become man and wife on 14th March 1654, and so well pleased was the minister with his wife that he bought for her and himself the lands of Hospitalfield and Kirkton in 1656.

James Philp, the son of the bailie, is retoured as heir to his father in various crofts[1] and lands on 17th August 1653, and by Precept of Chancery, on which sasine is taken[2] 11th February 1654, he is served and retoured, as mentioned before, as heir of his grandfather, Henry Philp. We also find that sasine is taken, 10th November 1655, on a Charter of Resignation, in virtue of a Procuratory contained in a contract of marriage between James Philp of Almerieclose and Margaret Graham. I presume that the interpretation of this mysterious sentence would indicate that the marriage had taken place before this last-mentioned date. Margaret Graham was the daughter of Walter Graham of Duntrune, who was the son of Walter, who again was the son of Sir William Graham of Claverhouse, the curator and friend of his cousin, the great Marquis of Montrose. Margaret Graham and Claverhouse were thus second cousins. Her mother was Elizabeth Guthrie. The estate of Almerieclose was now of considerable extent, and was still increasing; the family of the young laird was a

---

[1] He is retoured as heir to his father, Mr. James Philp, bailie of Aberbrothock, in the Elemosynarie croft of the lordship of Aberbrothock, with the teynd sheaves—E. 30/; the lands of Swestmedow (or Guestmedow), with the teynd sheaves—E. 3 bolls wheat of feu-duty; ane tenement of land on the east part of said croft; ane other tenement of land—E. 40/ of feu-duty; the land of Guthriehill, extending to 9 acres within parish of St. Vigeans and regality of Aberbrothock, feu £3.

[2] Napier's *Memoirs*, vol. iii. p. 731.

good one, well connected both in Fife and Forfar, and though his father was a bailie of Arbroath, the office at that time did not even suggest a mercantile position. We have nothing to guide us as to his personal attractions in the eyes of the fair Graham, in whose veins flowed royal blood. The politics and religion of the two families were identical. The following description by John Ochterlony, laird of Guynd, of the house of Almerieclose, in the year 1684, is of interest as showing the abode of this couple and the birthplace of our author.[1] 'The Almeshouse Chapple, as now possest by James Philp of Almryclose. His hous is built of the stones thereof, and has all the apartments belonging thereto. The fabrick was great and excellent, having many fyne gardines and orchards now converted to arable ground, about which is a high stone wall, and now by the King's gift belongs to the Bishop of Brechine.' The same author, speaking of Arbroath,[2] says, 'It is a pleasant, sweet place, and excellent good land about it. They have a shore, some shipping, and a little small trade. It hath one long large street with some bye streets. It is tolerably well built, and hath some good houses in it. Hard by the towne, upon the east syd is Newgait, belonging to a gentleman of the name of Carnegy, of the family of Southesk, a very good house and pleasant place. Almryclose is in the head of the towne, and good house and yards. Smiddie Croft is a little interest belonging to a gentleman of the name of Peirsone, who is ancient, and without debait, chief of his name.' I think the house of Almerieclose can be made out in Slezer's picture of Arbroath, 1693, standing at the head of the town, to the right of the Abbey, as one would look from it towards the sea. The times were trying for loyal families, but I read of no misfortunes befalling the Almerieclose household, and Arbroath came little in the way of the troubles.

---

[1] *Spottiswoode Miscellany*, pp. 343, 344. I suppose that it is the superiority of the property that the author speaks of as belonging to the Bishop of Brechin.
[2] *Ibid.*

The visit of Montrose to Arbroath was ten years previous to the marriage of Philp, and the attempt by Oliver Cromwell to land a portion of his troops at the shore was in 1651.[1]

Our author was born, as I have already said, in 1656 or 1657, and was the only child, as far as I know, of James Philp and Margaret Graham. Coming of such a stock, belonging to a town and county so loyal as Arbroath and Angus, and entering upon consciousness during the first enthusiasms of the Restoration, it was natural that the child should be a royalist from the first. It is disappointing that I am not able to give the name of the teacher who laid the foundation of our author's classics, and formed the handwriting which we see in the neat MS. in the Advocates' Library. The Grammar School of Arbroath may claim the credit of both, and it may be that George Grainger, who was the master in 1639, still reigned in the desk when the youthful Poet entered that seminary. Mr. Hay, in his chapter on Schools and Schoolmasters, supplies no name between Grainger's and that of James Hamilton, admitted in 1675, by which time our author had left college. The assistant of the school at the time, dignified by the title of 'Doctor of the Grammar School,' and who, like his superior, was expected to teach Latin, is also unknown to me. These offices were held under the express condition that their occupants 'made good service,' and in our author's case we may well consider that the condition was fulfilled. The education thus begun was continued at the University of St. Andrews, where we find the name of 'Jacobus Philpe' under the following heading in the Acta Rectorum of that University:—

'February 9, anno dom. 1672, Nomina incorporatorum in Collegio Salvatoriano Rectore Reverendiso: Do: Domino Waltero Comrio Collegii Mariani Praefecto Regente Mr. Geo. Thomsono.'

---

[1] For an account of the hire of big guns from Dundee, the hiding of them in Barry Sands in sight of the enemy's ships, and their subsequent capture, see Hay, pp. 154, 155.

PREFACE.

After giving a column of names of those 'Recepti in primam classem,' the Acta go on to say—'eodem tempore Recepti sunt hi adolescentes quorum nomina subsequuntur in classem semi-bachalaureorum dicti collegii alumni ac Mr. Patricii Strachoni discipuli

    Ja: Blair,
    Jo: Turnbull,
    Geo: Graeme,
    Jacobus Philpe,'

and sixteen other names follow, including two Ramsays— George and John—a James Ogilvy, Duncan Menzies, and other well-known Scotch names. In the list of the 1st class also we have three Fotheringhames, a family closely related to the Duntrunes, a Lindsay, an Urquhart, and thirteen other names, all Scotch. The name Jacobus Philpe seems to be a signature, and the writing, as far as I could judge without actual comparison, corresponds with the writing in the MS. of the *Grameid*.[1] Patrick Strachan, under whose special care the semibachelors of 1672 would seem to have been placed, matriculated in 1667, and graduated in 1669. Mr. Maitland Anderson writes to me that he takes this Patrick Strachan to have been regent of the 1st class in 1670-71, of the 2d class in 1671-72, the 3d class in 1672-73, and very likely the 4th class in 1673-74, although no record of such a class exists. He did not renew the circle, which was taken up in 1674-75 by a James Strachan. Patrick was the teacher of Philpe within the college in the ordinary curriculum.[2] On July 24th, 1675 we have the following entry:—

'Nomina candidatorum utriusque Collegii quorum nomina subsequuntur qui postquam secundum leges Academiae Re-

---

[1] I would here acknowledge gratefully the courteous and ready help afforded me by the custodian of the *Acta*, Mr. Maitland Anderson, the Librarian of the University of St. Andrews.

[2] Till I received Mr. Anderson's letter, I was inclined to think that this entry might indicate a recognition of extra-mural teaching, and that Philp, and perhaps others on the list, had been pupils of the well-known pious minister of

verend: D: Waltero Comrio Procancelario jusjurandum dedissent lauream Magisterialem consequuti sunt

> Alumni Sti Salvatoris.
> Joannes Lindesay.
> David Alexander.
> Jacobus Philip.
> Joannes Watsone.
> Jacobus Allanus.
> Alex. Barclay.
> Thomas Edward.
> Pa. Lyon.
> Alex. Caw.
> Thomas Martine.
> Johannes Dougall.
> Jacobus Campbell.
> David Kinloch.'

All of these, with the exception of Alexander and Campbell, were in the 1st class when our author was in the 2d. With his master's degree Philp left the University, and the spelling of his name is now Philip. Was the change due to the setting in at the University of a wind of fashion from the South? Did Philip indicate the equestrian order to which the youth belonged more successfully that Philp or Philpe? The University, with its social distinctions, may also have had something to do with the father of the student at this time, between 1672 and 1674, registering arms. James Philp of Almerieclose, son of the bailie of Arbroath, appears in the Register of the Lyon Office as registering arms between 1672

St. Vigeans, Mr. Patrick Strachan, a near neighbour of the Almerieclose family, strong Royalist and Episcopalian. He was minister of St. Vigeans from 1665 to 1693, thus holding his living five years after the Revolution. He was the author of a pious and now rare book, *The Map of the Little World, illuminated with Religion*, being a practical treatise directing man to a religious scope and right measure in all the periods of this life, with devotion suitable; with an appendix, *The Minister's Legacie to his Flock*, in Sermons on 2 Peter i. 12-16. Edinburgh, 1693. It is dedicated to the Earl of Panmure.

and 1678[1]—Azure, a chevron between three talbots' heads, couped argent; motto, 'Non dormit qui custodit.' That the registering took place before 1674 is evidenced by the monument in the Abbey Churchyard, erected (*see illustration*) in that year by the laird of Almerieclose, where the arms appear as given here, and where the fine shield of Margaret Graham also appears—the scallop shells and the three passion nails of the Graham.

The history of our author is a blank to me, from his leaving college in 1675, about the age of nineteen, till he joins Claverhouse in 1689. It may be that the title he gives himself— Panurgus[2]—indicates that he had tried many trades before he took to soldiering. It is clear that before 1691, when he wrote his poem, his reading in classical literature was very extensive, and that his skill in using his full vocabulary in Latin verse meant considerable previous practice in versification. His life in these years, between 1675 and 1689, must have had in it a considerable element of study and devotion to the Muses, and whatever employments of a practical kind his hand may have been set to, success in them was not likely to follow, with this strong bias towards Parnassus. The violence of feeling in matters ecclesiastical and political, and the romantic worship of his heroes, Montrose and Dundee, would also point in a direction away from the labours of a profession. The great Marquis was the hero of every Graham, and of every one claiming Graham blood, and it is not unlikely that the intimate knowledge of Lucan which our author displays is due to its having been a favourite book with Montrose. The Phoenix rising from his ashes, the dashing Claverhouse,

---

[1] [It is curious that another branch of the family of Philp, starting from a learned profession, and tracing through the burgess class, should have registered arms at the same time. David Philp, M.D., acquired the barony of Kippo, in which he was succeeded by his brother John, burgess of Cupar, who died in 1658. Robert of Kippo was father of David, who registered arms between 1672-1678—Azure, a chevron invecked between three talbots' heads erased or.]

[2] But see remarks below on title Panurgus.

much in court and camp, a man of mind and action, perfectly straight and perfectly fearless in attacking the powerful self-seeking diplomatists of his day, won the admiration of his younger relative, and the man of action claimed the Poet as his own. Professions, and he may have tried many, might go to the wind when the bonnie Dundee, with the toss of his bonnet, claimed all that loved honour and him. During these years he must not only have become familiar with the ways and byeways of Forfarshire, but the *Grameid* gives evidence that at the time it was written he was well acquainted with the geography of Scotland, with its towns, glens, rivers, and roads, and with the *locale* of the various clans, and the features of the various districts. He was also up in the history of the many families he introduces, and in many points of contemporary politics and feeling in relation to them. On the whole, I am inclined to fill up these years with study, with verses, with travelling, and with social intercourse and spasmodic efforts at more practical occupation. The *Grameid* supplies a few touches as to its author: his devotion to the Royal Family, especially the Prince of Wales, whom he invokes as the patron of his Muse, whose return to the ancestral throne he promises to celebrate in lofty song, his joining Dundee at Dudhope, as the Ennius of the campaign, and his steady adhesion to him as far, at any rate, as the broken-off narrative extends; his carrying the standard, and his guarding the fords of Spey, where he receives Lochbuy, and conveys the elated chieftain to the camp. The fugitive pieces at the end show his interest in the foreign wars, with the hopes which the Duke of Luxembourg's successes raised, and, withal, his readiness to seek comfort in seclusion, and in his Muse, under the trials of his time. The insertion of the lines 736 to 743, Lib. I., show that he lived to see the death of William in 1702. His epitaph on Aikman, prepared, we may suppose, very shortly before Aikman's death, shows that he was living in 1707. Between Killiecrankie and this date, 1707, he was engaged on his epic, and he tells us that he wrote 'arma inter media et squalorem carceris atri,' Lib. I. 793. No doubt he was in hiding for some time, or he may have stuck to Cannon and Buchan, which would account for 'arma inter media,' but he was at home in 1692 at his father's house, when he obtained an opportunity of writing some of his lines in prison. On 15th August 1692, in the Burgh Court of Arbroath, John Lamb appeared and declared that 'Almerieclose, younger, and John Guthrie, had, in a house in St. Vigean's, abused the magistrates, calling them base and rascals, and that they were not worthy to sit in judgment, with many other opprobrious things.' Almerieclose had also abused the clerk, saying he was not worthy of his office. He and Guthrie were fined, and were ordered to stay in prison till the fines were paid.[1] The magistrates were Provost Patrick Steven, and Bailies Ochterlony and Stevenson, all of whom had been appointed under an order of the Convention in 1689, which, declaring the throne vacant, required a new appointment of magistrates in burghs. They were not likely to suit the tastes of Philp, elder or younger. The father of the bard lived on to 1695 or 1696, as is witnessed by the later retour in the care of Susannah Philip, which see below. At his death our author became the laird of Almerieclose. Whether he built the old mansion-house, which still asserts its knowledge of better days, even in its now very reduced circumstances, I do not know. One or two talbot-head gargoyles still remain at the corners of the pavilion roof, which has a pitch upon it suggestive of Queen Anne, and I think it very likely that the building of this house gave another claim of the author to his title Panurgus.[2] Who his wife was I am unable to say, but no doubt a little more time and trouble than I

---

[1] Hay, p. 162. See also pp. 230, 231 for amusing account of the scolding of magistrates by Euphemia Ochterlony, spouse of John Aikman of Carnie. She scolded them publicly, 'they being sitting in judgment in a fenced court, calling them rascals, knaves, and carter fellows.' Kirk-session, presbytery, and magistrates alike failed to get adequate satisfaction out of the good lady.

[2] But see below.

have been able to give to the subject would fill up every gap which I have left in the Poet's story. His death, I think, occurred about the year 1713, or before that time. My inquiries also serve to clear the memory of the Poet from the only scandal supposed to affect it. Mr. Hay delicately puts the matter as 'giving trouble to the ecclesiastical courts,' and says that 'he was ordered to appear in the public place of repentance in Arbroath, but he declined to do so. He proposed to appear in his own seat in church to be rebuked, and the Presbytery condescended to allow this.'[1] Through the courtesy of the Rev. James Anderson, minister of Kirkden, the clerk to the Presbytery of Arbroath, I was allowed to examine the records, carefully preserved in the manse, and found the entry under December 6th, 1727. Had our author been the culprit, he would at the time have been over seventy years of age; and I felt, besides, that such an episode was in contradiction of the whole character of the writer of these verses, which, though full of violent feeling, and sinking in vituperation to coarseness of expression, yet, when the times are considered, are a marvel of purity. The terms of the retour of Susannah Philp indicate that the Poet was succeeded in Almericclose by a son James, who left no issue, and was succeeded by his brother John, the second son of the Poet, Susannah being the only child of the latter, whom she succeeds in 1752. The culprit of the Presbytery Record of 1727 was, I am convinced, James Philip, the son of the Poet. The succession to the Poet has caused me much trouble, but I have been greatly aided by the kind investigations of Mr. W. K. Macdonald, Town-Clerk of Arbroath, who has most generously searched the papers in his possession for any evidence bearing on the matter. I have not adopted his conclusion as to the Poet dying without issue, because of the evidence in the later volumes of retour, which I consulted under the eye of Dr.

---

[1] Hay, p. 164.

Dickson of the Register House. In these Susannah Philip is described as heir and only child of John Philip of Almerieclose, under 19th August 1752. In a deed quoted by Mr. Macdonald, dated 6th June 1734, her father is described as 'John Philips, Esquire, Governour of the Island of St. Martins, in America, brother-german and heir, served and retoured, to the deceased James Philips of Almeriecloss.' Now, on the 19th August 1752, Susannah is retoured, not only as heir to her father, but also 'to her *grandfather*, James Philp of Almeriecloss.' Again, on 1st September 1752, she is retoured as 'heir to her great-grandfather, James Philp of Almeriecloss, who died in 1695 or 1696, heir-in-line of part of Keptie, Dishland, and Lordburn.' It is therefore clear that the great-grandfather was James Philp, who married Margaret Graham, and died in 1695 or 1696, leaving the Poet to succeed him, who is described in 1692 as younger of Almerieclose. He is the grandfather of Susannah, her father being his second son, who succeeded his elder brother James, who died in 1734 without lawful issue. It is probable that the Poet had a third son, named Patrick or Peter, as, in 1746, Ann and Margaret Philip (the former the relict of Provost Allardice) are served heirs-portioners to a tenement within the burgh, as only children of Peter Philip, their father. Peter may have been a brother of the Poet, and perhaps this is more likely, as John Allardice, whose relict Anne was, had been Provost some time before 1718. The Island of St. Martins was a Dutch possession, and to see his son—if he did live to see it—Governor under such rule, must have been punishment enough for all the strong language used by the Jacobite Ennius. In the Lyon Register, John is described as grandson of the James Philp who registered arms in 1672. The Governor of the Dutch island, in the same Register is called chief of the name. The entries in the Register are due to the ambition of Susannah's husband to quarter the arms of Philp. In 1741 she married

c

Alexander Wilson,[1] merchant, Glasgow, and on succeeding to the old property in 1752, they took steps for its disposal. Accordingly, by a disposition, dated 29th August 1753, it was parted with by husband and wife to Robert Barclay, formerly (apparently) a merchant in Hamburgh, and Mrs. Anna Catharina Todd, his spouse. The Glasgow merchant was increasing his store, probably for the purchase of Glanderstoun, in Renfrewshire, for, in 1771, he appears as laird of that property, and claims arms, quartering with his own the talbots' heads of his wife's shield, with the motto of the Philp family.

As to the old property, Barclay conveyed it, in 1768, to William Graham of Morphie. In 1790 Robert Graham, his heir, conveyed Almerieclose to William Kerr of Dumbarrow, who sold it to Robert Lindsay in 1792. By arrangement, Lindsay gave off the mansion-house and garden and offices to Stewart Lyell of Dickmontlaw for a price of £1200. The trustees under the will of George Lyell, son of the purchaser of the mansion-house, sold the same to Dr. William Arrot in 1812. The trustees under the will of the son of Dr. William Arrot now hold the property. The house is now let out into workmen's dwellings, and it would be difficult to recognise the features of Ochterlony's description. The panelling of some of the rooms, the lead on the roof, together with the quaint leaden gargoyles, and the general air of the old place, bespeak the house of a burgess laird of some importance.

The late Miss Stirling Graham of Duntrune, the most interesting and gifted author of *Mystifications*, could have told us much more of the Philip connection with her family. She was a frequent visitor to her aunt, Miss Alyson Graham, a familiar figure in Arbroath, Mr. Hay tells us, through whom she made the acquaintance of her first Worthy, Meg Matthews —that admirable servant, who so well brought up her master's

---

[1] The Lyon Register by mistake calls him James.

fatherless, mitherless, pennyless bairns, after their father's death in 1754. Miss Alyson Graham was interred in the burying-ground of the Philps of Almerieclose, her kinsfolk, concerning whom no doubt she could have told her niece the whole tale out.[1]

We may now proceed to consider the work of our author, and in the first place the MSS. in which it has been preserved to us.

A. THE ORIGINAL.

The little duodecimo volume, bound in old brown calf, in the Advocates' Library, with the title 'Panurgi Philo-caballi Scoti Poemata,' and containing 139 pages of writing, and 36 blank pages, is undoubtedly the original MS. of these verses, and there is no reason to question the statement at the beginning of the principal piece, that the writing is in the hand of the author—*autoris manu*—and its date 1691.

The writing is very small and neat, and, for the most part, carefully done. The initial capitals of each verse are handsomely elaborated, and the punctuation is, as a rule, carefully and intelligently supplied. The ink varies from very good black to the palest brown, and sometimes to a feeble grey. These shades come in special blocks, and indicate that the author was copying into his precious volume his corrected lines when he had a good many ready, and it may have been that the ink varied from the good black of Almerieclose to the grey hue of the Arbroath lock-up, or the rusty shades of

---

[1] For much of the new information given above I have to thank Mr. Maitland Anderson, Librarian of St. Andrews University, and specially Mr. W. K. Macdonald, Town-Clerk of Arbroath, also Mr. Andrew Ross, S.S.C., the author of *Old Scotch Colours*; Messrs. Ferguson and Steven, Writers, Dundee; Mr. Hay, the author of the *History of Arbroath*, the last mentioned of whom went over the old house with me, and guided me to sources of information otherwise inaccessible. The owner of Duntrune, and Mr. T. Graham Murray of Stenton, have also contributed important information. The references to printed authorities are given in their places.

campaigning pigment.[1] The writing is in the same hand throughout, and is of the same character as the signature *Jacobus Philpe* in the roll of the Acta Rectorum at St. Andrews. Here and there it is illegible, partly through the running of the ink on the paper, and thus darkening the other side of the page. The piece entitled 'In Jacobum Carnegium de Balnamoone' is carefully deleted by a pen, not the author's, and as one of our copies, MS. B, contains the lines, and MS. C, the Balnamoon copy, does not contain them, as it was not likely that it should, and no subsequent copy has them, I gather that the pen which expunged the lines was that of the Balnamoon copyist. The original MS. has been in the Advocates' Library since 1742, but how long before is not known, and how acquired is equally a blank. Did Philip leave his little volume to the Advocates' Library? or did the Faculty acquire it at the breaking up of the household at Almericclose, when James, the Poet's son, died, and John his brother was out governing the Island of St. Martin? It was in their possession a year after the marriage of Susannah in 1741, and long before she came into possession of the property. I incline to think that the Faculty obtained the little volume either at the Poet's death in 1713 or between that date and 1732. The epitaph suggested for his neighbour Aikman is written in larger characters, but evidently by the same hand. It has not been copied into any of the other MSS. I think on the inside of the board of the

---

[1] As to the ink of the period the following recipe for its manufacture jotted down on an old pocket-book Almanack or Calendarium Astrologicum of 1677 in my possession, may be of interest :—

'August 20th 1688.

'Materials for making Ink : 1ˢ, Any of ye barals, they being 5 gallons large the peace —— 10 lbs good gals 12/ or 10/ per lb, 6 lbs good green copris 20 pennies ye lb., 7 lbs gummarabik 8/ per lb, fouir lbs fine candi broad shugar.

The galis are first put in,
Copris about 8 days therafter,
gum 8 days after the copris,
the suggar 20 days or a month
after the gum and it is most to
be stirred after gum is put in.'

little volume, I can trace the name James Philp, the capitals being formed in the same style as those of the poems, but with more extended flourish. There are also efforts at monograms, and a little account jotted of capital and interest, as well as some markings by an idle hand. The name Charles and initials D. Y. and M. D. are printed in capitals by such a hand, indicating careless custody of the MS. at some time.

The MS.[1] B is a small quarto, calf-bound, with ornamented back, and having originally had clasps, now wanting. There are 202 pages, 14 of which are not written on. The writing is seventeenth century or beginning of eighteenth century. It is a very early copy, probably taken during the author's lifetime, or very soon after his death. Some of the mistakes of the original are corrected in it, and the hand of a scholar appears from time to time, not unassociated with grave blunders. Some of the Latinised names of places are translated on the margin, such as 'Byrse, Aboyn, Cromar, Strathbogie, Arthur Syre, Inverness,' etc. It bears in an old hand, but later than itself, the name of Jo. Stevenson, M. D. Ayr, and at the beginning of the *Grameid* the same name appears, but this time Ayr appears as Air. At some time it would seem, from a jotting in pencil, to have belonged to Dr. David Laing. This copy contains the Balnamoon piece, and the translation of Quarles' paraphrase, and it has also on the fly-leaf at the end the following pasquil on John Stewart, Lord Traquair,[2] as I suppose, which does not profess to be the work of our author.

---

[1] The MS. is now the property of Mr. Richard Cameron, bookseller, 1 St. David Street, Edinburgh, who has kindly lent the volume to the Editor for the benefit of this edition.

[2] I had thought that the treacherous Stewart of Goodtrees might be the subject of these lines, but they are so like the verses of a pasquil on Lord Traquair, dated 1640, that they may be regarded as a reproduction of it. Balfour, as quoted in the *Book of Pasquils* referred to below, says, 'Ther anagrams were publicklie wented of the Thesaurer Traquair, first in Edinburgh, and then over all the countrey, in March 1640.

John, Earle of Traquair, a varrie effronted lyar—
" Thy face, thy tongue, thy harte are at a stryffe,
Wich of them to thy lyeis should ade most lyffe.

Quam formosa tua est facies, tenebrosa Stewarte,
Quam simplex, duplex, quam falsum pectus honestum,
Quam verax mendax, . . . oh quam suavis amarus,
Quam mitis, crudelis, quam pius, Athecus extas.
Quam coeleste tuum est meditans terrestria pectus,
Tuque colens Christum, coelum nec Tartara credis.
Non mirum, quamvis ludis utraque manu,
Hanc tibi vel similem cacadæmon mittit at olim,
Nill mihi rescribas, attamen ipse veni.

Paraphrased.

What painter can, misterious Stewart, trace
The various features of thy double face,
Where truth and guile by turns assume their place.
Each Proteus shape thou canst put on with ease,
All honey now, all gall just as you please.
Both mild and cruell thou art justly named,
Ranked Atheist, yet for piety are famed.
Thy visage is an emblem of thy heart,
Where every passion acts a different part,
A subtill serpent, or a harmless dove,
All fury now, but in a moment love.
A saint in show, but in thy carnall minde
A slave to Mammon's drossy part inclined,
Heaven thou pretends to probe, but Heaven does know
All thy desires are centered here below.
Weedling's thy trade, and spite of all command,
Thou finds the means to play with both ye hands,
For qch old Nicke will shortly wryte to thee,
'Send noe word backe, but come thyself to me.'

Apology.

Envy and malice may in vain invent
A thousand lyes, great Stewart's worke to taint,
Which, founded on a rocke, more firmly stands
Than to be moved by blasts of chimile [1] sands.

> Falsse is thy harte, perfidious plots conceavinge,
> Thy tongue unfaithfull, and thy lookes deceaving,
> The hearte affords, unto the other tuo
> Moe cusining shapes than Proteus ever knew."'

—Maidment's *Book of Pasquils*, p. 113.

[1] Is this word known?

Soe when the moon does dart her useful light,
The snarling curs, surprysed with the sight,
Torment themselves by barking all the night.
Let them rail on, thy merit clearly shines,
And no more harm can suffer by y^r lies
Than the Pope's capp from biggoted Divines.

FINIS.

The capitals are arranged without discoverable plan or purpose, and the punctuation is careless and irregular.

MS. C. This MS. and that which is noted next, are in the collection of Dr. David Laing's MSS. left to the University of Edinburgh.

It is numbered 461 in the collection. It is handsomely bound in calf, with red edges, and bears Mr. D. Constable's shield on both boards. He no doubt had it bound, and there is a note by Dr. Laing that he bought it at the sale of Mr. Constable's library, Dec. 13, 1828. Mr. Constable had acquired it, or it was acquired by some one, from the Balnamoon library, as it bears the inscription 'E Libris Robt Carnegy' (of Balnamoon is inserted in a later hand), and the name is again written on first page. Mr. Laing's note goes on to say that it was evidently transcribed from the Advocates' Library copy for James Carnegy of Balnamoon. He notices the obliteration in the original of the 30 lines on James Carnegy, and the 4 lines of Quarles' paraphrase. The paging is up to 140, and the lines are numbered in fives,—a new feature. It is a careful copy, and well done throughout. Its date, I should fancy, would be 1730 or 1740.

MS. D, in the same collection as MS. C, is a small quarto, written on old thick paper, in separate sheets, afterwards half-bound in paper boards, with leather back. Inside, on the board, is the book-plate of Gordon of Buthlaw, and David Laing's signature. The writing leaves a wide margin, which is used for several of the lines written up the page. There are

88 pages. The writing is very difficult. It is an early copy, but not so old as MS. B, and evidently follows the deletion of the Balnamoon piece.

MS. E belongs to the Library of the Theological College of the Scottish Episcopal Church. The large majority of the MSS. belonging to that Library, came into its possession with Bishop Jolly's books. It is probable that Bishop Jolly received it, with many other MSS., from his friend Bishop Alexander. There is a jotting on the last page of the word 'Meiklefolla,' which may indicate a connection with Bishop Petrie. It is a quarto, unbound, of 147 pages, clearly written. There are a great many mistakes in it, and capitals and punctuation are arranged with little method. Till Mr. Cameron kindly lent me his copy, this MS. was the only one I had to work from, as the original, and the University Library copies, could not be lent out, and my avocations prevented my working from home. My thanks, and the thanks of the Society, are due o the authorities of the Library, and especially the present Bishop of Edinburgh, for putting this MS., for so long a time, at the service of the Editor.

The evidence of the authorship of these verses may here be noted.

1*st*, The title 'Panurgi Philo-caballi Scoti Poemata' may, with good show of probability, be interpreted '*The Poems of James Philip, Scotchman.*' See below the interpretation of 'Panurgus Philo-caballus.'

2*d*, The name James Philp may, in a good light and with a glass, be made out on the board of the little volume, the capitals having the same flourish as those of the MS.

3*d*, The title-page has the early insertion, probably in Goodall's hand, of the interpretation of Panurgi Philo-caballi in these words, 'Jacobi Philp sub nomine,' and 'auctore Jacobo Philp.'

4*th*, The writing of the MS., which professes to be that

of the author, is similar to the signature in the Acta at St. Andrews.

5*th*, The author of Lochiel's Memoirs, who finished his work in 1737, says: 'I have before me a manuscript copy of an historical Latin poem called "*the Grameis*," written in imitation of Lucan's Pharsalia (but unfinished), by Mr. Philips of Amrycloss, who had the office of standard-bearer during that famous expedition'—meaning Dundee's campaign. *Memoirs of Lochiel*, Abbotsford Edition, pp. 235-236.—Balhaldy makes many extracts from the MS., and translates a few into English verse.

6*th*, The evidence afforded by the work itself harmonises with the external evidence. That it was written by an Angus man, nay, an Arbroath man, a strong Jacobite and Episcopalian, a connection of the Graham, the internal evidence goes to support, and that 1691, the date given on the MS., is the true one, has also internal support. See pp. 17, 21, 23, 45-218, 252-254, *et passim*.

7*th*, The authorship has never been disputed.

Next to Drummond of Balhaldy's influence through his Memoirs of Lochiel, in preserving a knowledge of the interesting work, we have to thank the late Mr. Mark Napier for reviving that knowledge, when Lord Macaulay had already pronounced the Epic *lost*. Such a statement by Macaulay was sufficient to provoke question, and Mr. Napier, by the help of Mr. David Laing, soon found the original in the Advocates' Library, and obtained from Mr. Laing himself a loan of the two copies, now in the University Library. The present Editor, at that time living in the family of Mr. Napier as tutor to his son, made a translation of some books of the *Grameid* for Mr. Napier, and that translation is the basis of the paraphrase which appears in the Memorials of Viscount Dundee. At Mr. Napier's death, his son, Mr. Francis Napier, returned the MS. translation, and it has been useful in the work of the present edition. It will be seen that the credit of the revival of the Epic is due to Mr.

Napier, and that his connection with the present edition is not indirect.

The name assumed by our author has been a puzzle to many, and not least to myself, but, after all, its meaning, as I think, lies on the surface. 'Philo-caballi Scoti poemata' clearly means the poems of Philip the Scot; and naturally one would expect that Panurgus standing before it, should indicate the first or Christian name of the author. James, Jacobus, and Jacob are the same name; and Jacob the patriarch, the pre-eminent possessor of the name, was so called from a root signifying astuteness or cunning, a quality which he certainly exhibited before he won the nobler name of Israel. Our author translates Jacob into its Latinised Greek equivalent 'Panurgus,' which ordinarily means a cunning fellow, and by dictionaries of the time, and as late as by Ainsworth's, he is upheld in treating Jacobus and Panurgus as equivalents. He may mean, as a subsense, that he was a man of many resources, a Jack-of-all-trades (and does not 'Jack-of-all-trades' rest on the versatility of Jacque or Jacob for part of its significance?), and not over scrupulous, but I am content to think that he meant no more than to veil Jacobus Philip by its Latinised Greek equivalent 'Panurgus Philo-caballus.' The moral character of the Panurge of Rabelais, if known to him, might well have made him hesitate in applying such a name to himself, but it is possible he had not read that author even in Sir Thomas Urquhart's translation. I submit the interpretation as one which seems to me the most simple and natural, but I submit it with diffidence. The word, 'Philocaballus' (used as an adjective), while translating, and at the same time concealing, Philip, may have had in the Poet's mind a subsense, recognising his love of the Muses. The fountain of Hippocrene is prominent in the author's thought, and on page 252 will be found his adoption of the unusual expression of Persius to indicate that inspiring stream. The 'fonte caballino' of the prologue of Persius is 'caballino flumine' in our author, and 'Philo-caballus' may thus have the second meaning of Philip the lover of Hippocrene.

The reader who is not prepared to toil through the Latin will obtain, from the paraphrase translation and notes of this edition, easy acquaintance with the historical matter contained in the work, of which it may be well perhaps to give now a short summary.

1. The contributions here made to the knowledge of personages of the period are very large. Besides many touches concerning well-known historical characters, our author presents in his pages quite a gallery of national portraits of individuals hitherto almost unknown, though their deeds had given character to their time.

2. The topographical references are valuable, as giving evidence to characteristic features of towns, rivers, roads, castles, moors, and country-sides, with their features of cultivation, woods, cottages, etc.

3. The contribution as to dates is scanty, but helpful as far as it goes.

4. The references to dress, weapons, and musical instruments, both of the Saxon and the Gael, are very numerous, and of value to the student of social history; while manners and customs, clan peculiarities and observances, heraldic uses and military ensigns, will be found prominent in these pages.

5. The events recorded by our author are divisible by a significant line of distinction, viz., those of which he was an eye-witness, or personally connected with, and those which he records on the witness of others. As he joined Dundee at Dudhope, on his first raising the standard for King James, and continued with him for the whole period of his narrative, and that narrative is mainly a poetic history of events, it will be seen that, for that short time at any rate, we have from our author history at first-hand. It is, however, to be regretted that the poetic element has sometimes obscured, if not perverted, history. With such powers of observation and

description in the author of the *Grameid*, we are constrained to ejaculate with the northern critic of a greater poet, 'What a pitie it wasna putten in prose!' As from an eye-witness, we have the interesting parting with Lady Dundee—a final farewell—and the riding off to Glen Ogilvy, the gallop through Angus and Mearns, and over the Cairn, and onwards by Dee and Don, Bogie, Spey, and Lossie, to Forres. Back again comes the little troop of cavaliers to the Cairn, whence Dundee surveys Mackay, and perplexing him by turning up the Dee, pursues his way from Aboyne by Kildrummie, Drumminor, and Huntly, by merry Keith, the Bog of Gight, where Lord Dunfermline joins him with the gay Gordon troopers, by Elgin, Forres, and Darnaway, to Inverness. Then, there is the frustration of his hopes of turning on Mackay with the Highlanders under Keppoch, through the conduct of that chieftain. The march by Stratherrick to Kilcummin, by Corryarrick to the Spey, and the halt at the humble hearth of Presmukerach (which still retains its place and name), whence went forth the order for the clans to arm, are graphically recorded. The swoop upon Dunkeld, Perth, and Dundee by the seventy sabres, augmented before the attack on the latter town by Pitcur, Fullerton, and Venton, and the terrible march afterwards by Rannoch to Glen Roy, is told as simple history, with the ring here and there of true poetry. These features of simple narrative are maintained throughout, encumbered no doubt by his classics, but ever and anon the Poet rises with his theme, and his hexameters give him wings. The gathering of the clans is meant to be highly poetic and picturesque; and he forces facts somewhat in assembling them altogether, at one time, on the plain of Dalmacommer; but the departures from history are slight, and the causes of the departures are apparent. The details of the march from Lochaber to the Spey, and the pursuit of Mackay to Edenglassie, with the characteristic preparations of the Highlanders for battle, by casting plaid and brogues, will all be followed with interest. The retreat to

PREFACE. xxxvii

Lochaber, with the affair of Knockbrecht, is historical; but the account of one so closely connected with the skirmish, and so capable of telling the story of it, is a valuable contribution to our knowledge of the event. The value of the author's history may be roughly gauged by the depth of the disappointment felt at the sudden breaking off of his tale.

Among the hitherto unknown, out-of-the-way bits of information which he gives on common report, we may note the reference to the horse which stumbled with King William —he speaks of it as the horse of Fenwick revenging thus the unjust death of his former master, no doubt Sir John; the custody of the Queen and Prince, committed to Dundee by King James; the fact that Dundee was of the party who saw James off in the French frigate; his bold attitude in the Convention, anticipating the words of the song, 'Ere the King's crown go down there are crowns to be broke.' Many such tales, accurate and inaccurate, evidently current in his time, are woven into the poetic narrative.

6. The witness borne to the culture of such provincial students, and the books read by them at the period, is another element of value in our author's work. In our criticism of the classical scholarship displayed in the *Grameid* and other pieces, we shall have occasion to refer to his reading in that field, but here we may note that Virgil has evidently been so thoroughly studied and absorbed by our author, that his parodies have often the freedom of spontaneity. Lucan and Ovid have many expressions in common, but Philip did not get his Ovid from Lucan alone, but had read Naso himself. Horace makes contributions to the work, and so does Persius. There may be references to less-known authors, as will be found suggested in the notes. But deferring for the present the consideration of the classical reading of Philip, it is evident that Buchanan and Boetius unfortunately formed his standard authorities in historical study, and the extraordinary etymologies of place-names of the former author were

receiving omage at the close of the seventeenth century. Where we fall back now on the Celtic so readily for the origin of place-names, the classic tongues were then resorted to for their derivations, and so we have Culnakyle thus rendered, 'Ad vada, queis Coilo deducta colonia nomen indidit.' We are reminded of the derivation of the Soutars of Cromarty from the Greek Σωτηρες, because they were the saviours of the bay from storms. Had our author read Fulgosus, at first or second hand, for his account of the bernicle goose? He had read Milton, and he paraphrases Francis Quarles. Rabelais may have had to do with the name Panurge. There are many expressions which suggest Dr. Pitcairn, his contemporary. The Pasquils of the time were evidently familiar to our author, and contemporary history generally, both home and foreign, noted at Almerieclose.

7. The superstitions of the time are duly honoured by Philip; and though he may be drawing his prodigies from Lucan and Livy, and giving them Monrimmon Muir as their locality, he was not going beyond, but only illustrating, the beliefs of his age. Gordon, in his *History of Scots Affairs*, gravely states as beyond question the following occurrences on the hill of Dunecht, in the year 1638: 'Upon the toppe of this hill, it was that, for the space of all the winter, almost every night, drumms were hearde beatne about 4 ocl, the parade or reteering of the gwardes, ther taptoos, their reveilles, and marches distinctly. And ear witnesses, souldiers of credite, have told me, that when the parade was beating, they could discerne when the drumer walked towards them, or when he turned about, as the fashion is for drummers, to walk too and again upon the heade or front of a company drawne upp. At such tymes, also, they could distinguish the marches of severall nationes; and the first marches that wer heard ther, was the Scottish marche; afterward the Irish marche was hearde; then the English marche. But before these noyses ceased, thes who had been trained up much of ther lyves abroade in the

German warres, affirmed that they could perfectly, by their hearing, discerne the marches upon the drumme of several forraine nations of Europe, such as French, Dutch, Danes, etc. The drumms wer so constantly heard, that all the countrey people next adjacent were therewith accustomed; and sometimes thes drummers wer heard off that hill, in places two or three myle distant. Some people in the night, travelling neere by the Loche of Skeene, within three myle of that hill, were frighted with the lowde noyse of drummes, struck hard by them, which did convey them along the way, but saw nothing; as I had it oftne from such as heard these noises, from the laird of Skeen and his lady, from the laird Eycht, etc., and my owne wyfe then living ther in Skeene all that winter, almost immediatly after that the people thus terrifyed, had come and told it with affrightment. Some gentlemen of knowne integritye and truth affirmed that, neer thes places, they heard as perfect shott of cannon goe off as ever they heard at the Battell of Nordlingen, wher themselves, some years before, had been present. I shall not give you so long an accompt of that visione of an army, seene within four myles of Banfe, upon the Hill of Manderlye, being but once seen, and the witnesses few and obscure, upon whose credit let it lye. About the same tyme, in winter lyckwayes, there was heard a greate noyse of songes, and musicke upon several instruments, in a parosh landward churche, in Buchanne, called the kirk of Rethine; but when the people opned the churche doors, and cam in to see what it was, they neither heard nor saw anything; only there was heard from a loft (or from the toppe of the pulpit, as some reported) within the churche, a greate long strocke, as it had been strucke upon a *viol de gambo.*'—See Gordon's *History of Scots Affairs*, pp. 57, 58. Also see, for prodigies very similar to those of our author, *The Spottiswoode Miscellany*, vol. ii. p. 521. While our author was writing the *Grameid* in 1691, Mr. Robert Kirk, minister of Aberfoill, was contending against the growing scepticisme of the age as to these prodigies, and issuing his work entitled, ' *The Secret Commonwealth, a Treatise displaying the chief curiosities as they are in use among diverse of the People of Scotland to this Day—singularities for the most Part peculiar to that Nation—a subject not heretofore discoursed of by any of our writers; and yet ventured on in an Essay to suppress the impudent and growing Atheisme of this age, and to satisfie the Desire of some choice Friends.*'

Burt, thirty years later, was charged with Atheism, because he laughed at an absurd witch story.

8th. The poems of Philip are a new witness, were such required, to the violence of contemporary feeling, political and ecclesiastical. Our author, in bitterness of invective, equals the most partisan satires of the time, and it cannot be said that he has heightened his large amount of such matter by much point. The Latin tongue gave him a veil for his vituperation, and so left him very free to indulge his spleen; but his use of it in these passages is so heavy that our regret for his misspent time is unmixed. The time thrown away on his First Book, and the concluding passage of the Fifth, would have given us Killiecrankie. The latter passage I conceive to have been written as a pasquil—a kind of composition much in vogue at the time, and he has put it into the mouth of his hero merely to bring up the book to the bulk of the others. The title of Dr. Pitcairn's *Assembly*, written at this time, though not printed till 1722, runs very much in the same line with our author. ' *The Assembly; a Comedy, by a Scots Gentleman*'— *Glomorantur in unum Innumerae pestes Erebi, quascunque sinistro Nox genuit Foeta.* Dr. Pitcairn, by his wit and the elegance of his composition, produced telling satire, and had many imitators, in whose hands the weight of the weapon is all we experience. Our author and Pitcairn were contemporaries, and ended their career in the same year, and it would be strange if they were quite unacquainted with each other. Many passages suggest that *Babel* and *The Assembly* had been seen by Philip. A book of Scottish Pasquils, 1568-1715—chiefly taken from the collections of Sir James Balfour of Denmylne, who cared to gather Presbyterian attacks on the Bishops, and such like, and of Robert Mylne, whose taste lay in the opposite direction—found an able editor in Maidment, and was republished in Edinburgh in 1868. The book will perhaps better illustrate than anything we can say the feelings of the time, and show Philip both in his superiority and inferiority to the contemporary exponents of political and ecclesiastical virulence. It is most extraordinary that Glencoe should not be alluded to in the *Grameid*, and goes to prove that the book, as far as it went, was written in the year 1691, as given on the title-page, before that event. Why, when he took up his pen again in 1702 to tell, in prophetic strain, the death of William, then a fact, does he not endeavour to finish his book ? and if a text for attack more pointed than the subversion of a father-in-law, or the execution of a Fenwick, were wanted, Glencoe would have given one which would have pierced any breastplate.

9*th*. A more pleasing contribution to our knowledge of contemporary feeling is the evidence of unquestioning loyalty —we had almost said reverence—for Claverhouse on the part of the learned author. Pitcairn was not alone among scholars in his admiration of the last Graham. The very labour of the composition of such an epic in praise of Claverhouse by a contemporary and neighbour, is a set-off against the volumes of abuse with which a later generation assailed the memory of that gallant Graham. Assuredly Philip saw in his hero a general brave and wise, patient and dashing ; a cavalier chivalrous, loyal, and generous, the centre of a circle of gay youths, the mover of the Highland heart, feared yet loved by the Scotch dragoon. The last long look of the bright eyes, which followed him while a glint of his armour or a toss of his plume could be seen on the road to the Glen of Ogilvy, tells the Poet's mind as to the love which glowed on the domestic hearth. There is almost a womanly sensitiveness thrown into the picture of Claverhouse, and one is tempted to rebel at times against the plaintive utterances which the author puts into the mouth of the 'fulmineus Gramus.' Assuredly it would be difficult to believe that the portrait by Wodrow and Macaulay, and that by Philip, had the same subject. The *Grameid* is entitled to an important place among contemporary witnesses to the character of Dundee, and must contribute materially in rescuing that character from the region of darkness to which polemical prejudice has doomed it in Scotland.

10*th*. The following criticism, extracted from a letter by Mr. H. F. Morland Simpson, M.A., of Fettes College, who has most generously aided me with his scholarship throughout most of my task, may be accepted as a note on the classics, and the historical value of the work, by one well skilled in judging of such compositions :—

'The author of this poem is evidently deeply impressed with the epic nature of the events he witnessed, and will spare us none of the pomp and circumstance of a great epic poem, adorned with all the artifice he has gathered from long and careful study of his Latin models. He is well provided with the machinery of classical mythology, and seems to take a somewhat pedantic delight in painting with the whole pot—invocations, similes, speeches, Furies, portents, comets, thunderbolts, sweating statues (simulacra *deorum*), prophecies, ghosts, talking beasts, and evil spirits, are introduced as solemnly as if Livy or Lucan had been the writer. It is difficult to say how much of this is mere "purple patches," and how much was really current in the superstitions[1] of the period, which were scarcely less gross than those of heathen Rome. But his epic ideal does not prevent him from falling foul of 'Presbyter' whenever he has occasion to mention him. These long digres-

---

[1] See our remarks on this subject above in Preface.

sions and tirades are tedious interruptions to the narrative, but in themselves interesting as an index of party feeling at the time.

'As a scholar he had read much and very carefully. It would be a task of much labour and research into contemporary Latin scholarship, probably no less than into classical Latin, to determine accurately how much is original and what was his debt to others. Such a labour could do little more than establish the writer's claim to scholarship and careful study of his models, which is patent enough on a first reading of the *Grameid*. The real value of the poem is due to the fact that here, when stripped of all verbiage and flourish, we have a very detailed story by an eye-witness,—perhaps still more to the strong side-lights it throws on many details of contemporary history and tradition, genealogy, social life and customs, dress and thought, party and religious feeling. The allusions to contemporary history in Book I. are especially interesting, being in the nature of "unconscious admissions," which make the most valuable testimony.

'The versification of the poem is polished and smooth-flowing. The sense is clear, and rarely obscure. The vocabulary is very rich and varied. I am disposed to think that he used a dictionary pretty frequently; and that this was probably Holyoke's (1677), which is English-Latin as well as Latin-English. Still it seems to me probable that he wrote *currente calamo:* the occasional mistakes in accidence, quantity, and mythology are indirectly strong evidence of this, as he might easily have corrected them by more frequent reference to his authorities. He writes with a freedom that could only be acquired by long practice and full confidence in the resources of his Latinity. The critical reader will observe proofs enough of this in the occurrence of rare, unclassical, or impossible words and forms, such as a less practised or fluent writer would hardly venture to use. The imitations of the classics are obvious, but read rather as "memories" than slavish imitations, such as a schoolboy might write.

'The syntax is often somewhat loose and irregular, especially in sequence. The "quantities" are on the whole carefully observed, and, if not the result of early training, show a very fine ear. Modern readers may be apt to stumble over the frequent violation of the rule which makes a final short vowel long before a word beginning with *sc, sp, st,* etc.; but the rule is narrow in its application to classical authors, and was probably unknown in our author's day. Milton ignores it very often.

'Perhaps his facility is most apparent in his treatment of Scottish names, notably in the march northwards in Book II., the gathering of the clans in Book IV., and his frequent descriptions of fire-arms (*e.g.* Book II. p. 47). His power of graphic description in detail is well shown in his account of Claverhouse leaving Edinburgh (II. p. 44), the march (II. p. 50), the night-alarm (Book V. p. 207), the fall of the officer (in Book V. pp. 212-13), and the scenery described in Book II. pp. 76-8 and 80. His birds and plants are native; and there are here many genuine touches of "local colour," for which his countrymen have a special gift. Occasionally his satirical humour reminds us of the lampoons of the period [Batavi obesi (II. p. 229); the advance of Mackay (II. p. 58); the surprise of Blair in Perth (II. p. 60); the dismay of the citizens of Dundee at Claverhouse's approach (II. pp. 67-8), etc.].

'In descriptions of persons he is not so successful. As a rule, he tells us little or nothing of the *complexion* of his characters —a very frequent defect in historical writers. His epithets tell us almost nothing of the appearance of his hero. An eye-witness, writing for the present rather than the future, is apt to assume much in the knowledge of his contemporaries. Thus the Gospels give us no details of Christ's appearance from which we could construct a *portrait.*

'Our chief regret in reading the poem is that our author did not avail himself of his splendid opportunity for a plain narrative in English; in which case his work would have proved one of the most valuable and interesting pieces of contemporary historical biography in the language, and might have taken its place worthily alongside of the great work of Clarendon.'

In illustration of his remarks on 'rare words,' 'errors,' and 'contemporary history,' Mr. Simpson notes the following [but see for this additional notes in Appendix to Preface]:—

Book I. 154. fimeta.
„ 164 and 344. fictitius (in Cooper's *Thesaurus*, without reference).
„ 191. amandant.
„ 359. masora.
„ 639. periscelide.
Book II. 271. transfictat.
„ 398. suburram.
„ 576 and elsewhere, 'sclopeta,' called in Holyoke 'an harquebuss, an hand-gun, a pistol, a snaphaunce.'
. 702. stiria.
Book III. 106. Libistidis.
„ 366. emaci.
„ 685. tabanorum.

Errors not of quantity or mere syntax—
Book I. 143. A Gade ad Gangem.
Book III. 361. macellos masc. in Martial, a gender recognised, without a reference, by Holyoke.

Contemporary History.—Turks, Moors (Ethiopae occidui Maurique), infidus Saxon; saevi Angli, and other nations are introduced. We have religious feeling preceding the Revolution; English treatment of royalty; divine right of kings dealt with. Charles the Martyr and Charles II. are eulogised. Ireland is spoken of as reduced to respect the law by Charles II. As to James II., the author regrets but excuses his Roman Catholic faith. He brings up the difficulties as to Italian— *i.e.* Roman Catholic—Ministers of State. The Bishops, the Queen, the birth of the Prince and rumours regarding it, and

James as an Admiral, come in for their share of notice. William of Orange is *signifer doli*. His great-grandfather and the Dutch war for liberty are spoken of. War in Germany; King Louis of France in his wars against Holland, Spain, Austria, and the Scotch in his service are also alluded to. The reader will also find many more references to Scotch history in the later Books.

It was my purpose in the Preface to give some account of the peculiarities of weapons and musical instruments mentioned in the volume, as well as some matter illustrative of military equipment and Highland dress, but space and time are both exhausted, and the reader must be left to make out what he can from the author and the notes already supplied. I also forego the intention I had formed of supplying a diary of Dundee's movements from his return to Scotland at the Revolution till his death at Killiecrankie. Any attempt at a summary of his life, or view of his character, is hardly within the scope of such a Preface as I have intended here, and the *Grameid*, as is already pointed out, does not supply much new complexion to the hero. For new matter which has been passed over hitherto, I would refer the student to the letters of Dundee in the *Red Book of Menteith* (Fraser), some extracts from which I had purposed to give here. I find, however, that such extracts have already been given to the public in an article in *Macmillan's Magazine*, November 1887. The *marginalia* written on the Duke of Gordon's copy of 'Balcarres' Account of Affairs of Scotland,' given in *Northern Notes and Queries*, Vol. i. No. 1—A statement full of domestic colour in the midst of war written by Alexander Stewart of Ballachulish soon after the battle of Killiecrankie, and printed in *The Stewarts of Appin*, a book referred to on page 144—Some letters in the *Thanes of Cawdor* (Spalding Club), giving an account of the fuss in Edinburgh on Dundee's leaving the Convention, I had noted for extract, but must now content myself with simple reference. My note on General Mackay must also be given up, with the exception of one remark. Though Philip indulges largely in hostile and contemptuous terms concerning this General, yet, from time to time, he speaks of him with high appreciation of his character and prowess. See, for instance, the spirited comparison of the two leaders at the conclusion of Book III., and specially the lines—

> ' Clari animis, clarique armorum laudibus ambo,
> Inter se totis obnixi viribus instant
> Quem Regem terris inferrent arma Britannis.'

The moment when I sacrifice the hope of adding interest to my work by these illustrations, is a fitting one for deprecating, to some extent, the adverse criticism which I fear that work must merit. When I was asked to edit the *Grameid* a translation was not contemplated, but only a running margin of contents and a few notes. I agreed towards the end of last year to make a translation which would give the English reader the matter of the book in a readable form, and to increase the notes so as to make one volume of the Society's publications. It will be allowed that the time has been short, and the amount of matter supplied has been large. It will also, I hope, be considered that the time at my disposal for this work has been snatched from the business of my profession, which is always heavy.

It now only remains for me to return my sincere thanks to those who have so readily aided me, and without whose ready aid the book would not now be where it is, nor what it is. Space forbids that I should name again those whose kind help I have already acknowledged in the Preface or Notes, though much more might be said regarding it. To the Rev. J. Faber Scholfield, I am specially indebted for revising the Latin text of some of the Books, as also to the Revs. Canon Keating, N. Green Armytage, and Geoffry Hill, for some help in the same way. To Sir William Fettes Douglas my thanks are due for a list of contemporary Scottish authors, and the loan of some scarce books from his valuable collection. I have already expressed my gratitude to Mr. T. Graham Murray of Stenton for some part of his kind assistance, but I have also to thank him for the loan of books, and for the valuable suggestions of his correspondents. To the Bishop of Edinburgh, to Mr. George Seton, to Cluny Macpherson, to Sir John D. Hope, to Mr. J. W. Young, and to the representatives of the various families referred to in the Notes, I have to tender my thanks. Mr. Clark of the Advocates' Library most kindly collated the First Book with the original, and has yielded me every assistance in his power. The courtesy of the Lyon Office I have also to acknowledge. The valuable contribution of Mr. Maitland Anderson, Librarian of St. Andrews University, I have already acknowledged; but the courtesy of the Librarian of the University of Edinburgh claims like recognition. The patience and the ready help which I have met with from our Secretary, Mr. T. G. Law, I am deeply grateful for; and but for his goodness in putting at my disposal his knowledge of books and the resources of the valuable collection of which he is the keeper, this edition of the *Grameid* would have been poorer than it is.

In conclusion, may I be allowed to recall the memory of my late dear friend, Mr. Mark Napier, whose enthusiastic admiration for the *Grameid* kindled in me the hope of some day gratifying him by its publication. The Scottish History Society has enabled me to do the work I had hoped to achieve; but alas! he for whose pleasure I desired to accomplish the task has passed away.

ALEX. D. MURDOCH.

ALL SAINTS' PARSONAGE,
    EDINBURGH, 1888.

APPENDIX TO PREFACE.

NOTE.—Where references are given throughout the work to Notes at end of Volume this Appendix is to be consulted.

ADDITIONAL CORRECTIONS AND NOTES.

Book I

LINE	PAGE	
78,	4.	'Quod,' better 'Quid.'
199,	9.	'Non armatae acies illam' would put this line right.
214,	10.	Delete comma after 'Tinnula'
230,	11.	Read 'Pollutam.'
257,	12.	'Tribuni' may generally be translated 'chieftains.'
282,	13.	Read 'Privatae.'
329,	15.	Read 'Exsuperans.'
531,	15.	Read 'Iraeque.'
	17,	note. Read 'tract' for 'track.' Add Liv. xxii. c. i. to Note 3.
384,	18.	Read 'stragesne virum'; won't scan otherwise.
421,	19.	Omit 'acies.'
	19,	note 2. Which comet pointed north with its tail?
482,	22.	'vindicet.' Translate 'Morinorum finibus' French or Flanders.
509,	24.	'Securigeris,' translate 'axe-bearing,' and in note read '*down* to James,' instead of '*up*.'
564,	26.	Insert comma after 'alii.'
568,	26.	'peregre venientem'=the foreign foe.
597,	28.	'repêturus,' blunder for 'repetiturus.'
599,	28.	Read 'totis' for 'toties.'
600,	28.	Read 'bella' for 'belli.'
612,	29.	Omit comma after 'cohors'; insert it after 'luxu.'
637,	30.	'Comitia,' false quantity.
639,	30,	note. Read 'pĕrīscēlĭdĕ,' and omit comma after 'ducis.'
651,	31.	'ductis' is suggested for 'auctis.'

APPENDIX TO PREFACE.

LINE	PAGE	
656,	31.	'Deis' is suggested for 'Divis.'
671,	32.	Read 'hyberno.'
674,	32.	Read 'pectori.'
690,	32.	Read 'foret.'
691,	32.	Read 'auferret.'
693,	33.	Better 'quum.'
704,	33.	Read 'caupone,' and translate 'hireling.'
744,	35.	Read 'imminuet,' and translate 'break,' in accordance with Holyoke.
792,	37.	Read 'proelia' here, and elsewhere, as word occurs.

Line 580, p. 27. I have translated 'siccabant' rather after a Scriptural example; but Herodotus, who was no poet, tells soberly that the army of Xerxes drank up the rivers, and our Poet may be following the historian. [See Herod. vii. 58.]

Line 683, p. 32. Translate 'straturus' either 'destined to strew,' in allusion to the dispersion of William's fleet on his first attempt; or, 'about to cover' the sea, in allusion to their number, see note, page 31.

Line 743, p. 35. 'Non aequa lege peremptum' has reference to the protests against the legality of Sir John Fenwick's trial, and the special bill of attainder.

Book II.

LINE	PAGE	
40,	39.	Read comma after 'fata.'
72,	41.	Read period after 'Reges.'
92,	42.	Read 'longinquum,' and translate 'from afar.'
124,	44.	Read 'elati' for 'alati,' perhaps.
193,	48.	'aereas turres'—Dudhope, which Ochterlony thus describes, 'ane extraordinare pleasant and sweet place, a good house, excellent yards, much planting, and fyne parks. It lyes pleasantly on the syde of the hill of Dundie, overlooks the town, and as of purpose built there to command the place. Dundie Law is at the back thereof, ane exceeding high mott hill.'
219,	49.	Read 'Jamque.'
	49.	Note 2. Ochterlony gives the following account of the house at Glen Ogilvy:—'Glen, belonging to the Laird of Claverhouse, Grahame, an ancient gentleman of good extraction and great estate in the

APPENDIX TO PREFACE.

LINE	PAGE	
		shyre—a pleasant place, a good house, and well planted; excellent quarrie of freestone and sklait; well furnished in peat and turfe; and in the hill thereof abundance of muirfoull. The sklait is carried to Dundie on horseback, and from thence by sea to all places within the river of Forth.'—*Spottiswoode Miscellany*, vol. i.
251,	51.	Line will scan only by taking liberties with Elgin.
277,	53.	Read 'radiis.'
285,	53.	Read 'amoenam.'
294,	54.	Read 'Nessique.'
297,	54.	Read 'cornipedes.'
309,	55.	Translate 'now accusing one, now another.'
325,	56.	'Insultus'—accusative plural; rare and late for 'revilings.'
326,	56.	'animam,' perhaps 'animum.'
327,	56.	Read 'invictamque.'
350.	57.	For note 1, read 'example of Synizesis, "alvêo."'
367,	58.	Read, perhaps, 'laetus.'
403,	61.	'Mala aurea'—note 2. The Lyon Office Register supplies some answer to the query in the note. Oranges were bestowed as heraldic badges, and would be carried on the ensigns of those companies raised by gentlemen who had received such an honour from William and Mary. The arms of Colonel Row of the 21st Regiment were enriched with oranges by special favour of the reigning powers, and I believe there is evidence of their use on the colours of the companies he commanded.
454,	64.	Read 'torosa' and translate 'brawny.'
511,	67.	Read, perhaps, 'trepidosque agitat.'
560,	71.	Read, perhaps, 'ut' between 'ibat' and 'altus.'
610,	73.	Omit comma after 'hesperus,' and insert it after 'lacessitum.'
681,	76.	Read, perhaps, 'ephippia.'
683,	76.	See note below on translation of 'ipse.'
685,	76.	Delete period after 'plantis,' and insert comma.

P. 47. More correct to say, *earliest event in author's life mentioned by himself.* He speaks of himself at end of Book I.

APPENDIX TO PREFACE.

P. 67. Yeaman is probably wrong here. Bailie Duncan was in charge at Dundee, and sent two 'missive letters' to the provost, then in Edinburgh, who took them at once to Lord Rosse. The committee was 'called extraordinarily at 6^{ocl} in the morning on the 14th May, when the two letters were read, bearing that Viscount Dundee had attacked the town of Dundee at 5^{ocl} yesternight.'

He may also be wrong in identifying Bailie Duncan with Duncan of Lundie. See *Acts of Parl.*, vol. ix., Appen. p. 22.

P. 68. 'Culullos' (see Horace, *Od.* i. 31), where the word is used in this sense, though its ordinary application is to cups baked of earth, and used by priests and vestals in sacred rites.

P. 72. 'Sclopeta.' 'Sclopetum' is given by Holyoke for a gun or pistol, and he derives it from *sclopus* or *scloppus*, a sound made by striking an inflated cheek. For survival of the word, see James's *Military Dict.* under Sclopetaria. Perhaps *scopette*, the old French blunderbuss for gendarmes, may take its name from the word.

P. 73. 'Uber apum'—a swarm of bees, very rare; a metaphor from the shape of a cow's udder. Holyoke has it, and doubtless our author got it there. He was not likely to have seen Palladius Rusticus Taurus, a writer of about 260 A.D., from whom the expression comes.

P. 73. The translation should have given 'that they pursue the enemy like the swift east wind, or like the bullet shot with gunpowder, and harass,' etc.

P. 74, line 633. 'Ninguida' or 'ningida,' a word not found before Ausonius, but Holyoke gives it under snow—full of snow, 'ningida' in the English-Latin part.

P. 74, line 634. Translate 'high Abria stretches north.'

P. 75, line 643. 'Ranocham' would look better with 'paludem.'

P. 75, line 652. Translate 'vecti,' *who have ridden.*

P. 76, line 683. 'Ipse' can hardly refer to the author; the full stop at *plantis* must go out, and *progreditur* will become the verb, of which *ipse* is the subject. It was Claverhouse who lost his horse. The author comes in at 'excutimur,' verse 697. The description of scenery in the concluding paragraph is very fine, and line 707 has the genuine ring of true poetry.

APPENDIX TO PREFACE.

Book III.

LINE	PAGE	
49,	81.	Read 'ninguida' for 'nimguida.'
120,	86.	Read 'inque' for 'in que.'
172,	89.	Read 'tolerare' for 'tollerare.'
367,	98.	'Viden' won't scan.
389,	99.	See Jacobite song—'Willie the Wag'—

> 'The tod rules o'er the lion;
> The midden's aboon the moon.'

406,	100.	Read 'Macte' for 'Macti.'
580,	108.	Read, perhaps, 'actutum.'
585,	108.	Connect 'ne' with 'sese.'
601,	109.	Read comma instead of period at 'volatu.'

Book IV.

Line 232, p. 138, is noted as very fine.

Note 1, p. 140. As the Dragoons are said to take their name from Dracones, there may be some reference to them here—
'*The twin dragoons uplift the standards.*'

P. 143 and 144. 'Ierna' may be an old name for Loch Leven, or Loch Creran, which arms of the sea bound Appin lands. The fur bonnets may mean bonnets of frieze, or woven bonnets. The Stewarts of Appin were much in advance in matters of military organisation and uniform, as is noticed by Philip. As to the device on the banners, there is no doubt that as given by our author it is bad heraldry, a colour being placed on a colour, but 'figures Or' would meet the difficulty.

P. 157. 'Niveas turmas.' In the *Historical Records of the Scots Greys* it is noted that in the journals of the period (about 1702) the regiment is sometimes styled 'the Grey Dragoons,' and on other occasions the 'Scots Regt. of White Horses.' The Editor says the order for remounting the regiment with grey horses exclusively has not been discovered, and I am disposed to believe that a fashion had by the time of our author set in towards grey mounts, which afterwards received sanction at headquarters. The practice of mounting *corps d'élite* on horses of one colour had been adopted before this in Continental armies. It may be of interest to note the rates of pay in this famous regiment in 1689, as given in the *Records*.

		Pay per Day.		
1 Colonel and Captain,		£1	6	0
1 Lieut.-Colonel and Captain.		1	0	0
1 Major,		1	0	0
4 Captains, each 11s.,		2	4	0
6 Lieutenants, each 6s.,		1	16	0
6 Cornets, each 5s.,		1	10	0
1 Chaplain,		0	6	8
1 Adjutant,		0	5	0
1 Surgeon,		0	6	0
1 Gunsmith,		0	5	0
6 Quarter-Masters, each 4s.,		1	4	0
12 Serjeants,	,, 2s. 6d.,	1	10	0
18 Corporals,	,, 2s.,	1	16	0
12 Drummers,	,, 2s.,	1	4	0
12 Hautboys,	,, 2s.,	1	4	0
360 Private men,	,, 1s. 6d.,	27	0	0
		£43	16	8

A mistake has been frequently made by confounding this regiment with the one which Claverhouse commanded. Many of the men and officers were his friends, and afterwards joined him; and it would seem that the regiment was placed under his orders at Reading on the retreat of James from Salisbury, but the regiment of which he was Colonel and Captain was *the Royal Regiment of Scots Horse*, the Scots Greys being then styled the Royal Regiment of Scots Dragoons.

Line 467, p. 165. 'Tuba' in the classical sense would mean some straight trumpet. I have translated it pipe—and tube may have suggested pipe—but I do not hold to the translation. Holyoke gives 'Tibia utricularis' as translation of Bagpipe. Bagpiper is 'Utricularius Pithaules.' Under 'Tuba' he does not mention bagpipes.

Line 512, p. 167. 'Cornua' may be bugles, or real horns, which were in use in Highland gatherings, as they are still in use: witness the assembling of crofters lately in Skye and Tiree by the blowing of horns. Altogether, I should prefer that the reader should make his own translation of these classical terms for musical instruments.

APPENDIX TO PREFACE.

P. 177, note. Some of the Ogilvys were with King James in Ireland. Witness Captain Ogilvy of Inverquharity, the reputed author of the pretty and touching song—

> ' It was a' for our rightfu' king
> We left fair Scotland's strand !
> It was a' for our rightfu' king
> We e'er saw Irish land, my dear,
> We e'er saw Irish land.'

P. 179. The translation 'the powder being fired in the terrible guns' is adopted in reference to the practice of applying fire to the powder by a torch.

P. 181, note 1. A friend would construe this doubtful passage— 'E'en as the herd of deer led by a stag fears the troops of lions led by a lion.'

P. 183. The custom of the Highlanders in casting off brogues and plaids on going into battle is well known. At Kilsyth, Montrose and his cavalry cast off their jackets, but the Highlanders cast off everything except their shirts. They were almost in a state of nudity, and their appearance added much to the terror of the Fife militia. See Browne's *History of the Highlands*, p. 406.

Book V.

P. 190. The figure [1] for note should have been attached to 'Cathari,' to which it refers. Holyoke translates Puritan —'Puritatis studiosus, hypocrita seditiosus.' Bailey's *Dict.*, 1783, gives 'Catharians—a sect of heretics, the spawn of the Manichees, who held themselves altogether free from sin,'— but this sect was not the Puritans or our Cathari.

P. 193, note. *Herring Bushes*, called also 'Burses.' The history of native fishery would be interesting. Most of the fishing on our coasts was carried on by Dutch, French, and Portuguese in large fleets. They probably established depots and fixed stations along the shores, which gave origin to our fishing villages and the peculiarities of race found in them. The natives, except on the west coast, had very little fishing enterprise.

P. 202. 'He wore a white plumach.' Was this the 'white cockade' in anticipation?

P. 207, note. The words obliterated may have been 'instantes agitatis vocibus hostes.'

APPENDIX TO PREFACE.

P. 209. The word 'streperous,' as an English word, may have been familiar to our author. Bailey gives it.

P. 211. 'Emisit jaculum.' Hand-grenades were in use at the time. Does the expression refer to them? On page 214, line 357, the words suggest some kind of grenade or shell. There is not now space to go into the question of weapons, but the student will doubtless find many contributions in this work to a knowledge of the subject.

P. 226, line 573. Perhaps 'Daci' should be 'Dani.'

P. 229, note 3. 'At Oxford, Falkland, to amuse the king, proposed to try this kind of augury, and the king hit upon Book IV. ver. 881-893, the gist of which passage is that "evil wars would break out, and the king lose his life." Falkland, to laugh the matter off, said he would show his majesty how ridiculously the "lot" would foretell the next fate, and he lighted on Book XI. ver. 230-237, the lament of Evander for the untimely death of his son Pallas. King Charles, in 1643, mourned over his noble friend, who was shot through the body in the battle of Newbury.'—BREWER's *Dict. of Phrase and Fable*, S.V. SORTES VIRGILIANÆ.

PANURGI PHILOCABALLI SCOTI
GRAMEIDOS
LIBRI SEX
ET POEMATA RELIQUA

PANURGI PHILOCABALLI SCOTI
GRAMEIDOS

LIBER PRIMUS.

BELLA Caledonios civiliaque arma per agros [1]
Instructasque acies, variisque horrentia signis
Agmina, et horriferae canimus certamina pugnae,
Magnanimumque Ducem, pulso pro Rege cientem
Arma, acresque viros, ipsumque in saeva ruentem
Vulnera, terribilemque in belli pulvere Gramum
Ingentemque heroem animis armisque potentem,
Pangimus et saeclis Mavortia facta futuris.
 Quis novus arctoum nunc o furor excitat orbem?
Sollicitatque feros in barbara bella Britannos
Ire iterum? et patriam civilibus urere flammis
Provocat? et tragici tot damna subire duelli?
Anne adeo veteres oblita Britannia clades?

WE sing the Scottish wars, and civil strife, the lines of battle, and ranks bristling with many standards, the encounters of a horrid contest. And we sing the noble Leader, calling brave men to arms for an exiled King, and himself rushing to meet cruel wounds. We sing the Graham, the great Hero, terrible in the dust of battle, mighty in spirit and in arms. We tell of warlike deeds for times to come.

Oh! what new madness now excites the northern world, and tempts again the fierce Britons into barbarous wars, to burn their country in civil flames, to endure the calamities of a tragic contest. Is Britain so forgetful of her past misfortunes? Raging in

---

[1] Cf. first line of Lucan's *Pharsalia*—
   ' Bella per Emathios plusquam civilia compos.'

Bella nefanda fremens convulso cardine rerum
Impia civili ruit in sua vulnera motû,
Condit et exertum sua rursus in ilia ferrum.
Hectoridumque genus fatali exscindere bello
Brutigenum quod nulli unquam potuere tyranni
Ipsa parat demensque suo se robore sternit?
Quod si adeo insani jam prurit amore Gradivi,
Nunc eat, et Geticum detrudat moenibus hostem
Pannoniis, patriaeque vehat victricia signa
Ethiopas ultra occiduos Maurosque feroces,
Pulchraque barbaricum circumferat arma per orbem.
Ite, animae illustres, incoctaque pectora honesto
Queis meliore animos finxit natura metallo,
Christiadumque jugo subducite colla profano,
Lassa diu, fessisque Europae accurrite rebus.
O invicti animi juvenes pia ducite signa
In Mahometicolas, quaque omnipotentis IESU
Busta Dei repetenda vocant, felicibus ite

impious war—the centre of things overthrown—she rushes in civil commotion to her own destruction, and again buries the naked sword in her own vitals. Does she herself prepare to cut off, in fatal strife, the British[1] race, whom no Roman[2] tyrant could ever overcome, and madly destroy herself by her own strength?

But if she longs for war with such an insane love, let her now go and drive the Tartar[3] host from the besieged walls of Hungary,[4] and carry her conquering banners among the Ethiopians and the fierce Moors, and encompass the barbarous world in honourable warfare. Go! illustrious spirits, unsullied hearts, for whom Nature has fashioned souls of the nobler metal, and loosen the necks of Christians—so long oppressed—from the yoke of the Infidel, and aid the wearied state of Europe. Oh! youths of unconquered spirit! carry your pious banners against the Moslem, where the Sepulchre of JESUS, the Almighty GOD, calls you to recover it. Go! under happy auspices—for, what will it avail you

---

[1] 'Brutigenum'=British. Brutus, according to *Historia Britonum*, quoted by Skene, *Four Books of Wales*, vol. ii. p. 99, was first King of Britain.

[2] 'Hectoridum'=Roman, I fancy. He may, however, mean hectoring tyrants, or heroic kings.

[3] 'Geticum,' probably applied to Turks and Tartars, who were at this time the masters of the Danubian Provinces.

[4] 'Pannoniis': Hungary probably referred to. Turks not expelled till 1686. Siege of Vienna raised only in 1683.

Auspiciis; quid enim toties furialibus ausis
Profuit horribili patriam lacerasse tumultu?
Et ferrum miserisque inferre incendia tectis?
Quid juvat et validas in viscera vertere vires?
Nulla triumphales dant civica proelia lauros,
Nec feret haec veram vecors victoria laudem.
Sed fera barbaries, cognato sanguine gaudens,
Exuit humanos, O secli infamia! mores.
Proh scelus! horrendos malesana Britannia motus
Concipit, et diros ardet renovare furores,
In sua damna ruens; nunc ira furorque tumultus
Concitat insanos, et tristia trudit ad arma.
   Hinc fera monstra vocat quotquot pallentia Ditis
Regna tenent, Furiasque, Erebumque, Chaosque fatigat,
Gorgones Harpyiasque ciet Scyllasque biformes
Centaurosque, ignemque vomentes ore Chymaeras;
Saeva quibus torto Nemesis bacchata flagello
It comes, et lacera gaudens Confusio palla
Insequitur, nigraque cohors sata nocte sororum
Advolat Eumenidum, Stygiasque resuscitat iras,
Atque iterum rupto laxantur Erinnyes Orco,
Et belli geminas Furiarum maxima portas
Rupit, et arctoas tremefecit turbine terras;

to have so often torn your country in these mad darings, and to have carried fire and sword to her unhappy roofs? What does it profit to turn your strength against your own bowels? Civil wars give no triumphal laurels, nor does the senseless victory merit praise.

But fierce barbarism rejoicing in brothers' blood casts off all human feeling. Oh, infamy of the age! oh shame! Insane Britain conceives fearful revolution, and, burning in desire to renew past fury, rushes to her own destruction.

Hereupon she invokes whatever monsters the gloomy realm of Pluto holds. She rouses up the Furies, Erebus, and Chaos. She calls up the Gorgons, the Harpies, the Scyllæ, and the biformed Centaurs, and Chymaera vomiting fire; as companion, comes the cruel Nemesis with her knotted lash, and Confusion follows her, proud of her torn cloak. And the black cohort of the Sisters Eumenides, born of Night, hither flies, stirring the Stygian Pool, and from Orcus—again burst open—are loosed the Erynnides, and the greatest of the Furies throwing open the double gates of

Et Stygiam quatit ore tubam Bellona Britannis
Plus quam hostile fremens, jurataque bella quietis
Inspirans populis, cognatas foedere gentes
Et consanguineas impellit ad arma catervas,
Armat et infensos in mutua vulnera fratres.
    Tantane Caucasiis in rupibus ira Leones
Possidet? Haecne tenet Lybicas truculentia Tygres?
Quid genus humanum tantas exarsit in iras?
Vertitur et tantam in rabiem scelerata virûm gens
Ut vincat feritate lupos et caede leones?
Non ita Getulas in sese vertere vires
Edocuit natura feras. Sic ebria Maenas,
Idaeûsque Chorus, Cybelesque altaria circum
Turba furens, rigido nudabant viscera ferro.
Heu miseros! quo fata trahunt? quo tenditis ultro
Damnatam in cunctas cervicem exponere poenas?
Innocuisque sacrum jugulis fudisse cruorem?
Haecne fides Superum? Restaurataeque verendus
Relligionis honos, pietas atque aemula coelo
Communem hanc patriam praedae abjecisse nefandae,
Et stimulasse novos in publica damna furores?
Cur miseram alterno properatis sanguine mortem
Effuso? patriusne in vulnera sufficit ensis?
    Quod conjurati Rhenus, Dravusque, Savusque,

war, makes northern lands to reel. Fierce Bellona sounds her Stygian pipe more madly hostile than ever, inspiring party strife among peaceful peoples, and impels races, united in friendship and blood, to war, and arms brethren for mutual destruction.
    Does such fierceness possess the Caucasian lion, or the Lybian tiger? What race of men exhibits a savageness surpassing the wolf in ferocity, and the lion in slaughter? Nature has not taught the Getulian wild beast so to turn his strength against his own. Drunken Bacchante and Idæan Chorus, a mad crowd around the Altar of Cybele, thus lay open their flesh with the hard steel. Alas! whither do the Fates draw us? Why do you seek by pouring out innocent blood to expose a neck doomed to the last vengeance? Is this religion? Is this the glory of the Reformed Faith and its lofty piety, to subject the common fatherland to unspeakable misfortune, and to have roused new furies to the public loss? Why hasten our end by pouring out each other's blood? And is not the native sword enough? Why do the Rhine, the Drave, the Save, flow united to our destruction? It is

Exitio accurrunt? Satis est, jam martia tellus
Fergusique domus, miseranda vel hostibus ipsis
Concidit, et propriis a culmine vertitur armis.
  Di quibus hoc sublime stetit per saecula sceptrum,
Et quibus imperii commissa est cura tuendi,
Vertite in hostiles haec bella domestica terras ;
Aerumnisque modum, nostrisque imponite finem
Cladibus, et miseri causas arcete duelli.
Jam satis humano maduerunt sanguine campi,
Nosque satis ludo lassarunt fata cruento.
Saeva quid ulterius miseros fortuna fatigas ?
Ecce iterum Arctoo bacchatur in orbe Megaera,
Arma Caledonios sparsitque Alecto per agros ;
Improba vis leges, et jura injuria vicit ;
Pulsa retro cessit pietas, civilis Erynnis
Civibus in cives atque impia porrigit arma.
Nunc et ad ultrices vindex Rhamnusia poenas
Excubat, et mentes stimulat rationis egentes ;
Tisiphoneque facem flagrantem fervida jactat,
Funereasque infert ardenti lampade taedas.
Jam graditur Bellona fremens, et tristis Enyo
Civiles inflat lituos, Marsque impius arma
Dira quatit, raptimque leves per aperta quadrigas
Aequora saevus agit, trux et Discordia dextram

enough ! the martial land and house of Fergus fall, by their own arms, an object of pity even to an enemy.
  Ye gods, who have upheld for ages this mighty sceptre, and to whom the charge of empire is committed, turn these domestic wars on hostile lands, put a measure to our adversity, an end to our destruction, and disperse the causes of this miserable strife ! Already with enough of blood have the fields been soaked, enough have the Fates worn us out in their pitiless sport. Why does cruel fortune still lash the miserable ?
  Lo ! again Megaera revels in the North, and Alecto scatters arms through the land. Unrighteous might has triumphed over law, and injustice over right. Stricken piety has yielded, and Erynnis in civil strife impiously arms citizens against citizens. Now, too, the avenging Rhamnusia waits to punish. Tisiphone casts her flaming fagot and lights the funeral torch. Already Bellona advances, and mournful Enyo sounds her clarion, and impious Mars shakes dread weapons, driving swiftly through the open plain his light chariot, while cruel Discord extends a mailed

Porrigit armatam, speque insultantia tollit
Pectora, et indomitas cognata flagellat ad iras
Agmina, flagrantemque infidi Saxonis oram
Concutit, infensosque parentum in funera natos
Suscitat, antiquos flammaque abolere Penates
Molitur, patrios et Marte evertere muros.
    Musa refer tanti funesta incendia belli,
Et causas accerse odii, civilis et irae
Semina, quid saevos et ad arma nefanda Britannos
Impulerat tantos patriaeque ciere tumultus.
Numina jam laetis nimium contraria rebus
Et revoluta novam seriem fortuna laborum
Saeva parat, rerumque alternus vertitur ordo.
Tristia succedunt laetis, sorsque aspera belli
Ingruit, et tragici trahit in ludibria Fati.
Astra inimica premunt, et jam surgentis in altum
Imperii tristem properant Fata impia finem,
Et rerum fatalis apex, conversaque retro
Fatorum series regalibus invida sceptris,
Attulit extremam summi discriminis horam,
Qua tria Regna suis jaceant tumulata ruinis.
Sic ubi summa dies perituro illuxerit orbi,
Cuncta Chaos priscum repetent, tellusque, fretumque,
Stellantisque poli moles, operosaque rerum
Machina coelestis flagrabit et ignibus axis.
Sponte sua in cineres mortalia cuncta redibunt;

right hand, and inflates her breast with rising hope. She lashes friends into opposition, goading on sons against their fathers, and strives to consume the ancient Penates in flame, and to overthrow the country's strength.
    Tell, oh Muse, the origin and cause of this anger which impels the Britons to such ruinous strife. A reversed fortune, now turned against our former too bright prosperity, prepares a new series of labours. Sadness succeeds joy, and the bitter lot of war presses on, drawing all things to be the sport of a tragic fate. The stars are hostile, and threaten a sad end to the reviving glory of the empire, and the fatal moment has come when three kingdoms are to fall together in ruins. Thus when the last day shall have shone upon a perishing world, all things will return to ancient Chaos, and land and sea and starry heaven, and the whole globe labouring on its axis, shall burn with fire. All things mortal will return by

Et metam magnis posuerunt sidera Regnis
Imperiisque modum, nihil et complectitur orbis
Aut gremio natura suo, nil Terra nec Aether
Protulit, aut liquidus Tethys complectitur ulnis,
Quod non praecipiti lapsu volventibus annis
Corruet, et senio tandem languente fatiscat.
    Hinc rapit ardentes studia in contraria mentes
Relligionis apex, et dissona sacra furores
Exacuere novos, et sic diversa secuti
Dogmata, fallaci laetamur imagine veri.
Ille vel ille suas magno molimine partes
Dum fovet, et fatuae dictat mysteria turbae,
Linquimur in caecis, dubio rectore, tenebris.
Et licet in terris, magni per moenia mundi,
A Gade ad Gangem, nihil est praeclarius usquam
Quam sincera fides, fraudisque ignara nefandae
Relligio, immensum toties cantata per orbem;
At simulata fides, pridemque renata Genevae
Relligio, extremas mundi jam concutit oras,
Brutigenumque dolis tria Regna coercet iniquis,
Alternisque odiis humano sanguine terram
Purpuream pinguemque facit, fluviosque cruore
Inficit, et thalami sociam praebere marito
Toxica, et innocui natos in busta parentis
Excitat, et solio Reges detrudit avito,

their own motion to ashes; the stars have placed a limit to great kingdoms, a measure to empire; and the world and nature, earth, air, and sea, hold nothing which in the revolving years fades not away.
Now religious controversy hurries men into opposing lines, and as they follow diverse dogmas, they grasp the false image of the true. While this one or that one supports his party with great eagerness, and casts mysteries before the fatuous crowd, we are left in darkness, doubt alone triumphing. And although within earth's bounds, from Gades to Ganges, there be nothing more illustrious, more worthy of song than a sincere faith, yet false faith, the religion long ago new-born at Geneva, is that which distracts the world, ruins the British realm, makes fat the empurpled earth with human gore, stains the rivers with blood, tempts the wife to poison her husband, the children to seek the death of the innocent parent; it drives kings from ancestral thrones, compels great

Magnanimosque duces putrefacta fimeta lacertis
Amplecti cogit tremulis, et sceptra potentum
Sternit humi, totumque movet fera bella per orbem.
O quam felices, Regesque habitura beatos
Insula magnorum genetrix foecunda parentum !
Tempora si priscum servassent nostra tenorem,
Proelia pro sacris cum Mars non intulit aris
Impius, et nullum pro relligione duellum.
Nec nisi cum saevis Regni pro finibus Anglis
Lis erat, externus vel quando lacesserat hostis.
At cum fictitium assumpsit pietatis amictum,
Et foedo infandum contraxit foedere bellum,
Albion ipsa suis ruit irreparabilis armis,
Sternitur et patrio confossa Britannia ferro.
   O male concordes indulgentesque furori
Axe sub arctoo populos, et in arma ruentes
Saxonidas ! queis nulli unquam de stemmate Regum
Sceptrigeri placuere viri, non Martyr et Heros
Carolus ipse licet, magnorum uberrima Divum
Progenies, nec uterque suo de sanguine natus
Insidias potuit populi vitare furentis ;
Gesserit invicto licet inclyta sceptra lacerto
Pulsus uterque novas exul sibi quaerere terras.
Et Pater ad Superos indigno funere missus

generals to embrace the dunghill; it casts to the ground the sceptre of the powerful, and rouses fierce war throughout the world. Oh how happy we, and our island, blest in her kings, the fruitful mother of great parents—oh would that our times had preserved their ancient tenour—when impious Mars roused no strife for sacred things, and religious wars were not; and when there was battle with the fierce English alone, for border-land, or when the external enemy attacked us. But when Albion assumes the fictitious garb of piety, and by the foul Covenant contracts an infamous war, she herself rushes to her own ruin, and Britain perishes, pierced with her own sword. Oh ye discordant Scots indulging in fury, and Saxons rushing to arms, to whom never any man of the race of kings was pleasing, not the martyr and hero Charles himself, the richest offspring of the gods, nor could either of the sons, sprung from his blood, escape the snares of this mad race. Both were driven to seek new homes in exile, and the father, sent to Heaven before his time by an unworthy

Ante diem, dubii Patriam in sudore duelli
Luctantem, et terras infames caede reliquit.
Quo magis illustrem vera aut pietate merentem
Phoebus ab extremis surgens non viderat Indis,
Dum petit Herculeas fesso temone columnas.
Namque aditum virtute nova super ardua Coeli
Stravit, et exemplo callem patefecit Olympo.
At nunc civilis post tanta incendia flammae
Totque procellosos infausto Marte labores,
Atque interfectum crudeli caede Parentem,
Haec eadem innocuis meditantur proelia natis
Saxonidae, et caecos populo immisere furores ;
Jam solio pulsum, rapto diademate, Regem
Amandant, patriisque vetant consistere terris.
Hinc fas atque nefas vertere nefanda potentum
Ingenia, et rapido permiscet cuncta tumultu.
Vana superstitio, et nomen pietatis inane
Impulit effrenes iterum in fera bella Britannos.
O mentita fides, et nigrae conscia fraudis
Relligio, in varias docilis transire figuras.
Infelix monstrum et Patriae fatalis Erynnis !
Non illam armatae acies non arma nec urbes,
Moenia nec coelo educta, aut maria alta coercent,
Nec cohibere valent fraudem munimina belli
Fortia, praecipiti sed transtulit omnia cursu
In Chaos antiquum, totumque coercuit orbem.

death, left his country stained with his blood, and struggling in the throes of a doubtful contest. Than Charles, Phœbus, from his rising in the extremest Indies, to his setting at the Pillars of Hercules, ne'er looked upon a prince more worthy, more illustrious for true piety. He strewed the steep ascent to Heaven with new virtues, and made easier, by his example, the narrow path to Olympus. And now, after so great a burning of the civil flame, after so many stormy commotions, the father being thus slain, the English people again meditate the same attempts against his innocent sons, and stir up blind fury in the popular mind. They drive the king into exile, and forbid him to return to his ancestral kingdoms. Vain superstition, and the empty name of piety, impel the fierce Briton again into these savage wars. Oh lying Faith ! and Religion conscious of black fraud ! skilled in assuming diverse forms.

Et jam Brutigenae Rex augustissimus orae
Saecla Caledoniae qui condidit aurea terrae,
Quique indignantem sub jura redegit Iernam,
Carolus et coelo et patriis jam debitus astris,
Aethereas felix Superum remeavit ad aedes,
Imperii summas fratrique reliquit habenas.
Ille reformatam dubia licet usque teneret
Mente fidem, saevos tranquilla in pace Britannos
Composuit ; quo sceptra manu gestante, per orbem
Arctoum pax alta fuit, non Martius horror
Tinnula, nec tacitos ruperunt tympana somnos
Agricolûm. At fatis postquam concessit iniquis,
Civica succensis fervescunt jurgia bellis,
Magnaque turbatis surgit confusio rebus.
Frater ut imperii trabeata insignia tanti
Induit, et solio ingentem sese intulit alto,
Dogmata Pontificum Romanaque sacra secutus
(Quae prius externis procul hauserat exul in oris)
Rite colit, patriisque eadem se inducere templis
Velle ministeria et cultus abolere priores
Rumor erat, populique levis vox alta tenebat.
Attolli Ausonios ad maxima pondera rerum
Gnaviter asseclas, nec jam locus ullus in aula,

And now when that most august monarch, whose reign was the golden age of Scotland, who reduced impatient Ireland to obedience, when he (Charles II.) had passed to the celestial mansions of the gods, he left the reins of government to his brother. Although he held the reformed religion with a dubious mind, he yet kept the Britons in tranquil peace. While his hand held the sceptre, a profound peace lay upon the country, no martial dread, no sounding drum broke the quiet dreams of the husbandman. But when he had yielded his life to the Fates, civil broils swell to fiery wars, and terrible confusion arises in the troubled State. When his brother donned the royal robes of the great empire, and ascended the lofty throne, he dutifully observed the doctrines and the rites of Rome, which he had first learned when an exile on a foreign shore, and soon there arose a rumour that he was determined to introduce the same into the Churches of the Nation, and to abolish the existing Ministry and Worship.

The light word takes deep hold of the mind of the people. They shout that Italian followers are being steadily promoted to

Vociferant, nullique adeo tribuuntur honores,
Qui non Romuleos veneratur transfuga ritus :
Hinc fremit, inque graves assurgit Episcopus iras,
Pollutum queriturque fidem, temerataque sacra
Jura, magistratus, positasque in pulvere leges.
Jam quatit iratis suggesta trementia palmis,
Atque ementitis populi rumoribus aures
Palpat, et ardentes succendit pectoris aestus,
Impia grandiloquas acuitque in jurgia linguas,
Regique infandum clangit ceu buccina bellum.
  Haec conjuratae quam primum tessera turbae
Insonuit, dubio fervet gens tota tumultu.
Extemplo stimulis haud mollibus excitat iras
Patricia de gente chorus summique Senatus,
Turba etiam tacitas male-cauto perfida Regi
Astruit insidias occultaque retia tendit ;
Accenditque animos Marti, dirosque tumultus
Suscitat, et motus ira stimulante rebelles ;
Et vocat externum qui sceptra capesseret hostem.

the chief management of affairs, that there is no longer place at Court, no honours, save for those who, as perverts, venerate the rites of Rome. Then the Bishop[1] murmurs, and rises up in grave anger. He complains that the Faith is being corrupted, that sacred things are insulted, that the Magistrate and the Law are thrown in the dust. Anon he shakes the trembling pulpit with his angry fist, and with lying tales he tickles the ears of the people and fires their breasts. He sharpens his grandiloquent tongue into impious railing, and, as a trumpet, he proclaims an unnatural war against his King.

As soon as this party-cry of the conspirators goes forth, the whole nation blazes into dangerous tumult. Nobles, and chief of the senate, are found, who apply no gentle spur to the rising feeling. A party, treacherous to the king, sets the snare, and spreads the secret net, whetting spirits already sharpened to rebellion, and invites a foreign enemy to seize the sceptre. Oh

---

[1] Probably referring to the attitude of the seven Bishops, or specially to that of Compton, Bishop of London, who not only condemned the action of James, but joined in the invitation to William to make a descent upon England. With him in this invitation were the Earls of Devonshire, Danby, and Shrewsbury, Lord Lumley, Admiral Russel, and Sidney.

O Populi furor! O Procerum male sana libido!
O secli impietas! O degener Anglia diris
Cladibus exposita, et civilibus obruta bellis!
In ferrum flammasque ruunt tria regna stupendis
Motibus, insanis Mavors nunc ardet in armis
Improbus. O quantos potuit suadere furores
Relligio! Patriaeque graves inferre ruinas.
Quis furor iste sacer? rabies quae tanta nocendi
Sternere praecipitem sublimi a culmine Regem,
Atque iterum patrios foedare in pulvere fasces!
Jam Proceres, primique Duces, ipsique Tribuni
Militiae, infausti pubesque ignava Gradivi
Regis in exitium, et Patriae irreparabile damnum
Conspirant, multumque animis discordibus ardent;
Irarum ingentes volvuntque in pectore fluctus,
Et furit insano belli civilis amore;
Atque agitur saevi Martis male sana juventus
Consiliis, rapiturque levi vertigine vulgus,
Convocat armatos et ad impia signa maniplos.

  Hos inter belli strepitus gliscente tumultu,
Regina Italidum decus ingens matronarum,
In Tyriis enixa toris feliciter almum
Haeredem Regnis peperit formosa Britannis.
Illa uteri felix, et fortunata laborum
Reddidit insigni felicem prole maritum.
Ante alias et laeta nurus quas Romula tellus
Dives alit, magnum magni patris incrementum

madness of the people! Oh mad lust of the nobles! Oh impiety of the age! three kingdoms rush to fire and sword, and impious Mars glows in wild fury. Nobles, leading Generals, and officers of lower rank, and the vile mercenaries, conspire to defile the sceptre in the mire, to destroy the King, and bring irreparable ruin on their country. In armed bands the common people assemble under impious standards.

  Amid the sounds of gathering tumult the beautiful Queen—the great ornament of Italian matrons—in the purple of the throne happily bore the sweet heir of the British realms. Happy in her womb, and fortunate in labour, she made glad her husband with an illustrious offspring, and rich beyond other women of her country, she, a joyous mother, brought forth this support to his

Progenuit, serae solatia blanda senectae ;
Atque equidem hunc ipsum olim oriundum ex gente Stuarti[1]
Esse reor, celsis famam qui terminet astris,
Imperium Oceano, et magni genitoris iniquum
Exilium, ereptos quique ulciscetur honores,
Quique iterum patrium sub leges mitteret orbem.
Namque Patris virtute sua mox damna rependet,
Cunctandoque, armisque urgendo restituet rem.
Ille etenim coelo missum ceu numen ab alto
Privati nil sortis habet, decor insitus oris
Et matrem referens specie, et virtute Parentem
Dat generis documenta sui, geniique futuri
Exhibet indicium, et, si quid praesagia possunt,
Non leve pignus erit, divini Principis ortus
Uno eodemque die quo Constantinus in auras
Edidit aethereas, magnum crescentibus annis
Omen habet superos[2] que jubet sperare faventes.

great father, a sweet consolation of advancing age. And indeed I deem this prince to be the one of the Stuart race, whose fame shall reach the stars, whose empire the sea alone shall bound, and who shall revenge the unjust exile of his great father, and his reft honours, and who again shall bring his country under law. Soon by his virtue will he repair the losses of his father, and by his counsel and prowess recover the state. For he, as a divinity sent from high Heaven, will have no ordinary lot. His countenance in its native grace, recalling his mother by its beauty, and his father by its goodness, gives the credentials of his race, and exhibits an index of future genius; and if presages mean anything, not light are their promises. The birth of the divine Prince on the same day as that on which Constantine[3] first breathed the air of Heaven, holds great omen for his future years, and bids us hope for the favour of the gods.

---

[1] Ver. 274 may be scanned with severe elisions.

[2] *Var. lect.* No 'que' after superos.

[3] The Prince was born on 10th June; Constantine the Great apparently on February 27th. The reference may be to Constantine II. of Scotland, who, according to Buchanan—the History most accessible to the author—retrieved something of the ruin caused by his uncle Donald in the kingdom, and restored it 'to the same bounds which had been left by his father,' Kenneth M'Alpin. The source of the author's knowledge of the birthday of either Constantine would be interesting. Innocent XII. transferred the Feast of St. Margaret of Scotland from 16th November to June 10th, as a compliment, it was thought, to the birthday of the Prince.

At Phlegetonteis jam fama innata cavernis
Daemonis arte ruit, terrasque effusa per omnes
Praepetibus volitat pennis et guttura mille
Solvit, et ora virûm fictis rumoribus implet :
Hunc ipsum heroem mentito ex semine nasci
Supposita de matre nothum, Regemque futurum
Fraude sacerdotum, toto qui imponeret orbi
Pontificum ritus et barbara sacra Quiritum,
Et solio Auriacum secluderet arte tyrannum,
Atque reformatos ferro flammaque Britannos
Vastaret, patrias et milite verteret arces.
   Talia fama levis volitans pernicibus alis
Ocyor et nymbis, rapidisque citatior Euris
Nunciat Europae populis, et ab Aequore Rubro
Usque ad stridentem Mauris in fluctibus axem
Fertur, et attonitum commentis commovet Orbem.
Signifer ipse doli, conjurataeque catervae
Ductor ut Auriacus Batavo de littore Princeps
Impia discordes ardere in bella Britannos
Praesensit, stimulos animis flagrantibus addit,
Edoctus proavum sceleris superare Magistrum,

   But meanwhile, a report born of diabolic skill issues from the caverns of Phlegethon, and spreading itself out over all lands, flies on beating wing, opening a thousand throats, and filling the mouths of men with lying tales—that this very hero was born of false blood, the fraudulent offspring of a counterfeit mother, designed by the fraud of the priests to become a king who might impose the papal rites and barbarous religion of Rome upon the whole world, and exclude by art the Dutch Prince from the throne, and who might destroy the reformed Britons with fire and sword, and overthrow the country's strength. Light rumour, flying on nimble wing, swifter than the clouds and winds, spreads these tales throughout Europe, from the Red Sea to the Moorish Straits, and, with such fabrications, stirs the astonished world. When the Prince of Orange, himself the author of the fraud and leader of the conspiracy, perceived that the discordant Britons were burning for war, he added fuel to the flame. Skilled to surpass his great grandsire [1] (that master of craft, who withdrew the

---

[1] William the Silent, the liberator of the Netherlands from the Spanish yoke. His youngest son was Frederick Henry, whose eldest son was William II. of Orange, who was the father of William III. of Orange and England.

Belgarum qui colla jugo subducit Ibero,
Et Domino insidiis detraxit sceptra nefandis,
Quae nunc illicitis male parta tuetur in armis.
Barbara bella parat, nova regnaque sanguine quaerit.
Nam sitis in sobole haec crescit vesana cruoris;
Qualis in Hyrcanis saxa inter inhospita silvis
Effera pollutas quae semper sanguine fauces
Tygris habet, cum jam facilis data copia praedae
Saevit in annosum stomacho latrante parentem,
Et fremitu ruit ingenti, et simul ore cruento
Involat in praedam pedibusque eviscerat uncis.
Sic ille in socerum insurgit nil tale merentem
Ambitione furens, et inanes mente triumphos
Somniat injustis dum cuncta patere rapinis
Posse putat, magno accendit tria regna tumultu,
Irritatque ultro heroes, Martemque lacessit.

    Est Dea Tartarei monstrum furiale barathri
Impia Gorgoneis Alecto armata colubris,
Cuncta cavernoso ex-superans portenta sub orco.
Huic caedes et bella placent, dirique tumultus,
Iraque insidiaeque, et sunt certamina curae;
Haec nunc Coccyti sedem Stygiamque paludem
Linquit, et anguicomum superis caput extulit arvis,

necks of the Belgians from the Spanish yoke, and by wicked arts won the sceptre from its lord, which now, wrongfully acquired, is held by unlawful power), he prepares barbarous wars, and seeks new kingdoms by blood—for this raging thirst for blood ever increases in the offspring. As amid the inhospitable rocks of the Hyrcanian forest, the fierce tiger, with jaws ever stained with blood, turns with rage—even when food is plentiful—against his sire, and with gory fangs falls upon the prey and tears it with his feet and claws; so that prince, raging with ambition, rises against his father-in-law (little deserving such treatment), dreams of empty triumphs, while he thinks that he is able to lay open all things to his unjust rapine, and setting fire to three kingdoms, he excites beyond measure their brave men, and provokes war.

    There is an impious goddess, a dire monster in the depths of Tartarus, armed with Gorgon snakes, Alecto by name, surpassing all the powers of darkness. To her, carnage, war, tumult, anger, treachery, are ever pleasing, and her chief care. She now leaves her seat by the Stygian Lake, and raising her snake-crowned head

Quaque ibat late terrorque metusque sequuntur;
Et petit aequoreas Tamisini littoris undas
Nube volans, magnam Luddique superstitit urbem
Ardua stridentes quassans serpentibus alas,
Tartaream clangitque tubam, et fremebunda per omnem
Evolat illa urbem, lateque patentia regna,
Inspirans passim populos furialibus iris.
Finitimasque ciens in tristia proelia gentes,
Perfurit infelix, turbataque pectora versat,
Fictitiisque virûm mentes sermonibus implet,
Erroremque animis ultro flagrantibus indit,
Inque sinus Stygios immittit protinus angues.
Saeva quibus totum monstris perterritat orbem
Et late sternit populos, regesque potentes
Disjicit imperiis, et magnas proterit urbes.
Haec ubi commotis immisit monstra Britannis
Liquit acerba solum, atque horrenda petivit Averni.
Continuo fremuere viri, simul omnis in arma
Conjurat regio, nec non proceresque ducesque
Plebsque lacessitum poscit certamine martem.
Nec tantum proceres, et plebs insana frementes
Instigant clamore animos, sed Episcopus audax
Ira ultrice fremit, furiisque accensus iniquis
Aestuat, et linguis civilia bella protervis
Exacuit, gaudetque tubas inflare rebelles.

above the earth—while terror and fear follow her—she seeks the shores of Thames, and rests over the great city of London. Aloft, beating her wings, rustling with serpents, she sounds her hellish trumpet, and, muttering as she goes, flies through every city, and far and wide through the land, filling men's minds with fury, and rousing neighbour races to dire strife. Implanting error and sowing lies, she casts her Stygian snakes into men's bosoms. With what prodigies does she terrify the whole earth in her cruelty! Far and wide she overthrows nations, dethrones mighty kings, ruins great cities. When she has done her evil work among the agitated Britons, she leaves the land and seeks the horrors of Avernus. Forthwith men rage, at once each district is sworn to arms, and nobles, generals, common people, seek the arbitrament of war. Nor are nobles and common people alone, but the bold Bishop rises up in vengeful wrath, and fired with fury, he stimulates to civil war with his wanton tongue, and eagerly blows the

Pro Masora, et sacri venerando dogmate Christi
Amplexus lituos, atque horrida castra secutus
Ante aciem Tyrio fulget conspectus in ostro.
　Jam manifesta dedit diri praesagia belli
Omniparens Natura, polusque elementaque mundi
Ostendunt nostrae fatalia signa ruinae;
Et Superi, in nostras jurataque numina clades,
Pectora prodigiis terrent mortalia miris.
Haud procul Oceano, qua longe Arctoa relinquit
Plaustra calescentes et Scotia vergit ad Austros,
Est locus Aeneadum dicta est de nomine tellus;
Hic ubi Roumondae latum se expandit in aequor
Planities, densisque solum vestitur ericis,
Agmina sanguineis utrinque minantia signis
Visa polo mediae per muta silentia noctis
Inter se infestis concurrere cominus armis.
Terribilis clamorque virum, atque hinnitus equorum
Armorumque sonus varius, sonitusque tubarum,
Auditi, et toto resonantia tympana coelo:
Diraque sulphureis vibrata tonitrua flammis

rebel trump, grasping the clarion instead of his Bible and the Sacred Creed of Christ; joining the rough camp, he shines before the line in his Tyrian purple.

Already Mother Nature had given manifest presages of terrible war, and the Heavens, and the elements of the world, were showing fatal signs of our ruin; and the gods, and lesser deities, sworn together for our destruction, terrify the breasts of men with marvellous prodigies. Not far from the ocean, where Scotland turns from the Northern Wain and verges towards the warming South, there is a place called the Land of Angus.[1] Here, where Monromond[2] stretches itself towards the broad sea, the plain is clothed alone with thick heather.[3] Through the deep silence of midnight, in the sky are seen on every side menacing hosts with bloody standards, rushing against each other with hostile arms. In the heavens there is heard varied clang of arms, sound of trumpets, shouts of men, neighing of horses, and rolling drums.

---

[1] Locus Aeneadum = Angus. Eneas = Angus, *Scotticè*.
[2] Monrimmon Muir — in old maps Monrommond — well-known track of moorland in Forfarshire.
[3] For like matter see Lucan's *Pharsalia*, Book I.

Horrendum caecas procul insonuere per umbras :
Voxque secuta ruit magno per inane boatu
Nil mortale sonans, 'Quid[1] saeva, Britannia, Divos
Infensos in fata vocas ? en horrida belli
Damna feres, strages virûm cladesque videbis.
Prima sed horrentes spectabit Iernia pugnas
Maestior, undantes et sanguine sentiet amnes
Grampius, et patrios in bella vocabit alumnos ;
Sed ducis incoeptos Mors impia sistet honores.
Hinc fremebunda pedem referet Bellona per omnem
Europam, bellique dabit Germania sedem.
Magnus at Hectoreis surget Ludovicus in armis,
Et conjuratas prosternet Marte phalanges,
Vastabitque solum disjectis oppida circum
Praesidiis, Batavaeque et Iberae insignia gentis
Delebit, pennasque aquilae mucrone secabit ;
Victor et in saevos mox transferet arma Britannos,
Atque armis opibusque in regna juvabit euntem
Haeredem, tandem defuncti Marte Britanni
Sceptra dabunt niveis pueri gestanda lacertis.'
Haec procul ut resonas late exaudita per auras,

Through the dark distance dread thunderings sound, with lightnings to be feared, and a voice following, of no mortal tone, rushes through the empty air with loud cry. 'Why, oh Britain, dost thou evoke to thy bitter fate gods hostile to thee ? Lo, thou shalt bear the dread calamities of war, and shalt see havoc and the slaughter of men. But Ireland first, the more sorrowful, shall behold fierce battles, and the Grampian land shall see rivers flowing with blood, and will call out her sons to war. But impious death shall arrest the rising honours of the general. Then shall raging Bellona pass throughout Europe, and Germany shall be the first seat of war. But the great Louis, in Hectorean arms, shall overcome the allied armies in battle, and shall devastate the land around the cities whose bulwarks have been destroyed ; and he will blot out the emblems of Holland, and the Spanish race, and clip the Eagle's wings. As a conqueror he will presently turn his sword against the fierce Britons, and with arms and money will he aid the heir returning to his kingdoms, and the Britons at length— war being at an end—will give the sceptre to be borne by the fair arms of youth.' As these words sounded in the air, victory

---

[1] *Var. lect.* Quod.

Cum prius incerto steterat victoria fato,
Una acies trepido vertit vestigia gressu,
Alteraque hostilem sequitur cum murmure turmam.
Desuper at lapsae jacuere per arva secures,
Loricaeque ocreaeque et duro hastilia ferro
Spiculaque in variis atque arma inventa figuris,
Terrent jam stupidi trepidantia pectora vulgi,
Tristia venturis praebentque oracula bellis.

   Haec mala nec dubiis licuit praenoscere signis,
Nam Pater Omnipotens stupidum prope terruit orbem
Fulgure, et insano rapidum procul impete fulmen
Torsit, et ardentes disjecit ab aethere flammas;
Et micuere faces, totoque sonantia coelo
Disjecere altas templorum fulmina turres;
Arsit et ignivomi sidus ferale cometae
Crinitam et gelidas caudam perrexit ad arctos,
Portendens terris civilia bella Britannis.
Phoebus et obscura nitidum ferrugine coelum
Texit, et horrendis noctis se immiscuit umbris,
Oppositaque suo fratrem lugubris opacat
Phoebe[1] soror, nigrumque abdit lita sanguine vultum,
Et stupuere, acie obtusa acies, vaga sidera coeli,
Horruit aeternas mundusque instare tenebras.

at first seemed uncertain. Then one line turns in rapid flight, the other follows the enemy with clamour, and, falling from above, axes, shields, greaves, iron-pointed spears, darts, and armour of varied shapes bestrew the ground, and terrify the timid breasts of the dull peasant, giving sad omen of the wars to come.

Nor are there only doubtful signs of coming evil, for God Himself terrifies the earth with lightning and thunderbolt, and glowing flame from Heaven. Towers of churches are struck down, and the deadly comet [2] blazes in the sky with tail streaming towards the chilly North, portending civil wars in British land. Phœbus also plunges the sky in darkness, and wraps the day in night. The moon, too, casts her brother into mournful shadow, and besmeared in blood hides a darkened face. The wandering stars of heaven, a confused band, are stupified, and the world trembles as she

---

[1] Final *e* in 'Phoebe' should be long.

[2] The comet of 1680 excited great interest throughout Europe. Its splendour and swiftness were very remarkable. Halley's comet of 1682 soon followed. The eclipses of the time made much impression, and are frequently referred to.

In templis sudasse ferunt simulacra Deorum,
Sanguineos alto delapsos aethere rores
Et tumulo egressos vitae se reddere manes.
Quorum (si qua fides) pietate verendus et annis
Unus erat qui se circum vada curva Timellae
Fluminis incautis, vertunt dum rura, colonis
Obtulit, et dictis sic est effatus amicis.
'Tristibus infestam Furiis jam linquite terram,
Adventat Bellona furens, fugite ocius,' inquit,
'Littore ab arctoo. Ferventem in proelia Martem
Fatalem et video stagnantem sanguine campum;
Victrici de parte cadet dux ipse cruento
Vulnere, et in mediis animam dabit ille triumphis,
Nec multum patriae victoria laeta futura est.
Belliger ille quidem et sumptis late inclytus armis,
Dent modo fata dies, Regem positurus avito
In solio, et Batavi fracturus sceptra tyranni.
Verum ultra fata ire vetant, gentisque Britannae
Ultimus Hectoridum Atholio tumulabitur arvo.'
Dixerat, et tenues evanidus exit in auras.
Tamque per attonitam vulgantur carmina plebem
Dira Liermonthi vatis, Gildaeque Britanni

seems to enter into eternal darkness. Report tells of sweating images in the churches, and that from high Heaven fell drops of blood, that the dead rose from their graves; of whom one, venerable from piety and years—if it may be believed—appeared by the fords of the Tummel to the peasants in the fields, and thus spoke in friendly words: 'Leave now this fated country; flee quickly from these Northern lands. I behold fatal contests, and the plains steeped in blood. The general himself, on the conquering side, will fall by bloody wound, and will yield up his soul in the midst of triumph, nor will his victory be of much future good to his country. That warrior indeed, so illustrious, would—had the Fates given time—have placed the King on his ancestral throne, and broken the sceptre of the Dutch tyrant. But further the Fates forbid to go, and the last hero of the British race will be buried in the fields of Atholl.' He spoke, and vanished into the thin air. And now, throughout the country, among the anxious people, the ominous songs of Learmonth the Prophet,[1] of Gildas

---

[1] Thomas the Rhymer, Gildas, Merlin,—all three much associated in Celtic and Scottish minds with dreary vaticination. Buchanan says that in his

Merlinique senis, qui nunc uno ore canebant
Affore Grampiacis miseranda pericula terris.
Mira quoque aethereas sunt edita monstra sub auras
Latrarunt lugubre canes, et bellua voces
Edidit humanas Lemuresque animaeque nocentes,
Et larvae in mediis insultavere tenebris.
   Heu Patria infelix, et iniqua Britannia magnis
Regibus, haud sacri venerando nomine Christi
Censeri jam digna satis : Quid jura fidemque
Conculcas toties et Regum sanguine gaudes?
Quo ruis oh demens? nec te tua vulnera tangunt?
Nec Patriae telluris honos, nec mentis honestae
Gloria, nec sacris reverentia debita sceptris,
Districtos cohibent Regum a cervicibus enses.
Haud secus insanis quam si fera vipera matrem
Lactantem eroso crudeliter enecet alvo.
Quid tam civili placet insanire tumultu
Mutuaque infensos animare in proelia cives?

the Briton, and of the ancient Merlin, are sung as with one mouth, telling of the miseries approaching the Grampian land. The air is filled with portents—brutes speak with human voice—ghosts and spectres rise in the darkness on every side.

   Alas! unhappy country! Britain, hostile to great kings, now unworthy to be ranked among Christian countries! Why so often dost thou spurn law and religion, and rejoice in the blood of kings? Whither madly dost thou rush? Dost thou not feel thy wounds? Neither the honour of the fatherland, nor the glory of an honourable mind, nor the reverence due to the sacred sceptre, withhold thy drawn sword from the necks of thy kings. Thus does the viper wound the breast that nourishes it. Why does civil tumult so delight you? or what avails it to set on fire

---

time the prophecies of Merlin were widely spread, but obscure, and that they were 'now daily interpolated and augmented by new additions.' He considers Merlin as an 'egregious impostor and cunning pretender rather than a prophet'; he puts his date about 479 A.D. As to Gildas, he considers him a good and learned man, held in high veneration, both while alive and since his death. 'The predictions which are circulated under his name,' he says, 'are so ridiculous in sentiment and language, and so rude and wretched in composition, that no person in his senses can believe them to be his composition.' He puts his date a little later than Merlin's. The editor remembers all three names in connection with the observances of Hallowe'en in Forfarshire, in his early days.

Quidve juvat patrios flamma vastare penates?
Felix qui Patria cineres commiscuit urna
Cerneret ante gravem Regi quam instare ruinam,
Et Patriam in tenues ambustam sponte favillas,
Equatosque solo muros, versosque penates,
Atque alio cives mundi sub cardine caesos
Et vacuas cultore domos. Tu causa malorum
Anglia tantorum meritas dabis impia poenas:
En funesta lues, tempestasque horrida belli
Ingruit (irati praesagia tristia coeli
Fulguraque, et longo feralem crine cometam
Conspectam, terris haud unquam impune Britannis
Vidimus) invictis ingens Jacobus in armis
Victor ab extremis Morinorum finibus, hoste
Perdomito, Batavum solio turbare tyrannum
Advolat, et sua regna gravi jam Marte reposcat,
Aut ferro populetur agros, et navibus ignem
Injiciat; totamque infestet littoris oram,
Et pelagi imperium, raptique insignia sceptri
Vendicet, et partis clarescat Marte trophaeis.

Jamne adeo eversis fatali fraude Britannis
Martia, quae claris surrexit ad aethera factis,
Haud semel experto saevi certamine Martis,

---

the Penates of the land? Happy he who died ere he saw ruin approaching his king, and his country in flames, its walls levelled to the ground, its religion overthrown, its citizens driven into other climes, and the homes of its peasants desolate. Thou, impious England, the cause of so great evils, shalt receive thy merited punishment. Lo! dread calamity, and the horrid tempest of war, hasten on (we saw the sad presages of an angry Heaven, the lightning, and the fateful comet, never seen over British lands but for evil). The great James, in unconquered arms, a victor from distant shores, his enemy vanquished, flies to dethrone the Batavian tyrant, and may he reclaim his kingdoms in glorious battle, devastate the country with the sword, and fire the ships. May he infest the whole seaboard,[1] lay claim to the empire of the deep, to the insignia of his government, and shine in the triumphs of his conquest.

---

[1] Does the Poet hope that he may appear off Arbroath, and free him from his troubles with the Magistrates and Ministers?

Gloria Scotorum, subducto sole peribit
Tot prius et tantis belli decorata trophaeis,
Imperiis nunquam externi parere tyranni,
Nec tolerare jugum, aut dominis servire superbis
Sueta, nec injecto servilia vincula collo
Passa, nec hostiles errare impune maniplos,
Scotia plebeios nec gesserat inclyta fasces,
Nullius aut duras sub leges venerat hostis :
Substitit hic domito Romana potentia mundo ;
Atque triumphatis utroque a cardine terris
Scotia limes erat, Romanaque repulit arma.
Quae toties Cymbrum, toties compescuit Anglum
Danorum toties et fregerat agmina, quorum
Pingue cruore solum littusque etiam ossibus album est
Et quorum decies millena cadavera nostris

Is it indeed so, that through a stratagem, the martial glory of the Scots—once so exalted by illustrious deeds, and so adorned with the trophies of war—shall suffer eclipse, without a struggle being once attempted? Scotland, never accustomed to the yoke or to endure servile chain—Scotland, the illustrious, never obeyed democratic rule, nor came under the law of an enemy. Here, Roman power stayed her course over a conquered world; Scotland was the limit of her triumph. How often did she beat back the Britons, the Angles, and the Danes, whose hosts she broke, enriching her soil with their blood, and whitening her shores with their bones, and of whom ten thousand bodies lie unburied[1]

---

[1] The author is here speaking under the influence of local tradition as well as from Buchanan. The districts of Barry and Aberlemno are remarkable for numerous traces of ancient sepulture, and the tales of battles with the Danes are still fresh among the people. The slaughter of the battle of Barry, in which Camus, the leader of the Northmen, was said to have been slain, is thus commemorated in local rhyme—

'Lochty, Lochty is red, red, red,
For it has run three days wi' bluid.'

Another local rhyme gives a supposed interpretation of the stones at Aberlemno which shows the moderation of our author in his numbers of the slain—

'Here lies the King o' Denmark's son,
Wi' twenty thousand o' his horse and men.'

See Jervise, p. 22, Edition 1861.

As to the unburied condition, Buchanan speaks of the Danes on one occasion buying a permission to bury their dead after a great battle, and says the sepulture took place on Inchcolm. This would suggest that they would lie unburied when this commercial transaction did not take place.

Congestim sine honore jacent incondita campis.
Hoc fatale solum, haec invictaque moenia Scoti,
Per medios bellorum aestus, Martisque furores,
Perque vices rerum varias, bis mille per annos,
Centum sex proavi Reges, Regumque parentes
Ferguso tenuere sati victricibus armis.
Nam neque tempus edax ferrumve nec horrida belli
Fulmina Scotigenam poterant evertere gentem.
Illa securigeris fuit olim gloria Scotis
Propria, legitimos vitae discrimine Reges
Sustentare manu, et Patriae reparare ruinas,
Remque decusque simul libertatemque tueri,
Externos nescire duces, domuisse rebelles,
Hostilesque acies, vastatricesque catervas
Trans maria, et nostri citra confinia regni,
Audaci pepulisse manu, atque ultricibus armis.
Cum Regum poscebat honos latera ardua lato
Cingebant ferro, et clypeis capita alta coruscis,
Praecipites ad pugnam ingente mole ruebant:
Atque illuc laetum referunt vel ab hoste triumphum
Aut cum laude suam posuere in pulvere vitam.
    Sed nunc degeneres animi nil praeter inanes

without honour in our fields. This soil so fatal, these walls so impregnable, a hundred and six[1] ancestral kings, and parents of kings, sprung from Fergus, held, by unconquered arms, for twice a thousand years, through so many outbursts of war, through so many changes. Neither corroding time, nor the sword, were able to overthrow the Scottish race. It was the special glory of the target-bearing Scots in the crises of history, to uphold with strong hand the lawful King, to repair the country's losses, and to guard the honour and liberty of the State. When the honour of the King claimed it, they girt the broadsword to their shoulder, and with the bright shield held aloft, plunged headlong into battle with mighty impetus. Thence they either joyfully brought home the trophies of the enemy, or left their life in the dust.

But now we, degenerate men, possess nothing but the empty

---

[1] Our author is moderate compared with the Scottish barons in Bruce's time, who claimed at that date 113 kings of Scotland. In an appendix to the translation of Buchanan (Edin. 1829) the names and dates of 113 kings are given up to James VII. for a period of 2000 years.

Gloriolae fumos, et inertem nominis umbram
Prendimus indecores. Pigroque sepulta veterno
Corda animosque metu resides, desuetaque bello
Brachia, et attonitas labefacto in pectore mentes
Gestamus, segnesque humili concussa pavore
Pectora, dum rebus Patriae Pater astat in arctis.
Nunc ubi gentis honos antiquae, invictaque bello
Dextera victrices quae fregerat ante cohortes
Romulidum, saevasque superbi Saxonis iras
Sustinuit, Danosque truces fera bella minantes
Perdomuit, turpique fuga dare terga coegit
Saepius, et claris famam tulit inclyta factis.
At mores abiere boni cum viribus, et jam
Fata Caledoniis finem posuere trophaeis.
Corruit ipsa suis tandem confossa lacertis
Scotia, nec saevum mage sese senserat hostem;
Ante invicta aliis, dominaeque immunis habenae,
Vincula contorto sibi nectit ahenea collo;
Haec eadem externum virtus quae reppulit hostem,
Quaeque prius magnis stetit inconcussa procellis,
Retulit et pulchras invicto milite palmas,
Scotorum toties expertam vincere gentem
Nititur illicitis evertere funditus armis.
  Jam socerum gener et proles petit ense parentem,
Vincitur insidiis et avunculus ipse nepotis;

vapour of glory, the dim shadow of a name. We carry hearts
buried in the sluggishness of age, trembling souls, arms unaccus-
tomed to war, and dull minds in shattered breasts. And this,
while the Father of the country abides in adversity. Where now
is the honour of the ancient race, whose right hand, unconquered
in war, had before broken the cohorts of Rome, and stood firm
against the fierce anger of the proud Saxon, and conquered the
savage Dane, and oft compelled him to turn in base flight?
Now our good ways, with our strength, have departed, and
already the Fates have put an end to Scottish triumph. Scotland
at length, pierced by her own sword, falls to the ground, not
knowing herself to be her own worst foe. Her strength, which once
repelled the enemy, is now used for her own destruction. Now
the son-in-law attacks his father-in-law with the sword, and the
child the parent, and the uncle is overthrown by the snares of his

Nil leges, nil jura valent, non sanguinis ordo
Sufficit humani fluvios cohibere cruoris,
Nil pietas, thalami prosunt nec vincula juncti ;
Alter ad alterius non est nisi funere felix.
Nulla fides, sacri nusquam reverentia sceptri,
Majestas sed laesa jacet ; fert obvia Regi
Tela manu miles, Regemque inglorius armis
Prodidit et, ruptis Patriae jam legibus aequis,
Vota damus rapidis tanquam ludibria ventis,
Solvimus et junctas aeterno foedere dextras,
Mutua jam patrios per viscera condimus enses,
Gnaviter adversis simul et concurrimus hastis :
Europaeque oculos in nos convertimus omnes.
Infami turpique adeo innotescimus orbi
Nomine, venturis et stigma nepotibus ingens
Linquimus innocuis quod nulla obliteret aetas.
Dum pia signa gerunt alii civilia nobis
Bella placent, sparsi fratrumque cruore lacerti.
Arma nec infidis tantum civilia dextris
Sumpsimus, et totis jam sistimus agmina campis ;
Sed peregre multis venientem millibus ultro
Accipimus mediisque vocamus in aedibus hostem.

nephew.[1] Law and right avail nothing, nor do ties of family withhold from bloodshed. Piety and the bands of married life are little regarded. One man is made happy only by the destruction of another. There is no fidelity, there is no reverence, towards the sacred sceptre. Majesty lies wounded, the soldier raises his armed hand against his King, and ingloriously betrays him and the country's laws. Our oaths we give to be the sport of the winds. The hands given in assurance of mutual loyalty are raised to bury the sword in each other's vitals. We bring the eyes of Europe upon us, and bid the world note our infamy. We leave a stain upon our innocent children which no lapse of time will obliterate. While others bear Christian standards, civil war delights us, and arms besprinkled with fraternal blood. Nor do we only with treacherous hand raise arms and take the field, but we eagerly welcome into our midst the enemy, coming in force, and invite him within our walls.

---

[1] William was the nephew of James, his mother being Mary, daughter of Charles the First.

Ille Caledoniis qui praesidit inclitus arvis
Rex Jacobus avis atavisque ingentior altis,
Bellipotens Terrae Dominus, Deus aequoris alti,
Cujus ab imperio vasti maris ora pependit,
Quem toties celsa residentem puppe magistrum
Nereiadum mirata cohors, clavumque tenente
Quo caput aequoreis sepsit Neptunus in undis,
Quo viso positis Mavors et inhorruit armis,
Signaque concussum cujus victricia mundum
Terruerint, vastumque satis vix classibus aequor
Olim erat, et plenos siccabant agmina rivos.
At nunc insidiis, et proditione suorum
Elusus fictae pietatis imagine falsa,
Subdole et[1] obducto simulatis fraudibus hamo,
Armatam ante aciem, et simulati in pulvere belli
Atque inter turmas et circumstantia pila
Deseritur, densosque inter sine caede maniplos
Pulsus abit, regnisque tribus post terga relictis.
Cogitur a solio profugus remeare paterno,
Et vento affines Gallorum exquirere terras.
Illic liligeri Ludoici munere Regis
Francorum illustri suffultus milite, et armis
Fortibus adjutus, multis comitantibus ultro

James, that illustrious ruler of Scotland, greater than the greatest of his ancestors, valiant lord of earth, god of the ocean, from whose vast empire hung the shores of the sea—whom, as often as he sat as master on the lofty stern, the band of Nereids gathered to admire—who, holding the rudder, Neptune veiled his head beneath the waves—who, being seen, Mars trembled and laid aside his arms, whose conquering standards frightened the stricken world, and for whose ships the vast sea was once scarcely sufficient, and the feet of his soldiers dried up the swollen rivers! But now, deceived by the snares and treachery of his own, by a fictitious piety, by an artfully laid trap, in the dust of a simulated battle, he finds himself alone in the presence of an army, and in the midst of his troops and surrounding spears. Beaten without bloodshed, he departs, leaving three kingdoms behind him. He is compelled as a fugitive to leave the paternal throne, and to sail to the neighbouring shores of France. There, supported by the generosity of the Lily-bearing Louis, illustrious King of the

---

[1] Subdole et (*sic*).

Millibus heroum, bellatorumque virorum
Agmine stipatus, multa et subnixus opum vi
Illicet ingentes magno molimine turmas
Contrahit, infidos domiturus Marte Britannos
Erepta et saevo repêturus regna tyranno.
Jam petit herbiferae vicinum littus Iernae
Navibus instructis, ubi toties agmina campis
Instruit, atque Tyro jam jam duce belli Conello
Instaurat, Martemque in vulnera saeva lacessit.
    Presbyter at Scotus, perjuri militis astu
Ut videt excelso dejectum a culmine Regem,
Primus ad arma viros ingentibus evocat ausis
Turmatim, trepido subvertit et omnia motu ;
Tempus adesse ratus, quo foedera laesa reducat,
Instauretque sacram violati foederis aram,
Effera jam sumptis certamina provocat armis,
Speque animoque fremens toto conamine causam
Promovet antiquam, perque oppida et arva tumultus

French, aided with men and arms, a thousand heroes voluntarily[1] accompanying him, and strengthened with a body of men-at-arms, and with much money, he drew together great forces, that he might conquer the faithless Britons by war, and recover from the savage tyrant his stolen dominions. Now he seeks the near shores of Ireland the green with his fleet, where he draws up his army on the plain, and where Tyrconnell,[2] his general, now renews the war.

But when the Scotch Presbyter sees the King, through the craft of a perjured soldiery, cast down from his lofty station, he first, with great presumption, calls men to arms in companies, and overthrows everything with his commotions, thinking that the time is come when he may bring back the overthrown Covenant, and renew the sacred altar of that violated bond. With arms taken up he provokes men to fierce strife; fired with new hopes and spirit he promotes the old cause by every effort, and through city and country stirs up horrid tumults, and fills the byways with

---

[1] James was accompanied by about 1200 British subjects and a good number of French officers. He refused the help of a French army. They embarked at Brest in a fleet of 14 ships of the line, 7 frigates, 3 fire-ships, and a good number of transports. From Louis he received great stores of arms for the Irish, much money and superb equipages and plate for himself and his household.— Smollett, Book I. chap. i.

[2] Made Lord-Lieutenant when Clarendon was recalled in 1686, and still holding that kingdom for King James.

Concitat horrisonos, et compita milite complet.
Cui procerum discincta cohors, et perdita luxu
Et juvenum scelerata manus se adjungit, et omnis
Turba sequax miseri objecta de faece popelli
Confluit, eque suis redit impia turba latebris
Errorum, coetumque omnes glomerantur in unum
Quos capitale nefas, alieni aut pondera nummi
Jam pridem patrias cogebant linquere sedes.
Proditor et ganio atque exlex eadem arma sequuntur.
E quibus infanda ex omni regione locoque
Colluvies collecta virûm sub nomine Summi
Conventus, qui jam praeter jus fasque nefando
Nec prius audito titulo, cum prole Monarcham
Expulit ingentem, quo pulso expellitur alma
Relligio, sacris et Episcopus exulit [1] aris.
Et successoris statuit de jure futuri
Artificum foeda illuvies (mirabile dictu)
Judicis et partes Regni de rebus agebat,
Et Regum, invitis naturae legibus ipsis,
Non interruptam [2] seriem bis mille per annos

soldiery.[3] To him, a dissolute body of nobles and a debauched band of youths ally themselves, and a whole crowd of the off-scourings of the people, together with vagabonds, coming forth from their hiding-places. And with them too are gathered into one crowd, those whom capital offences, or debt, had compelled to leave their country. The traitor, and the debauchee, and the lawless, follow the same standard. From these, out of every region and place, a vile collection of men was gathered under the name of the Supreme Convention, which now, without law or right, on an impious title never before heard of, drives from the throne the great Monarch with his son. With them went a benign Religion, and the Bishops became exiles from their sacred altars. And this vile gathering of artificers (*mirabile dictu!*) fixed the law of succession, and played the part of judge in the affairs of the kingdom. Though the very laws of nature forbade it, the Convention breaks the succession of kings, unbroken for two thousand

---

[1] exulit, ? exulat.

[2] 'interuptam' is the spelling of the original.

[3] General Mackay, on taking command in Scotland, reaped the benefit of this activity of the Presbyterians, and 'encouraged them in their method of forming themselves in companies, and continuing their weekly exercises of the handling of their arms.'—*Memoirs*, page 11.

Innovat, et solo transfert diademata nutu.
   Jamque adeo fictae caeco pietatis amore,
Nobiliumque dolis saevique furore popelli,
Per vim perque nefas, et falso nomine juris,
Auriacus gener atque nepos decernitur heres
Caesaris, et vivo jam Rege superstite gnato.
Ergo abjecta hominum de faece comitia regni
Constituunt, et lege nefas commune tuentur.
Auspiciis ductuque Ducis, periscelide[1] cincti
Res agitur, regnisque excluditur exul avitis,
Rex, ingens pietate, fori damnatus iniquis
Suffragiis, raptumque haud aequo nomine sceptrum
Imperii, contra Divina humanaque jura.
Albion at tali nunquam gaudebit alumno,
Perfidus infausto quo praeside Presbyter arma
Sumpsit, et audaces erexit ad aethera cristas.
Queis nec lege nefas tantum licuisse placebat,
Regis et infami famam laesisse libello
Nec satis usque fuit scelus exitiale supremi
Decretis sancire fori, sed atrocibus armis

years, and by its nod transfers the Crown. Now, through the blind ardour of a Religion so spurious, through the intrigues of the nobles, through the madnesss of the fierce people, by force and wrong, and in the falsified name of Justice, the Dutch Prince, the son-in-law, the nephew, is declared the heir of the Cæsar, and that while the King and his son still live. Then, from these miserable dregs of society, they constitute a commission of the kingdom, and uphold their crime by common law. Under the auspices and leading of the Duke[2] who wears the Garter, the thing is done, and, as an exile, the King—great in his piety—is banished from his ancestral kingdom, condemned by the iniquitous votes of the courts, and against law—Divine and human—the sceptre of the empire is ravished from his hand. But Albion will never rejoice in a son under whose unlucky presidency the perfidious Presbyter took up arms, and reared his bold front to the skies. To them it was pleasing, not only to make wrong lawful, and to injure the honour of the King by an infamous charge, and to sanction the horrible crime by the decrees of the Supreme Court, but having

---

[1] periscĕlĭdĕ (*sic*).

[2] William Douglas, Duke of Hamilton, was made Knight of the Garter, and placed in the stall of his late enemy, Lauderdale, by Charles II. His election as President of the Convention indicated the line of its action against King James.

Et peregre auctis Batavorum millibus ultro
Monstrum horrendum ingens regali in sede locatum
Iam stabilire parant, stirpemque abolere Stuartum
Aggressi, Regemque tribus detrudere regnis.
Impia terrigenae veluti gessere Gigantes
Bella adversa Divis, infesta atque arma tulere
In Coelum, et Superos, et lucida lumina mundi
Ardua Thessalicos ad sidera tollere montes
Conati, Superisque Jovem detrudere regnis ;
Sic scelerata cohors, conjuratusque Senatus
Praecipiti nimium fastu damnatur Olympo
Affectasse viam, et sceptrum rapuisse Tonantis.
 Talibus auspiciis bellantis fraude catervae
Ille Caledoniae Rex et Pater inclitus orae
Et pelagi Princeps, et formidabilis hosti,
Turpiter, atque suis sine honore relictus amicis,
Proditur insidiis. At nunc tenet omnia solus
Auriacus Princeps, Batavae qui robore gentis
Suffultus, Procerumque animis, vulgique favore
Nixus, in exitium soceri, quae instruxerat olim,

advanced to the abolition of the Stuart race, and the expulsion of the King from his three kingdoms, they prepare to establish the dread monster on the royal throne by the aid of over a thousand Dutch troops. As the earthly giants attacked the gods in impious war, and raised hostile arms against high Heaven, piling up the Thessalian mountains towards the stars, the bright luminaries of the world, striving to dethrone Jupiter, so this wicked company, and conspiring Senate, is condemned by a too hasty pride to attempt a way to Olympus, to seize the sceptre of thundering Jove. Under the auspices of a body working by intrigue, that King of Scotland, that illustrious father of his country, that Prince of the sea, formidable to the enemy, is basely betrayed and dishonourably deserted by his friends. And now the Dutch Prince alone holds the field, upheld by the strength of the Netherlands. Trusting to the temper of the nobles and the favour of the people, he makes ready the arms—already acquired—for the destruction of his father-in-law. He prepares a great fleet, and the chosen strength of his army.[1] Already ambition had added her sharp

---

[1] He put to sea on September 28th, 1688, the fleet consisting of 60 men-of-war and 700 transports, carrying 11,000 infantry and 4500 cavalry. The fleet was driven back in confusion, but after refitting, the Prince of Orange landed in Torbay, November 5th.

Arma parat; validamque hyberna sidere classem
Molitur, lectumque ex omni milite robur.
Jam vero ambitio stimulos superaddidit acres
Pectore, et aeratis instructis mille carinis
(Incassum Eoliis maria alta cientibus Austris)
Saxonis infidi petit infelicia regna
Olim intestinis misere decerpta duellis.
Nec semel adversis fati pulsata procellis
At nunc insano se ardent miscere tumultu
Atque iterum Patriis spargunt incendia tectis
Et conclamatis properant sua busta ruinis.
  Belgicus Arctoae Princeps praedo impius orae
Aequoreas vastis straturus puppibus undas
Et venalitio domiturus Marte Britannos.
Usque ementitis promittit magna libellis,
Et maria et montes, sub ovino vellere vulpes
Pollicitus, partes et primum judicis aequi
Insimulat, speciem prae seque ferebat honoris,
Ut Regem Populumque inter justissimus unus
Arbiter ipse feret litis, pacisque sequester.
Jurgiaque auferet querulaeque gravamina plebis
Tolleret, et saevas Procerum compesceret iras.

spur, and in a fleet of a thousand sail (the south wind raising the sea in vain) he seeks the unhappy kingdoms of the faithless Saxon, already torn miserably with intestine strife, and buffeted by the storms of fate. Now are they eager to mingle in mad tumult, to set fire to their country's roofs, and they make their own grave in her lamentable ruins.

 The Belgian Prince, the impious robber of the North, having got ready his fleet, prepares for the conquest of Britain by mercenary means. By lying letters he promises great things—seas and mountains—and, as the fox in the sheep's skin, he simulates the part of the just Judge, and assumes the appearance of honour, presenting himself as a righteous arbiter in the strife existing between the King and his people. Seeking peace, he would remove the causes of anger and the grievances of the people, and allay the irritation of the nobles.[1] But he changes his mind when he sees

---

[1] No less than 80,000 copies of William's Manifesto were published, and distributed broadcast among the English people. It set forth that William had nothing before his eyes but the preservation of the Protestant religion, protection for men's consciences, the securing of laws, liberties, and rights under a just and legal government.

Sed vafer ille animi, quam primum in littore classem
Viderat, irati maris evasisse procellas,
Et sua jam profugas venisse in castra cohortes,
Et conjuratos ex omni parte tribunos:
Clam cauponato in Regem jam milite tendit;
Signa movens soceroque trucem fert marte ruinam.
Non tamen ille animi abjecti jam segnior instat,
Sed spe bella parat, Martemque in praelia poscit,
Cum sceptri caupono[1] sui justa arma lacessens.
Impius et miles pretio corruptus iniquo
Churchilli ducis insidiis jam transit ad hostem,
Linquit et insignem summo in discrimine Regem;
Quem miserè abjectis armis dare terga coegit
Militis ignavi dolus, et temerarius error
Principis Auriaci, et dominandi insana libido
Insontem Regnis Socerum depellit avitis.

 Quae tibi digna satis reddant pro talibus ausis
Numina, terrigenum Nassovi pessime fratrum,
Improbe subversor soceri, gravis ira Deorum![2]

his fleet come safe to land, escaping the dangers of the deep, and when he finds the deserting troops with their conspiring officers coming into his camp, with the bought-up soldiery he turns upon the King, bringing cruel ruin on his father-in-law. He, however, of no downcast spirit, presses on to meet him, and dares the issue of a battle, trusting the just cause of the sceptre in contest with this trader enemy. But the impious soldiery, bought with a price through the treachery of General Churchill,[3] now passes over to the enemy; he too leaves the illustrious King in the greatest danger, whom miserably, the deception of an unworthy army and their rash error, compel to flee. The insane lust of the Dutch Prince for power expels his guiltless father-in-law from his ancestral kingdom. Oh thou Prince of Nassau, what shall the gods in their wrath render to thee for thy crime, thou most wicked of the sons of earth! Infamous subverter of thy father-in-law, heavy scourge from the angry gods, whence to thee so dread

---

[1] caupono (*sic*).

[2] 'gravis ira Deorum.' See Virgil, *Aen.* iii. 215, and Heyne's note, 'ira deum h.l. res, quae ab ira deum venit, a diis iratis immittitur.'

[3] Lord Cornbury, son of the Earl of Clarendon, deserted from the King's army with some officers and 100 privates. His example was followed by other regiments. Lord Churchill, and the Dukes of Grafton and Ormond, joined him shortly after.—Luckock's *Bishops in the Tower*, page 174.

Unde tibi tanti sceleris tam dira cupido
Purpureoque sitis Regum satianda cruore?
En erit illa dies, cum tu funesta laborum
Supplicia et meritas referes pro crimine poenas.
Teque tuosque manent scelerati praemia facti.
Tuque adeo tali conjunx o digna marito,
Tullia Tarquinio merito conjuncta superbo
Impia quae Patrios foedasti in pulvere vultus,
Non te foemineas credam suxisse mamillas;
Sed rapidae tygres infantem lacte ferino
Te sub Caucaseis enutrivere cavernis:
Te quoque nascentem nimis exitialibus astris
Sanguineo procul igne rubens Mars lumine torvo
Vidit, et infausto volucer Cyllenius ortu,
Et strix triste gemens summoque a culmine tecti
Noctua natalem devovit carmine lucem.
Heu nimium coeli sub iniquo sidere juncti,
Et dicti auspiciis Rex et Regina sinistris.
O pudor Imperii! Nate infelicibus annis
Tu licet arctoum quatias terroribus orbem,
Et soceri manibus teneas jam sceptra superbis,
Exitii venit hora tui cum triste cadaver
Projectum medios caesorum augebit acervos,
Aut Batavas saturabit aves miserabile corpus,

a love of crime; a thirst so insatiable for the purple blood of kings? Lo! there will come the day when thou shalt undergo the punishment of thy wicked deeds, and suffer merited vengeance for thy crime. For thee and thine there abides the reward of evil. Thou too, oh worthy consort of such a husband, a Tullia well mated with a Tarquin the proud, impious woman who didst defile a father's face in the dust! I will not believe that woman's breast nourished thee, but that thou wert suckled by the fierce tigress in Caucasian cave. On thee, at thy birth, ruddy Mars, shining in bloody fire, and swift Mercury too, turned baneful eye on thy unhappy birth, and the doleful owl, hooting from the house-top, cursed thy natal day in nocturnal song. Alas! too well united under the sinister constellations of Heaven, and entitled King and Queen under evil omens. Oh shameful rule! Born in unfortunate time, although thou shake the North with thy terrors, and now hold the sceptre in proud hands, the hour of thy destruction approaches, when thy miserable carcase, cast into the midst, shall increase the heaps of the slain,

Viscera vel vituli laniabunt nuda marini,
Truncus in ignota vel forte jacebis arena.
Aut si nulla valent bellorum fulmina contra
Hoc caput infandum, si tela nec aequoris undae
Hunc nil juris habent certe damnare ruinae
Praedonem, veniet nostro felicior aevo
Fenvicii sonipes Sejani ex stirpe caballi,
Ulturus Dominum non aequa lege peremptum,
Dira cruentati imminet qui colla tyranni,
Membraque in opposita rumpet magno impete quercu.
Dii te, qui socero civilia bella verendo
Inspirasti odiis, Regemque hostilibus armis
Firmaque tranquilli turbasti foedera mundi,
Turbatum Stygios trudant ad Tartara manes.

    At vos si qua pios respectant numina Reges
Coelicolae, si quid sancti meruere labores,
Si qua polo pietas, aut Regum cura piorum,
Jam sinite afflictis Gramum succurrere rebus,

or shall gorge the carrion birds of Batavia, or thy vitals shall the sea monsters tear. Thou shalt perchance lie a corpse on an unknown shore, or, if no thunderbolt of war, or weapon of the sea avail against this unhallowed head, to bring this robber to ruin, yet in our time, more happily, there shall arise, to avenge his lord, unjustly cut off, the horse of Fenwick, a steed of the race of Sejanus,[1] who shall threaten the ill-starred neck of the bloodstained tyrant, and shatter his limbs with mighty force against the opposing oak. May the gods hurl thee in confusion to Tartarus, to the infernal spirits of the Stygian Lake! thee, who didst fan the hatred of civil war, and burst the settled bonds of a peaceful world.

    But oh! ye heavenly gods—if indeed the gods regard pious kings, if holy effort merits anything, if piety and the love of pious kings mean anything to Heaven—suffer the Graham to succour

---

[1] Sejanus was the name of a steed, in fable, who brought ruin on its successive possessors. The author would seem to indicate that William had become the owner of the unfortunate Sir John Fenwick's horse, and that he was riding this horse when he met with the accident which so contributed to his death. Sir John was executed on Tower-hill in 1696.

In the original, the lines 736 to 743 are at the end of the book, but there is a direction to insert them here. They were evidently written after the death of William, but are prophetic in form.

Invictaque manu stabilire labantia sceptra,
Imperii regnisque heredem inferre paternis.
Tu vero undosas fortunae experte procellas
Alternasque vices rerum, populique furentis
Deturbate odiis, et iniquis obrute fatis,
Rex Jacobe ingens! si nunc te fervida Martis
Cura sinit, seu te Germani nobile fanum
Sive tenet blando nemoralis Iernia nexu,
Seu fera Flandriacis vibras jam fulmina campis,
In mea vota veni facilisque hanc aspice partem,
Qua nostri flos aevi, heroum ex sanguine cretus,
Arma tuis movet auspiciis victricia Gramus,
Teque parat patriis reducem jam sistere terris.
Quod si forte vices, et habet fortuna regressum,
Inveniant jam fata viam conversa trahentque[1]
Praedonem in praeceps et diro funere mergant.
Hoc satis; O superi faxint rata vota, nec ultra
Tristia conquerimur nobis incommoda belli.
Praemia magna ferent, placet hac mercede cruentas
Exeruisse manus, et sic periisse juvabit.
  Tuque Leonigeri proles animusque Parentis

our afflicted State, and to stablish with invincible hand the falling sceptre, and bring back the heir to his paternal throne. But oh! great James! who hast indeed experienced the storm waves and vicissitudes of fortune, overwhelmed by the hatreds of a raging people, and the evils of a cruel fate, if now the intense interests of war permit thee, whether it be the noble fane of St. Germains, or green Ireland that holds thee in soft chain, or whether thou be hurling the deadly bolts of war on the plains of Flanders,—come to my prayers, look favourably on this land where the Graham, the flower of our age, sprung from the blood of heroes—bears conquering arms in thy name, and prepares to establish thee, restored to the country of thy fathers. But if it be that fortune has thy return in store, may the converted Fates find now a way to hurl the robber headlong, and sink him in destruction. Sufficient this! and oh may the gods only bring about these our desires, and no longer will we complain of the miseries of our war! For such reward, it will delight us to have fought and to have died.

  And thou, offspring and soul of the Lion-bearing father, noble

---

[1] trahentque, (?) trahantque.

Magne Puer, (nec forma, genus moresve refellunt,
Neve ementitos mens degener arguit ortus)
Liligeri ditione soli licet usque teneris
Ingrata procul a patria aspectuque tuorum,
Haud aliam nostris Cyrrham, Puer inclite musis
Optarim, votisve alium deposcere Phoebum.
Huc ades, illustris magnorum splendor avorum,
O Puer, Auriaco jam formidate Tyranno,
Maxime Cambrorum Princeps, tu carminis hujus
Numen eris, magno Deus ipso et Apolline major.
Jam mihi Moeonias inspira in carmina vires.
Tempus erit, nec vana animum praesagia fallunt,
Cum dabitur veneranda Patris magni ora tueri
Jam reducis rerumque iterum tractantis habenas,
Et te cum terris videam dare jura Britannis.
Martia majori dicam tua bella cothurno;
Sic mihi ad Elysias feliciter ibitur umbras.
Interea magni cantantem praelia Grami
Arma inter media et squalorem carceris atri
Me fove, et in dubiis affer solatia rebus.

LIBRI PRIMI FINIS.

youth (neither form, genius, nor manners, nor mind degenerate argue false origin), although from thy tender years till now, abiding in the land whose emblem is the Lily, away from thine own country, and the sight of thine own people, yet no other Parnassus would I seek for my muse—no other Apollo. Hither come, oh! illustrious youth, the splendour of your great ancestors, already dreaded by the Dutch tyrant, and oh! great Prince of Wales, be thou the patron of this my song, a divinity greater than the great Apollo himself. Inspire now my song with Mæonian strength. The time will come—it is no vain presage—when it will be granted to us to behold the venerable face of thy great father, restored to his kingdom, and holding again the reins of power. And I shall see him with thee giving laws to British lands. In grander notes will I some day sing of thy martial glory, and then happily depart to the Elysian shades. Meanwhile, aid me as I sing, 'mid arms and in the squalor of a dark prison, the battles of the great Graham, and bring consolation to our distress![1]

END OF BOOK I.

---

[1] See Preface on life of the author.

LIBER SECUNDUS.

CIVILIS rerum Dominam discordia Romam
  Quae fines terris, famamque aequavit Olympo,
Perdidit, et fortes bella intestina Quirites
Fregerunt; toto dominataque moenia mundo
In se versa ruunt, Romae et civilibus armis
Gloria magna perit, cui nunquam barbarus ensis,
Parthorum missae nec post sua terga sagittae,
Tantam adeo stragem, nec vulnera tanta dedere
Infelix Trebia, aut Poenorum gloria Cannae,
Quam nimis infames civili sanguine Campi
Aematii, et sparsi Romana caede Philippi.
Corruit hinc mundi imperium, ceciditque superbi
Romulidae decus, et rerum pulcherrima Roma.
Haud aliam saevos convellere fata Britannos
Invenere viam, quos non domuere potentes
Ausonii, aut Latiae populator Vandalus orae.
Pallida Tisiphone, caecos discordibus iris
Saxonidum furians animos, jam perdere gentem
Promeritam parat, et patrio prosternere ferro.
Proh pudor! hostiles bello domuisse catervas!
Et pepulisse acies Romani Caesaris! ut nunc

BY civil strife fell Rome, the mistress of the world, whose limits were the limits of the earth, whose glory rivalled Olympus. Intestine wars broke down the bold Romans. The world subdued, they turn upon each other, and the great glory of Rome perishes in civil broils. Not Barbarian sword or Parthian dart, not Trebia nor Cannae, the boast of Carthage, made such havoc, or inflicted such grievous wounds, as Pharsalia, red with the blood of fellow-countrymen, or Philippi, covered with Roman carnage. Thus fell the world-empire and the glory of Rome; and thus, too, the Fates seek the ruin of the brave Britons, whom neither Rome, nor the Vandal, Rome's despoiler, could ever subdue. Pale Tisiphone, darkening their minds with discordant passion, prepares the overthrow of the guilty Saxon race with the civil sword. Oh shame! to have conquered in battle and expelled from our coasts

Deleret rabidos scelerata insania cives.
Heu belli civilis amor, nunc arma juventus
Apparat, et saevi violento Martis eunt res
Arbitrio, nostrisque procul pax exulat oris.
   Jamque ardent animi studiis discordibus acti,
Praecipitesque suae quoquo tulit impetus irae,
In commune nefas magno coiere tumultu.
Hinc turbata quies civilia vincula rupit,
Ingerit et stimulos, et fraena furentibus addit,
Et bellum civile placet, furor undique fervet.
Spumea seu surgunt luctantibus aequora ventis,
Obstrepit hinc Boreae Notus, inde Favonius Euro
Luctatur, Coroque ruit contrarius Auster ;
Undique jactatus diverso turbine pontus
Corripitur, quocunque trahit violentia caeli ;
Sic quatit Arctoum praeceps discordia mundum,
Et rapit incertam sententia dissona plebem.
Nunc quoque iniqua petit venalis praemia miles,
Et sceleri jam constat honos ; proh tristia fata
Proditor in pretio ! magni sed splendida Regis
Gloria mersa luto, legisque eversa potestas ;
Languet et ipsa fides, jacet et sine vindice virtus.

the armies of the Caesar ! that at length a wicked fanaticism should ruin us—a maddened race. Alas, that love of civil strife ! the youth of the country prepare their arms, our affairs fall to the arbitrament of Mars, and peace flies far from our shores.

   Already men's minds are in a flame, driven headlong in different directions whither the impetus of their passion sends them, and in great tumult they gather for the common hurt. Peace broken, the bonds of society are severed, and while the rein is flung loose, the spur is driven into the mad citizen. Strife alone delights, and madness blazes forth on every hand. As the foaming billows are lashed by opposing winds—Notus with Boreas, Favonius with Eurus, Auster with the north-west wind, contending—and the seas are carried whithersoever the violence of heaven drives them, so headlong discord rouses the Northern land, and differing opinions hurry on an unstable people. Now, too, a venal soldiery seeks unjust reward, and honour goes hand in hand with villainy. Shame on a miserable fate ! The traitor and his price ! And the splendid glory of a great King sunk in the mire, and the potency of the law overthrown, Faith itself languishes, and Virtue lies prone without an avenger.

Imperii decor ille ingens Jacobus aviti,
Atque leonigeri soboles generosa Stuarti,
Tempora Di¹ coeptis et si satis aequa dedissent,
Felicis fratris non infelicior haeres
Septimus, infando fugitivi militis ausu
Missus in exilium, longinqui littora ponti
Classe petit, terrasque alio sub sole calentes.
Qui simulac patriis abiit depulsus ab oris,
Quem dedit immanem scelerata Batavia Regem,
Legibus invitis, male gratum hominique Deoque
Accipiunt, monstrumque locant in sede suprema.
Sic Fergusiadum Domus alta rapacibus ultro
Praeda jacet Batavis, ruit et civilibus armis
Albion infelix; nec quisquam insurgere contra
Pro Rege, et patriae pro libertate tuenda,
Audet, inhumano neve arma inferre Tyranno,
Bellica sanguinei nec tollere signa Gradivi.

    Ecce autem mediis bellorum in motibus, ingens
Dum stupor iste tenet procerum mentesque manusque,
Et premit atra polum nox pulso sole Britannum,
Montrosio novus exoritur de pulvere phoenix,
Virtutis simul, et patrii cognominis haeres
Illius ad Varium cecidit qui Marte Sacellum,
Gramus, hyperborei decus et fax unica Scoti ³

James VII., that great ornament of the hereditary throne, the noble offspring of the lion-bearing Stuarts, the heir of his fortunate brother, himself no less fortunate, had the gods but given time to his undertakings, seeks as an exile (through the vile conduct of his treacherous army) the distant shores of ocean, and lands warming under another sun.² As soon as he had departed, driven from the paternal shores, they welcome and place on the throne a fierce King, hated alike by gods and men, a monster from Batavia. Thus the lofty house of Fergus becomes the prey of the rapacious Dutchmen, and unhappy Albion sinks in civil strife. For the exiled King no man dares to rise against the inhuman tyrant, nor yet for fatherland or liberty does any man unfurl the ruddy banner of Mars. But lo! while stupor of hand and mind holds the nobles, while dark night o'erspreads the sky of Britain, her sun having fled, lo! the Graham as a new Phœnix rises from the ashes of Montrose, the heir alike of the valour and

---

¹ *Var. lect.* Dii.   ² 'Classe' is a bold licence for a single frigate.
³ See Preface as to author's prosody.

Dundius, armisoni sobolesque invicta Gradivi,
Atque leonigeros attingens sanguine Reges.
Ille ingens veterum (quem secula nulla tacebunt)
Grampiadum Ductor, teneris qui semper ab annis
Assuetus veros ferro defendere Reges,
Millibus e multis solus pro Regis honore,
Et patria, sine praesidiis, atque agmine et aere,
Restitit Auriaci rabiem, titulumque tyranni,
Atque pio pro Rege stetit sine milite et armis,
Usque sub Atholiis posuit dum viscera campis.
Fama per attonitum cujus volat aurea mundum,
Qua mare fluctivagis terram circumsonat undis,
Quaque coloratis roseum caput exserit Indis
Luce nova exoriens Phoebus, Maurumque[1] relabens
Aspicit Oceanum, bellis exercita virtus
Magni magna cluit Grami; quem Gallica castra

the name of him who fell at Falkirk,[2] Dundee, the light and glory of the North, invincible son of Mars, descended from the lion-bearing kings.[3] He, the great leader of the ancient Grampian race (concerning whom no age will be silent), from his early years a defender of lawful kings,—he alone of many soldiers stood for King and Country against the title and the rage of the Dutch tyrant, without means, men, or defence, till he laid his body beneath the sod of Athole. His fair fame flies throughout the admiring world—to every shore of the ocean. Wherever Phœbus presents his rosy head—from his rising in new light in the Indies to his setting among the Moors—there is heralded the valour of the Graham. The French camp on the Loire,[4] where Orleans lifts

---

[1] *Var. lect.* Marum.

[2] The reference is to Sir John Graham, the friend of Wallace, who fell at the battle of Falkirk, 1298. He was buried here, and a monument with an inscription marks the spot. *Varium sacellum*, or *Varia capella*, is the Latin for the Saxon *Falkirk*, which itself was a translation of the Gaelic *Eaglais Breac*, the spotted or brindled kirk. By this name, I am told, Highlanders still designate Falkirk. See Skene's *Four Ancient Books of Wales*, vol. i. p. 93.

[3] 'Sir Wm. Grahame of Kincardine married, as his second wife, the Princess Mary, daughter of Robert III. By her he had a son, Sir Robert Graham of Strathcarron. His youngest son, John, was the first of the family of Claverhouse in Angus, commonly pronounced Clavers.'—Napier's *Dundee*, vol. i. p. 176.

[4] There could have been no fighting on the Seine or Loire. Probably camps of instruction were there, from which drafts of young soldiers were sent to the front. Claverhouse served under Turenne for some short period before the end of 1673. It would appear that there had been some service under his native

Ad Ligerim, celsas tollit qua Aurelia turres,
Sequana Parisiam quaque auctior alluit urbem,
Hostibus eversis toties videre superbum,
Saepius et saevi respersum sanguine belli ;
Cujus et auxilium, nimiumque inimica paratam
Sensit opem fractis sub Principe Belgia rebus.
Gallia quem toties victricibus extulit armis,
Inde triumphato suscepit Belgia Gallo.
 Mox tamen ad patrias longinquam attraxerat oras
Dulcis Amor Regum, quos et cum laude secutus,
Et studiis clarus civilibus acer et armis
Rettulit insignes et bello et pace triumphos.
Ingenii numne Hercle prior belline laborum
Laudibus ambiguum, sed certe magnus utroque,
Aequandus prisci magnisque heroibus aevi,
Atque inter summos Regum censendus amicos
Brutigenum, multis quibus et feliciter annis
Praestitit officium. Nec jam cum saeva tonaret
Fortunae alternantis hyems, se proripit instar

her towers,—on the Seine, where her increased waters lave the city of Paris,—has beheld him triumphant over the defeated enemy, stained with the blood-marks of a relentless war. His aid, too,[1]— a help, alas! too well given—hostile Belgium experienced in her adversity. Then began the Netherlands to triumph, whom France had so often defeated.

Soon, however, the sweet love of the Kings, whom with praise he had already followed, drew him back to his fatherland.[2] As distinguished in civil, as spirited in military, affairs, he brought back the trophies of peace and war. Waiving the question whether he surpassed Hercules in labours, it is certain he was as great as any hero of the ancient time, and he is to be reckoned among the greatest upholders of the British Kings. To them for many years he happily presented his service. Nor now does he shrink from his King when the cruel frost of changeful fortune seizes him, or

---

sovereign before his going abroad. The Duke of Monmouth joined Turenne with 6000 English and Scottish troops in 1672. At the peace with Holland in 1674 there were serving in France 10,000 English troops whom Charles did not recall, but whom he bound himself not to recruit.

[1] See note on Seneffe, Book v.

[2] He returned in 1677 with a reputation recognised by the Duke of York, who urged the young Marquis of Montrose to secure him for his new troop of horse. This he did. Claverhouse was then, it would seem, in his thirty-fifth year.

Ignavi, aut animo dat terga inhonesta remisso.
Verum et opes et opem tanto in discrimine Regi
Contulit, et rebus lateri comes haesit in arctis.
Tandem belligerae deceptus fraude catervae
Cogitur undoso Rex se committere ponto.
Dira Stuartorum fortuna o fataque Regum!
Caesaris heu patria pulsi sorsque aspera, Gramo
Tristis et illa dies, qua castris ire Stuartum
Viderat armatum, quaque hunc conspexit inermem
Furtivae dare terga fugae, vectumque biremi
Exigua patriae linquentem littora terrae.
Huic vero curam Reginae, et Principis ultro
Tutelam medias mittendi puppe per undas[1]
Discedens dederat, monumentum et pignus amoris.
Inde domum rediens castris cum laude relictis,
Fida Stuartaeis tulit et suffragia sceptris.
Conventu in medio procerum, summoque Senatu

betake himself to dastardly flight. With money[2] and strength he aids the King, and in his adversity cleaves to his side.

At length, betrayed by the treachery of his soldiers, the King is compelled to commit himself to the stormy waves. Oh sad fortune, sad fate of the Stuart kings! Alas! bitter was the lot of the exiled Caesar, and sad to the Graham was the day when he beheld the King, now armed in his camp, anon unarmed, turning his back in flight, and secretly, in a two-oared boat,[3] leaving the paternal shores. But to him the King had given the care of the Queen,[4] and the custody of the Prince, the monument and pledge of his love, that he might see them safely embarked. Then, returning to Scotland, the camp honourably left, he presented his faithful suffrage for the maintenance of the Stuart sceptre. In the midst of the Convention, at the head of the Senate, he declared

---

[1] *Var. lect.* Full stop at 'undas.'

[2] Balcarres in his Memoir, p. 47, Bannatyne Club Edition, says of Claverhouse that 'although a good manager his private fortune, he had no reserve when your (King James's) service and his own reputation required him to be liberal!' Elsewhere he says he distributed frankly when the service demanded it, though naturally more sparing than profuse.

[3] If this is historical at all, it may mean that Dundee saw James leave the shore for the French frigate on December 23d. Dumbarton, Arran, and a few others, went down the river with the King, and stayed with him at Rochester till the 23d, when he embarked.

[4] As far as I know, this is quite new to history, and is inconsistent with recognised facts and dates.

Innocuo factam Regi vim clamat apertam,
Testaturque Deos se invitum in praelia cogi.
Hinc odiis querulae turbae, tacitisque petitus
Presbyteri insidiis, paucis comitantibus urbem
Deserit, alati commendans moenia castri
Gordonio; at summam belli secum ipse ferebat.
Quem piger obtusis sequitur Buntinus in armis,
Coeptum ut sistat iter, captumque reducat ad urbem.
Talpa prius tygrem premeret, vel alaudula nisum,
Et petat accipitrem perdix et dama molossum,
Quam nebulo vetus iste instructo milite talem
Ausit adire virum, fulgentiave ora tueri.
Ille autem pontem Sterlingi [1] transiit altum

that open force [2] would be resorted to on behalf of the innocent King; and he took God to witness that he was driven unwillingly to war. Being endangered by the hatred of the hostile mob, and the secret designs of the Presbyterians, he left the city with a few companions,[3] commending the Castle to the Gordon,[4] and taking on himself the chief conduct of the war. The sluggish Buntine,[5] without spirit, follows to stop his journey, and bring him back a captive to the city. Sooner would the mole seize the tiger, or the lark the merlin; sooner would the partridge assail the falcon, or the doe pursue the hounds, than would that pitiful veteran dare to cross swords with such a man, or even venture to look upon his glowing brow. Dundee soon crossed the high bridge at Stirling,

---

[1] *Var. lect.* Sterlyngi.

[2] This statement of the author as to the line of open defiance adopted by Dundee, I think springs from the imagination of the Poet, or his enthusiastic gossips. King James's party were obliged, and by King James were directed, to be very cautious; and it is evident from Dundee's letter from Dudhope that he had taken no open step more decided than leaving the Convention, and that act he explains. If he said 'there are crowns to be broke,' it was not in the Convention, but when he was clear of the town.

[3] They numbered fifty or sixty horse, one nobleman, George Lord Livingstone, and a few officers, being among them. He left the city on Monday, March 18th.

[4] The first Duke of Gordon. For account of interview see Preface, and Napier, p. 506.

[5] Major Hugh Buntine of Kilbryde was despatched by the Duke of Hamilton with a party of horse to follow Claverhouse. There is no reliable evidence that he came up with him—the story of Creighton that Claverhouse fell back behind his own party and frightened Buntine being unauthenticated. Major Buntine became Muster-master-General of the forces raised by the Convention.

Impiger, inque suas se contulit ocyus aedes.
Decessu at vario trepidatur in urbe tumultu.
Pars stupet ingentes bellorum instare procellas,
Ingruere et tragicos per civica praelia motus.
Presbyter elapsum fremit indignantior hostem,
Et recidiva iterum procumbere foedera moeret.
   Ergo omnis belli studiis excita juventus
Arma fremit, proceresque insano Martis amore
Ardebant; quorum sequitur pars maxima dirum
Principis imperium, et Batavi fera signa Tyranni.
Rari autem fuerunt adversae partis alumni,
Caesaris afflictis ausi succurrere rebus;
Hi quibus incoctum est generoso pectus honesto,
Queis amor aut studium recti, patriaeque tuendae
Cura fuit, Regis soli pro partibus instant.
Ipse ego militiam, Gramumque in castra secutus
Regia. Sic medio bellorum in turbine fortem
Scipiadem ipse pater stipaverat Ennius olim.
Nec cecinisse Ducis mihi contigit acta minoris,
Cui Macedum magnus cedat Rex pectore et armis,

and quickly reached his own house.[1] On his departure from Edinburgh the city was disturbed. Some dreaded the outburst of civil war; the Presbyterians were wild with indignation at the escape of their enemy, and mourned that the reviving Covenant still lay in the dust. The whole youth of the country is stirred to war, and nobles burn with mad eagerness for the field. The greater part follow the command and fierce standard of the Dutch tyrant. A few there were who dared to stand for the King in his misfortunes—those whose hearts rang true to honour, who loved the right and their country's good. I[2] myself followed the Graham on the Royal side. Thus did Father Ennius, amid the storms of war, follow the heroic Scipio. Nor has it fallen to my lot to sing the deeds of a General less exalted. To him the great king of Macedon gives place in courage and conduct of war; and Manlius

---

[1] 'Dudhope,' then near Dundee, now within the town. Claverhouse acquired it, and became Constable of Dundee, after long waiting, in 1684. On his way to Dudhope he had tarried long enough at Linlithgow (though it was only for one night) to alarm the Convention, for on the 19th they issued an order to dislodge him. Next day they hear of him at Stirling, and order his arrest. At Dunblane he wrote to Hamilton, and, what was perhaps of greater moment, there met Lochiel's son-in-law, Alexander Drummond of Balhaldy, and had much talk with him.

[2] First mention of the Author by himself. See Preface.

Et Capitolinae defensor Manlius arcis.
Cui ferus ipse etiam eversor Carthaginis altae
Cedat, et Iliacos qui cinxerat agmine muros.
Ille (licet fractis infausto marte maniplis,
Et quanquam studiis procerum suppressus iniquis,
Et frustratus ope, et jam spe laetatus inani),
Nescius adversis tamen unquam cedere rebus,
Dundius arctoae Ductor Mavortius orae,
Alipedum jam Marte ferox rapit agmen equorum,
Et petit aerios, Grampi trans culmina, montes
Ad boream, aeternis horrentiaque arva pruinis,
Martia Grampiacos ut mittat in arma colonos,
Legitimi quibus est nomen venerabile Regis.
At Regum fasces quicunque inhiasset iniquos
Sive dolo, sive insidiis, sive arte vel armis,
Monstrum istud merito mittunt ad Tartara letho.
Jamque adeo totis late gradientia campis
Agmina ad arma vocat, celeresque ad praelia turmas
Acer agit, juvenumque globo comitante superbo,
Signa Caledoniis pro Rege attollit in oris.

too, the defender of the Capitol, and Scipio, the destroyer of Carthage, and the hero who invested the Trojan walls. Dundee, the heroic leader of the North, knew not how to yield, however adverse might be his fate—his troops disbanding, the nobles opposing, cheated of his hopes of aid, cajoled by expectations never realised. Now roused to war, he carries his troop of wing-footed horse over the Grampians, through regions of perpetual frost. He seeks those lands that he may send forth the sons of the hills to martial enterprise. In them there was a reverence for the name of the lawful King, and they regarded him, who by guile or force, laid hands upon the insignia of royalty, as worthy of despatch to Pluto's realm. And now Dundee calls forth his troopers, scouring over the plain, and takes the field. In a proud circle of youths, he raises aloft the Royal standard on Scottish soil.[1]

---

[1] The messengers of Hamilton and the Convention appeared at Dudhope on the 26th March, summoning him to lay down his arms and return to the Convention. He replied by letter, dated 'Dudhope, March 27th, 1689.' On the 30th he was proclaimed traitor at the market-cross of Edinburgh. On the 11th April William and Mary were proclaimed King and Queen of Scotland. It would seem that Leven was ordered to secure Claverhouse and Balcarres about the same date. Dundee must have raised the standard between the 12th and 15th April.

Interea arctois M'Kaius appulit oris,
Jussus ad extremos boreae penetrare recessus,
Sterneret ut fidum magno certamine Gramum.
Jam prius invictos circumdat milite muros
Arcis Edineae, atque alto satis undique ducto
Aggere, ferratas tormenta rotantia glandes
Collocat, atque arcis jam propugnacula bombis
Concutit ignivomis, quae dux pro Rege tenebat
Gordonius; verum ille armis inglorius arcem
Tradidit, amissa aeternum cum nomine fama.
Ergo iter aggreditur magnis dux Belgicus orsis
Dira fremens, cinctusque ingenti milite, et armis
Jam rapit adductos diversis partibus orbis
Sub sua signa duces, durique in praelia Martis
Explicat ingentes equitum peditumque catervas;
Monticolisque necem, Gramoque extrema minatur.
Nec mora; jam validas certatim utrinque phalanges
Instaurant, totisque in praelia viribus acrem
Martem acuunt, strictoque parant decernere ferro.
Dundius at campo primus se immittit aperto,

Meanwhile Mackay[1] advances towards the North, with orders to penetrate to its utmost bounds and defeat the Graham in a decisive battle. He already surrounds the hitherto invincible walls of Edinburgh Castle. Having led his works round it, and raised them sufficiently high on every side, he planted his cannon and shook the bulwarks of the fortress with iron balls. Gordon held it for the King, but, inglorious in arms, he yielded the stronghold, losing name and fame for ever. The Belgic general, elated with these great beginnings,[2] and surrounded by a strong force, hastens forward, threatening terrible things. He hurries up his officers from various quarters to his standard, and parades great companies of horse and foot for the war. He vows death and destruction to the Highlanders and the Graham. Gathering their strength on both sides, they make ready without delay to decide the matter with the drawn sword. Dundee first takes the field, and leaves his lofty towers. His beloved wife,[3] too, he leaves, though she had

---

[1] See Preface.

[2] Mackay hastened forward before the Castle was surrendered; it was yielded to Sir John Lanier, who had succeeded Mackay in the conduct of the siege.

[3] She was Lady Jean Cochrane, daughter of William, Lord Cochrane, granddaughter of Lord Dundonald. Her mother was a daughter of the Earl of Cassilis, and strong in Whig sympathies. They were married at Paisley, June

Linquit et aereas chara cum conjuge turres.
Illa, licet saevos Lucinae experta labores,
Rara sui sexus et nostri rarior aevi
Gloria, foemineum generosi exemplar honesti
Nobile, Amazoniis et par Mavorte puellis;
Sola sed egregii infelix virtute mariti,
Verum animis sexum superans, et mascula plus quam
Corda gerens, magnis animum virtutibus aequans
Expedit arma viro, et gradientem talibus ultro
Hortatur dictis: 'I nunc mea maxima cura
Felici auspicio, Superisque vocantibus ito,
Enceladi rabiem, et Batavum domiture Tyrannum;
I felix quo fata vocant, et quo tua virtus
Et pietas rapit, et generosi pectoris ardor,
Quo te Regis honos vocat;' et sic fata supremum
Ingeminans jam moesta vale dabat inscia, longe et
Quantum acres poterant oculi penetrare sequendo
Prosequitur votis ardentem Marte maritum.
Ipse invectus equo, Tyrioque insignis in ostro,

just experienced the cruel pangs of Lucina. She, the rare glory of her sex, and still more rare of her age, the grand example of female honour, in martial spirit equalling the Amazon—she alone is rendered unhappy through the exalted virtue of her lord. But surpassing her sex in spirit, and carrying a more than manly heart, equalling the mind of her husband in her great virtues, she prepares his arms, and at their parting addresses him in these words: 'Go now, my dearest one, under happy auspices; go under Divine guidance to quell the madness of the Dutch tyrant, another Enceladus. Go fortunate, whither the Fates call you, where your valour and devotion, and the ardour of your noble heart, carry you. Go where the honour of your King commands.' Thus speaking, she sadly took, unconsciously, her last farewell of her husband; and with her prayers she followed him as he went, ardent for the war, straining her bright eyes after him as long as he was in sight. He himself,

---

11th, 1684. These few days at Dudhope were all that the Viscount and his wife spent together after his elevation to the peerage. On March 27th he was looking for her confinement; by the 15th of April she was able to take some share in his preparation for departure. Their son must have been born about the beginning of April, 1689. He survived his father as second Viscount for only three months. He is buried in the tomb of the Grahams of Morphie at St. Cyrus. Lady Dundee married, secondly, William Livingstone, afterwards Lord Kilsyth. For interesting matter concerning her life, manner of her death, and the discovery of her remains, see Napier's *Dundee*, vol. iii. pp. 672-685.

Ante urbem, inque ipso Taoduni vertice montis,
Instruit audacem juvenum longo ordine turmam,
Signaque Grampiacis attollit regia castris.
Quem circum lecti comites, et laeta juventus
Omnes sublimes in equis fulgentibus armis
Agglomerant, Gramumque sequuntur in arma ruentem.
Jam inter medios per celsa cacumina Sidlae
Ibat ovans. Soles at tres cunctantur in arce
Vallis Ogilvianae, donec speculator in armis
Nuntiat adventum, et numerum exploraverit hostis.
Inferior longe numero, non viribus impar,
Flumina adhuc glacie quanquam concreta rigebant,
Et niveo celsos vestiret vellere montes
Tristis hyems; motis Phryxeo[1] sidere signis,
Carpit somniferas obscura nocte sub umbras
Laetus iter, tenditque extremae ad littora Thules.
Hic vero, quanquam M'Kaius agmine septus

mounted on his charger, brilliant in scarlet, in the face of the town, drew out in long line his band of brave youths, and on the very top of the Law of Dundee he unfurled the Royal banner for the Northern war. Around him gather his chosen companions, and young men, in high spirits. All mounted and in bright armour, they follow the Graham as he rushes to the field. Then triumphantly he led them over the lofty ridges of the Seidlaws. Three days they tarry at the Tower of the Glen of Ogilvy,[2] that the scouts may announce the approach and strength of the enemy. Finding himself greatly inferior in numbers—though not in vigour —he moves northwards, under the constellation of Aries, mid the deep shadows of sombre night, undaunted by the ice-covered rivers and the snowy hills. Mackay,[3] although surrounded by

---

[1] *Var. lect.* Phryxaeo. 'Vestiret' in preceding line, a bad sequence.

[2] Dundee had a strong house here. The name of the Ogilvy family is derived from this district. It was the home of S. Donovald and his nine daughters—the nine maidens. It was the scene too of the reputed interview between William the Lion and Gilchrist of Angus, when the King restored him to his estates. It is now the property of the Earl of Strathmore. The old road, by which Claverhouse travelled to the Glen, was by Balmuir and Tealing, and still exists. Mackay (page 6) says, 'Towards the 20th April, Sir Thomas Livingstone, having formed a design to surprise Dundee in a country-house of his called Glen Ogilvy, though very well and secretly led on, was nevertheless disappointed by the retreat of the said Dundee the day before Sir Thomas came out of his quarters.'

[3] Mackay was not on the march at this time. Sir Thomas Livingstone alone was in motion. Mackay afterwards advanced slowly towards Brechin with Colchester's dragoons and some Dutch foot—450 in all.

Saxonidum denso, et Batavis comitatus obesis,
Pone tamen vigilem nequiquam inglorius hostem
Insequitur, lentis a tergo et passibus instat.
   Gramus at antevolans montes agit agmen in altos,
Et salit immissis in vallibus acer habenis,
Perque undas scopulosque atque horrida tesqua frutetis
Irruit, et longum per campos dirigit agmen.
Non tempestates illum, non nubibus ignes
Elisi, celsisve voluti[1] montibus amnes,
Nec juga cana gelu, non motae aquilone procellae,
Saeva nec hyberni remorantur flumina cauri.
Jamque alacres omnes, Gramo duce et auspice Gramo,
Jejunae sterilem Kerymorae invisimus urbem.
Et simul Arctoi pontem transmittimus Escae;
Ardua praeruptis hinc per juga Carnea saxis
Scandimus, et rapidum Dejae tranavimus amnem.
Inde per Oneali villam, quo nomine dicta est
Carnea jam Regis, trajecto flumine Donae,

dense masses of English, and a regiment of gross Dutchmen, creeps on behind his vigilant enemy, ingloriously. But the Graham, far in advance, leads his band with loosened rein through the vales towards the mountains. They traverse torrents, rocky defiles, tangled thickets. The tempest, the lightning flash, the cold blast from the frozen north, delay them not. In high spirits, under the leadership and auspices of the Graham, we reach the bare town of Kirriemuir, and soon pass over the North Esk by its bridge.[2] Next we climb the rugged heights of the Cairn o' Mount,[3] and swim the swift current of the Dee. Then by Kincardine O'Neil[4] and the Don, we come to Keith,[5] famous for the gifts of Bacchus

---

[1] *Var. lect.* Soluti.

[2] Dundee took the road by Kirriemuir and the North Water Bridge, probably to avoid Forfar and Brechin. The road from Dudhope to Kirriemuir, through Glen Ogilvy, is in a straight line, due north. The old North Water Bridge was said to have been built by Erskine of Dun, the Superintendent of Angus. It bore his coat of arms.

[3] The great North road passed over this hill, where there is still considerable traffic.

[4] The direct route lay through this place. The Poet's skill in rendering the name into Latin deserves more praise than his etymology: 'O'Neali villam quo nomine dicta est carnea Regis.'

[5] There were many mills in the district; were breweries and distilleries as plentiful as now? The Poet further on refers to the pleasant time spent here. On the 21st April Dundee wrote to Lord Murray, Athole's son, from this place.

Ad Bacchi Cererisque insignem munere Ketham
Venimus, et pulchram pinnis sublimibus arcem
Gordoneam, et celsas post terga relinquimus aedes.
Hinc celeri undantem remeamus gurgite Speiam,
Turrigerasque aedes, atque Elgini nobile fanum
Linquimus, et flavis Lossum[1] tranamus arenis.
Tandem inter dulces Forressae insedimus agros,
Monstrat frugiferas ubi laeta Moravia messes.
Jam vero auxilium sperabat ab hoste paratum,
Et sua jam profugas sub signa redire cohortes
Scotigenum cupiebat. Ut arte illuderet artem
Flectit equos retroque eadem vestigia campo
Jam relegit, nigrumque ad Dejae substitit amnem.
Marte ferox, atque arte potens, haud inscius armis
Hosti aptare dolos, vitare pericula cautus
Audierat Batavum multis jam millibus auctum

and Ceres. Fair Gordon Castle,[2] with its lofty battlements and towers, we soon leave behind us, and ferry the surging current of the rapid Spey. Elgin,[3] with its towering roofs and noble fane, we pass, and ford the Lossie with its yellow sands. At length we rest mid the sweet fields of Forres, where gladsome Moray is wont to show her rich harvests.

Now there arose a hope that the enemy might yield us a ready aid, and Dundee began to think that the Scotch Dragoons,[4] lost to us, might return to the Standard. That he might meet art with art, he wheels about and retraces his steps, till he rests by the dark waters of the Dee. Fierce in arms, and subtle in art, was Dundee; not unskilled in meeting the strategy of an enemy, watchful in avoiding dangers. He had heard that the Dutch

---

[1] *Var. lect.* Lossam.

[2] Founded by George, Earl of Huntly, 1507, and by the year 1726 much added to at different times. It was best known in the North as the 'Bog of Gight.' The passage of the Spey on the post-road was called the 'Boat of Bog.'

[3] For unwarrantable intercommuning with Dundee, Provost Stewart of Elgin, Sir John Innes, and two Bailies, were summoned to appear before the Estates in June 1689.—*Act. Parl.* vol. ix. p. 86.

[4] The Scotch Dragoons had sent him promises that they would declare for the King, and this movement was to give them encouragement. He designed to go near the town of Dundee, where they were stationed. On his way south he intercepted a messenger from the Master of Forbes, and learnt something of Mackay's movements. He waited for Mackay at the Cairn o' Mount, and turned northward when Mackay reached Fettercairn. Instead of crossing the Dee at Kincardine O'Neil, he kept up the river, through Birse to Aboyne. His movement puzzled Mackay, who feared that it might mean a descent on Angus,

Adventare ducem, boreaeque extrema petentem
Ut sine honore animam vel nunc effunderet aegram,
Aut daret aeternam praesens victoria famam.
    Dundius instantem praesensit ut impiger hostem,
Hinc atque hinc densas et circumstare catervas,
Castra movet, rursusque ad Byrsam flumine Dejae
Transmisso, nitidas Abboyni praeterit aedes.
Et nemora, et montes Cromarrae transilit altos
Acer equis, Donaeque rapacem transfretat amnem,
Ardua ubi ingentem attollit Kildrimmea molem
Murorum, et vacuam Forbesi ignobilis arcem
Pervolat; hinc dulces quos Bogius alluit agros
Invisit, pulchramque ad Bogi flumina vallem,
Atque ibi laetus equos, defessaque corpora curat.

general, his force now increased by many thousands,[1] was approaching, seeking the North, that he might part with his life in failure, or, by present victory, merit undying fame. Dundee, ever vigilant, soon felt the approaching enemy, and perceived a movement to surround him by strong divisions. He moves his camp, and crossing the Dee at Birse, speeds past the beautiful place of Aboyne. Through the woods, and over the mountains of Cromar, he gallops, and where lofty Kildrummie[2] rears its huge towers he crosses the devouring waters of the Don, and speeds past the empty house of ignoble Forbes.[3] Then he visits the sweet fields which the Bogie waters, and the fair Strath,[4] and there he gladly

---

in his rear, by Glenshee. Claverhouse, however, went north by the route given by the Poet.

[1] Poetical licence. Mackay was only 1000 strong altogether.

[2] Castle of the Earls of Mar, described in *View of Diocese of Aberdeen*, Spalding Club, as the 'noblest castle in all the diocese, formerly consisting of seven towers, the highest called the "Snow Tower," though remains only of six now discernible, . . . looks still noble and grand.' The Statistical Account describes the ruins as 'stupendous and magnificent.'

[3] 'Vacuam Forbesi ignobilis arcem pervolat.' The reference is to Druminnor, then the chief house of Lord Forbes. See note on Suy Hill, Book v. The Master of Forbes was a great supporter of the Government, and ally of Mackay's. Soon after Dundee passed his empty house he was able to join Mackay at Kincardine with 'forty gentlemen of his name, on horse, and about five or six hundred country foot, who were so ill armed, and appeared so little like the work that Mackay ordered them to be dismissed.' He and Sir George Gordon of Edinglassie were the chief supporters of Mackay in Aberdeen and Banff.

[4] The great Gordon stronghold, Huntly Castle, in Strathbogie, was doubtless the resting-place.

Crastina sed rediis ut lux effulsit eois
Aurea, clangit iter rauco cava buccina cantu.
Jam lepidam rapidis Ketham praetervolat alis,
Demum Gordonii perventum ad moenia castri.
Illic praecipitem Spejae prope fluminis undam
Fermelodunus adest, stipatus robore gentis
Gordoniae, socia arma ferens, atque agmina jungens.
Inde alacres omnes, superato flumine, pulchram
Elginum, atque urbem Forressae intramus amaenam,
Aereasque arces, et Tarni nobile vallum
Linquimus, antiquae et fanum transcurrimus Ernae.
Hinc procul invicti castrum sublime Stuarti
Emicat, et flavis Rossaeum littus arenis,

bids man and horse take rest. But no sooner did the morrow's golden rays brighten the east than the harsh clang of the trumpet sounded to horse. Next, he sweeps through merry Keith, and on to Gordon Castle. There, by the headlong waters of the Spey, Dunfermline [1] meets him, bringing with him some strength of the Gordon Clan to join the Standard. Speedily we cross the Spey, and enter again fair Elgin and sweet Forres. Then to Darnaway,[2] a noble castle with its airy turrets, and onwards past the Kirk of Auldearn [3] we move, till we view in the distance the lofty castle

---

[1] James Seton, fourth and last Earl of Dunfermline, grandson of the Chancellor, was brother-in-law of the Duke of Gordon, and represented him in the North. In his younger days he had served with the Prince of Orange in several memorable expeditions. He was a faithful supporter of Dundee, and showed much gallantry at Killiecrankie. Outlawed and forfeited by Parliament in 1690, Lord Dunfermline followed the King to St. Germains, where he died without issue four years afterwards, about the age of fifty. According to M'Kay he received very bad treatment at the hands of his exiled sovereign. He is lauded by the author of *Proelium Gilliecrankianum*. Lieutenant Nisbet, one of the prisoners taken at Killiecrankie, afterwards deposed to his having been examined in a low room in the Castle of Blair, by the said Earl of Dunfermline, and states, 'that he was middle-sized, weel-favoured, and high-nosed.'—*Acts of Parliaments of Scotland*, 1690, App. p. 56. I am informed by an eminent member of the Seton family that the above description indicates a strong resemblance to Charles, the second Earl, his father, whose aquiline nose forms a very prominent feature on his medallion in the British Museum, as well as in his portrait by Vandyck at Yester.

[2] 'Tarni nobile vallum.' Darnaway, in old deeds spelt Tarnway or Tarnaway. Bp. Pococke spells it Tarnaway. See Pococke, p. 183, and notes.

[3] 'Antiquae Fanum Ernae.' The scene of Montrose's great victory in 1645.

Arthurique fretum, turritaque culmina Nessi
Apparent longe, et caput inter nubila jactant.
　Fama erat ingentes pro Rege instare phalanges
Monticolum, medios passimque errare per agros,
Agmina picta croco, Nessi haud segniter urbis
Ad portas ruere, atque urbem obsidione tenere.
Gnaviter ergo premit ferrata calce citatos
Corripedes, levibusque immittit lora caballis.
Tandem in conspectu atque ipsis sub moenibus urbis
Constitit, atque oculis circumspicit agmina laetis.
Olli inter turmas equitum clamore frementes
Obvius occurrit Donaldi filius audax,
Quodlibet in facinus spoliorum impulsus amore,
Kapochus, et chlamyde et clypeo conspectus ahenis

of the unconquered Stuart,[1] the yellow shore of Ross, the Firth of Arthur,[2] and the cloud-capped towers of Inverness.

Now there came intelligence that great bodies of mountaineers, standing for the King, arrayed in saffron,[3] were pressing forward from all sides, and hurrying to the gates of Inverness, and were even holding it in siege. Quickly Dundee gives the rein and applies the spur. He stopped at length in sight of the town, and under its very walls, and beheld, with glad eyes, the bands gathered on every side. To meet him advances, amid the cheering troopers, the bold Macdonald of Keppoch,[4] a man whom

---

[1] Castle Stuart, a house of the Earls of Murray. In 1762 Bp. Forbes says it was uninhabited and going to ruin. In 1665 a correspondent of the Laird of Cawdor tells him that Lord and Lady Duffus are at Castle Stewart, and they are all good company.

[2] 'Arthuri fretum.' The parish of Ardersier bounds on the south that part of the Moray Firth lying between Fort George and Kessock Ferry, and gave it the name of Firth of Arderseir. Arderseir was corrupted into Arthursire, and appears in deeds of the sixteenth and seventeenth centuries in that form. Arthur was naturally suggested by this form of the word, and, when latinised, the Firth would become 'Arthuri fretum.' The learned author of *Celtic Scotland* has supplied this explanation. The oldest form of the name was Ardrosser.

[3] 'Agmina picta croco,' alluding to the saffron dye with which the shirts of the Highlanders were coloured. Camden says that the words of Sidonius, describing a Goth, exactly described the Highlanders of his time: 'they shine with yellow.' See Preface.

[4] It would seem from Lochiel's Memoirs that Dundee had sent an express from Gordon Castle to Lochiel informing him of the situation, and that, after consultation with neighbouring chiefs, a detachment of 800 men, under Macdonald of Keppoch, was sent to conduct Dundee into Lochaber. Keppoch was at feud

Bullato clavis, pictisque insignis in armis.
Dundius ut numerum, et vires et militis ora
Cominus inspexit, jubet ocyus arma parari
Adventumque ducis Batavi expectare superbi.
Kapochus at furto, spoliisque assuetus iniquis
Nunc hos nunc illos causando turpiter haeret,
Innectitque moras; namque illum sola cupido
Praedandi adversum, non gloria, ducit in hostem.
Jam vero miseram Nessi premit acriter urbem,
Detinet et vinctos intra tentoria cives,
Praetoresque ipsos, quos omnes aere soluto
Liberat, et trepidos solvit formidine mentes.
Hinc celeri in montes secum rapit agmina cursu,
Abripit ingentem pecudumque boumque catervam,
Praedonum stipante manu, villasque domosque
Et late populatur agros, et inertia carpit
Armenta, atque humiles praedando exhauriit aedes.

love of plunder would impel to any crime. From his shoulder hung the tartan plaid, and he carried a shield studded with brazen knobs. Dundee, when he beheld the number, the vigour, and bearing of these warriors, bade them quickly prepare for battle, and be ready for the approach of the proud Dutch general. But Keppoch, accustomed to pillage and unjust rapine, basely makes delay, adhering now to one view, now to another, for the thirst for booty alone, and not glory, had drawn him out against the enemy. Even now he was sharply pressing the miserable town of Inverness, and holding its citizens and its magistrates within his tents, whom he liberates and sets free from their fear, only for money paid down. Thence, quickly to the mountains he leads his bands, and carries with him immense booty in sheep and cattle. With his band of robbers he devastates hamlets and homes, and fields far and wide, seizes the quiet flocks, and harries the humblest dwell-

---

with the Macintosh, and Inverness had taken part with the Macintosh, and Keppoch, instead of joining Dundee, used his force for his own ends. Dundee had counted on Keppoch joining him, and on turning on Mackay in strength, for he wrote to the magistrates of Elgin from Inverness to prepare quarters for 900 or 1000 Highlanders besides his own cavalry. See Mackay's Memoirs, page 14; Lochiel's Memoirs, pages 236, 237. Keppoch is described by Balhaldy as a gentleman of good understanding, of great cunning, and much attached to King James, but indulging himself in too great liberties with respect to those with whom he was at variance. Dundee had great difficulty in controlling this chief. See description of him, Book IV.

At postquam rapidis permiscuit omnia flammis
Avius ipse fuga se rupibus abdidit altis.
　　Et quamquam in mediis circumdatus hoste periclis
Stabat, fortunae non cedere suetus iniquae,
Dundius, ut rupes circumstagnantibus undis
Mole sua pelagi insultus immota retundit,
Audacem usque animam, promtamque in vulnera dextram,
Invictam gerens generoso in pectore mentem,
Fert aegre amissam tanti certaminis ansam.
Haud sine laude tamen linquit jam cerula Nessi
Flumina, sulphureis pelago labentia lymphis.
Inde lacum, rigidae spernit quae frigora brumae,
Saxa per et celsos ascendit inhospita montes.
Perque Herichum graditur, vallem Tarsumque nivalem
Scandit, et aeternis boreae juga cana pruinis.
Invia pulsat equis, ubi cincta paludibus atris
Arxque superba alto jacet Invergarria saxo.

ing. But when he had reduced the country to ashes, he betook himself to his unapproachable mountain fastnesses. As a rock amid the billows repels the onslaughts of the sea, immovable in its mass, so Dundee, surrounded by dangers, in the midst of enemies, stood firm, bearing in his noble breast a bold unconquerable spirit, and a hand ready to strike. Yet is he grieved to lose so great an opportunity of giving battle to the enemy. Not however without praise[1] does he leave the blue waters of the Ness, gliding in sulphur-mingled[2] streams to the sea. Thence he ascends the lake which despises the frosts of hard winter, and by rock and mountain he advances through Strath Errick[3] and the snowy vale of Tarf, and over ridges, white with perpetual snow. His horses trample the untrodden paths where Invergarry Castle[4]

---

[1] He had got rid of Keppoch, and had promised the magistrates of Inverness, that the money they had lost should be repaid them on the King's return if they did not declare for the Prince of Orange.—*Nairne Papers*, quoted by Napier, p. 547.

[2] 'Sulphureis lymphis.' It was supposed that Loch Ness owed its freedom from ice to sulphur in its waters.

[3] A road in this district is described, eighty years later, by Bishop Robert Forbes, as 'the most rugged in the world—a narrow sheep or goat road along which the Highland garrons made their way, stepping like dogs over huge stones.'—Bishop Forbes's Journal.

[4] Its attempted destruction in 1746 was unsuccessful; the walls, according to Bishop Forbes, were only rent with the gunpowder.

Hinc redit, atque eadem loca rupibus horrida vastis
Transit et ad sacram sistit Kilyghymenis aedem ;
Utque diem campis aurora reduxit eois,
Phoebus et oceano auricomum caput extulit alto,
Dundius audacem nunc ipsa per ardua turmam,
Cornipedemque citum per devia rura fatigat,
Perque humiles nullo signatàs tramite valles,
Arva per et rigidis Badenothae horrentia saxis
Ordine agit, celeres et per dumeta phalanges
Aspera, surgentes et celsa ad nubila montes
Transvolat. Hinc Batavo duce jam post terga relicto
Ad boream, tepidos sensim se vertit ad austros.
Impiger et Spejae superato fluminis alveo[1]
Ad vada, quae patulis prospectat Clunia campis,
Presmochorae tenues dignatur adire penates.

stands proudly aloft, girt with black bogs. Thence he returns by rugged ways, mid vast rocks, and halts at the Kirk of Kilcummin.[2] But when Aurora returned, and Phœbus raised his golden locks above the sea, Dundee led on his bold troopers through the mountains by devious paths,[3] and where no path appeared in the frozen wastes of rugged Badenoch, through thickets and over hilltops. Then, having left the Dutch general far behind in the North, he leisurely turns towards the warmer South. Quickly he passed the Spey at the fords, where Cluny[4] looks out on his wide plains, and deigned to visit the humble hearth of Presmochora.[5]

---

[1] An example of Synapheia: 'fluminis alve(o) ad vada.'

[2] The Church of St. Coemgen, where Fort-Augustus now stands. It was here that Montrose and the chiefs of the Highland clans signed their bond in 1645. It is spelt in the bond 'Killiewheimen.'

[3] His route evidently lay by the Pass of Corryarrick to the Spey, along which river he would pass, from where the Bridge of Laggan now is, to the fords near Cluny. From thence there was a straight road to Loch Garry by Dalwhinnie.

[4] Throughout this march Dundee succeeded in 'engaging most part of the men of note to be ready at a call to join in his master's service.' 'He found the Macphersons very keen and hearty in their inclinations for that service.' Duncan Macpherson of Cluny, the Chief, was at this time on uncomfortable terms with the gentlemen of his clan, through their fear of the results of the marriage of his only daughter to the second son of the Laird of Cawdor. Sixteen of them had entered into a bond to resist his supposed intentions as to the entail. See *Book of the Thanes of Cawdor*, Spalding Club, p. 377.

[5] Probably the farm of Presmukerach, on the Truim, between Cluny and Dalwhinnie, now the property of Col. Macpherson of Glentruim, but formerly

Regia Grampiacis ibi epistola missa Tribunis
Quos prius expertus tam fidos Regibus omnes,
Sub magni imperiis Grami cum pube paratos
Rex sua castra sequi ad Maii jubet esse calendas.
 Parte alia lento M'Kaius agmina gressu
Tardus agit, tepidi latitatque ad flumina Nessi,
Mentis inops animique levis, pavet usque fragorem
Motorum nemorum, seu quassa cacumina quercus
Nutavit, tenuive insibilat aura susurro,
Obvia quaeque timet, patuloque errantia campo
Jumenta, et densis armenta emissa latebris,
Hostica sublatis formidat ut agmina signis.
At nunquam fatis animo concussus iniquis
Gramus iter tutum per inhospita tesqua tenebat
Latos ad Atholios trans Grampica culmina campos,
Perque Lacum Gereum triplici se fonte secantem,
Per densas coryli silvas, et curva Timellae

There he issued the Royal letter to all the faithful clans,[1] bidding them be ready with their men by the Kalends of May, to follow the orders and the camp of the Graham.

On the other side, the tardy Mackay, with slow step, makes his advance, and skulks about the mild waters of the Ness. Without mind or spirit, he fears even the creaking of the woods when the oak-tree bows his head before the blast, or when the breeze whistles in gentle note. The herds of cattle straying over the plain alarm him, and he sees hostile bands in the flocks appearing from among the bushes. But the Graham, never losing heart under hardship, briskly holds on his way through inhospitable deserts, and over the Grampians to the wide plains of Athole. He passes Loch Garry, issuing in triple stream, and on through dense woods of hazel, and reaches, by the winding Tummel,[2] the Castle

---

belonging to the Dukes of Gordon. The presence of Lord Dunfermline and the Gordon cavaliers, as well as the privacy of the secluded situation, would make Presmukerach a natural halting-place. The Latin in length of syllables exactly follows the Gaelic pronunciation.

[1] The letter was issued probably on 6th or 7th May, and fixed the meeting with the chiefs, in Lochaber, for the 18th.

[2] The Tummel is here named for the Garry. The Garry becomes the Tummel below Killiecrankie. The dense hazel woods give a feature of the country in 1689. Does the river still issue from the lake in triple stream?

Flumina ad alta Blari tendit munimina castri.
Inde Caledoniam subito provectus ad urbem,
Irruit occiduae patefacta ad limina portae,
Atque hic hostilis ductorem forte manipli,
Regia finitimis qui vectigalia villis
Hauserat, incautum premit, et sine sanguine sternit,
Exque improviso simul aere atque exuit armis.
Mox defessa virum tum corpora curat equorum.
At postquam oceano nitidum caput abdiderat sol,
Noxque polo rutilum stellarum induxit honorem,[1]
Rursus anhelantes cogit sub frena caballos,
Et durum molitur iter gressuque citato
Per vada caeca Tai Perthanam tendit ad urbem.
Jam vero ad lapidem progressus ab urbe secundum
Sistit, et ex omni bis denos agmine lectos
Secum ducit equos, portisque illabitur altis,

of Blair,[2] with its lofty battlements. Thence, advancing to Dunkeld,[3] he dashes at the open door of the western gate, and there, unexpectedly, came upon the captain of a hostile troop, who had been gathering the revenues of the district. Without bloodshed, he prostrates him, depriving him of the money, and his arms. There he rests to refresh man and horse. But as soon as the sun had hidden his glowing head in ocean, and night had bespread the heavens with the radiant glory of the stars, the horses are bridled, and, by the hidden fords of Tay,[4] he makes forced march on Perth. Having advanced to the second milestone[5] from the town, he halts, and, selecting twenty men from his troop, he steals through the lofty gates of the city, before the lark had sung his

---

[1] *Var. lect.* Period after ' honorem ' in original.

[2] Patrick Stewart of Ballechin held the men of Athole loyal to King James, though the Marquis and his son wavered between both parties. Ballechin probably was already holding the Castle of Blair, for the guardianship of which Dundee afterwards gave him formal appointment, to the exclusion of Lord Murray. Dundee was at Blair on the 9th May.

[3] The descent on Dunkeld was on the 10th; he moved on to Perth that night. By two o'clock on Saturday morning, the 11th, he had entered Perth. His force was about seventy sabres, though the Provost of Perth in his letter to the Convention nearly doubles the number.

[4] ' Caeca vada.' This may mean that the water was deep, hiding the fords, or that his course was by private, less-known fords.—Virgil, *Aen.* i. 536.

[5] ' Ad lapidem ab urbe secundum.' Were milestones a feature of the Perth roads two hundred years ago ?

Quam prius aut solitum cecinisset alaudula carmen,
Aurora aut croceos tinxisset in aequore crines.
Atque forum vigilumque domos simul occupat, acri et
Vectus equo mediam victor dat lora per urbem.
Caetera sub variis legio dum instructa magistris
Certatim ruit ad muros, atque ilicet omnes
Illi aditus fecere sibi portasque patentes.
Inde vias omnes abjecto milite complent,
Hinc atque hinc, densaeque fremunt per tecta catervae,
Degeneres pars quaerit opes, pars colligit arma,
Alter equos, alter captivam detinet hostem.
Ipsum inter spolia ampla ducem jam lecta juventus
Forte Blarum somno stertentem suscitat alto,

wonted song, or Aurora gilded the sea with her yellow tresses. At once he occupies the market-place and the watch-houses, and, as a victor, rides freely through the town. Meanwhile, the troopers, drawn up under their officers outside, rush to the walls, and there make entrance for themselves by the open gates; then they fill all the streets where the soldiers lie; here and there strong bands storm the houses, some seize the ill-gotten money,[1] others collect arms, some horses, others guard the captive enemy. Now a band of youthful cavaliers rouses up, amidst his ample spoil, Blair,[2] the

---

[1] 'Degeneres opes.' I have ventured on this translation with some hesitation. He may mean filthy lucre in general, or the revenues wrongly acquired by an agent of the new Government. Browne, in his *History of the Highlands*, without giving his authority, says that Dundee took a sum of 9000 merks of the public revenue on this occasion. He however prohibited interference with private property, and left behind him, in the same room where he found the cess-money, £500, understanding that it was private property.

[2] William Blair of Blair, a man of importance, who had married into the Duke of Hamilton's family, his wife being Lady Margaret Hamilton, youngest daughter of William, second Duke. He and his lieutenant, Pollock, were both taken prisoners in their beds. The spoil of this raid included forty horses, some arms, gunpowder, public money, besides numerous prisoners, including officers, one of whom, Lieut. Colt, gives interesting evidence in the process of forfeiture. They were all carried on with the party, and most of them afterwards sent as prisoners to Duart in Mull. Blair and Pollock were raising a troop in the shire of Perth for the new Government. On Blair's remonstrating, Claverhouse is reported to have said, 'You take prisoners for the Prince of Orange, and we take prisoners for King James, and there 's an end of it.' In the detailed account sent from Claverhouse to King James by M'Swine, we have the following: 'He (Dundee) took occasion to slip down through Athole to St. Johnston, where he surprised the Laird of Blair, seized him, his lieutenant Pogue (Pollock) of that ilk, trumpet, standard, and all the troopers that were in the town, with two

Cum nondum hesternam decoxit mane suburram.
Undique mox captam cogunt uno agmine turbam,
Cum ducibus, turmamque equitum, peditumque catervam.
Gramineo posuere solo, praedaque potiti
Hostica cum magno tollunt vexilla cachinno,
Malaque de victis convellunt aurea signis.
　Jam[1] adeo spoliis induti hostilibus omnes
Victores celsique in equis, armisque superbi,

commander himself, snoring in deep sleep, not having yet shaken off the effects of the night's debauch. From every side they now gather the captives together, with their leaders, a band of horse and foot, on the green sod, and having possessed themselves of the booty, with great laughter they raise aloft the ensigns of the enemy, and pluck the golden apples[2] from the conquered standards. And now all the victors, clothed with the spoils of the enemy, mounted on their horses, proud in arms, return in order to

lieutenants of M'Kays, and two or three officers of the new levies, most of which are sent to an island of the MacLeans, which is said to be like the Bass.'

The island was Cairnburg, one of the Treshnish islands—a high rock, of some considerable extent at the top, inaccessible on all sides excepting by one narrow pass. See *Letters of Viscount Dundee*, edited by George Smythe, for the Bannatyne Club, pp. 56, 57.

In the Decreet of Forfeiture, *Acts of Parliament of Scotland*, Appendix, p. 61, Dundee and others are charged with 'coming to the toune of Perth, in fear of wear, and that therein in ane hostile manner they did seize and carry away the Laird of Blair and other officers of their Magesties' forces, and detained the Lajrd of Blair prisoner in the Castle of Dowart, in a cruel and sad conditione till he dyed.'

The prisoners having been carried along with Dundee's party through Angus and Perth, and on the fearful march described by the Poet to Glen Roy, were afterwards lodged in Lochiel's house. Lieutenant Colt accompanied the force in the march to Badenoch, where he saw the taking of Ruthven Castle, and the pursuit of M'Kay to Edinglassie. Afterwards he and the other prisoners were carried from Lochiel's house, where they had been well cared for, under the charge of Hector MacLean, younger of Lochbuy, to Mull, and were sent to Cairnburg. They remained there till after the engagement at Dunkeld, when Sir John MacLean brought them to Duart Castle, where Blair died.

Pollock was Robert, younger of Pollock. He survived his imprisonment, and was made a Baronet in 1703, partly in consequence of his having been 'confined in the most barbarous and uncivilised places of the Highlands during the space of nine months.' It is satisfactory to find Wodrow corresponding with him at Oldman's Coffee-house after such an experience.—See *Wodrow Correspondence*, vol. ii. p. 405.

[1] No elision of the 'am' before 'adeo.' See Lucretius ii. 466 and iii. 1095, and Ramsay's *Prosody*, on subject of 'Elision.' 'Jam' and 'adeo' should not have been brought together, however.

[2] 'Mala aurea,'—probably gilt balls on the tops of the standard poles. Were

Ordine compositis redeunt ad signa maniplis.
Utque in procinctu densae micuere phalanges,
Fulmineus medio victor stetit agmine Gramus,
Jam sublimis equo et fulgentibus arduus armis.
' En,' ait, ' auspiciis olim felicibus usi
Regia jam sequimur castra, et pro gente Stuarta
Hostibus eversis, ultricia sumpsimus arma,
Et Perthae insignem spoliis intravimus urbem.
Nunc quocunque vocant laeti data fata sequamur.'
Dixit ; et instructis generoso milite turmis,
Signa jubet placido tolli victricia vultu.
Ipse simul campo vestigia figit aperto
Martia heroo praetervolat agmina gressu.
Inde Tai rapidam transmittit fluminis undam,
Stant ubi Regificae turrita palatia Sconae.
Protinus ad sacram Cargillae fertilis aedem

their own ensigns. And as the squadrons formed up in a circle, Graham, the fiery victor, mounted, and towering aloft in shining arms, in the midst, thus addresses them: 'Again we follow the Royal camp, and the fortunes of the Stuart, under the happy auspices of former days. We have taken up avenging arms, and have entered Perth, a city rich in spoil, the enemy being overthrown. Now let us gladly follow whither the Fates call us.' He spoke, and the troops being formed under a noble soldier,[1] with calm dignity he gives the order to march. He himself at the same time moved to the open plain, and speeds at the head of his martial line with heroic mien. Then he passes the rapid Tay, where stands the turreted palace of royal Scone.[2] Quickly he advances to the Kirk of fertile Cargill,[3] and stops at the fair Castle of Stobhall.[3]

---

they a special feature of the Orange regiments? Their meeting with special derision would seem to indicate special significance.

[1] Probably Lord Dunfermline.

[2] The lines here suggest that Dundee passed on in front, leaving the command to the noble soldier who hurried on to Stobhall with the troopers. Dundee himself dined at Scone. Through this dinner Lord Stormont came under the suspicion of the Convention. He explained that 'Dundee had forced his dinner from him on Saturday last.' His father-in-law, Scott of Scotstarvet, and his uncle, Sir John Murray of Drumcairn, were on a visit at Scone at the time, and had much trouble through the same dinner.—Napier, p. 552.

[3] Stobhall, a seat of the Earl of Perth, at this time a prisoner in Stirling Castle. The Kirk of Cargill is further from Perth than Stobhall; but probably the advanced party of the troop went on to Cargill, while Claverhouse himself stayed at Stobhall. The route taken from Perth would be by Scone and the old

Fertur, et ad nitidam Stobhalli substitit arcem.
Et jam census agit rationem, et nomine fisci
Exigit, immissis vicina per oppida turmis,
Publica finitimos et colligit aera per agros.
Sed jam Phoebus equis declivior exit anhelis,
Et nox atra polo nigrantibus incubat alis.
Indulgent placido dum cuncta animantia somno,
Et curas animo et duros posuere labores,[1]
Gramus equos atque arma vigil rapit ocius, acres
Et rauco ciet aere viros, illi ilicet omnes
Circumstant, saltuque ingentia membra caballis
Subjiciunt, et nota ducum vexilla sequuntur.
Ipse praeit, socios et sic hortatur euntes:
' Erigite in dubiis mavortia pectora rebus,
Invicti validis et fortia forte lacertis
Arma viri, duroque manus assuescite Marti.
Me deturbati patria de sede Monarchae
Torquet amor, qui nunc ignotis exulat oris,
Et cura innocui tangit praecordia nati,
Cogit et horrisoni tentare pericula belli.
Et magni jam Regis honos et gloria nostram
Poscit opem, simul et patriae titubantis imago

Here he makes valuations of cess,[2] and raises the taxes in the name of the Exchequer, parties being sent out to the neighbouring towns; and he collects the public dues in the surrounding country. When night had settled down upon the sky, and all things were finding repose, the wakeful Graham quickly arms and mounts, and calls up his men with trumpet sound. They soon gather around, big men, yet taking the saddle at a bound, and forming up under their various leaders. He himself goes before them, and thus exhorts his friends: ' Rouse ye, and prepare to meet danger with stout heart and hand. The love of the dethroned and exiled King, and the welfare of his heir, stirs my heart, and moves me to try the issues of war. The honour and glory of a great King claim our aid, and the picture of our country falling, or, by our arms,

---

Roman road above the river. Does the word 'nitidam' mean that Stobhall was then a white-washed house?

[1] *Var. lect.* A colon after ' labores.'

[2] ' Census agit' will not scan. The reference is to the *cess* or assess taxes which we know Claverhouse seized at Dunkeld, Perth, and Dundee, and collected throughout parts of Angus and Perth.

Quae cadat, aut nostris nunc ardua surgat ab armis
Excitet ipsa viros ; nec nos pia signa secutos
Caesareis olim castris meruisse pigebit.'
Sic fatur: subitoque a tergo moenia Coupri,
Et Miglae linquit turres, fanumque Colassi
Praeterit, et laetos quos alluit Illia campos.
Inde viam secat ad fumantia culmina Glammi,
Ardua porticibus, pinnis exstructa superbis
Atria magnifici genium testata Magistri.
Hic vero in viridi dum membra terosa reponit
Gramine, quaesitum Regis sub nomine nummos
Emittit celeres turmas, missique repente
Jam redeunt, et equos, atque aera, atque arma reportant.
Ergo dato graditur signo, durisque lupatis
Cornipedem premit, et patulo quatit agmina campo.
    Haud procul infensus Batavi jam nominis hostis
Obvius it, procerum decus Haliburtonius,[1] ingens

rising aloft, itself should give spirit to men. It will not shame us to have served in the camp of the Caesar, following pious standards.' Thus he spoke ; and quickly he leaves behind him the walls of Cupar, the towers of Meigle, and the Kirk of Collessie,[2] and the gladsome fields which Isla waters. Onward he pursues his way towards the smoking chimneys of Glamis, with its lofty porticoes and halls reared aloft in superb turrets, all testifying to the genius of its magnificent master.[3] While here, on the green grass, he rests his wearied limbs, he sends out, in the King's name, light troopers to collect the revenues, who quickly return, bringing back horses, money, and arms. The signal being then given, he presses on his horse and speeds over the plain. At no great distance Hallyburton[4] meets him, the foe of the Dutchman, the flower of nobles, lead-

---

[1] The Poet has taken a liberty with the length of the *u* in this proper name. It is given as ' Hallburtonius' in one MS.

[2] This must be the Kirk of Eassie, which lay in the direct route to Glamis. Collace lay quite out of the route, and several miles behind them.

[3] The first Earl of Kinghorn, the builder of the magnificent castle, I suppose, is alluded to. He did not live to see it finished. The smoking chimneys indicate the presence of the family. I am informed that there is no documentary evidence at Glamis of this visit, but the legend of the place is that the Lord Strathmore of the day rode over the hills with Claverhouse from Glamis. Lord Livingstone, who left Edinburgh with Dundee, went to Glamis on a visit to his half-brother, Lord Strathmore, and there affected illness. He had returned to the Convention by this time.

[4] David Hallyburton, of Pitcur, a prominent man in this rising. It would

Agmen agens, totoque ipse altior agmine surgens.
Addit se comitem Gramo Mavortius heros.
Huic juxta patriis nomen qui sumpsit[1] ab arvis
Fullertonus adest, atque ipse acerrimus armis
Ventonus socium se infert, eadem arma secutus ;
Clari animis omnes, clari armis fortibus omnes
Incedunt, Gramumque in bella sequuntur euntem.
Ille rebellantem Taoduni tendit ad urbem,
Ut fugitiva suis induceret agmina castris,
Aut secum in dubiam descendere Martis arenam.

ing with him a great band, himself towering above his whole line. This warlike hero allies himself to the Graham. With him comes Fullerton,[2] who took his name from his paternal acres. The eager Venton,[3] too, most ardent in arms, joins the same standard as an ally. All in high spirits, all illustrious in arms, they make their advance, and follow the Graham as he goes to battle.

He moves towards the rebel town of Dundee, that he may bring back the deserted troopers to his standard, or try the doubtful issue of battle. He at once approaches the town, to the very

---

seem from Colt's evidence that he joined Dundee first at Stobhall, where Major Middleton also joined. He may have ridden back to his own house after an interview at Stobhall, and brought up his men to join Claverhouse on the road to Dundee. He was at the attack on Dundee, and was with Claverhouse throughout the campaign, and fell with him at Killiecrankie. He was buried by the side of his beloved leader. Lieutenant Nisbet, when a prisoner at Blair, saw the party of Highlanders who had just returned from his burial at the Kirk of Blair, and Lieutenant Hay, another prisoner at Blair, had a visit from the Laird of Strickmartin, who told him he had just been burying Pitcur. His faithfulness and patient endurance of hardship is referred to by Claverhouse in his letters. His strength and prowess made havoc among M'Kay's men at Killiecrankie. He is described in the process of forfeiture by James Malcolm as sometimes during the battle riding on a grey horse wanting an eye, and sometimes on a bay horse with a white face. Elsewhere he is described as a moving castle in the shape of a man.

On the process of forfeiture, Sir Patrick Murray, Commissioner of Stranraar, protested that his process might be without prejudice of the Lady of Pitcur, her liferent, and of her children's provisions, which protestation was admitted.

The family of Hallyburton of Pitcur was an old one in Angus and Perth. The property has now passed into other hands. Judge Haliburton (*Sam Slick*) was proud of his connection with the race.

[1] The spelling of original is 'sumsit.'

[2] Fullerton of Fullerton. The property is near Meigle. See note, Book IV.

[3] Renton of Renton, according to Napier; but I do not see any ground for such identification. See note, Book IV.

Continuo ruit ad muros, urbique propinquat.
Et jam fama volans pavidam pervenit ad urbem,
Ingentem signis volitantibus affore Gramum.
Attoniti subito trepida formidine cives
Discurrunt, tremulisque implent ululatibus auras.
Pars aditus plaustris, saxisque ingentibus obdunt,
Stipitibusque vias, et muros aggere vallant;
Ast alii crates, et dura repagula portis
Injiciunt, foribus addunt praegrandia claustra.
  Gramus at emissis, quaterent ut compita, turmis,
Ingruit, insani Martisque ardebat amore.
Loricam ingentem et munimina fortia dorsi
Induit, et nigri galeam sub pelle galeri. ·
Insigni alipedum turma stipatus equorum,
Surgentis jam celsa petit fastigia montis,
Dum fraenata acies, equitumque exercitus omnis
Radicem tenet, et surgentem vertice collem.
Jamque Tai properans juga scandit, et imminet urbi,

walls. Already the report[1] that the great Graham was approaching with flying banners had reached the trembling city. The affrighted citizens turn every way in their fear, and fill the air with their cries. Some block the approaches with wagons and huge stones, and the streets are barricaded. The walls are strengthened with earthworks and fascines, the gates are barred and blocked. The Graham—having sent out an advance party to clear the way—now approaches eager for the fight. He puts on his armour, breast-plate and back-piece of strength, and a helmet under a covering of black fur. Surrounded by a brilliant staff of horsemen, he at once seeks the top of the Law, while his horse and the rest of his force hold the base and declivities. Now he climbs the ridges above the Tay, and threatens the city. He seizes the mound,[2] and drives in the outposts. As when the bird of Jove,

---

[1] He approached Dundee on 13th May. A man named Moir, the servant of a Mrs. Maxwell at Tealing, hastened into Dundee with the news that Claverhouse was coming over the Seidlaws. He only appeared before the town at five o'clock in the evening, if Lord Ross is correct in his letter to Hamilton, dated May 14th. On this occasion Claverhouse seized the drums and baggage of the the Laird of Dun, and other of the Earl of Mar's officers, and dispersed and frightened whole companies. He also seized £300 of cess and excise.—*Nairne Papers*; Dundee's *Letters*, Bannatyne Club.

[2] Is the tumulum, the Hill of Dundee, called the Bonnet Hill, where was the suburb of the Hilltown or Rottenrow, which a local historian, without giving any

Et tumulum capit, excubitoresque expulit hostes.
Qualis ubi nebula veniens Jovis ales ab alta
Fertur in imbelles penna plaudente columbas,
Illae ut terribilem prospectant eminus hostem,
Dant sese magno liquidum per inane volatu
Aut humiles tectis, aut densae vimine sylvae
Abscondunt sese, donec nox humida terras
Nigrantes furvo nebularum involvit amictu.
Haud aliter praemissi equites formidine torpent.
Audacem ut rutilis Gramum speculantur in armis,
Atque illum longe gradientem atque arma ferentem
Ut videre, metu conversi terga dedere,
Et sese portis pavidi sepsere sub altis.
Interea vario complentur moenia motu,
Et vigilum summo pulsus de monte satelles
Ingentem rediens terrorem civibus aegris
Incutit, et duro populum rumore fatigat.
Ingruere infestum subito sub moenibus hostem
Qui face fumantem ferroque exscinderet urbem.
Jam cecidere animi, tremefactaque pectora vulgi,
Fit plangor confestim ingens, et in urbe tumultus
Exoritur, tepidosque[1] agit discordia cives.

descending from high heaven, is borne on sounding wing against the timid doves, they gaze aloft upon their dreadful enemy, and fly to the shelter of roof or grove until dark night involve the sky in gloomy vesture. So are the advanced troopers of the enemy benumbed with fear as they look up upon the Graham in glittering armour, and as in dread they behold his approach, they fly within the gates, where all is terror and confusion. The scouts, driven in from the hill, fill the townspeople with dismay, and harass them with terrible reports. They dreaded that the fierce foe would at once fire the town and put the inhabitants to the sword. Wailing, discord, tumult arose on all sides. Some in

---

authority, says Claverhouse fired and reduced to ashes. It lay on the way of Claverhouse's approach. The fact of this assault on the town was communicated to the Committee in Edinburgh that same night, Bailie Duncan of Lundie being the express. In consequence six firekings (firkins) of powder were ordered to be sent from Bo'ness to Dundee, and Hastings' infantry and Berkley's horse were ordered to proceed thither.—Yeaman's *History of Dundee*, p. 86.

[1] 'tepidosque agit' will scan if there be no elision, which however there ought to be.

Pars mare sollicitant remis et in aequora currunt,
Secumque ingentes asportant aeris acervos,
Et turpi dant terga fugae ; pars altera magno
Gramo urbem, portasque jubent praebere patentes,
Et titulum Batavi execrantur et arma tyranni.
Arma alii expediunt, Bacchique[1] furoribus acti
Discurrunt trepido per proxima tecta tumultu,
Perque vias vicosque ruunt, mustoque madentes
Hortantur socios ; illi ferrugine scabra
Arma attrita parant, hic ruptam corripit hastam,
Et ferrugineam tectis rapit ille securem ;
Alter et exesum rubigine protrahit ensem.
Et jam scabra locant tormenta ad limina portae,
Sanguineumque alti vexillum in vertice saxi
Tollitur, et plenos exsiccant ore culullos.
Sic madidi ad muros insana mole ruebant
Longaevi juvenesque, et fossas agmine cingunt.
Verum inter strepitus, et tanti fulmina belli
Diriguere metu, nec lapsos pocula Bacchi
Sustentant animos, conspecto cominus hoste
Urbs fremit, in varias et scinditur impia partes.
  Ductores ipsi, studia in contraria versi,
Qui tenuere altos Batavo pro principe muros

dastardly flight take to their boats, carrying with them their valuables; others bid the gates be opened to the great Graham, renouncing all allegiance to the Dutch tyrant. Others prepare arms, running about, mad with drink, from house to house, and through the streets, calling to arms. Some take down the broken spear and axe, and rusty sword and arms, useless with age. Now they place the old ordnance at the gate, and hoist a red banner on the top of the rock, and drain deep cups of liquor. Thus they rush to the walls, a drunken multitude, and old and young surround the ditches in a body. But the cup of Bacchus could not uphold their spirits mid the real darts of war, and, in the presence of the enemy, the impious town is divided into two parties.

  The commanders themselves, who held the town for the Batavian Prince, took different lines, and remained inactive and confused.

---

[1] The drinking in Dundee about the period was not all on the Dutch side. There is a petition and bond among the Dundee papers by Robert Lindsay, merchant and burgess, dated from the prison, an inmate of which he became for drinking 'King James his health, or for being in the company where the samen was drunken.'

Attonitis haesere animis. Balfourius urbem
Linquere, nec patulo patitur concurrere campo.
Rollocus et, turmam qui ductor agebat equorum,
Ante metu fugiens hostem vicina reliquit
Oppida, et insanam pavitans advenerat urbem ;
Noluit ille pedem nota extra limina ferre,

Balfour[1] will not move outside the walls. Rollo,[2] who was raising a troop of horse in the district for his own command, hurried in from the neighbouring villages in fear, sought the shelter of the town, and refused to move a step outside his door. The name of

---

[1] Claverhouse writes 'that he went to Dundee thinking to gain the two troops of dragoons, but could not prevail because of Captain Balfour, who commanded them.' Lord Rosse, writing from Lanark, 2d May 1679, to the Earl of Linlithgow, says, 'Last night a horrible abuse hath fallen out, and of such a nature that could not but give your Lordship notice of it by express. Some eight or ten soldiers belonging to Captain Ogilvy's and Captain Balfour's companies, being gone to the country, to the parish of Pitenen, of purpose (as it seems) to rob, took occasion at night to fall out with some country people, who having fled to a house where there was a good strong gate which the soldiers not being able to break open did threaten to burn, and accordingly did actually set fire to it; and thereafter, not being able to fire it by reason of the people's diligence by throwing water upon it from within, they went away breaking open a poor widow woman's house which was near by, taking three pieces of cloth which were in the house.' The Balfour of this letter was the Honourable John, second son of the third Lord Balfour of Burleigh, and, though of the same regiment as the captain of our Poet, may not have been the same man, for the Honourable John Balfour was a Jacobite, and appears as Governor of Perth under Lord Mar in 1715.—See *Letters of Dundee*, p. 21.

[2] Andrew, third Lord Rollo. He was raising a troop of horse in Angus, but hearing of Blair's misfortune at Perth, hurried into Dundee for safety.—Balcarres' *Memoir*, p. 40. His troop cost him much difficulty, for the Master of Forbes had been over the ground before him, and the Angus and Mearns district was most loyal to King James. The following extract from a lettter from Hamilton to the Master of Forbes illustrates the matter: 'And sieing yow have taken up so many of the horse levied in these shyres which were allocate for making up the Lord Rollo his troup, the Estates doe expect your careful endeavours in assisting the Lord Rollo in making up his troup out of that part of your former localitie which you have not called for to make up your own.'—*Acts of Scot. Parliaments*, vol. ix. p. 84.

The following 'order' refers to the same difficulty: 'The Committee of Estates, having had information that these of the shyre of Forfar, Kincairdine, and Marishell's part of Aberdeine Shyre lyable for outreicking of their proportiones of horse for making up of my Lord Rollo's Troop, raised for their Majesties service, have not obeyed the Act of the Estates made thereanent, they therefore doe heirby ordaine and require the Shirreff Deputts of the respective Shyres aforsaid to give tymeous intimatione to the leaders of horse in the bounds to meet

Sed latet infelix ; audito et nomine Grami
Tecta petit, caecis et sese condidit umbris.
Ductor at a vivo ducit qui nomina saxo
Inclyta, jam Regi tacite Gramoque favebat ;
Utque sub antiquis conjungeret agmina signis
Ille equitum turmas, ter centum civibus auctas,
Ire jubet, strictoque viam prorumpere ferro.

Graham being heard, he seeks his dwelling and conceals himself in darkness. But the illustrious Captain,[1] who derives his name from the living stone, was secretly favouring the King and the Graham. That he might bring back his force to their old standards, he commands them—increased with 300 citizens—to make a sortie, and force a way with the drawn sword.

---

at Dundee, the 23rd day of May instant, to give obedience to the said Act of the Estates in delyvering to the said Lord Rollo ffourtie fyve horses with sufficient ryders and mounting as they will be answerable on their highest perill.'—*Acts of Parl.*, vol. ix. App. p. 27.

The following letter I have extracted from *Municipal History of Dundee*, Yeaman, p. 87 :—

'Duncrub, 11th Sept. 1689.

'Sir,—I give you the troble to desyre you may put my Trouper William Wallace, whom you have in your prisone as ane remaining from my troup, at freedom, providing he give beall to act honestly and to return to Duncrub with his sadle and furnitur and arms, against Wednesday's night next, and upon your letter with him he shall be allowed to ryd in the troup as formerlie. Als I desire he may not go out of prisone till he pay for the tyme he has been in yr.

'This is all, expecting you will doe me this favor, restis, Sir, your most affectionate and humble servant,   ROLLO.

'The Provost of Dundee, and in his absence Wm. Oliphant, Mercht, yr.'

Wallace gives his bond to return, and doubtless did return to Duncrub. The old and common spelling of Rollo was Rollock.

[1] Lieut.-Col. Livingstone, afterwards Lord Kilsyth. He was one of the officers engaged in the plot for recovering the Scotch Dragoons for King James. The regiment—formerly Lord Dunmore's—was now commanded by Sir Thomas Livingstone, who was with Mackay. Two troops, under Livingstone and Balfour, were left in Dundee. Mackay says that Dundee 'braved the two troops of dragoons left there under the Lieut.-Col., by which occasion he showed that he was either a traitor or a coward.'—*Memoirs*, p. 20. Livingstone was afterward arrested in the north, and condemned, but on his appealing for mercy he was liberated. He afterwards married Dundee's widow, and narrowly escaped her fate, as will be seen from the following letter :—

'Extract of a letter from Countess of Wemyss in her own right, to her sister (*daughter?*), the Countess of Leven, dated London, October 26, 1695:—"I doubt not but you have heard or this time of my Lady Dundee, hir sad death at Holland. It seems she was newly come to the place, and could not get lodgings, which made her to go to a little hous for a night ; but in the midle of the night,

Talibus inter se studiis sub moenibus urbis
Certantes stupuere duces, stupuere cohortes.
Dumque anceps trepidam torquet sententia turbam,
Dundius, expulso custode, cacumina montis
Occupat, invictas atque instruit ordine turmas,
Ante urbem, pulchris et sese ostendit in armis.
Huc atque huc celerique volans obit agmina cursu;
Evocat et mediis cunctantem moenibus hostem
Prodire, in campo martemque poposcit aperto.
Sed trepidi rerum, et saevi formidine Martis
Perculsi summique duces, urbisque juventus
Moenia tuta tenent, et portas obice firmant.
Gramus et ante aciem nitidis ibat altus in armis,
Hinc atque hinc dubiosque aditus explorat, et omnes
Excutit anfractus, urbemque impune rebellem
Aspicit, et muris stantes denso agmine cives.
Nec quenquam instantem turmis, aut arma ferentem
Contra stare videt, graviter commotus, et ira
Concitus adversi peragrat vestigia clivi.
Rursus et ad dextram quadratum dirigit agmen,

Mid such opposing designs the leaders and troops remain inactive, and the people are in suspense. Dundee having driven in the defenders of the hill, occupies it, and forms up his troops in order before the town, and it was a sight fair to see. On this side and that he presents his men in rapid formation, and challenges the enemy—keeping to their walls—to the open field, and demands battle. But cautious and timid leaders, and youth alike, cling to the safety of their defences and well-barred gates. The Graham in gleaming arms rides out before his line, and explores every approach and corner in the defences of the rebel city. With impunity he closely views the citizens crowding the walls. He finds no one ready to meet him, and in grave anger and disappointment he retraces his steps to the hillside, and moves his force in square[1] to the right. Having surmounted, or gone round,

---

the hous fell, and killed hir and hir sone and hir woman. The V. of Kilsith escaped, but was very ill hurt; so it is doubtful if he will live, with grife and pain togither. This is very sad news" (*Leven and Melville Papers*).'—Napier's *Dundee*, p. 673.

He died in exile, loyal to the Stuarts. He is to be distinguished from Captain Livingstone of the same regiment, and from his Colonel, Sir Thomas, afterwards General Livingstone of Glencoe notoriety.

[1] This may mean 'in fours.'

Transilit et colles, et montes circuit altos,
Accessusque omnes superat, campumque tenebat
Surgentem unde omnem late est prospectus ad urbem.
Quatuor hic juvenes ferventi sanguine venas
Inflati, rigidum gaudent accendere Martem,
Sublimesque in equis inimica lacessere castra,
Aggressi ducis imperio non ante rogato,
Ad portas magno incurrunt hostesque fatigant
Clamore, et rapidum sclopeta rotantia plumbum
Immittunt, clausasque vocant in praelia turmas.
Illi intus septi muris et turribus altis
Defensi, sat iniqua viris responsa remittunt.
Horum unum longe torquentes glande petitum
Sulphurea juvenem sternunt, et pectora dura
Transadigunt plumbo; ille accepto cernuus ictu
Concidit in terram, moribundus et arva cruentat.
    Dundius at tonitru ignivomae succensus acuto
Bombardae, hostiles credens instare cohortes,
Bellica signa movet, properansque adventat ad urbem
Et campum tenet, atque aciem simul instruit arvis.
Ipse duces longeque incessit in urbe morantes
Increpitans, portasque ingens rapit agmen ad altas.
Utque in conspectu expansis apparuit alis
Prima acies, cumulo glomerantur et agmina denso,
Panicus infidam subito tremor occupat urbem,

the hills, and made himself master of all the approaches, he occupied a high tableland, from which all the town could be seen. Now four hot-blooded youths on horseback, thinking to provoke a battle, without orders from their commanders advance to the hostile garrison, to the very gates, firing their pistols and challenging the beleaguered enemy. Those within, defended by walls and towers, send an answer sufficiently hostile. They prostrate one of their challengers with a volley from a distance, and pierce his breast with the hard lead. He falls to the earth, and, dying, stains the plain with his blood. But Dundee, aroused by the sharp thunder of guns, thinking that the enemy were approaching, moves his force, and hastens towards the city. He holds the plain, and forms in order of battle. He himself advances, contemning the leaders for dallying so long within the city, and leads his line to the high gates. But when the force appeared, with its centre massed and wings extended, a sudden panic seized the faithless town, and fear and trembling held both

Horror ubique duces, labefactaque pectora plebis
Invadit, propiusque necis grassatur imago.
Non arma expediunt, nec jam per compita currunt,
Ora nec obsessis tollunt trepidantia muris,
Sed jam septa tenent et limina tuta domorum,
Et pavidi mediis cunctantur in aedibus omnes.
Haud secus uber apum rigido sub sidere caeli,
Dum jam saevit hiems, et densae grandinis imber
Incubuit, caelique fragor cum jam intonat arvis,
Triste silet requiemque favis ignobile carpit.
Non illae pennis stridentibus agmine vectae
Extra tecta volant, nec circum limina mussant,
Sed portis pigrae latitant fessaeque recumbunt.
Sic pariter trepidi cives se moenibus abdunt,
Miles et obscuris condit se ignobilis umbris.;
Horrendo dum Marte duces Kilychranchius heros
Urget, et invictis urbem circumsonat armis.

    Jamque lacessitum cum venerat hesperus, hostem
Incassum expectans duri in certamina Martis,
Carpit iter, cursuque volans dat lora secundo.
Bis seni juvenes cristati, armisque corusci
Erumpunt portis, tergumque exercitus urgent.
Dundius ut denso fumantem pulvere campum
Prospexit, totidem emittit fulgentibus armis;
Illi continuo volitant, hostemque sequuntur
Euri instar volucris, aut pulsi pulvere plumbi

leaders and people under the threatening nearness of death. No longer they lift their weapons, no longer fill the streets nor raise their terrified faces above the walls, but keep close under cover, and within the safe threshold of their homes. As bees in winter, or during the crashing of a thunderstorm, keep within the hive and venture not out to the fields, so these timid citizens and ignoble soldiers keep within doors, while the Killiecrankian hero dares the leaders to battle, and the circuit of the town resounds with his unconquered arms. As the shades of evening came on, Dundee—having waited in vain for the foe—began his march, and gave rein to his horses, for the second time. Then, indeed, a dozen youths in glittering armour and floating plumes rush out at the gates to harass the rear. Dundee, when he saw the plain in clouds of dust, sent out an equal number in shining arms to meet them. Swiftly they fly, and pursue the enemy like the

Sulphureo, cursuque viros armisque lacessunt
Ignivomis, donec portarum ad limina laeti
Accipiunt illos socii sub moenibus altis.
Ergo iter inceptum peragunt, et signa sequuntur
Una omnes, laetique viam sub nocte silenti
Per vaga rura tenent, atque alti ad moenia castri
Vallis Ogilviacae jam corpora lassa reponunt.

   His in diversa penitus regione peractis
Dum procul arctois M'Kaius otia terris
Lenta terit, nectitque moras inglorius armis,
Dundius alipedum cursu provectus equorum
Martia finitimas circumtulit arma per urbes,
Et rerum trepidos successu territat hostes.
Nunc et victor ovans gressum tendebat ad altos
Ingentis Grampi trans ninguida culmina montes
Abria qua vastis boream petit ardua silvis,
Agmina Grampigenum ciat ut clypeata gygantum.
Ergo iter accelerans Couprum jam pone relinquit,
Atque Caledoniam raptim praetervolat urbem ;
Inde Tai pulchram piscoso flumine vallem
Permeat, et nigri campum transcurrit Apini,

wind, and with bullet and sword attack them, till their thankful friends receive them safely within the gates. The journey is then pursued, and all briskly follow their standards through the open fields, till under the high walls of the tower of Glen Ogilvy they rest their wearied limbs.

   Thus while Mackay, inglorious in arms, still lingers in the North, and frames reasons for delay, Dundee, in a distant region, borne along by swift-footed steeds, carried his arms through the towns of the South, and terrified the trembling enemy with his success. Now as a victor he advances to the Highlands, over the snow-clad Grampians, to where rugged Lochaber courts the cold winds with her vast forests. Thither he speeds that he may call out the target-bearing giants of the hills. He hastens on by Cupar and Dunkeld, and traverses the beautiful valley of the finny Tay, crosses the field of dark Appin,[1] passes the castles of

---

[1] These places are all on the road from the Tay to Loch Rannoch. Weem Castle is Castle Menzies, where Mackay was soon to sleep, if sleep he did, the night after the battle of Killiecrankie. The old castle of Comrie remains, as also Garth, in ruins. The latter was originally a seat of the 'Wolf of Badenoch.' The road attains a height of 1262 feet above the sea.

Et Vemiae Comraeque domos, et moenia Garthae
Transit et hirsutis squalentia rura frutetis,
Ferturque ad Ranochum loca per salebrosa paludem.
Inde lacum longe fluctantem gurgite vasto
Circuit, et tristes boreali turbine silvas;
Ingrediturque viam Nessi quae ducit ad urbem.
Fessaque gramineis dum corpora curat in arvis,
Praemittit lectos juga per vicina maniplos,
Qui nemora et montes et rura latentia lustrant.
Illi jussa ducis peragunt, missique reportant
Nullum in conspectu, aut latitantem vallibus hostem.
Gramus signa jubet tolli et sic incipit ore:
'O socii mecum per densa pericula vecti,
Haec est illa dies, qua duri in praelia Martis
Hostem expectabam infestis concurrere signis.
Si quidquam in laeva saltaret parte mamillae
Ductori huic Batavo, nobis sese ille dedisset
Obvium, et adversum, cum nos via ducit ad arcton
Invia, et infractas cohibent nemora alta cohortes.

Weem, Comrie, and Garth, and thence through wilds, and by rugged paths, to Loch Rannoch. Then, making a circuit round the long reach of its waters, he moves through thickets stunted by the cold blasts, and emerges upon the road[1] to Inverness. While here, on the sward, the weary troopers find rest, the scouts reconnoitre hill and dale, and report no enemy in sight. Again he bids the standard be raised, and thus speaks: 'Oh my comrades! borne with me through the thick of danger, this is the day when I looked for the enemy with floating banner. If the Dutch general possessed any spirit he would have been here to oppose our march

---

[1] The route lay, I think, by a short but rugged cut towards Kinloch Rannoch, and as he advanced round the loch he would cut the road—if such existed —towards Tummel Bridge, from which there lay a track to Dalnacardoch, on the great north road to Inverness. Perhaps, as he advanced along the road on the north side of the loch, he would strike the wild path from Annat to Dalnaspidal on the same road to Inverness. This path might be called, by a euphemism, the road to Inverness. Claverhouse was here in a position where Mackay might have attacked him from the north road. Passing along the north side of Loch Rannoch, he would find a track towards the south end of Loch Treig answering in its features to the description in the text. From Loch Treig-head, by going a little to the west, and then nor'-west-by-north, his track would bring him, through such scenes as are described, to Glenroy.—See Preface, *on Roads*.

At nunc ille fugax incertis motibus errat,
Aut vaga praecipiti mutat tentoria cursu,
Aut latitat tacitis clausus convallibus inter
Praeruptos scopulos, et concava viscera terrae.
Degener ut mediis fodit cunabula silvis
Delituitque lepus, venantum incursibus actus,
Jam mea signa timet, fataliaque arma tremiscit,
Linquit et arva metu, longeque per avia tendit.
Me si caelicolae incolumem mortalibus oris
Praestiterint, tacito lateat licet abditus antro,
Ignotove solo, defensae aut moenibus urbis,
Praedonem hunc patriae terrae a radicibus imis
Eruam, et extorrem trans Belgica littora mittam.'

Haec fatus; turmas montana per ardua ducit,
Rura secans, scopulosque, et saxa minantia caelo;
Et loca senta situ peragit, liquidasque paludes
Transmeat, et largo fluctantes aequore fossas,
Quaerit iter longo perque arva palustria tractu.
Jam multi in foveas fessi jacuere caballi
Immersique luto glauca stabulantur in ulva,
Quos socii frustra certatim attollere tentant,
Sed graviter lapsos, mediaque palude trahentes
Ilia quadrupedes linquunt, et ephippea lato
Imponunt humero, et terram pede praepete pulsant.
Ipse coactus equo tandem pedes ire relicto
Tesqua per, atque altos scopulos et confraga saxa,
Atque amnes atque arva pedum transmittere plantis.
Tandem per fluvios, udasque uligine valles,

through these wild forests. But he now flees, or wanders with uncertain purpose, or hides mid mountains and glens. As the hare, frightened by the sportsman, buries itself in the woods, so he now fears my banners, and trembles at my dread arms. If the gods preserve me on this mortal stage, I will root out this robber of his country, and send him as an exile to his Dutch home, though he lie in secret cave or walled town.' Thus speaking he led his troops through the mountains, forcing his way by plain and rock and cliff, by sweltering bog and gully. Now many of the wearied horses sink into the marsh, and are lost in its depth. Failing to raise them, the riders place the saddles on their own shoulders, and pursue their way on foot. I myself, having lost my horse, have to tramp by rugged path and hill, by rock and river. At

Limososque lacus, et stagna fluentia musco
Progreditur, silvasque, arbustaque diruta ventis
Transilit, et saxis vaga flumina foeta fragosis.
Inter inaccessos terrarum atque ardua montes
Collocat ad Traugum sublimia castra paludem.
   Inde ubi solis equi radianti luce corusci
Flammiferum vitreo revehebant aequore currum,
Et patulis rutilum sufflabant naribus ignem,
Dundius excitas rauco clangore cohortes
Ire jubet, totisque cubilia linquere castris;
Excutimur somno confestim et frigore pigri.
Verna licet patulos vestiret gloria campos,
Tyndaridumque polo sidus praefulserit[1] alto,
Membra pruinosis convellimus algida stratis;
Incompti glacie horrentes riguere capilli,
Diraque ab intonsis pendebat stiria barbis.
Jamque viam carpit, scopulosaeque ardua rupis,
Excelsosque apices scandit, praeruptaque saxa,
Perpetuo damnata gelu, loca nullius ante
Trita pede, et nullis equitum calcata catervis.
Tristiaque aeternum spirantes frigora montes
Tranat, et exesis juga cautibus invia transit.
Rupibus imposuitque jugum, caeloque minantes
Submisit scopulos, et ferrea claustra reclusit
Naturae, celsos et saxa aequantia nimbos

length, by stream, by marsh, and quaking bog, by forest blocked with uprooted trees, by precipice and mountain height, we reach Loch Treig, and there fix our lofty camp. Then, when the horses of the Sun in flashing light—breathing forth golden fire from their nostrils—brought back his flaming chariot, the trumpet sounds and the camp is struck. Though the glories of Spring were clothing the Lowlands, and the Tyndaridæ[2] were shining in the high heavens, we have to tear our limbs from frozen couches, and our hair and beards are stiff with ice. We pursue our way through regions condemned to perpetual frost, and never before trodden by the foot of man or horse. By mountains, rising above the airy flight of birds, and cliffs towering to the sky, by devious paths among the time-worn rocks, our march unlocks the iron bolts of Nature.

---

[1] Bad sequence.

[2] The sun enters the Gemini a little after the middle of May. Dundee had fixed the 18th for the rendezvous in Lochaber.

Transiit aereis volucrum vix pervia pennis.
Hannibal haud tanto contrivit saxa labore
Cum flamma aereas et aceto rumperet Alpes.
Transvolat hinc densis deserta horrentia dumis,
Apparent ubi nulla domus vestigia structae,
Aethere nec potis hic glomerantem cernere fumum,
Sed nemora, et montes, caelum undique atque alta ferarum
Lustra oculis toto videas immania tractu.
Haec loca Martigenae nunquam videre Quirites
Non Cimbri furor, aut rabiosi Saxonis arma
Attigerant ; non ipse suo sol lumine lustrat.
Tandem iter, extremum campique peregerat aequor,
Difficilesque aditus, scopulosque amnesque sonantes,
Angustasque vias, saltusque emensus opacos,
Marmoreo demissa solo vestigia figit ;
Calce premit foetas et molli gramine ripas ;
Transmittensque altam Glen-Roae fluminis undam,
Abria jam gremio Gramum accipit ardua laeto.

LIBRI SECUNDI FINIS.

Hannibal, with less labour, clave his way, by vinegar and flame, across the lofty Alps. Here, no smoke or sign of human dwelling appears, but only the lair of the wild beast, and a chaos of mountain, wood, and sky. Roman, Cimbrian, Saxon, ne'er reached so far, and here the sun itself scarce darts a ray. At last our march is ended, and Dundee plants his foot on level ground, and presses with his heel the verdant bank, as he crosses the deep waters of Glenroy. Gladly Lochaber receives the Graham into her bosom.

END OF BOOK II.

LIBER TERTIUS.

POSTERA puniceis Aurora invecta quadrigis
    Lampade fulgentem rutilanti tinxerat [1] axem.
Ilicet Arctoi nudo sub fornice coeli
Humentes quos terra toros dabat ipsa nivoso
Algida vestitu, constrataque stragula rore
Grandineo, nivibusque altis, et ninguida [2] crudo
Linquunt castra gelu; missisque per arva caballis,
Hispida qui rigidis carpebant pabula dumis
Jejuni, longaque fame ilia lassa trahebant.
Jam boreae rigidis tentoria cana pruinis
Egressi, lustrant nemora, et pernice pedum vi
Scandunt nimbiferi praerupta cacumina clivi,
Et juga celsa petunt, unde omnis rite videri
Jam poterit regio; qua Kapocha respicit austrum,
Corpocha spumosum vel qua glacialis Iernae
Vergit ad Oceanum, vel qua Balnavius ingens
Emicat, et [3] salebris, durique crepidine [4] saxi
Arduus,[5] et magno attollens fastigia mole
Exsurgentem apicem stellanti immittit Olympo;

NEXT morn's Aurora, carried along in roseate car, had tinted the glowing pole with radiant light. Forthwith they leave the dripping couches, with coverlets of hail, which the earth clothed in snowy vesture was affording them. The horses were sent out over the plain to swell, as best they might, their famished flanks with the prickly shoots of the surrounding bushes. Leaving their tents, white with hoar-frost, the men speed on foot through the woods, and climb the steeps of the cloud-capped hills, to view the surrounding region. There Keppoch extends towards the south, and Corpach to the Irish Sea, while here Ben Nevis towers aloft, raising her massive summit to the sky. Beneath their eyes

---

[1] *Var. lect.* tinxerit. [2] *Var. lect.* ninguidi.
[3] *Var. lect.* Emicat et et. [4] *Var. lect.* dure crepidine.
[5] *Var. lect.* Arduis.

Quaque lacus liquido diffunditur amne Spaini ;
Et qua magna Gluae, vallisque sonantia Roae
Flumina, non uno currunt in caerula cornu ;
Quaque pruinosis boream secat Abria saxis
Cernere erat, camposque oculis haurire patentes.
Jam scopulos super assurgentes aetheris oras,
Atque cavas tacito permensi lumine valles.
Quocunque ingenti torserunt ora rotatu,
Nil praeter montes, et saxa, amnesque lacusque
Collustrant, spinisque et vepribus obsita densis
Tesqua patent, raris et rura habitata colonis.
Frigoribus durescit humus, concreta rigebant
Arva gelu, assiduis algetque aquilonibus aer,
Horrebantque rubis late omnia, et undique sentes,
Dumique et tribuli incultis dominantur in arvis.
Vestit erica solum, montes nixque alta tegebat,
Pigraque ferratis concrescunt flumina crustis.

are seen the lake [1] which pours its waters into the Spean, and the great waters of the Gloy, and the sounding streams of the Roy, as they flow to the sea by separate mouths.[2] Here, too, they behold Lochaber parting the north wind with its frozen ridges, and expanding its wide fields. Cliff rises above cliff, and the deep-lying straths are bathed in soft light. Wherever they turn, mountain and rock, river and lake, dense thickets of bramble and thorn, with here and there a peasant's cot, meet the eye. The ground beneath their feet is hard with frost, the air is freezing with the keen north wind, and the whole region is a wilderness of briar, thistle, and heather, while snow covers the mountains, and ice the rivers.[3]

---

[1] Loch Laggan. The scene is evidently somewhere near Roy Bridge, from a hill near which the objects mentioned would all be visible, Keppoch lying south, and Corpach west.

[2] 'Non uno currunt in caerula cornu.' The idea is that they reach the salt water together, but in different ways, the Gloy falling into Loch Lochy, the Roy into the Spean, which, falling into the Lochy, there meets the waters of the Gloy, and both flow together into Loch Eil.

[3] Drummond of Balhaldy, from his MS., attempts some poetic translations of our author. The following has been admired as rendering well this scene :—

> ' Arrived on Abria's skirts we nothing spy,
> But mountains frowning in the clouded sky,
> And rugged rocks which round in fragments lie ;
> Impetuous torrents rage in vales below,
> And pools and lakes their lazy waters show.

Continuo exclamant; heu nunc quibus orbis in oris
Ignotis fato advehimur, tepidoque remotis
Sedibus axe procul gelidas erramus ad arctos,
Dumosos inter scopulos et inhospita tesqua.
Inter et horrentes aeterno frigore cautes,
Riphaeis ubi cuncta rigent damnata pruinis,
Horriferoque gelu; meta est certe ultima longe
Abria terrarum, quascunque liquentibus ulnis
Astrorum nutrix amplectitur[1] Amphitrite.
Jam quibus in terris infandos sistere cursus?
Aut ubi in exhaustos dabitur superare labores?
Sauromatumne ultra montes, ultraque Niphatem
Tendimus algentem, et rigidi juga nimguida Tauri?
Jam certe extremis terrarum insedimus oris,
Orbis et arctoi fines,[2] spatia ultima mundi
Emensi, terras longinqua sede repostas

'Alas!' they cry, 'to what unknown land has our fate carried us, to what ungenial clime?' Mid wood and rock and desert we wander, in regions of eternal snow, where Russian winter holds all things in its icy grasp. Lochaber, surely, is the extremity of that earth, which Amphitrite, nurse[3] of the stars, holds in her watery bosom. When and where shall these labours cease, this unfortunate journey end? Is our march directed beyond the Sarmatian mountains,[4] or the Niphates, or Taurus? We have surely come to the limits of the North, and to those islands where indomitable races

> Thin cottages the unequall fields adorn,
> O'erspread with briars, and rough with prickly thorn;
> With warring winds and storms the air is toss'd,
> And the ground hardened with perpetual frost!
> A desart wild, impatient of the plough,
> Where nought but thistles, shrubs, and bushes grow,
> And barren heath: and on the mountains high
> Deep snow in frozen beds afflicts the eye;
> While streams benumbed with cold forget to flow,
> Stiffen in ice, and into solid grow!'
>
> *Memoirs of Lochiel*, p. 239.

[1] For scanning of this verse cf. page 89, verse 180 and note.

[2] *Var. lect.* finis.

[3] This poetical expression I have not met with elsewhere. Whether we regard the stars as rising from the sea, or embosomed by reflection on its surface, the idea of 'nutrix astrorum' is pretty.

[4] Carpathian Mountains, or perhaps he means Caucasus. The Niphates— snow mountains—an eastward prolongation of the Taurus.

Oceani, penitusque alio sub sidere gentes
Vidimus indomitas, toto et procul orbe revulsas,
Hebridas, et populos incinctos cernimus usque
Montibus aëreis, gelidoque sub axe jacentes.
Gens ubi progeniem materno a ventre calentem
Et simulac teneris feriit vagitibus auras,
Usque pruinosi gelido sub gurgite Roae
(Haud secus ac chalybem candentem flumine vivo)
Immergit, coelique minas, boreaeque procellas
Grandineas, tenera jam primum aetate docebat
Spernere, et immanes durare in vulnera vires.
Utque tener gelidis infans immergitur undis,
Obstetricis ope, magicis quae docta susurris
Nascentis pueri casus aperire futuros,
Ille excantatis stygio cum murmure verbis

of men have settled under another sky, the Hebrides—torn off from the rest of the world. We see around us peoples enclosed by lofty mountains, under a bitter climate. These are they, who under the waters of the frozen Roy—like the red-hot iron plunged in the flowing river—dip their new-born babes,[1] and teach their offspring in their tender years to despise the hailstorms and tempests of the North, and to harden themselves against wounds. The infant is plunged in the wave by the midwife, skilled to unfold the future of the babe in mystic mutterings. Suspended in the air, he

---

[1] In *Letters from a Gentleman* (*English*) *in the North of Scotland to his Friend in London*, written before the year 1730 (Mr. Skene says 1716), and published by Pottinger in 1759, there is this remarkable testimony to the accuracy of our Poet in this matter. In Letter XI. he says: 'The moment a child is born in these northern parts it is immerged in cold water, be the season of the year never so rigorous. When I seemed, at first, a little shocked at the mention of this strange extreme, the good women told me the midwives would not forego that practice, if my wife, though a stranger, had a child born in this country.'

A practice called Dessil—from *Dess*, 'fire'—was in use in the Western Isles up to the time of our author. Fire was carried round about women before they were churched after child-bearing, and about children till they were baptized. This ceremony was performed in the morning and at night, and was practised by some of the old midwives in Martin's time. Some of them told him that the fire round was an effectual means of preserving both mother and child from the power of evil spirits. Browne's *History of the Highlands*, vol. i. p. 14; Glasgow, 1838.

Doubtless the author is accurate enough in his account of passing the child round the fire, and three times was the regular number, and sunwise the direction in similar rites.

Vertitur accensum ter circum pendulus ignem.
Gensque haec picta croco, glastoque infecta tremendos
Hostibus attollit duro in certamine vultus;
Oris et horribiles ostentat in arma figuras.
Gorgonei vultus hominum, cava lumina torvo
Fronte micant, priscos aequant et mole gigantes;
Immanesque Scythas referunt, pictosque Agathyrsos.
Nudi humeris, nudique pedes, non vulnera terrent,
Non ferrum, chalybesque feri, non machina glauco
Fulgure, non certam sclopeta[3] minantia mortem
Pectora prosternunt, sed et ipsa in vulnera gestant
Corda immota metu, statque imperterrita virtus
Rebus in adversis, et quando in proelia ventum est
Pugnae ardent studio, flagrantque cupidine praedae
Captandae, raptimque ruunt per tela per enses
Intrepidi invalidis fiducia sola lacertis,
Aut superare hostem, mediove occumbere campo.
  Olim siderea cum nondum sede potitus
Jupiter, aut patrio pulsus Saturnus Olympo,
Fama refert vacuos sine tecto errasse per agros
Semiferum genus hoc hominum, et si credere dignum,

is turned thrice round a fire, mid Stygian murmurs and words of incantation. This race, in yellow and blue,[1] presents a fearful front to the enemy in face and form. The deep-set eyes of the Gorgon visage sparkle in the savage faces of the men, and in height they equal the giants of ancient days, and recall the Scythians and the painted Agathyrsi.[2] Though naked as to feet and shoulders, no wounds affright them, nor do they flinch from sword or bullet or any hardship. Eager for battle and for booty, they rush headlong against spear and sword, and, trusting to strength of arm alone, they conquer or die.
  The story goes, that before Jupiter possessed the throne, or

---

[1] 'Picta croco glastoque infecta.' This must refer to their garments, though the author from time to time suggests tattooing. Yellow and blue were common dyes in the Highlands, obtained from the ragweed and madder respectively.

[2] Picti Agathyrsi. Virgil, *Aen*. iv. 146. A painted or tattooed people of European Sarmatia. Sacheveril, in 1688, says they—the Highlanders—remind him of the ancient Picts; '. . . their thighs are bare, with brawny muscles, . . . a thin brogue on their feet, a short buskin of various colours on the leg, tied above the calf with a striped pair of garters.' Camden says they remind him 'of the Scythian and Goth.' See Preface.

[3] See Notes at end of volume.

Gens erat illa prior Luna, et radiantibus astris,
Quae nata e ramis, et duri robore trunci
Sponte sua ad terram, Zephyro motante cadebat.
Qualis hyperboreis anser silvester in oris,
Qua maris undisono natat ultima Thule profundo,

Saturn was driven from Olympus, this semi-barbarous race was already wandering naked in these desolate regions, and (if it may be believed) that it existed before the moon and the light-giving stars, and that it sprang spontaneous from the branches and trunk of the oak, and by the movement of the zephyrs was shaken to the ground. Thus the wild goose[1] of the North, which swims on the roaring waves of Thule, has her origin. In the beginning of

---

[1] The bernicle or barnicle goose is here alluded to. In the time of the author there was no doubt in the popular, and but little in the scientific, mind as to the origin of this bird from the barnacle, adhering to decaying timber, or from the willow, or such tree. It was in 1636 that Gerard, in his *Herbal*, maintained from his own experience the reality of this transmutation, and concludes by offering to satisfy any doubting persons if they will repair unto him. Ray, in his *Willughby*, 1678, combats the views formerly accepted, and accepted by such men as Bishop Leslie, Torquemada, Odericus, the Bishop Olaus Magnus, and others of greater name, including Scaliger. The account given by Fulgosus harmonises with that of our author; he says, that 'the trees which bore these wonderful fruits resembled willows, producing at the ends of their branches small swelled balls containing the embryo of a duck suspended by the bill, which, when ripe, fell off into the sea, and took wing.' The bird was called the 'tree goose,' and one of the Orkneys, the scene of the prodigy, has received the appellation of Pomona. See *Penny Cyclopædia*, article 'Bernicle.' The subject is of interest in the history of science, in its relation to religious beliefs, as witnessing to the contention that Milton and Ray are responsible for the hard-and-fast view of species and special creations, and that transmutation was, previous to them, a common idea. My attention has been called to the following amusing extract from Robertson's Preface to his *Statuta Ecclesiae Scoticanae*, page xcv.-vii. He is quoting from Æneas Sylvius his Cosmographia—De Europa, cap. xlvi, *Opera* p. 443. Piccolomini had visited Scotland in 1435. 'He had heard of a tree which grew on the banks of rivers and yielded a fruit having the semblance of a goose; if the fruit fell on the land it rotted away, if it dropped into the stream it took life, feathers, and wings, swam in the water, and flew in the air. But when he asked where he could see this marvellous tree, he was told it was no longer to be found in Scotland, although it still flourished in the Orkneys,' so far Robertson. The original has a touch of Papal humour : 'De qua re cum audivimus investigaremus, didicimus *miracula semper remotius fugere*, famosamque arborem non in Scotia sed apud Orcades insulas inveniri.'

As to the origin of the men of Lochaber given by our author, though some touches are taken from Ovid's *Metamorphoses*, I have not been able to discover any likely source of his ideas. He may be able to claim all the credit himself.

Vere novo cum silva comas, et brachia pandit,
Nascitur e foliis, et de Jovis arbore rostro
Pendulus irriguae pubescit in aggere ripae,
Mollibus inclusus viridanti ex cortice capsis.
Deciduis donec nudatur frondibus arbos,
Et silvae posuere comas, mox frigore primo
Labitur autumni, liquidoque volutus in altum
Amne ruit, mediis animamque invenit[1] in undis.
Sic fere Grampiadum stirps edita frondibus, altis
Ut ramis delapsa solum simul attigit, artus
Induit humanos, vitalesque hauserat auras.
Hinc genus antiquum in silvis, nulla arte politum,
Monstrum informe, ingens, seu cruda Libistidis ursae
Progenies manibus primum raptabat aduncis.
At postquam vires maturior attulit aetas
Pondere terra gemit, fert et capita ardua caelo.
Huic jam nulla humeros hyacinthina lana tegebat.
Sed pardi ex spoliis, aut caesi pelle leonis
Asper amictus erat, nudoque sub aethere tristem
Herba dabat thalamum, domus et spelaea fuerunt.
Praebebant vulsae victum radicibus herbae,
Et Bacchi liquido potabat ab amne liquorem.
Alma Ceres ignota fuit, sed sola voluptas

spring foliage, she is born of the leaves, and, hanging by her beak from the tree of Jove on the river's brink, grows to maturity within her green covering. At the fall of the leaf, in the first frost of autumn, she drops into the stream, and is carried along to the sea, where she finds her life. So—it is said—did the fierce races of the Grampians spring from the leaves, and, falling from the branches, assumed human form and life on touching the soil. This ancient race, monstrous, mis-shapen, immense, as the rough progeny of the Libyan bear, polished by no art, at first crept along through the woods with clawlike hands. By and by, a later age beheld them as men. The earth groans under their weight, and they lift heads towering to the skies. No hyacinthine wool covered their shoulders, but the slaughtered pard or lion gave them their rough robe, and they made their bed under the open sky, or the cave served for their dwelling, their food the roots, their drink the stream. Ceres the benign was unknown. To rob the traveller,

---

[1] 'Invēnit,' perfect tense required for scanning.

Grassari, et praedas agere, atque impune vagari.
Et montana colens errabat more ferarum
Anfractus inter caecos, tacitosque recessus,
Segniter in que cavis exegit rupibus aevum.
Tandem decursi post longa volumina sêcli,

and drive the booty, was their delight, and like wild beasts they wandered idly amid the deep recesses of the woods and mountains. At length, after the long lapse of ages, Fergus the First,[1] coming

---

[1] This is Fergus Mor, son of Erc, the first of the Dalriadic kings in Scotland. The importance attributed here, and throughout the book, to this king, falls in with the recognised view of him current in the author's time, in such histories as that of Buchanan. The true date of Fergus is 498 A.D. or 501. His father was head of the Dalriadic Scots in Ireland, and was converted by St. Patrick. Fergus, in his youth, was blessed by that Saint, and his future rule in Alban foretold. He first settled his colony in Isla and Kintyre, but his dominion soon extended as far north as the Linnhe Loch, and Dunadd in the Crinan Moss became the capital of Dalriada, the people being Scots from Irish Dalriada. The progress of this growing kingdom was arrested in the reign of Gabran, grandson of Fergus, by the powerful Pictish monarch Brude, son of Mailchu, who drove the Scots back within their original limits of Kintyre, slaying their king Gabran. These Scots were Christians, and it would seem that their reduced circumstances, and subjection to a Pictish king, had an important influence in bringing St. Columba, one of their race, from Ireland. In the Prophecy of St. Berchan, it is said of Columba:

> 'Woe to the Cruithnigh to whom he will go eastward,
> He knew the thing that is
> Nor was it happy with him that an Erinach
> Should be king in the east under the Cruithnigh.'

Columba and Iona vastly increased the importance of the tribe, and brought the name of Scot to the front in the literature of the time, though the Pictish monarch ruled from Caithness to the Firth of Forth. St. Columba aided in making Scotch Dalriada independent of Irish Dalriada, and crowned King Aidan. Kenneth MacAlpin united both kingdoms under his rule, and through clerical, as well as race, influence, Scotland gradually took the place of Pictland and Albania, Kenneth ruling from Scone, and not Dunadd, over both peoples. This was in the year 842. It was the claims later on of the English kings for sovereignty over Scotland which brought the name of Fergus, son of Erc, into prominence. The antiquity of the kingdom of Scotland had to be proved, and it was no good to plead before papal courts, a descent from Brude the Pictish king, when it was a Scottish kingdom that was in question. The national independence turned upon the name Scots, and Fergus, though his kingdom was but a spot on the west of the island, was the first king of Scots, and at once evoked a national enthusiasm, which soon clothed him with poetic fictions, and as to antiquity made him a contemporary with Alexander the Great. Fordun gives his date as 330 B.C. The celebrated letter of the Barons of Scotland to

Primus ab aequorea veniens Fergusus Ierna
Prisca Caledonii posuit fundamina Regni ;
Et sibi belligeras late victricibus armis
Addiderat gentes, terrasque in fronte Britannae
Dorides[1] imperio, et magna ditione tenebat.
Martius at juveni postquam deferbuit ardor,
Jam meliora sequens, et rebus pace sequestra
Compositis, placidas sese convertit ad artes.
Jura dabat populis aequa jam lance subactis,
Terram omnem et parti peragrans confinia regni,
Ardua semotos ubi porrigit Abria tractus,
Audierat gentem indomitam per secula celsis
Insedisse jugis ; subito inflammatus amore
Augendi imperii fines, iterum induit arma,
Et pubem vocat armatam, silvasque fatigat.
Jam sonitu armorum insolito de sedibus imis
Exciti tremuere viri, cursuque citato

from sea-girt Ireland, laid the foundation of the Caledonian kingdom. Under his sway he brought the warlike races of the seaboard, and when martial ardour had cooled, he guided his people into the peaceful arts. To the conquered peoples he gave just laws, and moving through his kingdom he reached its confines, where lofty Lochaber extends her plains. Hearing that amidst these mountains an indomitable race had been settled for ages, he again donned his armour in hope of conquest. The mountaineers, roused in their dens by the unwonted sounds of war, seek in swift flight the deeper recesses of the woods. Fergus presses on in

---

the Pope in 1320 asserts that the kingdom of Scotland 'had been governed by an uninterrupted succession of 113 kings, all of our own native and royal stock, without the intervening of any stranger.' It is plain that the Barons were caught by the fictions and not by the facts of the national history. There is no doubt however that Fergus brought with him from Ireland much that would influence for good the wilder people to whom he came. He brought Christianity and much besides, and he prepared the way for the great missionary St. Columba, which entitles him to a gratitude equal to that described by the Poet. It was universally believed in Scotland that he brought with him from Ireland the coronation stone which Kenneth MacAlpin is said to have removed from Dunadd to Scone, and which Edward I. carried to Westminster. Its previous fabulous history brings it from Egypt to Spain by the hands of Scota, Pharaoh's daughter, and thence to Ireland by her descendants. See Skene's *Celtic Scotland*, also his Preface to Fordun, and D. Laing's Preface to Wyntoun, in *Historians of Scotland*. [1] *Var. lect.* Doridos.

Spelaea, et caecas nemorum petiere cavernas.
Ille instat contra cursuque ictuque lacessit,
Et saevas ratus esse feras indagine saltus
Circumdat, rapidisque quatit nemora alta molossis.
Illi turmatim variis assultibus urgent
Defessum, trepidique fugam meditantur inanem.
Precipiti demum sese effudere procella
Balnavi ad celsos magno cum murmure montes.
Insequiturque heros priscaeque haud immemor artis
Qua dumis agitare feras, silvisque solebat,
Speluncam ingentem glomeratis omnibus una
Excutit, et lato figens venabula ferro
Montivagum, positis hinc atque cassibus, agmen
Egit in insidias tacita convalle locatas,
Implicuitque plagis laqueisque ingentibus, illi
Clamores tollunt horrendos, unde profundae.
Insonuere umbrae, crebrisque ululatibus ingens
Silva gemit, resonantque cavis e vallibus antra.

 At Pater arctoae domitor clarissimus orae
Fergusus, victorque virum, Mavortius Heros,
Hos sine lege viros palantes montibus altis
Constituit, captosque domat, tectisque coercet,
Leniit effraenes et iniqui pectoris aestus,
Indomitosque animos, et corda ferocia mulcet,
Impiger, et longo docuit mansuescere cultu.
Instituitque modum vitae melioris, et artes
Tradidit ingenuas, legesque et foedera rerum
Edidit, et duri commercia saeva Gradivi,
Et lunare arcum, nervoque aptare sagittam

swifter course, and, taking them for wild beasts, surrounds their lairs with nets, and wakes the echoes of the woods with the baying of his hounds. Bursting forth like a storm, they seek the heights of Ben Nevis, and Fergus, skilled in woodland craft, follows with men and weapons, and various toils, and, at length, in the deep valleys snares them, and the shades resound with their wails and groans and horrid clamour.

But the illustrious Fergus, father and lord of the North, reduces these lawless men to obedience, softens their savage hearts, compels them to dwell in houses, and by a long course of culture raises up a civilisation. A better mode of life, the liberal arts and laws, he teaches them, as also the art of war. They fit the arrow and

Instruit, ancipitemque manu vibrare securem ;
Et pecori cultum, Cererique impendere curam
Edocuit, curvique usum monstravit aratri ;
Venatu assiduo jejunia longa domare,
Et tollerare famem male gratam, et frigora et aestus
Erudiit, mentem et docilem simul imbuit almis
Praeceptis, monitisque et relligione Deorum.
Hinc innatus amor, perituraque tempore nullo
Gratia Sceptrigerum per secula longa nepotum,
Et Fergusiadum generosa potentia Regum,
Atque Caledonii studium inviolabile sceptri
Tutandi, seros demanat ad usque nepotes.
Hinc et hyperborei[1] magnum Jovis incrementum
Ad natos natorum aeterno foedere surgit,
Et facti decus, et soboli jam rebus egenis
Inconcussa fides manet, aeternumque manebit,
Quam nec longa dies, dubii aut discrimina fati,
Solvere nec possunt violenti fulmina belli,
Ambitiove levis, nec duro mota tumultu
Seditio, aut dubiis anceps fortuna procellis.
Sed temeratus honos, et Regum laesa potestas,
Et civile nefas, vetitique licentia ferri,
Et struere arte dolos, fraudemque innectere Regi
Irritatque animum, et generosas provocat iras.
Gloria quin Regum mentes accendit honestas,

bend the bow, and wield with the hand the double-edged axe. They learn the care of flocks, and the use of the plough, and skill in hunting, and he imbues their docile minds with the benign precepts of religion. Hence sprang that love and reverence for the royal descendants of Fergus, never to perish in the lapse of ages, and that protecting care of the Scottish sceptre. Hence, too, this great and never-failing Highland contingent appears to uphold the throne, one generation succeeding another, in glorious deeds and uncontaminated fidelity, and will for ever be steadfast through hardship, changes of fortune, fierce war, and the tumults of sedition. The defaming of their King, the attack upon his power, civil treachery, the purchased desertion of his soldiery, all enrage their minds and provoke a generous wrath. The glory of their King fires

---

[1] *Var. lect.* hyperboreis. Cf. Virgil, *Ecl.* iv. 49. See also p. 81, verse 45, and page 121, verse 52.

Et decor infandos impulsat adire labores,
Pro quibus egregiam haud dubitant per vulnera mortem
Oppetere, et certae caput objectare ruinae.
Namque ab avis, et avorum atavis ab origine prima
Fida leonigeros venerata est Abria Reges.

Hic procul extremis Arctoi in finibus orbis
Belliger adversis animi insuperabilis armis
Dundius, et Regis pulsi asserturus honores,
Et Patriae illatas cupiens sarcire ruinas,
Culmina nimbiferi superaverat ardua Grampi,
Fortuna monstrante viam, per mille labores
Hosque adit indomitos duri Mavortis alumnos
Grampicolas, Batavo indociles servire tyranno.
Posthabitis patuli trepidis cultoribus agri,
Ignavum bello genus, et mercedibus emptum ;
Turbamque imbellem, molles et spernit agrestes,
Respuit infidos et culta per arva colonos,
Prava pusillanimi fastidit et agmina vulgi,
Versaque contemnit fugitivi militis arma,
Et scelere infamem, atra et proditione profanam
Colluviem bellantum odit, quae regia liquit
Castra fuga, et versis petiit contraria signis ;

their noble minds, and his honour impels to desperate labours, to wounds and death. From their first ancestors, from the origin of the race, they derive their veneration for the lion-bearing kings.[1]

To these indomitable sons of Mars, untaught to obey the Dutch tyrant, to these confines of the North, came the warlike Graham, crossing the cloudcapped Grampians, that thence, following fortune in a thousand labours, he might maintain the honour of an exiled King, and repair the ruin of his country. He despised the Lowland race, slow to war and ready for a bribe—the cowardly herd of easy-going rustics, the faithless inhabitants of the well-tilled lands. He loathes the poor-spirited commons, and the treacherous soldiery—that vile, fighting scum, who basely left the royal camp for the enemy, and who, without shedding a drop of blood, deserted their prince on

---

[1] 'The first of Scottish kings that Albion boasts,
   Who oft to victory led the Scottish hosts,
   Was Fergus, Ferchad's son, whose mighty shield
   Bore a red lion on a yellow field.'
                    Fordun, vol. iv. (*The Historians of Scotland.*)

Quaeque olim infausti Sarum super aequora campi
Prodidit insignem fuso sine sanguine Regem.
Nunc vocat in dubii certamina tristia belli
Praestantes virtute duces, qui fortibus armis
Ventura aeternam peperere in saecula famam.
Atque acres quatit aere viros quos Abria mater
Nutriit in duris, saxa inter inhospita, silvis.
Jamque croco pictas missurus in arma catervas,
Undique cogendis dat idonea tempora turmis:
Castraque ad undisoni metitur flumina Roae.
Hic tristem saliente sitem restinguimus unda,
Et manducamus nigrum cum furfure panem;
Horrentemque casis defendimus aera nudis,
Molliter hic dulces et sub Jove carpere somnos
Edocti, et rapidos tonsis sub pellibus imbres
Vitare, et duris soliti tollerare sub armis
Ferratas hyemes, et iniquae frigora brumae.
   Hac indamnata fatis regione sub Arcto,
Quae Cererem, Bacchumque viris non praebet alendis,
Ora pruinosis lenibant torrida lymphis,

the ill-omened plain of Sarum. He now summons to the strife valiant chiefs who had already earned in arms undying fame, and the sons whom Mother Abria nourishes in her savage woods, among inhospitable rocks. He measures out his camp by the sounding Roy, and sets a time for the assembling of the bands, stained with the crocus dye, whom he is about to lead forth to war. Here we slake our burning thirst in the leaping river, and devour our bread black with bran.[1] We shelter our bodies—thinly clad—from the sharp wind and driving shower under rude huts, well experienced how best to meet the winters of the North.

This drear region yielding no corn or wine for the use of man, he slakes his thirst with cold water, and finds his bread in acorns

---

[1] In Letter xxv. of *Letters from a Gentleman*, we have the following: 'In part of the Highlands people never rub out a greater quantity of oats than what is just necessary for seed against the following year; the rest they reserve in the sheaves for their food, and as they have occasion, set fire to some of them, not only to dry the oats, which, for the most part, are wet, but to burn off the husk. Then by winnowing they separate as well as they can the sooty part from the grain, but as this cannot be done effectually, the Bonnack or cake they make of it is very black. . . . They seldom burn and grind a greater quantity of these oats than serves them for a day.'

Et sterilem querna victum de glande petebant,
Languidaque arbuteo saturabant viscera fructu.
Illa fames duram queat expugnare Saguntum,
Et Numantinam concederet hostibus urbem;
Traderet et Phrygios nullo certamine muros.
Quam si adeo infelix invicta mente tulisset,
Haud profugus patrios fudasset Scylla triumphos;
Castra nec exutis cessisset Afranius armis.
Tristia jejunae jam passi incommoda terrae,
Haec socii tacitis incusavere quaerelis.
At non audacem concussit inedia Gramum,
Nec caeli rigor, aut boreae violentia frangit
Devotum jam Regi animum, nec martia corda
Imminuit duri saeva inclementia Fati.
Sed nitet in dubiis animi constantia rebus,
Et nunquam labefacta fides, visque ignea mentis
Invictae per acerba eluit; jam martius ardor
Incaluit, multumque animis, et viribus audax
Ductor ovat, bellique moras interritus odit.
Ceu Lybica de gente leo jam concitus ira

and berries. Such hunger could conquer a Saguntum, and yield Numantia to its enemies, and would have overthrown the Trojan walls without a contest. If Sulla could have endured such privation, he would not as a fugitive have so defiled his father's triumphs;[1] could Afranius have borne this thirst, he would not have yielded his camp, laying down his arms. Under the miserable hardships of this barren land secret complaints arise among the companions of the Graham, but he himself neither hunger nor cold nor tempest affect, strong in his devotion to his King. Unmoved by the bitterness of his fate, in the midst of difficulties and hardships he maintains his martial bearing, his fiery vigour, his steady constancy of mind, his unswerving fidelity. He frets only against the delays of war. As the Libyan lion roused to wrath tosses his mane,

---

[1] Scylla, or rather Sylla, was the spelling used incorrectly, through confusion with the spelling of the monster, by some writers not long ago, and probably inherited from the author's time, for Sulla. The Sulla alluded to here is Faustus Cornelius, the son of the dictator, who followed his father in his self-indulgence. His flight on hearing the name of Caesar is alluded to by Lucan, Book II. 465. Afranius and Petreius commanded for Pompey, but surrendered their army to Caesar, who had entrapped them between the Sicoris and the Iberus, in such a position that though they could see the water they were yet perishing from thirst. See Lucan, *Phar.* Bk. VI.

Attollit cervice jubas, seque erigit omnes
Protinus in vires, et saevae verbere caudae
Se stimulat, pugnaeque exultat mente propinquae.
Magnanimi sic surgit honos herois, et alto
Gloria se tollit caelo, jamque ardua virtus
Inconcussa locum tenuit, seque omnia contra
Intulit, obnixisque animis audentior ibat.
Qualiter obnitens adversa in pondera palma
Altior assurgit, seseque attollit in auras.
Quanquam jam laeti series transversa sereni,
Ingrueret tragico fortuna indigna tumultu,
Hosti nunc acies, et fortia bella parabat,
Intimaque armisonum spirant praecordia Martem.
Igneus et menti vigor insitus ardet in armis,
Illicitum Batavi imperium delere tyranni.
    Caesaris et partes depulsi totus anhelat
Dundius, impatiensque morae spe fervidus instat
Extorrem patriis Regem jam sistere terris.
Illum adeo rutila lustrat ceu Cynthius orbem
Lampade, nigrantes ceu nox tegit humida campos,
Mente agitat, memorique absentem pectore volvit.
O quoties flagrantem animum generosa cupido
Incessit, Regem quascunque eat ille per oras
Velle sequi, comitemque etiam se adjungere castris.
Verum alio nunc fata vocant ; et longa locorum
Sejungunt spatia, et vasti maris unda coercet.
Ergo ubi Grampiacis jam lenior intulit arvis

lashes his tail, and fronts the foe, so does honour move the spirit of the great-souled Hero, and his glory rises to the heavens. His lofty valour abides unsubdued, and bears him up against every evil, as the palm-tree rises higher the more it is weighed down. Although fortune seems adverse, he prepares his lines and strong array, and his soul longs for the din of battle, and the destruction of the Dutch tyrant's sway. He pants to do service to his King, and, glowing with hope, he is impatient till he restore the exiled monarch to his own land. By day and night his thoughts turn ever to the absent King. Oh! how often had the noble desire filled his breast that the King would determine to join his forces, and unite himself to his camp. But now the Fates call in different ways, and a vast distance, and the waves of the mighty sea, separate them. When already the gentler breeze is bringing the light

Aura levis Zephyros, tranquillaque littora cori,
Arvaque lenifico verrebant laeta susurro.
Alta sedens tacite labentis ad ostia Roae
Gramus ab undosa non flexit lumina Ierna,
Atque hinc innumeris necquicquam moenia turmis
Derria cingentem flagranti pectore Regem
Evocat, ignotaque procul tellure morantem
Inclamat, talique absentem voce fatigat.
' Septime Brutigenum soboles Mavortia Regum,
Lenta quid arma moves ? totumque agitanda per orbem
Agmina iniqua novis pateris coalescere regnis ?
Nunc quid in ignotis nimium teris otia terris ?
Deque die menses, de mensibus extrahis annos ?
Immemor heu nostri demandatique laboris,
Aequa reposcendis incassum tempora sceptris
Extrahis. O lentae nimium tardaeque Calendae !
Usque adeone times patrio te credere Scoto ?
Irrita numne fides, vana aut fiducia nostri ?
Ante Tai in fontes tumidi maris unda recurret,
Thraxque Caledoniis segetem metet efferus arvis,

zephyrs to the Grampian fields, and the tranquil shores and glad plains of the north-west are growing verdant [1] under its gentle whisper, the Graham, sitting silently by the mouth of the gliding Roy,[2] turns not his eyes from rainy Ireland. Hither he bids come the King—now besieging Derry in vain—with his numerous bands ; and in his burning breast he bewails his tarrying in that unknown land, and in this strain he reproaches the absent one: ' O seventh scion of British kings, why movest thou such torpid arms, and sufferest hostile bands, raised throughout the country, to unite for new kingdoms ? Why dost thou waste time in unknown lands, and from day to day and month to month draw out years ? Forgetful of our labour and commission, you wait in vain for a fitting time to retake your sceptre. O Kalends, too slow, too long ! Dost thou fear so much to trust thyself to thy native Scotland ? Hast thou no faith in our valour ? The waters of the sea will flow back to the swelling fountains of the Tay, and the

---

[1] Prosaic critics might remark on the rapid changes in Glenroy between the 18th and 23d May—the frosts of winter, and the plains growing verdant under light zephyrs.

[2] Probably where it enters the Spean,—or is Roy the name of the united rivers ?

Quam tua signa vago linquam nunc splendida cursu,
Aut mea mutatis vertam vestigia castris.
Rumpe moras: nostris quantum o decus adderet armis
Adventus, Rex magne, tuus. Quid Iernia belli
Segnia regna tenes, et molles Marte colonos,
Imbellesque in bella vocas, qui sanguine fuso
Pabula praestabunt tantum civilibus armis.
Sunt tamen ensifero nobis devota Gradivo
Pectora, sunt animi, duroque exercita luctu
Corpora, et assiduo durati Marte lacerti.
Quae nova tam subitam vertit sententia mentem?
In longum quid mittis iter? quid pendula torques
Corda mora? blandaque foves spe languida castra?
Te ver purpureum, mollique favonius aura
Invitat, sternitque tuae placida aequora classi.
Plena Caledonius vehat o tua carbasa pontus!
Terrarum satis exhaustum est, perque ardua rerum
Stratum iter, et vasti via facta per invia mundi.
Magne veni, victorque tuis illabere regnis.'

wild Thracian shall mete out corn in Scotia's fields, before your glorious standard shall see my flight, or my steps turn to another camp. A truce to this delay! how great an honour would your coming, O great King, add to our war! Why dost thou cling to unwarlike Ireland, and call out its peaceful rustics to yield up their blood as food for civil feuds? Here are souls devoted to sword-bearing Mars, and veterans well inured to war. What new opinion has changed your mind so suddenly? Why engage in so distant a journey? Why in hesitation do you frame delay? Do you buoy up your dispirited camp with merely a pleasant hope? Thee the purple spring[1] and the zephyrs invite with soft breeze, and the sea lies calm before your fleet. Oh may Scottish waters float thy full ships! We have marched over mountains, and the trackless regions of the earth, and it is enough; come, O great King! and, as a victor, enter thy kingdoms.' Such words he spake,

---

[1] 'Ver purpureum'—the Poet is quoting Virgil, *Ec.* ix. 40. *Purpureus* has the force of anything bright, young, vigorous, in classical literature, and therefore its presence here does not, I fear, indicate that our Poet had felt the purplish glow that hangs over hedges and woods in the early spring, before the green leaves burst from their warmly-tinted sheaths. The larch 'tufted with its rosy plumelets,' which now colours the spring in many Highland districts, was then unknown in Scotland.

Talia dicta dabat; sed vota feruntur in auras,
Irritaque in tenues abierunt omnia ventos.
　　Interea totum Grami vulgata per arcton
Fama volat, raptimque ruens pernice volatu,
Oceani extremas it fulminis instar ad oras.
Extemplo Arctoi diverso a margine ponti
Sedibus exciti patriis duce et auspice Gramo
Heroes, proceresque securigerique tribuni
Grampiadum, rigido gens dedita sola Gradivo
Arma parat Batavi contra agmina iniqua tyranni.
Primus ibi ante omnes Donaldi filius ingens,
Gloria Grampiadumque decor Glengarius heros,
Qui saevum teneris Martem spirabat ab annis,
Nominis ad magni famam et praeconia Grami
Auxilium rebus Regi laturus in arctis
Advolat, et nitidis Gramum comitatur in armis.
Inde alii proceres diverso tramite ducti
Claustra per Oceani extremaeque a littore Thules

but his prayers were borne on the breeze, and vanished in the empty air.
　Meanwhile the fame of the Graham flies on swift wing through all the North, and like lightning rushes to the furthermost coasts of the sea. At once the heroes are aroused, and chieftains and dunivassals and martial clansmen make ready to take the field against the Batavian tyrant. First, before all others, the son of Donald, the great glory of the Grampians, the heroic Glengarry,[1] who in his early years had borne the brunt of battle, appears to tender his aid to the King, and, in shining arms, allies himself to the Graham. Then other chiefs, from every region of the North, by

---

[1] This is Alastair Dubh Macdonell, at this time younger of Glengarry, his father, Ranald Macdonell, being still alive, though old and frail. He was practically Chief of the house, and commanded the clan, and is styled Glengarry. He was old enough to have a son, Donald Gorm, who is said by the historian of the family to have killed single-handed at Killiecrankie no less than eighteen of the enemy before meeting his own death. Glengarry was one of the most distinguished chiefs of his day; 'he was brave, loyal, and wonderfully sagacious and long-sighted, and was possessed of a great many shining qualities, blended with a few vices, which, like patches on a beautiful face, seemed to give the greater *éclat* to his character.'—*Memoirs of Lochiel*, p. 261.

　He afterwards fought at Sheriffmuir, and died in 1724. In addition to the description of him given by our author, he is represented by witnesses in the process of forfeiture, as 'a tall man, somewhat black.' See note, Book IV.

Conveniunt ; Gramique petunt sublimia castra.
Quos procul ut densa juvenum stipante corona.
Adventare videt, venientes ordine longo
Excipit amplexu heroes ; et talibus infit :
  'Vos ego belligeri prisco de sanguine Scoti,
Grampigenae fortes, et duri Martis alumni,
Caesaris arctoi jussu procul usque remotis
Finibus Oceani excitos, perque ultima mundi,
Nunc in bella voco, socialiaque agmina posco
Grassantes contra furias et iniqua superbi
Arma ducis Batavi, conjuratasque cohortes
Saxonidum, quae jam funesto viliter auro
Vendiderint libertatem, Regemque stupendo
Mancipio prius expositum, tacitisque petitum
Insidiis, dare terga fugae, tristique paternum
Exilio mutare solum, proavitaque sceptra
Impulerint, cursuque novas sibi quaerere terras.
O viles animae ! venaliaque agmina ! et Orco
Vendita mancipia, atque emptae mercede catervae,
Degeneresque viri victor quos respuet, et nunc
Venales tanquam Sardos versa agmina ridet,
Atque exarmatae veluti ludibria gentis
Secum Flandriacos rapit impletura macellos.

various paths seek the camp. As he beholds them advancing in their various companies, he receives the chiefs with an embrace, and welcomes them in these words :—
  'Ye warlike Scots of ancient blood, ye martial sons of the mountain, roused from your distant homes, I call you now to battle, and claim your aid against the Batavian general, and the conspiring band of Saxons who have vilely sold their liberty and their King for cursed gold, and have compelled him to leave the sceptre of his ancestors, and pass as an exile to foreign shores. O degenerate men ! O mercenary soldiery, sold to Orcus ! O mean spirits ! whom the victor already slights and laughs at, and now treats as the treacherous bands of Sardinians[1] were treated, carrying them, a disarmed race, to swell the empty Flemish ranks. But the father of his

---

[1] 'Venales Sardos :' a proverbial expression for anything cheap and worthless, arising out of a Sardinian revolt, which, when quelled, overstocked the slave-market with numbers of Sardinians. Already William was raising levies in England and Scotland for Flemish wars, and carrying them with him to the seat of war.

At patriae Pater ipse dolis suppressus iniquis,
Et misere a summis venundatus acre tribunis
Militiae, proavoque inhonesti militis ausu
Turpiter elusus, cognatis proditur armis
Turpius, et genero fraude interceptus emaci
Succubuit.   Viden' capiti diadema revulsum
Arripuit gener, et sceptris impune potitis
Exultat fidens, et proditione nefanda
Regna tenet, socerumque injusto Marte fatigat.
Et nunc Abriacis M'Kaius imminet arvis
Agmine Saxonidum, et Batava comitante caterva,
Et profugi versis Scoti circumdatus armis,
Haud procul undantem Speyae subsidit ad amnem,
Exitium patriae minitans patriaeque parentis.
Cogit ad arma viros, totamque a sedibus imis
Campestrem terrore quatit truculentior oram.
Scaurius, extremae prope natus ad aequora Thulae,
Atque eadem patriae retinens commercia linguae
Irruit Hyrcano jam tigride saevior omni
In patriam, patriaeque Patrem, qui ferre supremum
Nomen militiae, et primos concessit honores.

country, oppressed by their treachery, and, O shame! sold and basely cheated by the leading generals and soldiers of his native army, succumbs through the fraud of his son-in-law, who had bought them. Already has he seized the crown torn from the father's brow, and holds the sceptre proudly, though treason yielded it to him, and now wages war against his father-in-law. Mackay threatens Lochaber with a host of English, Dutch, and traitor Scots, and is already on the Spey vowing doom to his King and country. He of Scourie,[1] born near the waters of Thule, and speaking the native tongue, forces men to arms, and fills the plains with terror, and, more fierce than the Hyrcanian tiger, he attacks his country, and the father of it, who had bestowed upon him the highest military rank,[2] and had given him his first com-

---

[1] General Mackay was a younger son of Mackay of Scourie, a branch of Lord Reay's family, which 'long enjoyed extensive possessions in the northern counties of Scotland.'

[2] Mackay received his first commission in 1660, in the Royal Scots, termed Dumbarton's Regiment. Probably the Duke of York gave him his commission. He was promoted to the command of the Scotch-Dutch Brigade in 1680, and in 1685 he came, at the desire of James the Second, with his corps, to aid in suppressing Monmouth's Rebellion. He arrived too late, but the King advanced him to the dignity of a Privy Councillor in Scotland.—*Memoirs*, Prem. Notice.

Oh pudor! a propriis patria alta ardescit alumnis!
Interitura suo flagratque Britannia fato.
In Reges perjura nimis, jam sacra resolvit
Jura, et legitimi renuit moderamina sceptri.
Insultat jam verna duci, milesque tribuno;
Imperitatque patri gnatus; res horrida dictu,
Corvi aquilam, vulpesque dolo stravere leonem.
O quem non miseri facies tristissima regni
Commoveat, justasque insurgere cogat ad iras?
Nemo adeo est tam abjecti animi cuique unica tantum
Palpitat in mediis generosi guttula venis
Sanguinis, haec nostri cernens ludibria sêcli,
Atque impendentum discrimina tristia rerum,
Qui jam fulmineis mortem non mallet in armis
Oppetere, et certis caput objectare periclis,
Nudaque lethiferis exponere pectora telis,
Quam Fergusiadem clarum toto orbe Jacobum,
Tot magnis prognatum atavis, tot Regibus ortum,
Venalem Batavo serviliter aere sub hasta,
In praedam genero exponi, aut miseranda videre
Excidia imperii ruituri, atque ultima fata
Caesaris, et positum Regali in sede tyrannum.
Quare agite, o magni Fergusi clara propago,

mission. O shame! our noble land blazes by the hands of her own children, and Britain perishes by a fate which she has brought on herself. Perjured against her King, she dissolves the most sacred law of legitimate succession. Now the slave insults the general, the common soldier his officer, and, horrible to say, the son rules the father. By guile the crows have killed the eagle, and the foxes the lion. Oh, who is not moved by the miserable aspect of his country, and roused to anger! Is there a man of spirit so abject, who has a drop of blood in his veins, that can look upon these mockeries of our time, and its critical condition, and not prefer death to the enduring of them. Rather than that the illustrious James, the son of Fergus, the descendant of mighty ancestral kings should be sold for Dutch gold, to become the prey of his son-in-law, who would not meet the flash of arms, and present his breast to the darts of death? Who can look upon the close of an empire falling to ruin, on the last fate of the Caesar, and a tyrant seated on the royal throne? Wherefore lead on, bright sons of the mighty Fergus, ye heroes of unstained soul, ye

Macti animi heroes, simul et virtutis avitae
Heredes, factisque superbi fortibus omnes,
Tollite pro pulso victricia signa Stuarto,
Et patria extorrem cum prole reducite regem.
En erit auxilio nobis dilecta juventus
Militiae, venient atque omni ex parte manipli,
Qui nunquam Auriaci dextram tetigere tyranni;
Proximaque innumeras transmittet Ierna catervas.
Et Gessoriaci rex littoris, armipotens Rex
Liliger Almanici sceptri subversor, et orbis
Terrarum domitor victricia suggeret arma,
Et pro Rege pio, et consanguinitate propinquo,
Gallia Grampiacis praefiget lilia castris.
Nunc res ipsa vocat, vestris namque imminet hostis
Aedibus, et rapidis ardet vicinia flammis.
Jungite mansuras aeterna in foedera dextras,
Cognatasque acies; defensae ut fortiter armis
Crescat honos patriae, nomenque et gloria genti.'
    Dixit; et ingenti procerum caelum undique plausu
Personat Abriadum. Tandem Glengarius heros
Surgit, eo dicente attentas surrigit aures
Grampiadum manus omnis; et haec in verba profatur:

heirs of your father's valour, ye who rejoice in brave deeds. Raise the conquering standard for the exiled Stuart, and restore the King and his heir. Lo, a chosen company of youths will come to our assistance, and from every side troops who have never touched the right hand of the Dutchman. Neighbouring Ireland will send her multitudes, and the powerful King of France[1]—the lily-bearing conqueror of the German sceptre and the world—shall raise the victorious lilies of France on Grampian fields, on behalf of his kinsman, our pious King. Urgent is the case, for already the enemy threatens your homes, and wraps the country in flame. Join your right hands in eternal bond, that the honour of your country, bravely maintained, may increase with the glory of your name and race.'

He spoke, and the heavens re-echoed the shout of the nobles of Lochaber. Then arose Glengarry, and every hand was raised to the listening ear, while thus he spoke: 'O

---

[1] Gessoriaci Rex. Gesoriacum, the place in France whence in Roman days persons embarked for Britain. It was subsequently called Bononia, and now it is Boulogne. Here it stands for France.

'O patriae decus! O Scotorum maxime ductor,
Grame, (evertendis nomen fatale tyrannis)
Gratior Abriacis nuncquam venit advena castris,
Usque a primaeva nascentis origine mundi;
Sospite quo pulsum sublimi a culmine Regem
Haud metuam, imperii temeratave jura Britanni,
Sceptra nec Albionis, nec regna fatebor Iernae
Impia sub Batavi juga succubuisse tyranni.
Atque equidem quia Regis honos, et publica nostram
Libertas deposcit opem, nos magna secuti
Majorum documenta, damus socialia castra,
Et firmam pro rege fidem; tractusque per omnes
Ardua Grampiacae qua se plaga porrigit orae,
Undique collectos in bella ciemus agrestes.
Jungemus pubemque animis et viribus acrem,
Symbolaque in Regem grati referemus amoris.
Nos et militiam simul et pia signa sequamur
Caesaris, et junctis in publica commoda turmis,
Te duce, mancipii triste hoc enabimus aequor,
Frigida perpetuus condet vel lumina somnus.
O Fergusiadum semper domus ardua regum
Abria, magnorumque altrix animosa virum gens,
Cum prius acer Iber, rueretque in bella Sicamber,
Et ferus Ausoniae populator Vandalus orae,

Graham! (name fatal to tyrants) O glory of your country! noblest leader of the Scots. Never came to Lochaber since time began a stranger more pleasing. While you are safe I fear not for the King, though driven from his throne, nor for the laws of Britain's empire, though ruined; nor will I admit that Albion's sceptre has fallen, nor yet the Irish kingdom, beneath the Dutch yoke. Since the honour of the King and the public weal claim our aid, we, following the manner of our ancestors, shall present a united front, and offer a fidelity firm to the King. From every region of the Grampians we shall gather the clansmen, strong in heart and limb, and declare our loyalty and love, as we follow the standard of the Caesar. With hands joined for the common good we shall, with thee for our leader, swim this stormy sea of liberty, or the everlasting sleep shall close our cold eyelids. O lofty Lochaber, always a home for the Kings of Fergus' line, already the bold nurse of great men, before the fierce Iberian and Sygambrian and savage Vandal, despoilers of the Latian coast, rushed to battle. This

Hunnusque Europam vastaret caedibus omnem,
Haec sola est magni regio intra moenia mundi
Quae nunquam hostiles accepit victa secures.
Cumque aliae gentes domitae victricibus armis
Mutavere suas turpi formidine sedes;
Et cum barbaries domitum suppresserat orbem,
Haec eadem patrios tutata est Marte penates,
Fortunae insanis haud succubitura procellis.
Jam vero laesi cum Caesaris alta potestas
Praedonis pede pressa jacet, cape fortiter arma,
Victricesque acies, proavitasque exere vires.
Nunc nunc ille tuus ductor multo agmine Gramus
Caesareis venit auspiciis, atqua arma capescit,
Et patriae vindex pro libertate laborat
Impia sacrilegi contra molimina Belgae.
Hic ille est tanti solus qui pondera belli,
Et conjuratos Europae sustinet ictus
Intrepidus, pulsoque gerit pro Caesare bellum.
O quam te memorem, quantoque amplector honore
Grame, Leonigeri spes et tutela Stuarti?
Dum valet ancipitem manus haec vibrare securem,
Atque anima in mediis ebullit fervida venis;
Non ego te Batavas metuam ductore catervas,
Saeva nec Auriaci formidem tela tyranni.

is the only region of the earth which never bowed before an invading sovereign. While other nations left their settlements in base fear, and when barbarism was oppressing the world, this race by its sword maintained the paternal Penates, and yielded not to the storms of fortune. Now, when the heel of the robber tramples on the violated power of the Caesar, seize your arms, and call out the conquering tribes of the ancient race. Now, now the Graham comes as your leader with a great force under the auspices of the King. He labours as the avenger of his country for her liberty against the impious designs of the Belgian. Here is he who alone fearlessly sustains the weight of so great a contest, and conducts the war for the exiled monarch against the allied force of Europe. O Graham, the hope and guardian of the lion-bearing Stuart, how can I speak of thee, with what honour do I embrace thee! While I can wield the double-headed axe, and life-blood throbs in my veins, thou being our leader, I will fear no Batavian force, no dart of the Orange tyrant. Whether you bid me follow to the

Me si forte jubes penetrare vel ultima mundi
Littora, qua refluus concrescit frigore pontus ;
Ire vel extremas Lybiae sitientis ad oras,
Bagrada flaventes qua vertice volvit arenas,
Te sequar ; et quocunque vocat fortuna paratus
Dura pati, vitamque volens pro rege pacisci.'
  His dictis ; mox tota ducum clypeata corona
Grampiadum, laetas tollunt super aethera voces,
Exultantque animis, et ovanti plena tumultu
Castra sonant, eadem omnes uno ore fremebant ;
Unanimesque ducem magno clamore salutant.
Conjunctasque acies atque auxiliaria spondent
Agmina militiae, et tanto rectore superbi
Promisere fidem, quaecunque in bella vocaret
Regis honos ; jamque erectis ad sidera dextris

utmost limits of the earth, where the ebbing sea freezes into ice, or where, in thirsty Africa, Bagradas[1] in her course rolls her yellow sands,—wherever fortune calls I am prepared to suffer and give my life for my King.'

At these words uprose the shield-bearing circle of Grampian chiefs, and from their exulting souls went up their glad voices to the sky, and the whole camp resounded with triumphant tumult. With one voice and mind they salute the general with a cheer, they answer for their friends and allies, and proudly promise fidelity to the service, under so great a general, wherever the King should summon them. In solemn rite, with right hand raised to heaven,[2]

---

[1] See Lucan, *Phar.* Bk. IV. 588 : 'Bagrada lentus agit siccae sulcator arenae.' The river, in Lucan, is the 'plougher-up' of the sands ; here she 'rolls them along.' The Bagradas (Mejerdah) falls into the Gulf of Carthage, near Utica. Glengarry's speech has the benefit of our author's knowledge of Lucan and his geography. Virgil is also quoted here (see *Aen.* V. 230) : 'Vitamque volunt pro laude pacisci.' Heyne's note here is—'pacisci exquisite pro reddere impendere.'

[2] In Letter xxiv. of *Letters from a Gentleman*, etc., we have varieties of Highland oaths. After mentioning the oath on a drawn dirk, kissed, he gives other forms. He says, 'In taking whereof they do not kiss the Book, but hold up their right hand, saying thus, or to this purpose, "By God Himself, and as I shall answer to God at the great day, I shall speak the truth. If I do not, may I never thrive while I live, may I go to hell and be damned when I die, may my land neither bear grass nor corn, may my wife and bairns never prosper, may my cows, calves, sheep, and lambs all perish." Very much depended as to the value of an oath, whether it was taken in Highland fashion or not. A man who had readily forsworn himself on taking an oath on the Bible refused to take the Highland oath when offered to him on the occasion, saying, "Thar is a hantle o' difference betwixt blawing on a Buke and dam'ing one's saul."'

Mutua solenni jungebant foedera ritu.
Ipse in concessu medioque sub agmine Gramus
Constitit, et superos vocat haec in foedera testes.
Atque ait, 'O prisci Mavortia pectora, Scoti,
Quorum adeo in dubiis virtus spectata procellis
Enituit, totiesque tulit pulso hoste triumphum
Audite, atque animis mea jussa facessite laetis,
Septima cum roseos Aurora reduxerit ortus,
Praecipites in bella viri ferte horrida tela,
Ite et in arma alacres, et acerbo tempore Regi
Promissam servate fidem, et struite ordine campis
Agmina picta croco, fulgentesque aere phalanges.'
Dundius ista prior.   Glengarius inde secutus;
'Testor' ait 'caelum, et caeli spirabile lumen,
Nulla dies unquam nos foederis arguet hujus
Immemores, non si stagnanti Grampius alto
Exundet, caelumque gravi premat infera lapsu.
Nos, duce te, rigidum clangunt cum classica Martem,
Et fremebunda vocat Bellona in Caesaris hostes
Ibimus, intrepidique viam mucrone corusco
Sternemus.   Tua nec quo publica cunque vocat res
Jussa retractamus.   Caeli per numina juro,
Per superos, Stygiamque domum stagnantis Averni,

they pledge their mutual faith. In the midst of the assembly and surrounding troops, the Graham called the gods to witness these bonds, and thus he speaks, 'O Scots of ancient race! O warlike spirits! whose valour is seen most in the crises of affairs, you who so often have triumphed in the past, hear, and with willing minds obey, my commands. When the seventh morning has brought back the light, gather in force with your dread weapons of war. Move swift to battle, and preserve your faith to the King in an evil time. Draw out your clans in their saffron array upon the plain, and your battalions shining in brass.' These words spake Dundee, and Glengarry followed: 'I take Heaven to witness that no day shall prove us forgetful of this league, though the Grampians sink into the sea, or the sky falls upon us. While you are our leader, when the trumpets sound their notes of war, and raging Bellona summons us against the enemy of the Caesar, where the public weal demands, there we shall go, and at your command open the way with the sword. I swear by the gods of heaven, and by the powers above, by the Stygian home of dank

Quisquis Grampiadum chlamydata ex gente gigantum
Magnanimi jam signa sequi fulgentia Grami
Abnuerit, nostris pubemque inducere castris,
Horum ego maturis immittam frugibus ignes,
Incendamque Lares, armentaque poplite scisso
Convellam, totamque domum face et igne cruento
Persequar; ignavas animas ad Tartara trudam.'
  Finierat; noxque atra diem nigrantibus alis
Abdiderat, fessosque gravis sopor occupat artus.
At nunquam patiens somni, placidaeque quietis
Immemor, urgebat nocturnis pectora curis
Gramus, et insignem vocat ex bellantibus unum,
Qui mandata ferat Regi. Ille haud impiger acri
Castra ducis gressu petit, et se limine sistit.
Cui Gramus sic orsus ait. 'Sate stirpe Suini
Insignis Dionysi, tuae pete littora Iernae,
Quaque procul celsas tollit Dublinia turres.

Avernus, whosoever of the plaided race of Grampian giants shall refuse now to follow the glorious standard of the great-souled Graham, and to bring his clansmen to the camp, I will send the fire into their ripe corn, and burn their homes. I will hamstring[1] their herds, and pursue their whole house with fire and sword, and send their cowardly souls to Tartarus.'

He finished, and dark night hid the day with gloomy wing. Dundee, forgetful of rest and sleep, loads his breast with nocturnal care. He calls an illustrious youth from among his warriors, who may bear his words to the King. He, quick with light tread, sought the tent of his commander, and stood upon the threshold, to whom the Graham thus began: 'O illustrious Denis,[2] of the race of Suinus, seek the shores of your own Ireland, where far distant Dublin rears

---

[1] I fear this cruel custom prevailed to some extent among the Highlanders. When driving a herd from an enemy with whom they were at bitter feud, they would hamstring the cattle if they found they could not successfully escape with them.

[2] 'Sate stirpe Suini insignis Dionysi.' Dennis M'Swyne is mentioned in Privy Council Register, 27th January 1687, as 'one of the gentlemen of Major-General Graham, his troop of horse.' He carried important despatches from Dundee at Gordon Castle to the King in Ireland towards the end of April. In a letter of Dundee's to Melfort, dated Moy, in Lochaber, June 27, 1689, he refers to the information that he had sent by M'Swine, and further on says, 'M'Swyne has now been away near two months,' and it is one of his complaints to Melfort that he had not sent expresses, and that, at any rate, he might have hastened the despatch of 'these we sent.' It is therefore clear that Dennis

Carpe viam, nec te commotum flatibus aequor
Terreat, occultis latitansve in vallibus hostis,
Ne te turrigeris vallatae moenibus urbes
Detineant, requiesque tui sit nulla laboris.
Ut simul optatos dabitur contingere portus,
Haec mea sceptrigero narrabis dicta Stuarto,
Tuque meo multum Regi dabis ore salutem ;
Tempus adesse refer, quo debita sceptra capesset,
Et sua regna gravi depressa tyrannide Belgae
Liberet, et solium rursus conscendet avitum.
Dic fortes coiisse viros, sparsosque per aequor
Hinc atque hinc populos ultro in fera bella ruentes,
Auspiciisque meis Regi narrare memento
Fervere Grampiacos generoso milite colles.
Ipse modo adveniat, decus et tutamen in armis
Sentiet, et magnum patriae experietur amorem.
Sed reditum si fata negant, Marsque impius axe
Detinet ignoto implicitum civilibus armis,

her lofty towers, speed your way, nor let the stormy waves affright you, nor the enemy ambushed in the valleys; let not the walled towns with their fortifications dismay you, take no rest till you reach the wished-for haven. You will relate these things to the sceptre-bearing King, and offer my salutation as from my own lips. Tell him the time has come when he may seize his rightful sceptre, free his kingdoms from the oppressive tyranny of the Belgian, and mount his father's throne. Say that brave men have assembled, and that tribes from every region are rushing eagerly to arms. Remember to tell him that under my auspices the Highland clans are burning for war. Let him come himself, our only glory and protection, and let him experience the great love of the country. But if the Fates forbid his return, and impious Mars detains him in unknown lands, engaged in civil war,

---

M'Swyne could not have been sent on the occasion, and at the time our Poet indicates, as he had not returned from his first commission to Ireland. We are now at a date between the 18th and 25th May 1689. A poet may not be tied down to dates, and probably he is transferring the departure of M'Swyne from Gordon Castle to this point of departure in Lochaber. Mr. Hay, a King's messenger, had returned to Dundee on the 22d June, and carried back despatches to the King, dated 27th June, which were received by the King on the 7th July. Balhaldy gives the substance of an account sent to the King between the time of Dundee's arrival in Lochaber and the general rendezvous. It is very much on the lines of our Poet's statement. A verbal message may therefore have been sent at this time by some accredited messenger.

Caesaris et vultu patria est caritura sereno,
Oro per superos, et spem crescentis Ephebi,
Exulat ignotis qui nunc vagus hospes in oris,
Det mihi in arma viros, mavortiaque agmina mittat,
Praestet et auxilium, et rebus solamen in arctis.
Jamque vale, et memori sub pectore dicta reconde.'
Ille autem remis, et equi pernice pedum vi
Carpit iter, mora nulla volat perque arva per undas.

   Scaurius interea veterano milite cinctus,
Germanisque feris, promptisque in praelia Suevis,
Cimbrisque, Holsatisque, et desertore Britanno,
Undique tot turmis atque auxiliaribus auctus,
Perdomuisse ratus prisci picta agmina Scoti,
Caesareamque aciem campo pepulisse patenti.
Nulla quod horribilem cecinerunt classica Martem,
Credit inexperto magnum certamine Gramum
Cessisse, et dubio vitam concredere ponto.
Et quod in accessis praeclusit rupibus hostem
Otia securis carpebat languida castris.
Ductor ut ignavus longinqui ad littora ponti,
Hoste procul multo distans maris intervallo,
Cum fremit insanis Mavors furibundus in armis,
Credit se aequorei tutum munimine valli.

and if his country is to lose the serene aspect of Caesar, I pray by the gods, by the hope of his growing son, now in exile, a stranger guest in foreign lands, that he will send me men-at-arms and veteran troops, and yield us comfort and aid in our distress. Now farewell! bury these words in your faithful breast.' With oars, swift horse, light foot, he hastens on his way, and speeds through flood and field.

   Meanwhile he of Scourie, surrounded by a veteran soldiery, fierce Germans and Swabians, prompt to battle, and Cimbrians, Holsatians, and the British deserters, increased by new levies on every hand, concluded that he had subdued the tartaned bands of ancient Albion, and that he had driven the army of the Caesar from the open plain. Because no clarion sounded the dread notes of war, he thought that the Graham had given in without a struggle, and had betaken himself to the treacherous deep. Because his enemy was shut in by inaccessible rocks, he took a sluggish ease in a secure camp. Thus an incapable general, as yet separated from the war by the wide ocean, believes himself safe, and though fierce Mars be raging madly, he yet remains inactive,

En hostis trahit arte moras, et praelia differt,
Sed jam classe potens vicinum navigat aequor,
Et parat hostiles quam primum irrumpere portus.
Ille sed instantis quae sint molimina belli
Inscius, haud sensit venientem puppibus hostem,
Carbasa dum plenis cernit turgentia ventis,
Hostemque in mediis vestigia figere campis.
Sic ubi fama volans magni praenuntia Grami
Actutim attonitas Batavi ducis impulit aures,
Ingruere infestum nigri instar turbinis hostem,
Quem prius inclusum sperabat montibus altis,
Externumve solum patria petiisse relicta,
Ille animi dubius nunc huc, nunc flectitur illuc;
Anne fugam teneat, sese ne in bella remittat.
Ira metusque simul sub pectore fluctuat, et jam
Hostica cum nondum conspexerit agmina, solo
Rumoris sonitu trepidantia castra relinquit;
Saxonidumque globo et Batavorum inglorius armis
Terga dabat, mens ipsa mali sibi conscia facti
Horret, et occulto pavitantem verberat ictu.
Jam torpent in bella manus, non arma, nec ulla
Castra placent, pavor ora viri, pavor occupat artus.
Non jam cornipedum terram pede pulsat equorum,

trusting to the protection of the sea. Yet his enemy, only delaying the battle in subtlety, prepares his fleet, and, crossing the sea, bursts into the hostile harbours. The dull defender of the coast, knowing nothing of his enemy's preparations, is only apprised of his coming by his presence, his sails swelling full in the breeze, and his foot planted on the plain. Thus when report, as the herald of the Graham, reached the ears of the Dutch leader, telling him that the enemy was upon him like a thunderstorm (the enemy whom he had thought shut in by the mountains, or escaped to a foreign soil), he vacillates in mind, and is perplexed. Shall he take to flight, or meet the foe? Anger and fear burn together in his breast. At length, however, he left his camp, trembling; though he had not yet looked upon his adversary, and, on mere rumour, with his troops of English and Dutch, he betakes himself to inglorious flight. His own spirit, conscious of a bad cause, frightens him, and, with a concealed stroke, lashes him while he trembles, and his hands hang unready for the war. Neither his force nor any camp pleases him. Fear is in his face, and in his limbs. No longer his cavalry scours the plain, no longer does he

Agmina nec patulis infert gradientia campis;
Sed petit aereis extructas rupibus arces
Tuta tenens, Nessique tegit se moenibus altis.
Haud secus atque fugax per prata virentia perdix
Quae socios magno increpitans clamore vocabat,
Ut Jovis armigerum jam prospicit eminus acrem
Praecipiti ruere in terram per inane volatu.
Haud primum caelo pennis se credit aperto,
Sed trepidante viam pede carpit, avia longe
Rura petit, densisque fuga se vepribus abdit.
    Dundius e contra nullo terrore minacis
Fortunae, aut dubii commotus turbine belli,
Magna animo volvit, Martisque accendit amore
Grampicolas, vocat et gentes populosque propinquos,
Undique in auxilium durosque in bella colonos
Conclamat, campoque ardet concurrere aperto,
Indomita virtute furens, quicunque sequatur
Exitus, invidiae nec jam latratus iniquae
Territat audacem ingenti desistere coepto.
Et licet ipsa suis hostiliter ardeat armis

deploy his foot, but holding to the hills, he at length fortifies himself at Inverness.[1] Thus the partridge skimming over the green meadows summons together her companions by the flapping of her wings, as she beholds the bird of Jove stooping from aloft, and trusting not herself longer on the wing, she speeds along with trembling foot through the trackless fields, and hides herself among the thick briars.

Dundee, on the other hand, without any fear of threatening fortune, unmoved by the whirlwinds of doubtful war, revolves great projects in his mind, and calling the neighbouring tribes on every side to his aid, he also fires the Highlanders with the desire for battle. He assembles the clans inured to war, and, seeking for an outlet, with indomitable valour he longs to reach the open plain. Nor does the howl of the enemy intimidate the hero to the desertion of his cause, though Scot-

---

[1] Mackay himself does not seem to have returned to Inverness after leaving it to effect his junction with Ramsay. On his march with 640 men towards Ruthven he heard of the retreat of Ramsay to Perth, and after some hesitation he struck into Strathspey, so as to lie between Dundee and the Gordon country. Mackay's force hitherto had only been represented on the Spey by the Laird of Grant's men, who, under Captain Forbes, also garrisoned Ruthven Castle.

Albion, ingentique rebellis Ierna tumultu
Flagrabat, magnoque infensa Britannia Gramo
Instrueret totis inimica examina campis.
Despicit ista tamen Grami Mavortia virtus
Tanquam latrantes per compita nocte molossos.
Jam magis arma fremit, bellique cupidine flagrans
Arma arma ingeminat, Mavortemque increpat ultro,
Praelia sola placent, spemque omnem ponit in armis.
Tempora maesta trahit, pereuntesque autumat horas
Armorum studiis quas non impendit honestis.
Non genio indulget segnis, nec marcida luxu
Otia nec somnos deses sectatur inertes.
Sed Martem campo exercens praeludit aperto,
Spumantes aut versat equos, densasque phalanges
Laxat, easque iterum gyro breviore coarctat ;
Ludicraque ostendit belli simulacra futuri,
Pulvereo in campo et plena sudoris arena.
Et grave Martis opus, metuendaque fulmina belli
Assultu crebro alipedum sublimis equorum
Ferre docet, pugnasque simul inferre pedestres,
Fraenatas acies. At nunc mora longa videtur
Dum promissa dies fulgenti surgat Eoo.
    Mos Fergusiadis fuit olim regibus, et nunc

land rises against his arms, and Ireland blazes in rebellion, and hostile Britain on every hand was raising her levies. The warlike Graham regards all this as the barkings at night of dogs on the highway. Burning for war he strengthens his forces, and of his own accord gives the signal for battle, in which alone is his hope and joy. He thinks the days are dreary, and the hours lost, when unspent in the pursuits of war. With him there is no pampering of himself, no sluggish ease or luxury, no listless sleep, but practising for the battle, he reviews his troops, and turns out his foaming squadrons on the plain. He deploys his compact columns, and wheels them again into formation, displaying the image of the future battle on the heavy and dusty plain. Mounted on horseback, he teaches the toilsome task of Mars, and how to meet the fire of the enemy, and the heavy charge of swift cavalry, and how to charge by horse and foot. Yet the time seemed long till the sun should arise on the appointed day.[1]

    There was of old a custom among the Kings of Fergus's race,

---

[1] The 25th May or thereabout.

Abria majorum tenet hunc in secula morem.
Si quando externis meditantur gentibus arma,
Sive etiam arctois Mavors flagrasset in oris,
Grampiadum e numero procerum praestantior unus
Et chlamyde, et clypeo, galeaque accinctus, et ense,
Ignitae crucis effigiem solenniter hastae
Suffixam, magna juvenum comitante caterva,
Tinnituque tubae, et sonitu Bacchantis aheni,
Circumfert, Martemque vocans hastile coruscat.
Belliger hanc patrio Gramus de more comantem
In sublime crucem vicina per oppida pilo
Attolli jubet, atque omnem jam ferre per Arcton,
Classica venturi signum referentia belli.
Illi magna ducis laeti mandata facessunt,
Et primum e speculis aurato cuspide fulgens
Lancea transversim, flagrantibus undique taedis,
Tollitur; hinc cerae miniatae impressa per omnes
Ista Caledonias crux mittitur ignea gentes,
Tessera sanguinei salientis ad arma Gradivi.
Perque domos perque arva volat, gliscitque tumultu
Martis amor, nunc arma fremit chlamydata juventus.

which Lochaber still holds, receiving it from the past. When war is meditated by a foreign power, or breaks out in the Northern land, the first of the Grampian chiefs, in plaid and shield, helmet and sword, girt by a great company of his men, and to the sound of pipe and trump, solemnly carries round the symbol of the fiery cross affixed to a spear, and waving it aloft calls to arms. The warlike Graham following the custom of the country, bade the flaming cross be borne throughout the neighbouring townships, and through all the North, while the pibroch gives the signal of the coming war. Gladly they obey the orders of their chief, and at once a spear, shining with gilded point, crossed by wooden javelins, is raised aloft mid flaming torches. Then, covered with red wax,[1] that fiery cross is sent through the Caledonian clans, and flies as a symbol of bloody Mars, calling to arms through homestead and field, and the love of battle rises to wild excitement, and the plaided clansmen bristle in arms.

---

[1] Is not this a contribution to the many forms by which the fiery cross is already represented? The red wax I have not noticed elsewhere. Brown mentions a burnt or burning end, and on the other end of the arm a white rag dipped in blood.

Jamque Caledoniam litui sonuere per omnem,
Undique et horribilem strepuerunt cornua Martem;
Bellorum sonitu exciti juvenesque senesque,
Pro se quisque, ruunt, diversaque castra sequuntur.
Belgicus excelsam Nessi M'Kaius arcem
Deserit, et subito collectis omnibus una
Castra locat rapidi currentis in aequora Spejae,
Ad vada, queis Coilo deducta colonia nomen
Indidit: hic Batavi primum vexilla tyranni
Extulit, et duros in bella vocabat agrestes.
Mox ruit, invisum diis et mortalibus aeque,
Caesaris in jugulum juratum turpiter agmen.
Hunc levis ambitio, lucrique immensa cupido,
Illum dira Venus, Bacchusque, atque alea pernox,
Hos malesuada fames, durisque in rebus egestas
Impulit arma sequi, et multis nunc utile bellum.
Jam scelerata manus juvenum ruit omnis ad arma,
Colluviesque hominum rerum spe illecta novarum.

Throughout Scotland the pipe and the trumpet sound forth the dread notes of war. Young and old, each for his side, follow the opposing camps. The Dutch leader, Mackay, leaves the castle of Inverness, and quickly parading his troops, he pitched his camp by the surging waters of the rushing Spey, at the fords to which a colony once settled there had added its name to the name Coile.[1] Here, first, he raised the pennons of the Dutch tyrant, and called forth the natives to war. Presently a body of men, justly hated by gods and men, join him, vowed to the destruction of the Caesar. Here light ambition and greed of gain move some; there lust, wine, gambling move others; while the temptations of hunger, poverty, misery lead others to follow his standards. Now a despicable band of youths rushes to arms, and offscourings of men, drawn together by revolution, and moved by the desire of a

---

[1] This is Culnakyle. I suppose the author considers Cul or Col short for Colonia, and adds it to the name Coile. King Coilus was supposed by Buchanan to have given his name to Kyle in Ayrshire, to the Kyles of Bute, and all the many Kyles or Coils in Scotland. I believe the word is Gaelic for a narrow passage or strait, and Cul is the back or sheltered side of it. Mackay, advancing from Inverness to effect a junction with Ramsay coming from the south, had moved as far as Carbridge, or thereabout, when he was informed of Ramsay's retreat. After some hesitation he decided to pass into Strathspey, and Culnakyle would seem to have been his first camp. When he was at Carbridge, Dundee was in Badenoch, twelve miles above Ruthven Barracks. See notes, Books IV. and V.

It velut ad praedam, atque opulentae ardore rapinae,
Ex profugis ganeisque ingens congesta gregatim,
Turba volat, Batavique ducis petit impia castra.
Sic ubi putre jacet per devia rura cadaver
Accipitres, aquilaeque et edaci gutture corvi,
Cum jam vergit odor patulae ad spiramina naris,
Conveniunt, circumque volant dulcedine praedae ;
Aut ubi jam plenis spumat vindemia labris,
Agmina muscarum, et tabanorum stridula turma
Convolitant, unaque omnes spumantia circum
Musta volant, praedaeque inhiant stridentibus alis.
Haud aliter totis fervent examina campis
Ad Batavum glomerata ducem. Pars una citatis
Provehitur sublimis equis ; pars altera campo
Jam pedes ire parat densis instructa maniplis.
Atque equites peditesque simul glomerantur, et una
Transmittunt denso fumantes pulvere campos,
Praecipitesque in bella ruunt ; et uterque superbo
Milite ductor ovans fulgentibus intonat armis.

   Hos jam fata duces diversae partis alumnos
Rivales dubii posuere in pulvere belli.
Non tamen auspiciis (sic fert sors dura) secundis,
Nec coiere pares, nec diis nec partibus aequis.

rich booty, go forward on their prey. A great number of deserters from the haunts of debauchery are gathered together, and eagerly seek the camp of the Dutch General. Thus assemble the eagles, hawks, and carrion crows, when once the odour of a rotting corpse has reached their nostrils from the distant field, and gather around their sweet morsel. Or, as when the wine foams from the overflowing bowl, swarms of flies, and humming insects, hover around, and in buzzing crowds seek their booty. Thus all over the plains bands of youths are swarming, and there gather to the standards of the Dutch General squadrons of horse and companies of foot, and both together formed[1] into one army, rush impetuous to war, and each commander, exulting in a proud soldiery, in shining arms, gives the word of command.

Already the Fates have brought into the dust of a doubtful war these leaders of the opposing sides, and these rival youths. Not, however, do they meet (as the hard lot shows) under equal auspices,

---

[1] It is not clear from the original whether the commanders are Dundee and Mackay, or Mackay and his various brigadiers.

Scaurius Auriaci dux agminis impius acri
Marte premit patriam peregrino milite fretus,
Et conjurati subnixus viribus orbis,
Intonat horrendum, et magna se mole ferebat.
Jam fremit incassum totas effundere vires
Exultansque animo vana spe praecipit hostem,
Atque illum crebris assultibus irritus urget.
Nunc trahit arte moras, qua vi quove hostica possit
Sternere castra dolo, crudoque exscindere ferro.
Haud aliter lassus longo certamine taurus,
Quemdudum totos armenta secuta per agros
Constituere ducem, nunc intra septa reclusus
Aestuat, et saevi laniandus dente molossi,
Torva tuens campum ingreditur, mugitque tremendum ;
Nunc pede pro subigit terram, nunc cornua duris
Postibus infigit, sed ab omni parte cruentus
Hostis adest, fumant atque atro sanguine fauces
Et madet albenti spumarum aspergine cervix.
Ast ubi jam non plura videt se posse, suasque
In ventum effundi vires, se vertit ad artes

nor equal divinities, nor is their cause alike. Scourie, the impious Dutch General, comes as the oppressor of his country, trusting in a foreign soldiery, and backed by the strength of the allies.[1] Dread is his thunder, and with great might does he bear himself, while he fruitlessly burns to put forth his whole strength, and exults in the vain hope of a first advantage over his enemy. But to no effect does he press him with frequent assaults. Now does he frame delay by art, that he may consider by what force, by what strategy, he may be able to destroy his enemy, and cut him off by the sword. Thus a bull which in the open country was hitherto the accepted leader of the free herds which followed him, now at length enclosed within a field, wearied out after long resistance, and wounded by the savage tooth of the dog, turns with gloomy ferocity, and advances with loud bellowings. Now he tears up the turf with his feet, now he drives his horns into the palings, but wherever he goes there is his enemy. His mouth reeks with dark blood, his neck is flecked with white foam. But when at length he sees he can do no more, and that his strength is wasting away in the air, he betakes himself to arts, by

---

[1] 'Subnixus viribus conjurati orbis.' The Poet makes very frequent allusion to the allies of whom William of Orange was Generalissimo.

Queis vafer elusum crudeliter opprimat hostem.
Pronus humi jacet, et caput inter crura recondit,
Huc atque huc volvitque oculos, ut cornibus hostem
Adpetat incautum, et media prosternat arena.
  Dundius hinc murus pro Caesare stabat ahenus,
Inque hostem dubii sufflantem incendia belli
Ire parat, rara quanquam stipante caterva,
Et sine praesidiis, sine defensoribus ullis,
Fertur in adversum Batavi jam principis agmen.
At duce fortuna, et melioris numine causae,
Sola magnorum famaque innixus avorum ;
Et virtute potens, factisque et nomine clarus,
Militiae partisque insignis Marte trophaeis,
Ipse trahit secum chlamydatam in praelia gentem.
Atque pio pro rege pius pia sustulit arma,
Et conjurati solus vim sustinet orbis
Intrepidus, patriaeque et pulsi regis honorem
Fortiter asseruit, donec per vulnera vitam

which he cunningly but cruelly may overcome his deluded enemy. Prone on the ground he lies, his head between his legs; hither and thither he turns his eyes that he may watch his incautious enemy, and with his horns prostrate him on the ground.

Here, on the other hand, Dundee, like a wall of brass, was standing for the Caesar, against an enemy fanning the fires of a doubtful war. In anger he makes ready, and though accompanied by only a slender force, and without fortifications or other defences,[1] he is borne against the opposing army of the Dutch Prince. But fortune leading, and the blessing of a good cause, and relying on the fame of his great ancestors, himself great in valour, illustrious in name and deed, and glorious in trophies won in battle, he leads with him to the war the plaided tribes, and himself pious, for a pious King, he raises pious arms. Intrepidly, he alone meets the power of the allied world, and undaunted upholds the honour of his country, and of his exiled King, until by fatal wound he parted with his life, and poured out with his blood his faithful spirit.

---

[1] 'Sine praesidiis.' I gather from the various contexts in which the expression occurs, that the author means that Dundee has no cities or fortresses to fall back upon, nor the wealth of the country to support him. With his sword and his cavaliers he takes the field.

Amisit, fidamque animam cum sanguine fudit.
Qualis magnanimi soboles generosa leonis,
Quem pater accepto prius a venantibus ictu
Saucius, et longe semotis exul in arvis,
Lactantem obscuro jam forte reliquit in antro.
Postquam dura fames, atque impulit ardor edendi,
Tendit in arva furens, et justas surgit in iras,
Attollitque jubas, atque obvia quaeque feroci
Dente petit, lateque greges formidine sternit;
Utque indignantem venantum murmure turbam
Circumstare videt, contra truculentior ardet,
Rugitus ciet, et vasto fremit oris hiatu.
Ira referre pedem vetat, et speciosa pudendae
Haud dare terga fugae patitur Mavortia virtus.
Ore atque ungue minax, et nunc interritus hostes
In medios ruit, et venabula sanguine tingit.
    Jamque adeo infestis concurrere cominus armis
Orbis in extremo dux ardet uterque recessu.
Nunc et in arma ruunt, multum indignantibus astris
Atque etiam imparibus properant decernere fatis,
Clari animis, clarique armorum laudibus ambo,
Inter se totis obnixi viribus instant,
Quem Regem terris inferrent arma Britannis.

Thus the generous offspring of the great-souled Lion, left perchance in dark cave while still a cub, his sire lying wounded by hunters' spear in far distant wilds, impelled by hunger, goes forth raging to the fields, roused to fierceness. His mane bristling, he attacks with savage tooth whatever opposes him, and scatters the flocks in fear, far and wide; and when he discovers by their noise the hostile crowd of hunters surrounding him, his ferocity increases, and with mighty roaring and grinding jaw, he challenges them to the fight. His wrath forbids retreat, while his splendid courage suffers him not for very shame to turn his back. With fang and claw he threatens, and now undismayed he rushes into the midst of his enemies, and stains the hunter's spear with his blood.

    Now both Generals, in these remote regions, forthwith eagerly prepare for the attack, and under opposing stars and unequal fates, they hasten to the arbitrament of battle. Both, illustrious in spirit and in deeds of arms, put out their whole strength as they press forward to the decision as to who shall be the King to rule

Scaurius urget et hinc, atque hinc Kilychranchius Heros
Fulminat, et duri certamina Martis anhelat.

LIBRI TERTII FINIS.

the British lands. Here Scourie presses on, and here flashes the hero of Killiecrankie, and pants for the fierce strife of battle.

END OF BOOK III.

LIBER QUARTUS.

JAM belli signum, et dirae praeludia pugnae,
　　Flammantem procul igne crucem Glengarius heros
Extulit excelsi turrito a culmine castri;
Raucisonas sonuitque tubas, quibus ilicet omnes
Excivit Grampî populos, acuitque feroces
Marte duces, et ad arma viros cantu impulit acres.
Abria continuo flagranti concita motu
Tota coit, variaeque fremunt circum undique gentes,
Excitae Arctoae diversis partibus orae.
Skya potens, vastisque horrens Badenothia sylvis,

AND now the flaming cross, the signal and prelude of fierce war, Glengarry has raised on the topmost turret of his distant castle, and has sounded the screaming pipes. Thus he summons all the Grampian Clans, excites the wild chieftains to war, and with the notes of the pibroch urges on the clansmen, keen for the strife. Forthwith all Abria, aroused, gathers in bright array, and the various clans, from every part of the North, are coming with the wild sounds of war. Skye,[1] in its might; Badenoch, savage with her

---

[1] In this list of localities supplying Dundee with his army, though topographical order has not been strictly adhered to, under the demands of Latin prosody, the historical accuracy is sufficiently maintained. From Skye came the Macdonalds of Sleat, from Islay came Macdonalds and Macleans (though a Campbell, the Laird of Calder, was attempting to rule the island by his 'loveing cousin, Archibald Campbell of Octomor, Baily off Ilay,' in the Orange interest, as well as his own). Ilanterrim I take to be the Ilanterum, or the Ilanterrim of the Clanranald Papers, which is to be identified with Castle Terrim, the Clanranalds' stronghold in Moydart. It would send Macdonalds of Clanranald. Ionia I have translated Iona, thinking that the Poet's classics had biassed him to that spelling of the Island of Hy. In one of the copies the commas come before Ionia, and after Knapdale, so that it might be translated the Ionian Knapdale, or the Knapdale of Hy connection, the district having been much influenced by the Island and its Saints. If any fighting men came from Iona, I presume they were of the Maclean name. Knapdale sent MacAlisters and others; Jura, Macneils and Macleans; Knoydart and Moydart, Macdonnells; Raasay,

Ylla, Yllanterimque, Iona, Knapdala, Jura,
Knoydara, Rachliniumque, Raersaque, Moydara, Mulla,
Baraque, finitimis cum gentibus undique junctas
Agglomerant in[1] arma manus. Rapit arma juventus,
Grampiadumque duces Mavortem in praelia poscunt.
Ille securigeros vocat ad sua signa clientes,
Atque pharetratas rauco ciet aere phalanges.
Hic chlamydata furens peditum quatit agmina campo,
Conglobat alter equos, cogitque ad fraena ferocem
Verbere cornipedem, et duris premit ora lupatis.
Jamque omnis variis Grampî gens ardet in armis.
Pars patrios furvis fornacibus excoquit enses ;
Hi rigidum versant mordaci forcipe ferrum
Flammivomisque alii fundunt liquida aera caminis,
Et chalybem dura stridentem incude fatigant.
Expoliunt alii galeas, bifidasque secures,
Gesa novant alii, latoque hastilia ferro,

vast woods; Islay, and Ilanterim, and Iona, Knapdale, Jura, Knoydart, and Rachlin, and Raasay, Moydart, Mull, and Barra, gather their bands for war, and link them with their neighbouring clans. The youth of the country seize their arms, and the chiefs call them to the field. Here one gathers the axe-bearing clansmen to his standard, and the quiver-carrying companies he summons with the hoarse trump. There the fierce captain urges his plaided legions of foot over the plain, and there another collects his horse, and forces with the lash the wild steed under the bridle, and curbs him with the hard bit. And now every clan of the Grampians glows in varying arms. Some temper again their fathers' swords in the dusky smithy. There some are turning the hard iron with the gripping-tongs; while others pour out the rushing wind upon the glowing hearth, and fashion the ringing steel upon the hard anvil. Others again polish helmet and double-headed axe, and some are heading long javelins and spears with broad iron, and on the whetstone they sharpen sword and spear,

---

Macleods; Mull, Macleans; Barra, Macneils. From Badenoch some Macphersons may already have joined Dundee's army, and some of the Gordon tenants in that district. From Rathlin or Rachlin Island came many of the Macdonnell connection in the former wars, and doubtless they would appear in this. The Earls of Antrim, on the coast of which county Rathlin lies, were Macdonnells, and there was constant communication.

[1] 'in' should be short.

Cote terunt frameasque et cuspide tela trisulca,
Spiculaque exacuunt, et tegmina ferrea dorsi
Rite cavant, clypeosque parant ex aere corusco.
　　Est locus Abriacis fama celebratus in oris
Ardua qua latos pandit Dalcomera campos
At vero aequoreae qua littora spectat Iernae
Asper et incultis horrens vestitur ericis.
Planities ibi vasta jacet, lateque patentem
Aspicies campum, quem nuncquam Memnonis atri
Obtegerent acies, magni non agmina Xerxis,
Non Agamemnoniae poterant complere catervae.
Hic coiere duces, hic belli buccina signum
Dira dedit, Martemque ciens rauco ore pithaules
Inflarat plenis marsupia turgida buccis.

and dart with triple-grooved[1] head and arrow's point, and duly curve the iron back-plate, and stud the shield with gleaming brass.

In Abria's coasts there lies a place of great fame, where high Dalcomera[2] expands her wide plains, and turns towards the shores of sea-girt Ireland. Rough and rugged, it is clothed with the wild heather. There lies a great plain, and there thou mayest see an expanse widening out on every side, which the army of black Memnon could not cover, nor the hosts of Xerxes, nor the bands of Agamemnon, fill. Here gather the chiefs, here the trumpet gives the dread signal for war, here the piper,[3] calling to the battle with hoarse note, blows up the swelling bags with inflated cheeks.

---

[1] 'Trisulca cuspide': three-sided spear-head, the sides being lightened by a groove running up them, as in a bayonet.

[2] Dalcomera or Dalcomra. Balhaldy spells it Dalmacommer, and says it was 'near Locheill's house.' In April a meeting of Highland chiefs had been fixed to be held in this place on 13th May to support King James. Dundee's coming delayed, but increased the dimensions of, the gathering. Dalmacommer is, no doubt, Macomer, where the falls are which were made in connection with the construction of the Caledonian Canal. Though the size of the field will hardly justify the Poet's language, yet I am told that it is large, and that more than one battle was fought on it. The Mackintoshes, Camerons, and Macdonalds were well acquainted with Dalmacommer as a fighting ground.

[3] The peculiar feature of the Scottish bagpipes as distinguished from the common Irish and Continental type—namely, that the wind is supplied by the mouth of the piper, and not by bellows—is here indicated by 'plenis buccis,' and 'rauco ore' speaks unmistakably of the drone. On *pithaules* see Notes at the end of the volume.

Dundius, ut radiis jam septima fulsit Eois
Orta dies, mediisque jubar dispersit in undis,
Dalcomrae ad campum multis cum millibus heros
Ibat ovans, magna procerum stipante caterva.
Jam vero qua dira sonum dedit aere recurvo
Buccina, conveniunt armati ad signa manipli,
Heroesque Ducesque simul et plebeia juventus
Grami castra petunt. Nuncquam majore paratu
Tot coiere viri, nec sparsae in littore gentes
Tanto Grampiacos complerunt agmine colles.
Sed neque belligeros tot Cimbrica Chersonesus[1]
Effudit populos, septem[2] licet illa trionis
Foeta virum fuerat genetrix, vaginaque mundi.
Nec tot in herbiferae foecundis saltibus Hyblae

When the seventh morn,[3] arising in Eastern light, had now shone forth and poured its rays over the waves, the hero Dundee, girt with a circle of chiefs and with his thousands around him, moved to the camp of Dalcomera; where the dread trumpet from brazen curve was sounding, the armed bands were gathering to their standards, and heroes and chiefs and peasant youths together were seeking the camp of the Graham. Never with greater note of preparation did men assemble in such force, nor scattered clans cover the hills with so great a company. The Cimbrian Chersonese, mother of the races of the North,[4] womb of the world, ne'er sent out so many warlike hordes, nor do the bees, despoilers of the blossoms, gather in such numbers to their rosy food when they rob the fresh honours of the groves on the fertile slopes of flowery Hybla. Here one leaves a desolate home, the dear Penates,

---

[1] Syllable wanting for scanning, but cf. page 89, note.

[2] Septemtrionis—an instance of tmesis—cf. Virgil, *Georgics* III. 381.

[3] This was 26th or 27th May. The author's account of a previous gathering about the 18th May (see Book III.) is supported by the following extract from a letter of the Laird of Cawdor, dated Edinburgh, 29th May 1689: 'We hear that Dundee made a rendevouz in Lochaber of sevin or eight hundred men, but they are dissipate since, and he gone, we know not whither.' He adds: 'Severall English regiments of horse, foot, and dragoons, with severals of ours, are ordered North, and its lyke may go to Lochaber ere they come back.'—*Thanes of Cawdor*, p. 378.

[4] Jutland, the home of the Cimbri. In one of their migrations they are said to have numbered 300,000 fighting men, besides women and children. Had our author read Milton, *Par. Lost*, i. 351?—

'A multitude like which the populous North
Pour'd never from her frozen loins.'

Florilegae glomerantur apes ad roscida florum
Pabula, cum virides nemorum praedantur honores.
Deserit ille domos vacuas, charosque Penates,
Grandaevumque patrem, parvosque sub ubere natos
Et nollente gravem jam conjuge corripit hastam.
Et nati invitis rapuere parentibus arma.
Hic clangore tubae audito linquit aratrum,
Et galeam capiti laterique accommodat ensem,
Loricamque humeris confestim fortibus aptat.
    Pandite Pierides fontes Permessidis undae,
Et juga Parnassi, totumque Helicona ciete
Ut meminisse queam, cantuque referre sonoro,
Ingentem virtute Ducem, pro Caesare qui tum
Exule Grampiacis picta intulit agmina castris.
Exciti quique aere viri, quae quemque secuta est
Ductorem chlamydata cohors, quibus Abria mater
Floruit alma viris, quibus et gaudebat alumnis.
Non tamen haec dubia referam mihi tradita fama,
Sed quae oculis coram vidi, quaeque auribus hausi,
Pandere fert animus, saeclisque aperire futuris.
    Primus hyperboreis Glengarius acer ab oris

the aged father, the little children at the breast, and seizes his heavy spear though his wife refuse it. There the sons have torn their weapons from the resisting hands of parents. When the pibroch sounds they leave the plough, and forthwith gird sword to side, fit helm to head, and mail coat to their brawny shoulders.

Flow ye Pierian springs, Permessian waters! open ye heights of Parnassus and summon all Helicon that I may recall, and in sonorous verse relate, the story of the General, great in virtue, who then for the exiled Caesar gathered the tartaned host to the Grampian camp, and whom the plaided clansmen—with trumpet sound aroused—now follow as their leader; men through whom their nursing-mother Lochaber attained her fame; sons in whom she gloried. No doubtful tales,[1] brought to me by report, will I relate; but it is my purpose to unfold, and to open to future times, that only which I have seen with my own eyes, which I have heard with my own ears.

First, from his northern shores, the brave Glengarry leads three

---

[1] The lifelike descriptions which follow betoken the records of an eye-witness.

Tercentum validae primaevo flore juventae
Conspicuos ducit juvenes, quos discolor omnes
Penula Maeandro triplici, Phrygioque labore
Texta tegit, laxosque sinus pro tegmine vestit.
Cetra latus, munitque virum cava tempora cassis,
Picta chlamys velatque humeros, at caetera nudi.
Ipse inter medios armatus acinaci dextram,
Auratoque micans sagulo, cui balteus ingens
Cingebat laevam mordaci dente papillam,
Spumanti subvectus equo, et fulgentibus armis
Arduus ingreditur campum, quem pone secuti
Centeni cum fratre animi praestantis Alano,

hundred illustrious youths in the first flower of vigorous manhood, each of whom a tartan garb covers,[1] woven with Phrygian skill in triple stripe, and, as a garment, clothes their broad chests and flanks. A helmet defends the temples of the men. A coloured plaid veils their shoulders, and otherwise they are naked. The chief himself, mounted on a foaming steed, and towering in glittering arms, advances into the plain, claymore in hand, his cloak shining with gold, and a broad baldric with buckled clasp crossing his left breast. Following him closely comes his brother Allan,[2] the brave, with a hundred men all clothed in garments interwoven with the red stripe, their brawny calves bound with the

---

[1] See previous note on Glengarry, Book III. 'Discolor penula' may mean the belted plaid which was worn as a garment covering the body, and hanging down in folds after the manner of the kilt. It was called the Breacan. The Lenicroich or Highland shirt was also 'discolor,' and may be referred to here. Glengarry is the chief hero of the North in the Poet's eye, and the leading mind among the Highland chiefs. The slight notice taken of Lochiel, who was really the man of most weight in the councils of the war, and in the strength of his following, is remarkable. The Glengarry family is descended from John, first Lord of the Isles, and his first wife, Amy M'Rory, through Reginald or Ranald, their third son (the only one showing heirs-male). Ranald's eldest son, according to Skene, was Donald, from whom descended the family of Knoydart and Glengarry. The family rose to a peerage in the person of Æneas Macdonell, the ally of Montrose, who, at the Restoration, was created Lord Macdonell and Aros in the Peerage of Scotland, with succession only to heirs-male. He died without issue, and the peerage lapsed, though his lands still formed the barony of Macdonell. The representation of the family reverted to Ranald Macdonell, the descendant of the grandfather of Lord Macdonell and Aros. He was alive at this time, but old and frail, and his son, Alastair Dubh, the hero of the poem, was in command of the clan.

[2] Our author here is in conflict with the family historian, who gives no Allan as a brother of Alastair Dubh Macdonell, the Glengarry here referred to. It is probably a mistake of the author for Angus or Æneas, the brother of Glengarry

Ostro inter pictis induti vestibus omnes
Altaque puniceis evincti crura cothurnis,
Horrebant longe telis, et corpora scutis
Protecti, crudo succinctique inguina ferro,
Defensique cavis umbonibus aere rigebant.
Quos juxta egregiis Glencoius ibat in armis,
Horridus, et bibulo contectus pectora tergo,
Os humerosque super totum longe eminet agmen.
Illum in bella viri centum comitantur euntem,
Mole superbi omnes, horrendi et viribus omnes.

red buskin. Afar they bristle with spears, and they stand firm with sword belted round their loins, with shields strengthened with brazen knobs protecting their bodies. Next came Glencoe[1] terrible in unwonted arms, covered as to his breast with raw hide, and towering far above his whole line by head and shoulders. A hundred men, all of gigantic mould, all mighty in strength, accompany him as he goes to the war. He himself, turning his shield in his hand, flourishing terribly his sword, fierce in aspect, rolling

next in age to himself, and on whom his now aged father had settled the lands and barony of Scotus. He would thus naturally be second in command to his brother, and his independent property would contribute the separate company of one hundred men referred to. Till 1868 the chiefship of Glengarry went on in the family of Alastair Dubh, when it passed to the descendants of the younger, Angus of Scotus, through the failure of male issue. The present representative of Alastair Dubh is Mrs. Cunninghame of Balgownie, daughter of Æneas Ranaldson Macdonell of Glengarry, who parted with the estates of the family. Another brother of Glengarry took the field with him, Donald, who was killed at Killiecrankie. [Since the above was in print, Mrs. Cuninghame has passed to her fathers, leaving an only son, John Alastair, who now possesses the 'Craggan-an-fhithich,' with the ruin of the old castle, the old family burying-ground, and other interesting relics of his family.]

[1] This is Alastair Macdonald or M'Ian, the chief who suffered in the massacre. He is described by Balhaldy as 'strong, active, and of the biggest size; much loved by his neighbours, and blameless in his conduct. He was a person of great integrity, honour, good-nature, and courage, and his loyalty to King James was such that he continued in arms from Dundee's first appearing in the Highlands till the fatal treaty which brought on his ruin.'—*Lochiel's Memoirs*, page 321. The family is descended from Angus Og, the faithful supporter of Robert Bruce, against his own brother, Alastair, Lord of the Isles, and the M'Dougals of Lorne. Angus succeeded to the whole possessions of his brother, and, dying early in the fourteenth century, left two sons, John, his successor in the Isles, and John Og or Fraoch, the ancestor of this family of Glencoe. James Malcolm, a witness in the process of forfeiture, 'depones that he saw a man called the Laird of Glencoe in arms with the rebels at Badenoch, Strathspey, and several other places, and that he had a brass blunderbuss, and a buff coat.'. —*Act. Parl.*

Ipse manu clypeumque rotans, ensemque coruscans
Terribilis, vultusque truces et turbida volvens
Lumina, contortae revolutaque cornua barbae
Circumquaque ferens iras spirare videtur.
  Parte alia magni Donaldi clara propago,
Et gentis Princeps et Regulus Aebudarum[1]
Egregius bello, et florentibus insuper annis,
Orbis ab extremis terrarum Slatius oris,
Acer in arma ruit, secumque in bella furentes
Aere ciet juvenes quingentos, ensibus omnes
Cominus armatos, rigidisque hastilibus omnes,
Insula quos longis transmisit Skya carinis.
  Hinc Reginaldinae Ductor clarissimus orae,

his wild eyes, the horns of his twisted beard curled backwards, seems to breathe forth wrath wherever he moves.

Again the noble offspring of the great Donald, chief of the race, and Lord of the Isles, he of Sleat,[2] illustrious in war beyond his youthful years, rushes, brave in arms, from the extremities of the land, and with bugle summons with himself to the war five hundred fiery youths, all girt with sword and rigid spear, whom Skye has sent in her long boats across the water. Then comes the exalted Captain of Clan Ranald,[3] in the first flower of his age,

---

[1] By treating *Ae* in 'Aebudarum' as two syllables the line will scan, but see page 89, note.

[2] This is Sir Donald Macdonald of Sleat. Balhaldy says that he brought 700 men with him, and describes him as 'conducting all his actions by the strictest rules of religion and morality. He looked upon his clan as his children, and upon the King as the father of his country, and as he was possessed of a very opulent fortune, handed down to him by a long race of very noble ancestors, so he lived in the greatest affluence, but with a wise economy.' Sir Donald lost five near relations at Killiecrankie. The family is descended from John, the eldest son of Angus Og, mentioned in a preceding note. John was twice married, first to Amy, daughter of Roderick of the Isles, by whom he had three sons, John, Godfrey, and Ranald, from the last mentioned of whom comes the Clan Ranald, including the various Macdonalds of whom Glengarry would seem to be the chief according to blood. His second wife was the daughter of the Steward of Scotland, afterwards Robert II., and by her he had four sons, Donald, John, Alastair, and Angus. The Macdonalds of Sleat are descended from the first named of these, who succeeded his father as Lord of the Isles. The family was raised to the peerage in 1776, and is now represented by Lord Macdonald. The witness mentioned in the last note in process of forfeiture, 'depones he saw a young gentleman, Sir Donald Macdonald of Sleat, command a regiment at the fight of Killiecrankie, and that he had a red coat.'—*Act. Parl.*

[3] This is Allan Macdonald, twelfth of Clan Ranald. He was about sixteen years of age, and was under the tutorship of Donald Macdonald of Benbecula,

Primo in flore aevi, et studiis juvenilibus ardens,
Ante annos animi ostendit praeludia magni,
Et vixdum prima pingens lanugine malas,
Ingenti patriae laudis succensus amore,
Ibat in arma ferox tota cum gente suorum
Quos Reginalda cohors, et quos nigra insula misit,

glowing from his youthful studies, showing the preludes of a mind great beyond his years. While scarce the first down tints his cheek, he, fired with a great love of his country's glory, moved keenly to battle with his whole race. He bears along, rushing into the fight, races whom the Black Isle[1] has sent, those whom

---

known as the Tutor of Clan Ranald. James Malcolm 'depones (see note on Glencoe) that he saw a young lad, called the Captain of Clan Ranald, in Lochaber in arms with my Lord Dundee, and that he had a dirk, and that he dined several times with my Lord Dundee, and that he saw a company of the lusty men with him, whom he called his guards.'—*Act. Parl.* He is said to have joined Dundee with 700 men, who were formed into a regiment under the tutor's command, with the rank of Colonel. He refused to take advantage of the proclamation offering protection on taking the oath before 1st January 1692. He went abroad, and is said to have completed his education under the eye of King James, at the Court of St. Germains. He afterwards held a commission in the French service under the Duke of Berwick. Through the influence of Benbecula his estates were preserved to him. He married Penelope, daughter of Colonel Mackenzie, who had been Governor of Tangier under Charles II. She was a lady of great beauty, brilliant wit, and sweetness of temper, and though shining at the Court of St. Germains, she preferred Clan Ranald's offer to many others, and accompanied him to his native hills. They arrived safely in South Uist, where they 'drew around them company from all parts of the kingdom, and a little court, well befitting that of a chief, was actually formed.' See Mackenzie's *History of the Macdonalds of Clan Ranald*, p. 57. He joined the Earl of Mar in the rising of 1715, and was killed at the battle of Sheriffmuir, and buried at Innerpeffery, in the burying-place of the noble family of Perth. He left no children, and was succeeded by his brother Ranald. The family of Clan Ranald is descended from the Ranald mentioned (in previous note on Macdonalds of Sleat) as the son of John, eldest son of Angus Og, but a bar sinister has intervened. Ranald had five sons, of whom three only left issue, viz., Donald, from whom descended the family of Knoydart and Glengarry, Allan, the ancestor of the family of Moydart, and Angus, from whom came the family of Morar. In the troubles which befell the principal branch of Clan Ranald—that of Knoydart and Glengarry—the family of Moydart escaped, and in consequence of the reduced state of the rival branch, and the forfeiture of the Lords of the Isles, they placed themselves at the head of the Clan. This was effected principally by John Mudortach, an illegitimate son of the laird's brother, who assumed the title of *Captain* of Clan Ranald only, which afterwards was converted into that of Macdonald of Clan Ranald. See Skene on *the Highlanders of Scotland*, Part II. p. 104; also *Macdonalds of Clanranald*, by A. Mackenzie.

[1] Black Isle, probably Dark Isle. They came from Uist.

Knoydara quos vastis et Moydara nutrit in arvis,
Marte rapit populos in praelia saeva ruentes.
Post hos insignem ducens longo ordine turmam
Kapochus in campum geminis cum fratribus ibat

Knoydart and Moydart nourish in their vast fields. After these
Keppoch[1] in gilded array, with his twin brothers, advances into

---

[1] Keppoch—called sometimes Colonel Macdonald—to whom Claverhouse gave the name of 'Colonel of the Cows,' because 'he found them out when they were driven to the hills out of the way.' He has a very distinct personality among the Highlanders of the time.

I presume he is Ranald, son of the Archibald Macdonald of Keppoch for whom, with twelve others of his name, Æneas, Lord Macdonald of Aros, is required to find caution 'that they shall commit no murder, deforcement of messengers, reiff theifts, receipt of theifts, depredations, open and avowed fireraisings, and deidly feids, and any other deids contrar to the Acts of Parliament.'—Act of Privy Council, 18th July 1672. Ranald himself appears as the victor in the battle of Mulroy, when he defeated a strong body of the Macintoshes, taking their chief prisoner. The quarrel was an old one, and based on a somewhat interesting question of tenure. The Macdonalds had held long possession of the lands of Keppoch without title. The Macintosh had received a grant of the property from James IV. under royal charter, as well as under an old charter from the Lords of the Isles, and the Macdonalds became thus tenants of the Macintosh. From time to time, as they were compelled by circumstances, they made some trifling payments, but the Macintosh of this time determined that they should be tenants in fact as well as in name, and with a thousand men, supported by a company of royal troops under Captain Mackenzie of Sudry, marched into the Keppoch country, where they found no enemy. The Macdonalds, however, soon appeared, strengthened by the Martins of Letterfinlay and other Camerons, as well as Macdonalds of Glencoe and Glengarry, and utterly routed the Macintoshes. The life of the Macintosh was only saved through the generous action of Macpherson of Cluny, who brought his force to rescue his old enemy because he belonged to the Clan Chattan.

Keppoch next appears in command of the force of Macdonalds and Camerons, 800 in number, sent by the Highland chiefs towards Inverness to conduct Claverhouse into Lochaber. He used this force, as we have seen, in besieging Inverness, and extorted from the poor town a sum of 4000 merks. The town recovered this sum in 1695 on petition to Parliament. Instead of joining Claverhouse with his force, he used it for 'reiff theifts' on his way home through the Macintosh lands and those of their friends. He eventually joined Claverhouse in Lochaber with 200 men.

Our author presents him, later on in this book, as besieging Ruthven Castle, and without authority burning the house of Dunachton, and ravishing the country with fire and sword. He confesses that Dundee could not at all times control this wild soldier. We learn, however, from the *Memoirs of Lochiel*, that on this occasion Dundee had him up, and, in presence of all the officers of his small army, he told him 'that he would much rather choise to serve as a common

Aureus, et galea caput altum tectus ahena,
Et gemino mucrone minax, clypeoque coruscus
Martis amore furit, cujus latera undique cingunt
Bis centum torvo ore viri, quibus omnis in armis
Vita placet, praedasque juvat ductare recentes.

the plain, leading a great following in long line. His head is covered with a helmet, he flourishes his two-handed sword, and his shield flashes, as with the love of war he comes wildly on. Two hundred men of fierce aspect are gathered around him, to whom life in arms alone is pleasing, and to drive the new booty a

souldier among disciplined troops, than command such men as he, who seemed to make it his business to draw the odium of the country upon him. That though he had committed these outrages in revenge of his own private quarrel, yet it would be generally believed that he had acted by authority; that since he was resolved to do what he pleased, he begged that he would immediately begone with his men, that he might not hereafter have ane opportunity of affronting the General at his pleasure, or of making him and the better-disposed troops a cover to his robberies.' Keppoch humbly begged his Lordship's pardon, and told him 'that he would not have abused Macintosh so if he had not thought him ane enemy to the King, as well as to himself; that he was heartily sorry for what was passed, but since that could not be amended, he solemnly promised a submissive obedience for the future, and that neither hee, nor any of his men, should at any time thereafter stirr one foot without his Lordship's positive commands.'—*Memoirs of Lochiel*, p. 243. He is said by the writer of a Family Memoir of the Keppochs to have commanded 700 men at Killiecrankie. In the bond of 24th August 1689 he promises to bring 100 men.

Later on, after the battle of Cromdale, out of which Keppoch managed to keep himself, he joined the fugitives who took shelter in the upper Craigellachie, and made an attempt to seize the Castle of Lochinclan, which was repulsed with loss by the proprietor and his tenants. Shaw, in his *History of Moray*, notes it as worthy of remark that 'Col. Macdonald of Keppoch, who was ever keen for plunder, had never once fought for his King, would not encamp with the other rebels, but with his men, quartered at Garolin, half a mile distant, and thereby escaped without loss.'

He and his sept were doomed to the same fate as the Macdonalds of Glencoe, but escaped through timely submission.

He married a daughter of Macdonald of Glengarry, and by her had two sons, the eldest of whom, Alexander, succeeded his father, and was known, at any rate in the family, as 'the mirror of martial men, who immolated himself at the Battle of Culloden, to the inexpressible loss and affliction of his family.'—*Family Memoirs*, by Angus Macdonald, M.D.; 1885.

The descent of the Keppoch family is from John, Lord of the Isles, through his second family by the daughter of Robert II.

For additional information see Browne's *Hist. of the Highlands*, Napier's *Dundee*, Skene's *Highlanders*, *Acts of Parl. Scot.*, vol. ix. Index; also our note, Book II.

Hi rigidam gestant tereti mucrone securem,
Lucida gesa alii, et nodosam robore clavam,
Dextra alii frameam ostentant, clypeumque sinistra,
Machinaque horrisono tonat omnibus aerea bombo.
His ducibus claro Donaldi sanguine cretis
Illi inter sese bis denas ordine turmas
Constituunt, pubemque una facto agmine jungunt,
Et paria arma ferunt, gentisque insigne paternae
Fascem in bella gerunt omnes silvestris ericae
Suspensum tremuli summa de cuspide conti.
Atque alacres, junctis aeterno foedere dextris
Agmina sub patriis mittunt socialia signis.
   Hinc procul arctoi veniens a littore ponti
Evenus Cameronus Eques, Marte inclytus Heros,

delight. These carry the hard axe with keen point, and others the gleaming javelin and the knotty club. Others again show in their right hand the spear, in their left the shield; and the brazen gun thunders in the hands of them all with loud report. These all being chiefs sprung from the blood of Donald, they among themselves form twenty companies, and unite the clansmen in one battalion. They all bear similar arms, and carry into battle, as the emblem of their race, a bunch of wild heather[1] hung from the point of a quivering spear. All briskly—having clasped right hands in eternal bond—send forth their allied bands under their country's standard.

Here now Sir Ewen Cameron,[2] a hero of martial fame, coming

---

[1] The badge of the Macdonells is 'Heath.' The force apparently sent by them was 1900. In 1427 they mustered 2000; in 1715, 2800; in 1745, 2350. Skene's *Highland Clans*, chap. iv. As to the carrying of a bunch of heather on the top of a pole, cf. Ovid, *Fasti*, Lib. iii. 117, 'Pertica suspensos portabat longa maniplos.' The axe with tapering point refers to Lochaber axe.

[2] The celebrated Sir Ewen Cameron of Lochiel, chief of clan Cameron, the most remarkable Highland figure of the time. He was the grandson of Alan M'Conell Dhu, the fierce chief, 'warrior and seer' of James VI.'s time and the Regencies. Sir Ewen was born at Kilchurn Castle in February 1629, his mother being a Campbell of Glenorchy. His father, John Cameron, died soon after, leaving the child in the hands of old Alan. His fosterage was with the head of the Cameron tribe of M'Martin of Letterfinlay till he was twelve years old, when he was handed over to the astute Marquis of Argyll. This nobleman's kind, careful, and generous treatment of the boy comes as a pleasant surprise among the recognised features of the character of 'Gillespie Grumach.'

The principles of his guardian—if they ever had any chance of success with such a mind as Lochiel's—not only failed to influence him, but through their

Secum mille viros in praelia saeva ferebat,
Aspera belligeros quos Abria nutrit alumnos,
Infractos et in arma Duces, semperque recentem

from the distant shores of the northern waters, carried with him to
the field a thousand men, whom, a warlike offspring, rugged Abria
nourishes, chiefs unconquered in war, whom it ever delights to

---

connection with the many executions of loyal gentlemen, which Lochiel had to
witness in the company of the Marquis, roused at last his fierce opposition. Sir
Robert Spottiswood, before his execution, had a long conversation in his prison
with the boy, and practically fixed for him his future as a royalist. After the
execution of that gentleman, and his two companions, Nathaniel Gordon and
William Murray, he began to insist on his return to Lochaber, and Argyll did not
thwart him. In December 1646 he started for the Highlands, and was received
with wild delight by his clansmen. He was then not quite eighteen. Though
he never served under Montrose, as the Poet would seem to suggest, yet it was
one of the sayings about him, that 'Montrose was ever in his mouth,' and he
resolved to join him should he ever have the opportunity. Getting his clan
thoroughly into order kept him in much employment for a time, and the clearing
of his country of wolves and foxes was his useful diversion; he is said to have
killed the last wolf that was seen in the Highlands. After the battle of Worcester, the only body that stood out for the King was in the North under the
Earl of Glencairn. Lochiel joined him in 1652 with 700 men, and had the chief
honour in the defeat of Lilburn in Braemar, and in the saving of Glencairn's
force. He maintained his independence through many adventures, narrow
escapes, and skilful diplomacies, acting throughout under Middleton, till he
marched with Monck to London for the Restoration. He was knighted by the
Duke of York in 1682 with Lochiel's own sword, which James tried but failed to
draw. Lochiel drew it, when the Duke cried, 'See, my Lords, the sword of
Lochiel obeys no hand but his own.' When the King's crown went down,
Lochiel employed himself during the winter of 1688 and 1689 in forming a confederacy of the clans, and was encouraged in his work by a letter from King James.
His son-in-law, Balhaldy, met Dundee at Dunblane on his way from the convention to Dudhope, and no doubt negotiated the meeting of the clans and
Claverhouse in Lochaber. Lochiel was now sixty years of age. The picture of
him by our Poet conforms to the portrait possessed by the present Lochiel.
His face in the latter is described as swarthy and gipsy-like; the Poet speaks
of his Spanish countenance. In the picture he is a young man, so the
beard and moustache have not the remarkable development described by our
author. In this connection of Lochiel's beard a story characteristic of the times
and the Highlanders is told. In 1675 the then Marquis of Argyll invited Lochiel
to Inveraray, and observing the condition of his beard, offered him the services
of his own French valet, as one adroit with the razor, an offer which he readily
accepted. While the process of shaving was going on in the Marquis's presence,
two Camerons were observed to place their backs firmly against the door, and
to keep their eyes steadily on his Lordship. Lochiel having escaped from
the hands of the valet was asked by the Marquis for an explanation of the
conduct of these men, and was referred to themselves. They answered that as

Quos agitare juvat praedam, atque assuescere furto.
Ipse securigero sublimis in agmine surgit
Aere rigens, geminumque latus cinxere clientum
Agmina Grampiadum, cognatorumque suorum
Fida cohors ; unaque gener Balhadius ibat.

lift the recent prey, and to apply themselves to robbery. He himself, stiff in brazen armour, rises high above his axe-bearing line, and on each side of him a faithful guard of kinsmen and Grampian clansmen are gathered. And with him goes his son-in-law, Balhaldy.[1] The Cameron chief himself, mounted on a grey

---

Lochiel had a man of his own for shaving, they suspected that when the valet was called for it was to murder the chief, as there had been a difference with Argyll, and they meant, if the suspicion was true, to kill his Lordship and the valet. When asked what they thought would become of themselves after doing such a thing, they said, 'That we did not think upon, but we were resolved to avenge the murder of our chief.'

Sir Ewen brought 1000 men to the Royal cause, and by his own and their valour contributed greatly to the victory at Killiecrankie. He had never led his men except to victory. After this he retired to Lochaber, leaving his son John, with 500 Camerons, to support General Cannon. He died in 1719, at the age of ninety. He had married three times : first, the sister of Sir James Macdonald of Sleat ; second, the sister of Sir Alan Maclean of Duart ; and, third, the sister of Robert Barclay of Ury, the Quaker. This lady, I presume, is the dame with the 'mark on her eye,' which Lieutenant James Malcolm noticed when he supped at Lochiel's house.—*Acts of Parl. of Scotland*, ix. App. p. 58. He had at least three sons, John, Alan, and Ludovic. Alan was the son of his second wife, at whose birth she died. He had also eleven daughters, all married to chiefs or landed proprietors. If his character was equalled by any one of the family, it was by his grandson, the hero of the '45.

The clan, in an ancient MS. history, is said to be sprung from the first race inhabiting the country. Mr. Skene assents to the truth of this statement, and says they formed part of the extensive tribe of Moray. The family is traced up to Angus, who married Marion, one of the daughters of Kenneth III., and sister of the famous Banquo. Skene makes Cameron of Lochiel the oldest cadet of the family, and says that the chief, previous to the fifteenth century, was M'Martin of Letterfinlay. The strength of the clan in 1715 and 1745 was 800. See Skene's *Highland Clans*, Napier's *Montrose* and *Dundee*, *Temple Bar*, Nov. 1887, and, above all, *Memoirs of Sir Ewen Cameron*, Abbotsford Club edition, 1842.

[1] Alexander Drummond of Balhaldy married Margaret, eldest daughter of Sir Ewen Cameron, about the year 1688, and took a prominent part in the negotiations for the rising of 1689. He also distinguished himself at Killiecrankie. After Cannon's weak conduct at Dunkeld, he stole privately to his own county, and receiving a letter from the Council to attend their pleasure, he made his submission, and took the benefit of the indemnity 'till King James his affairs should be better conducted.' He and his eldest son William, in 1715, 'assumed or rather resumed the name of M'Gregor, and were by a number of persons declared hereditary chiefs of that ancient sept, in order to enable the clan

Puniceo Pater altus equo Cameronus amictu
Tricolore[1] micat, tenuis quem bractea fulvi
Auri obit, et rutilum circumdedit[2] orichalcum.
Casside frons tegitur, laterique accingitur anceps
Framea,[3] sanguineaeque volant in vertice cristae,
Pectora cingebat thorax adamante morocci
Durior, a laevo dependet parma lacerto ;
Discolor et medias subnectit fascia suras.
Obnubit lorica humeros, et ahenea dorsum
Tegmina munierant, solidoque ex aere rigebant
Arma, coruscantem jactantque ad nubila lucem.
Ipsa vel indomitum frons aspera terreat hostem,
Obtutusque ferox, ater et color oris Iberi,[4]
Ardentesque oculi, barba et mystace reflexa
Cornua seu lunae, aut ansatae forcipis instar,
Agmina semiviri poterant terrere Sycambri.
Ille olim ut calido stagnabant sanguine venae,
Et juveni viguere animi, Duce Monte Rosarum
Regia castra petit, Midletoniumque secutus

horse, shines in a tri-coloured tunic trimmed all round with gold lace. A helmet covers his head, to his side is girt a double-edged brand, blood-red plumes float on his crest. A cuirass of leather, harder than adamant, girds his breast, and on his left arm hangs his shield. His tartan hose are gartered round his calf, mail covers his shoulders, and a brazen plate his back. All his trappings are rigid with solid brass, and throw back to the clouds the reflected light. His very look, so fierce, might fright the boldest foe. His savage glance, and the swarthy hue of his Spanish countenance, his flashing eyes, his beard and moustache curled as the moon's horn, or the handle of the tongs, might terrify the bands of the half-human Sycambrians. He, ere age had chilled his blood, and while youth was still hot within him—Montrose being his leader—sought the royal camp, and when fierce Cromwell raged in the North, he followed Middleton, and dyed with

---

to receive the pension then paid to every chief.'—Preface to *Memoirs*. It is probable that the author of the Memoirs is the same person as the Jacobite agent previous to 1745, William Drummond, the son of Alexander, and grandson of Lochiel. The Latin spelling of the Poet follows the common pronunciation of the name, not the spelling of it.

[1] If we insert *In* before 'Tricolore' the line will scan.
[2] See page 89, note. [3] Frămĕă.
[4] Line will scan with 'et' omitted.

Cum ferus arctois fremeret Crombellus in oris,
Infecit patrios hostili sanguine campos.
Nunc quoque cum Batavi rabies scelerata Tyranni
Ingrueret Socerum, sexagenarius ultro,
In conjuratos sacrati Caesaris hostes
Induit arma ferox, et aperta in bella ruebat.
Maximus huic natu paribus comes ibat in armis
Filius egregiae primaevo in flore juventae,
Et generis decor, et gentis tutela paternae
Assuescit duros castrorum ferre labores;
Militiaeque locum tenet a genitore secundum.
Emicat hinc toto sublimior agmine natus

hostile gore the paternal plains. And now, when the Dutch tyrant in his cursed madness assails his father-in-law, Lochiel, though past his sixtieth year, fiercely dons his armour, and rushes into open war against the allied enemies of the sacred Caesar. In like arms his eldest son [1] accompanies him, in the first flower of peerless youth. He, the ornament of his race, and guardian of his father's clan, has accustomed himself to bear the hard service of the camp, and holds the place in command, second to his father.

Here, too, is MacMartin [2] rising high above his whole line.

---

[1] John, the eldest son of Sir Ewen. He commanded the clan after Killiecrankie while they still held the field under Cannon. He again commanded the clan in 1715. His father made over the estates to him, reserving his liferent, in 1696. Before going out in the '15, he took the precaution of making over his estates to his son Donald. He retired to France, and died an old man at Boulogne in 1747. His servant, Duncan Cameron, was sent with Prince Charlie to facilitate his landing by his knowledge of the coast.

[2] The picture of this chief, younger of M'Martin, is a very vigorous one, and though following Virgil in word, the Poet has Highland incident in view. The uprooting of the old ash is not beyond possibility, if we suppose it a mountain-ash on a rocky hillside; and it is possible that the tearing away of the iron with the bite alone may refer to the following incident in the early life of Lochiel among the M'Martins, or when he returned to his mountains, and this chief as a lad probably his companion. I take it from the fragment printed in the Preface of the *Memoirs of Lochiel:* 'His (Lochiel's) blood was never drawn either by the enemy or a chirurgeon, and but once that we hear of by an accident of tramping upon a sharp small-pointed knife, which ran quite through the thick of his foot, and which befell him in his younger days while he kept the mountains. This knife chancing to break at the handle where it joins the blade, he caused one of his attendants to pull it out with his teeth, and the blood following it with a great gush struck the gentleman full in the mouth, which gave Lochiel so much diversion that he said merrily, that if the knife had given him a sore foot, it had likewise given that gentleman sore teeth and a foul

Martini, cui fusca genas lambitque tegitque
Caesaries, fulgentque micantibus aemula[1] stellis
Lumina, candidulis certant et colla corymbis.
Quem genitor, longeque clientum exercitus ingens
Ambiit, et fratrum sequitur pulcherrimus ordo,
Atque illum ex omni circumstant parte manipli.
Ipse colorato graditur succinctus amictu
Arduus incessu, cui pendula fascia crurum
Corrycio fucata croco, Tyrioque rubebat

His dark locks hang around his face and cover his cheeks, and his eyes shine like the stars, while his neck rivals the white flowers. His father and a great force of dependants accompany him, and an illustrious company of his brethren in their ranks surround him on every side. He himself in variegated array advances with lofty mien. The garter ribbons hanging at his leg[2] were dyed with Corycian saffron, and with the tint of the Tyrian shell, as was his plaid. The crest of his helmet glows with

---

mouth.' If the keeping the mountains meant the time when Lochiel was out with his men operating with Glencairn and Middleton, the ages of the chief and the M'Martin would very well suit the incident. I have translated 'solo morsu' *with teeth alone*, because of the length of the first *o* in 'solo.' If it had been short, one could have translated it *from the sole* without much violence.

The tribe is supposed by Skene to be the original stock of the Clan Cameron. The traditional origin of the Camerons ' derives them from Cambro, a Dane, who is said to have acquired his property with the chiefship of the clan, by marriage with the daughter and heiress of M'Martin of Letterfinlay. . . . There is little room to doubt that the M'Martins were the old chiefs of the clan, and the Lochiel family were the oldest cadets, whose after position at the head of the clan gave them the title of Captain of the Clan Cameron.'—Skene's *Highland Clans*, chap. vii.

We find it a common custom among the Lochiels to give their eldest sons, soon after they were weaned, to be fostered among the M'Martins. The foster-father of the unfortunate Ewen M'Connell Cameron of Lochiel, who in 1560 was stabbed under the table by his keeper in his prison on an island in Lochawe at the moment of his rescue, was Martin M'Connochey of Letterfinlay, his rescuer. In 1533 a Duncan M'Martin signs a marriage contract of Lochiel. There are two signatures to deeds about 1514-1519 by the M'Martins.—*Book of Thanes of Cawdor* and *Memoirs of Lochiel*.

The family was much allied with the M'Donalds of Keppoch, and required a strong hand to keep them in order.

[1] The rule of strict prosody making a short vowel long before 'st,' 'sp,' etc., is commonly disregarded by the author. He is, however, supported in this violation of rule by good Latinists. See Preface.

[2] The passage is very difficult to translate. I only offer this, and much besides, as a suggestion.

Murice tincta chlamys, pinnisque volantibus ardet
Cassidis altus apex, et pixidis ornamenta
Sulphureae phalerata micant procul aere corusco.
At tunicam rutilo soror intertexerat auro,
Et geminata humeros circum Meliboea cucurrit.
Terribilis, membrisque valens, et viribus ingens,
Eruere annosas poterat radicibus ornos,
Et solo rigidum morsu convellere ferrum.
Et quocunque caput mota cervice rotasset
Arma sonant, rupesque cavae mugire videntur
Dum graditur, nimioque gemit sub pondere tellus.
Hinc Tanachaeus adest Cameronae stirpis alumnus
Horridus in jaculis, qui tendere[1] spicula cornu
Noverat, et certis transfigere pectora telis.
Seu libuit celeres nervo intentare sagittas,
Machina sulphureo reboat seu ferrea bombo,
Nemo illum sumptis impune lacesseret armis.
Post hos ingenti Glendishrius agmine campum
Arduus ingreditur, magnoque per agmina plausu

floating plumes, and the trappings of his mounted powder-horn gleam in shining brass. But his sister had embroidered his tunic with the red gold, and a doubled line of purple went round his terrible shoulders. Mighty of limb, mighty in strength, he could uproot the old ash-tree, or with his teeth alone tear away the hard iron. Whenever he turns his head and neck his arms rattle, and the hollow rocks seem to moan, and as he treads the plain the earth groans under his weight. Here also is Tannachy,[2] a scion of the Cameron clan, bristling with darts, who knew how to speed the arrow from the bow, and by bolt or bullet transfix the breast with deadly aim. No one might attack him when armed, with impunity. After these, stalwart Glendessary[3] with his company advances on the plain, and with applauding shouts he unfurls mid his clans-

---

[1] See note [1], p. 134. This use of the author will not be further noted.

[2] I have been unable to identify this hero. The only family that would be simply named Tannachy was Tulloch of Tannachy, but even the author of *Celtic Scotland* in his kind search has not been able to trace their connection with the Camerons. They were a Morayshire family.

[3] Cameron of Glendessary. The founder of the family was Donald, uncle and tutor of Lochiel. The tribe became very numerous. This chief was cousin of Lochiel, and, in company with John, Lochiel's son, brought up 500 Camerons three days too late for Killiecrankie. Note 'Nemo impune,' etc.

Explicuit patrio vexilla rubentia ritu.
Quem Lonochaea tribus, lateque effusa Gregori
Progenies stipata Ducem, tum deinde secuti
Nabide prognati, Cowloque et Gibbone, quorum
Horrescunt Latiae tam barbara nomina Musae.
Haudque[1] operae est pretium, venienti tradere famae,
Nec meminisse vacat confusae plebis acervum.

men his ruddy banner, with ancestral rite. Him the tribe of Lonoch,[2] and the widely spread clan of M'Gregor, accompanied as their leader. Then follow Macnabs,[3] Cowals,[4] and Gibbons,[5] barbarous names at which the Latin Muse shudders, nor is it worth while to hand down to future fame, or to record, the names of the mixed multitude.

---

[1] Are 'haud' and 'que' ever conjoined?

[2] The Lonoch tribe I take to be the Lennox tribe—chiefly the scattered tribe of M'Gregor, between whom and the Camerons there was great friendship, owing to the kindly attitude of old Alan M'Connel at the time of their greatest calamity. Old Alan's son, another Alan, married, in 1666, Jean M'Gregor, sister of the laird of M'Gregor. Drummond of Balhaldy, Lochiel's son-in-law, was really a M'Gregor, and afterwards claimed to be chief. M'Gregor of Boro brought up a party after Killiecrankie; a Colonel Donald M'Gregor signs the bond of the Highland chiefs after the Dunkeld affair, and promises to bring 100 men. The original seat of the clan was Glenorchy. There were many septs of the clan. Their force in 1745 was 790 men, but at the time of our author the clan was proscribed and scattered. Their possessions lay mostly at this time in the Lennox.

[3] The Macnabs were an independent clan settled in the heart of Campbell possessions, but generally opposed to their politics. The line of their chiefs has now become extinct, and their property is in possession of the Breadalbane family. The clan is one of those said to be descended from Kenneth Macalpine. They followed Lorn in opposition to Bruce, and consequently suffered much in their possessions. The barony of Bowain in Glendochard was their chief property.—Skene's *Highland Clans*, chap. viii. In 1677 the property was held by a tutor called the tutor of Macnab. I notice the signature of Finlaio Maknab of Powayne as witness to a deed of 1497.

[4] The Cowals here given, as under the Lennox tribe, I suppose to be the Macaulays. Duncan Fasselane who succeeded to the earldom of Lennox was supposed to be a link between Aulay and Lennox. They were of clan Alpine, and united in friendship and blood with the M'Gregors of Glenstray, whose misfortunes they would have shared had they not had the protection of the Earls of Lennox. The chief property was Ardincaple.

[5] Gibbons. There was a sept of Camerons called M'Gillery (Gilbertson or Gibson) who may have followed the standard of the chief from a distant property. Charles M'Gillery, the ancestor of the tribe, was killed in one of the many tribal battles which eventually brought about the great combat

Ecce satellitio circumdatus undique denso
Aequoreis procul a scopulis, et littore Mullae,
Magnanimo cum fratre venit Dowartius heros
Belliger, antiqui proles generosa Cleani,
Nobile par fratrum, prisci duo lumina Scoti

Lo, then, surrounded on every side by a dense following from the distant isles of the sea and the shores of Mull comes the warlike hero of Duart,[1] with his great-souled brother, the noble offspring of the ancient house of Maclean, a noble pair, two illustrious lights of the old Scottish race, like the double star

---

on Perth Inch. The reference, however, is probably to the M'Gibbons of the Lennox.

Glendessary seems to have had all these under his command. Charles Stewart in his evidence says that John Cameron of Glendessary was called Lieut.-Colonel to Lochiel, which answers to the position our author gives him. The special rite for unfurling the banner would be of interest.

[1] Sir John Maclean of Duart. He was only nineteen at this time. Several witnesses refer to the personal grace of this young chief—speaking of him as 'a well-favoured handsome young man.' Baldaldy says of him, 'There was a natural vivacity and politeness in his manner, which he afterwards much improved by a courtly education, and as his person was well made and graceful, so he took care to set it off by all the ornaments and luxury of dress. He was of a sweet temper, and good-natured; his wit lively and sparkling, and his humour pleasant and facetious. He loved books, and acquired the languages with great facility, whereby he cultivated and enriched his understanding with all manner of learning, but especially the belles-lettres.' He joined Dundee with a portion of his force in Lochaber. After Killiecrankie, where he and the Macleans greatly distinguished themselves, he continued to adhere to the Jacobite cause, and maintained himself in independence in Mull till after the Massacre of Glencoe, when he petitioned for a safe-conduct to Flanders or to England, that he might 'throw himself at the king's feet.' This was granted on condition of his conveying his house, *i.e.* Duart Castle, to Argyll. This he did, and on going to England he was received into great favour by Queen Mary, who had a 'warm side to all her father's friends.' He was the only man of his party who went to court, and he was frequently distinguished by special marks of royal favour. This favour from the Queen somewhat surprised William, and he gave him a commission, very much because of this singular attention on the part of Her Majesty. He became a favourite with William, but after the battle of Landen, in which the French were victorious, Duart was missing, to William's grief, but turned up at the Court of St. Germains. William, who was about to settle the disputed estates upon him, and to clear off Argyll's claims, at once conveyed them to Argyll. He became a favourite at St. Germains, and Lord Lovat claimed his interest as his cousin, when he was received with suspicion there. He fought in the centre of the first line at Sheriffmuir, and escaped abroad after the failure of the enterprise of 1715.

Inclyta, Tyndareo geminum ceu sidus ab ovo.
Ambo elati animis, titulis et equestribus ambo
Conspicui, Geticique insignes laude Gradivi.
Clarus in Abriacis frater Dowartius armis
Provehitur Scythica nive candidiore caballo
Coccineo fulgens sagulo, minioque rubentem
Pictus acu Phrygia tunicam conspectior ibat
Ante aciem, ferroque rigens, et squameus auro.
Atque una insignis plumato casside frater
Ibat Alexander, Tyrioque superbus in ostro
Horrebat rutilis toto velamine squamis;
Quem sonipes maculis subvectat discolor albis,
Ardua gramineo glomerans vestigia campo.

of the Tyndaridæ. Both of exalted spirit, both of knightly rank, and distinguished in the Hungarian war. Duart, the chief, famous in Highland wars, is borne on a steed whiter than Scythian snow,[1] and shines in scarlet. He moved conspicuous before his line in a tunic dyed red, and embroidered with Phrygian needle, stiff with steel, and scaly with gold. His brother Alexander[2] also moved conspicuous in helm with single plume, superb in Tyrian purple, his whole vesture stiff with scales of gold. A piebald steed, flecked with white, carries him, prancing over the plain. The

---

[1] The author gives these heroes the white horses of Castor and Pollux, but there is sufficient variety in the piebald to indicate that he speaks historically. He is not historical however in bringing these chiefs together on this occasion, but as a poet he is entitled so to present them to us.

[2] Sir Alexander Maclean, said to be of Otter, 'commisar of Argyle,' is called cousin by Sir John, which was no doubt the relationship. The Poet is anxious to work out his Castor and Pollux idea, and calls them brothers. He was the son of Bishop Maclean of the Isles. Dundee speaks of him in a letter to Macleod of Macleod, dated Moy, June 23d, 1689, as being with him 'all this while.' He met Dundee at Keppoch on his return to Lochaber from the Strathspey and Edinglassie movement, and brought with him 200 men from Argyllshire, mostly men of Macdonald of Largie, whom Dundee kept with him till the march to Blair. He took an important position at Killiecrankie, and began the battle. He also seized the standard of M'Kay's army. In 1691 he was appointed to intercept the English ships of war approaching Inverlochy. He seems to have maintained his independence till he went abroad. Previous to the gathering in Lochaber he had gone to operate against Young in Kintyre, and against the Glasgow frigates in the waters about Islay and Jura. This accounts for his having a number of Largie's men with him. Largie himself joined in Lochaber, and his tutor was killed at Killiecrankie. The burial of the tutor of Largie was observed by the prisoners in Blair Castle.

Et chlamys aurato circumtegit efflua limbo
Sublimes amborum humeros, amboque citatis
Huc illuc vehebantur[1] equis, atque aere rigentes
Ostentant longe galeas, pariterque feruntur
Turbinis in morem, clypeisque micantia mittunt
Fulgura, quadrupedumque urgent calcaribus armos.
Ille animis hic mole ingens sublimis ab omni
Parte coruscat apex, et sideris instar uterque
Emicat, et celso capita alta ferebat Olympo.
Seu duo coniferae celsa de rupe cupressi
Aemula sidereo tollunt fastigia caelo.
Utque super tenues cedrus procera myricas
Surgit, et exiles superant arbusta genistas,
Et silvae frutices ; sic compar nobile fratrum
Grampiadum proceres, Fergusiadumque tribunos,
Pictaque peltigeri superemicat agmina Scoti.
Fratribus his socium sese Torlisquius acer
Addiderat, Batavis Martemque secutus in oris.

flowing plaid with yellow stripe covers the shoulders of both the brothers. Borne hither and thither on 'swift chargers, their helmets, stiff with brass, show from afar. Like the whirlwind they fly, and like lightning-flashes come the gleams of their shields, as they urge forward their steeds with the spur. That one great in spirit, this one in height, their lofty crests are seen in every direction, each bright as a star, each with head lifted to the sky. Or they are as two pines on the lofty rock, lifting their rival tops to the starry heavens. As the cedar surpasses the tamarisk, or as the vine excels the broom, and the trees the shrubs, so did this noble pair of brothers outshine the Grampian chiefs, and chieftains of the house of Fergus, and the gay hosts of the target-bearing Scots. To these brothers the brave Torloisk,[2] a soldier from the Batavian war, allied himself. Coll[3] too, is here, and other chiefs of the clan

---

[1] Vectantur?

[2] Macleans of Torloisk—a property in Mull. A Lachlane Maclean of Torloisk would seem to have been the principal enemy of Sir Duncan Campbell of Auchinbreck, as he is mentioned first in that gentleman's 'petition for himself and his distrest friends,' for compensation for the depredations caused by the Macleans and others. See *Acts Parl. Scot.*, App. vol. ix. p. 44, and Note on MacNeill of Barra. This Lachlane was dead in 1690, and may have been killed at Killiecrankie.

[3] The Macleans of Coll were an ancient and powerful branch of the family. John, son of Lachlan Maclean of Coll, witnesses a charter of the Earl of Ross,

Colus adest, proceresque alii de gente Cleani,
Quos longum memorare fovet, quosque ordine longo
Mille manus juvenum post intervalla sequuntur,
Compositae in turmas, humeris quibus arma secures
Fortibus aptantur, validisque hastilia dextris.
Signaque cyaneo coelos imitata colore
Sparsa volant, geminique levant vexilla dracones.

Maclean, whom it would take long to name. These, in long order, a band of a thousand youths follows at intervals, formed into companies, on whose stalwart shoulders rests the battle-axe, and in their strong right hands the spear. Ensigns, blue as the heavens, float out on the breeze, and the Twins[1] as leaders uplift the standards. These men do not go into battle attacking the

---

Lord of the Isles in 1449. In 1626 I find Maclean of Coll required 'to search, seek, and take all and sundrie Jesuits repairing to his bounds, and to make open doors, and use his majesties;keys.' The island is ten miles long—has many remains of religious buildings, and the old castle with some tombs of the family.

The Macleans mustered 1000 strong, coming up, as the Poet says, after intervals. The Morven Macleans arrived first under Maclean of Ardgour. Then came Lochbuy with 200 men, who joined Dundee on the Spey, as he was retiring from Edinglassie. The brilliant skirmish of Knockbrecht covered him with glory, and much of material gain besides. Later on came Sir Alexander, accompanied by Macdonald of Largie, who joined at Keppoch with 200 more. Macleans of Coll and Torloisk formed companies in the force. The clan was in much greater strength here than at any other rising—from 500 to 800 men being their rating. They are supposed to have belonged originally to Moray, and to have been transplanted to Argyllshire by Malcolm IV. The first of the family with a name that has come down, according to Skene, was Gilleon, surnamed ni tuoidh from his battle-axe. In 1296 Ragman's Roll bears the name of Gillemore Macilean, who is supposed to be the ancestor of the Macleans. John MacGillimore in Bruce's time had two sons, Lachlan Lubanich, the predecessor of the house of Duart, and Eachin Reganich, the predecessor of the family of Lochbuy. For much interesting matter connected with the clan see Skene, *Highland Clans*, chap. vii. 'Red Hector of the battles,' the Lochbuy chief, was second in command at Harlaw, and died by the hand of Irvine of Drum, whom he also slew.

Before the 12th of July 1689 'Murdoch Maclean, younger of Lochbuy, had fallen into the hands of Sir Hugh Campbell of Cawdor, who is required to bring over his person (from Islay, I presume) to Edinburgh betwixt that date and the 1st day of August, to be disposed of by the Government as they shall think fit.' *Thanes of Cawdor*, p. 379.

[1] 'Gemini levant vexilla dracones.' 'Draconarius is a standard-bearer, and I presume that 'dracones' is here used poetically for the bearer of the 'draco,' and the Gemini are the standard lifters, Castor and Pollux being still the idea; or take 'dracones' in apposition to 'vexilla.' I do not know whether the Macleans ever carried dragons on their banners, as Napier suggests by his translation.

Non illi jaculis longe fallentibus hostem
Aggressi pugnas ineunt, sed cominus ense
Stricto bella gerunt, nunquam statione relicta
Terga inhonesta dabant victi, sed fortiter isto
Quo steterant cecidere loco, vitamque perosi
Indecorem pro Rege alacres in bella ruebant.
   Turba minor procerum cinctu conspecta Gabino
Insequitur, campoque ruit chlamydata juventus
Cognatos stipata duces; nunquam agmine tanto
Tot diversae acies, habituque armisque tremendae,
Undique complerunt campos. Gens cardine nusquam
Subjacet Arctoo quae non in proelia fortem
Juverit auxilio Gramum. Nunc ultima Thule,
Thule[1] Caledonio circumvallata profundo,
Gens et hyperboreis quaecunque trionibus alget
Intulit Abriacis chlamydata examina castris.
Omnis et occiduum, quaeque aspicit insula solem
Surgentem, refluo quaeque undique cingitur aestu
Tetheos,[2] Oceanum supraque infraque Britannum

enemy from a distance with erring bolts, but hand to hand with the drawn sword they make their war, and, if conquered, they never turn their backs, dishonoured, from a post deserted, but there, bravely, where they stand they fall, abhorring life without honour. Eagerly for their king they rushed to battle.
   A lesser band of chiefs, conspicuous in Gabinian toga,[3] follows, and a plaided company, under kindred leaders, rushes to the field. Never did a host so varied in aspect, so terrible in arms and habit, take the field. There lay no clan beneath the Northern sky which brought not aid for the struggle to the bold Graham. Now Ultima Thule walled in by Northern Scottish seas, and the races chilled under the Northern Wain, send their plaided swarms into Lochaber. The isles which see at once the setting and the rising sun, and are surrounded on every side by the flowing tide of the ocean, those within and without the British seas, sent forward their patriot bands to the war. Now

---

   [1] False quantity.

   [2] The original, and most of the copies, have here and elsewhere 'Tytheos' pronounced by a critic a *vox nihili*.

   [3] The 'cinctus Gabinus,' a peculiar mode of wearing the toga at Rome derived from Gabii in Latium. It was brought over the head and girded round the body. Here the reference is to the belted plaid. See Ramsay's *Roman Antiquities,* and Virg. *Aen.* vii. 612.

Ora omnis patrias accivit in arma catervas.
Jamque maris per claustra volant, perque invia tendunt
Praecipites, panduntque viam per saxa per undas.
Non juga perpetuis boreae tumulata pruinis,
Flumina non ruptas late exundantia ripas
Horrida nec subitis elisa tonitrua nimbis,
Aeternusque rigor coeli cohibere feroces
Tot poterant populos, pelagi non caeca profundi
Stagna tenent, longo non obstitit obice pontus.
Illos nubiferae vastis non mollibus Alpes
Impediunt, adamante licet via durior omni
Invia nulla viris, cum Jupiter indidit altae
Virtutis stimulos, et gloria spondet honores.
Ergo Caledoniae variis ex partibus orae
Turba ducum, pulchra pro libertate ruebant
In bellum: primusque Stuartus Apinius acer

over the trackless deep they speed headlong, and over mountain and flood. Not the mountain tops heaped with perpetual snow, not the rivers bursting their banks, not the dread thunder crashing in sudden tempest, nor the eternal severity of the clime, can hold back these fierce races. The dark depths of the deepest sea cannot restrain them, nor can its measureless extent. The cloud-clapped mountains with their rugged wilds, though harder than adamant, are no hindrance. The way is not pathless to men in whom Jove has implanted the pricks of lofty virtue, and to whom glory promises her honours. Therefore, from the various regions of the Scottish coast there gathered to the war for fair liberty a band of noble leaders. And first brave Stewart[1] of Appin prepares his arms, and, with the whole

---

[1] Robert Stewart of Appin was only a lad at this time. He hurried from college to join his clansmen, who were under the command of the Tutor of Appin, John Stewart of Ardsheal. Lochiel had been energetic in preparing the clans for the rising, and had visited Appin, meeting with Ardsheal and Ballachulish, and spending the night with the last-named Stewart. They were all on the alert, and the clan was one of the first to join Dundee, under its chief and his Tutor. At Killiecrankie, the chief, with 130 men, took part in the battle, Ballachulish, his kinsman, being wounded there. John Stewart of Ardsheal came up with the rest of the force, about 200 men, two days after the battle, and marched to Dunkeld, where his brother Alexander was killed in the attack on the Cathedral. The young chief, Robert Stewart, succeeded his uncle, Duncan Stewart, in the position as head of the clan in 1685. Duncan had been out with Montrose, had taken a prominent part in the battle of Inverlochy, and had been faithful to that commander throughout his career. Robert was no less faithful to his principles, and only escaped the fate of his neighbours

Arma parat, totaque instructa gente clientum
Littora piscosae contermina linquit Iernae,
Caerula signa ferens croceis distincta figuris.
Quem funesta viri bis centum in bella secuti
Omnes sublimes immani corpore et armis,

body of his clansmen, he leaves the shores bordering Leven, rich in fish, carrying blue banners, charged with yellow figures. Him two hundred men follow to dread war, all of them tall, terrible in form and in arms, and wearing on their lofty heads fur bonnets.

---

of Glencoe by making submission at the last hour. In 1714 he was summoned to Edinburgh to give security for his good behaviour. He did not go, but, instead, he and his clansmen busied themselves in making new targets. Campbell, who held the castle of Stalkair, reported that the Stewarts were preparing 'eighty more targets in addition to the great number they already had.' On the 27th August 1715 he attended the famous hunting on the Braes of Mar, which ended in Sheriffmuir, and in the attainder and flight of the Appin chief. He was still living in 1730, but had died before 1739. He married first a daughter of MacLeod of MacLeod, and second a daughter of Campbell of Lochnell. A son, Dugald, succeeded him, and he left daughters married to MacLachlan of MacLachlan, and to Alexander M'Donald of Glencoe.

John Stewart, the leader of the clan on the occasion of the rising in 1689, was a brave and skilful commander. He took the castle of Eilean Stalkair, and held it for King James against the forces of Argyll till October 1690, when he capitulated on very honourable terms. Colonel Hill, governor of Inverlochy, writing in May 1690 to Menzies, the laird of Weem, enjoins him 'to be strict with the Tutor of Appin, as he might be apt to be blowne up with stories, and might think to stand out still.'

The Stewarts of Appin are descended from the Norman stock of Fitzallan, and from the common stock whence came the Royal Stuarts. Skene says they are descended from the Stewart Lords of Lorne, through the illegitimate son of Sir John Stewart, last Lord of Lorne. The historians of the family seek to remove the bar sinister, and maintain that Sir John brought home the mother of his son Dugald—she was a MacLaren of Ardveich—with much ceremony, and was proceeding to the chapel of his castle for the marriage, when he was stabbed by a M'Dougall of Lorne. Young Dugald was about to pursue the murderer, when the wise priest of the family showed him there was a matter of more importance in hand, viz., the using of the few remaining moments of Sir John's life for the marriage. Sir John was able to take the MacLaren to wife, and to put the ring on her finger, before he died. Dugald was thus made heir to the small kingdom of Lorne. All, however, that he was able to hold of it was Appin, which he did successfully, and he avenged the death of his father by slaying his murderer. The chief descendants are the families of Ardsheal, Ballachulish, Invernahyle, and Fasnacloich. The colours borne by the Stewarts at the rising were referred to by witnesses in the forfeiture of Dundee, as well as by our Poet. It is curious that almost the only flag of the Highland clans that escaped from Culloden was the Stewart banner, which the bearer tore from the pole and wrapped round his body. It is now in the possession of the representative of

Nec non villosis tecti capita alta galeris.
Ipse inter medios ingenti mole Stuartus
Cum nondum flava lanugine vestiit ambas
Prima juventa genas, patrii dux agminis ibat
Cum patruis, totamque trahens in praelia gentem
Arduus ingreditur florenti milite campum.
Jam quoque belligeri proles praeclara Nigelli
Ibat ab aequoreae sinuoso littore Barae.

Stewart himself, in their midst, is of great stature, and though so young, that the yellow down does not yet cover his cheeks, he went forth, the leader (with his uncle) of his 'father's clan, and carrying with him its whole strength. Grandly he advances into the camp with his splendid force. Now, also, the illustrious son of warlike MacNeill[1] comes from the winding shore of Barra's isle,

the Ballachulish family. The helmet of the Stewart chief of our Poet is in the possession of Dugald Stewart of Lochcarron, as I gather from the work on the Stewarts of Appin, by John H. I. Stewart, F.S.A., and Lieut.-Colonel Duncan Stewart, late 92d Highlanders, privately printed by Maclachlan and Stewart, Edinburgh, 1880, from which work I have gathered most of the information in this note. See also Skene on *Highland Clans* and our Preface for further matter. The heraldry of the colours, as given by our author, requires the examination of an expert, for whose remarks see note at end of volume. The banner from Culloden is of blue silk, with a golden saltire. The authors of the above-named work claim the well-known tune called *Sheriffmuir* as the Stewart march.

The 'Ierna,' to which is attached the adjective ' piscosa,' I cannot identify. I have tried to read the original as *Levna*, and I believe that is what is meant, though it involves some violence towards the caligraphy of the author. Levna would, of course, be Loch Leven, which arm of the sea bounds the Appin lands. Loch Earn is far from the Appin lands, though the Stewarts and the maternal clan of MacLaren held property in Strathearn.

The clan was rated at 300 fighting men. The representatives of the various families still remain, but the lands have, for the most part, changed hands, very much through the loyalty of the clan to their kinsmen, the Royal Stuarts.

[1] MacNeill of Barra. His initial is R. in his subscription to the Bond and letters after Killiecrankie. Another MacNeill is Donald of Gallachallie, who is frequently referred to in the process of forfeiture evidence. In the petition of Sir Duncan Campbell of Auchinbreck—see Appendix to vol. ix. *Acts of Scot. Parliaments*, p. 45, this MacNeill is described as taking a very active part in the harrying of that gentleman's people and property, along with ' Lauchlane M'Laine of Torloisk, Lauchlane M'Laine of` Coll, M'Laine of Ardgour, M'Laine of Kinlochaline, M'Laine of Lochbuy, and their barbarous accomplices. They did, in the first place, hang Dugald M'Tavish, fiar of Dunardarie, and murdered Alexander Campbell of Strondour—the petitioner's uncle—and did wound above 20 of the souldiers of the garisone, and did carry off from the house of Carnasarie three score horse led of goods and plenishing, and then burnt it to ashes.' Lieutenant James Colt depones that he saw Donald Mac-

Quem circum juvenum patrii cognominis ingens
Turba secuta ducem dextra laevaque fremebat.
Ipse pedes sumpta spirans immane securi
Agmen agit, tyrioque humeros coopertus amictu
Emicat ingentes ingentior inter alumnos.
Tot chlamyde intextos ostentat et ille colores
Sole quot adverso curvata in nubibus iris.
Casside conspicuus rutila clypeoque coruscus

around whom, as their chief, a great company of the youth of his name presses on the right hand and on the left. Carrying his immense battle-axe he advances on foot, panting as he goes, leading his tall clansmen, himself the tallest, and his shoulders covered with a Tyrian mantle. He displays as many colours woven into his plaid as the rainbow in the clouds shows in the sunlight. Conspicuous with his gleaming helmet and flashing shield

---

Neill with his sword upon him at Mull, after the engagement at Dunkeld, and that he went in company with the Laird of MacLean when he brought the Lairds of Blair and Pollock from the isle of Carnburg to Dowart Castle. The chief of Barra does not come so prominently into the evidence as Donald of Gallachallie, but Claverhouse mentions him in his letter to MacLeod, dated Moy, June 23d, 1689. According to Skene, the family appears first in 1310, and had become a powerful clan by 1410, and held property in Knapdale, with the custody of Castle Swen. The family of Barra seems to have originated in the marriage of a MacNeill with a MacLean, who brought the distant island to the MacNeill. The Lord of the Isles gives a charter of it in 1427 to Gilleonan MacNeill. The family of Gigha appears in 1478, but it would seem from Skene that the chiefship lay still with the people of Castle Swen. The property on the mainland passed to the Macmillans, probably by the last of the Castle Swen family being a female, and marrying a Macmillan. Both Barra and Gigha claimed the chiefship after this, and Mr. Skene inclines to yield it to Barra, but Burke gives it to the Gigha family, which has descendants.

The island of Barra derives its name from St. Finbar of Cork, and the ruins of a chapel dedicated to him are still found on the island. There are several other ecclesiastical remains, and the burial-place of the MacNeills is within one of the churches. See Muir's *Ecclesiological Notes*, p. 282. Martin, as quoted by Muir, says, 'The natives have St. Barr's wooden Image standing on the altar covered with linen in form of a shirt: all their greatest asseverations are by this saint.' The image would not stay in the first church built for it, but was invisibly transported to the place where the people were obliged to build 'the present church.' For a description of this island in 1580 or thereabout see the exceedingly interesting 'Description of the Isles of Scotland' printed as an appendix to Skene's *Celtic Scotland*, and supposed by him to be an official report intended for the use of James VI., who was preparing to attempt the improvement of the Isles.

Ante aciem longe effulget,[1] Martemque lacessit.
  Quin etiam extremae properabat ab aequore Rarsae
Acer in egregiis Malcolmi filius armis,
Insignem ducens juvenum longo ordine turmam
Aere coruscantem, atque humeris gravia arma ferentem.
Quorum pennigeris surgunt capita ardua cristis,
Atque humeros succincta chlamys circumdedit altos,

he shone in front of his line, and roused them to martial ardour.

Here also from the distant shores of Raasay hastens, in striking arms, the bold son of Malcolm,[2] leading in long line a noble band of clansmen, gleaming in brass, and bearing on their shoulders their heavy weapons. With plumed heads erect, and shoulders

---

[1] *Var. lect.* effulgit.

[2] Malcolm, or Makgillichallum, *i.e.* Macleod of Raasay. I am not able to supply any additional information concerning this chief to that given in the text. The Macleods of Raasay belonged to the Lewis branch of that family, and, till lately, possessed the island, which has now passed out of their hands. The clan Macleod, and the clan Campbell, would seem to have had the same origin in the old earldom of Garmoran, and their chief possessions at first appear to have been Glenelg and Harris, and afterwards Dunvegan in Skye. At an early period a younger son gained possessions in Lewis, and Raasay was a cadet of that house. The force which the Macleods could bring into the field was estimated in 1704 at 700, in 1715 at 1000, but in 1745 again at 700. In the earlier civil war they distinguished themselves, and at the battle of Worcester were dreadfully cut to pieces, but few of them making their way home. The head of the clan was, and is, Macleod of Macleod. See the extremely interesting letter of Dundee to the Laird of Macleod, dated Moy, June 23, 1689, in 'Letters of Viscount Dundee,' collected by C. Kirkpatrick Sharpe, and edited by George Smythe, for the Bannatyne Club. The reader is requested to study for himself the Latin describing the garments and accoutrements of Raasay. I have not ventured to go beyond the Latin, but doubtless we have here the belted plaid, forming a kilt as well as a covering for the shoulders, the hose and garters, and probably an outer cloak of the skins of wild animals, after the manner of Hercules. The snake on his crest I leave with the heralds.

In the 'Description of the Isles of Scotland' referred to in previous note, 'Raarsa' is said ' to pertain to the Bishop of the Isles, and to be occupiet and possest be ane gentleman of M'Cloyd Lewis kin, callit clan Gillechallum of Raarsa. He hes ane strang little castell in this Ile, biggit on the heid of ane heich Craig, and is callit Prokill. It is but 8 merk land, and will raise 80 men. It pays yearly to the Bishop 16 merks, but to the captain thereof it payis of sundrie tributes better nor 500 merks. There is na woods, but great heich craigis in this Ile. It is commodious for corn and all kinds of bestiall, and chieflie horses.'

Et tunica ex corio latus ambit utrumque bovino.
Hi jaculis gravidam gestant de more pharetram,
Fulmineumque ensem, fulgentemque aere securem.
Cunctique oblongis protecti corpora scutis
Ibant, a teneris assueti gnaviter annis
Saxa super nudis vestigia ponere plantis.
Et dociles tolerare famem, perferre labores,
Morborum ignari, vitamque in longa trahentes,
Saecula centenos implent feliciter annos.
Rarsius Abriacis nulli cessurus in armis
Belliger et mira membrorum mole superbus
Emicat, et cunctis ingentior ibat alumnis.
Ille manu taurum potuit retinere furentem
Atque pedum plantis cervos anteire fugaces
Cornipedemque cito solitus praevertere cursu.
Cui pharetra ex humero pendebat, et aereus ensis
A femore, atque ambas cingebant vincula suras,
Et picturato circumdata crura cothurno.
Cuique pedum crudus texit vestigia pero,
Substrinxitque ingens discinctum balteus inguen,
Et chlamys immanes velamine vestiit artus,
Aurataque minax in casside sibilat anguis.
Jamque ferox torvis obtutibus ora ferebat,

covered with girded plaid, they advance. A tunic of ox hide covers their bodies. According to their custom they carry quivers full of arrows, the flashing sword and the axe shining with brass. They all advance protected by oblong shields. From their tender years these men are accustomed, with naked feet, to traverse the rocks, and patiently to bear hunger, to endure fatigue, free from disease, drawing out their life to great length, they attain happily a hundred years. The warlike Raasay himself would yield to none in the camp of Lochaber, and superb in the mighty mould of his limbs he heads his clan, higher than them all. He could hold back the wild bull in his grasp, outstrip the flying deer in fleetness of foot, and turn the steed in its swift course. From his shoulder hung a quiver, and on his thigh a brazen-hilted sword. Garters went round both calves, and the tartan hose enclose his legs. Raw hide covers his feet, a broad belt girds his loose garment at the waist, while a plaid clothes his brawny limbs, and a threatening snake hisses from his gilded crest. Now fierce with sullen gaze he shows his face, and savagely on

Turbidaque ingenti rotat undique lumina gyro
Horridus, hirsutisque minax in fronte capillis,
Herculeoque humeros circumvestitus amictu
Sic ut erat tota circumsistente caterva
Grampica magnifico subiit tentoria plausu.
  Jamque aderat patriis Herichae convallis ab arvis
Fraseria de gente satus natalibus amplis
Foyrius, arctois quo clarior alter in oris
Non erat, aut sumptis quisquam praestantior armis.
Ille audax animi nutat dum incerta futuri

every side he casts his rolling eyes in a great circle, while his brow with its shaggy locks seems to threaten. His shoulders have a covering fit for Hercules. Thus he stood, and with his whole band accompanying him he advanced amidst the Grampian tents with mighty applause.

And now approached from the paternal fields of Stratherrick, with many clansmen, Foyers,[1] sprung from the Fraser clan, than whom there was none more illustrious in Northern land, nor any excelling him in arms. He, bold in spirit, while the house of

---

[1] I suppose this to be William Fraser of Foyers, who, soon after 1696, signs the address of Thomas of Beaufort to Argyll, putting favourably the conduct of Simon, in the matter of the forcible marriage of the Dowager Lady Lovat, and the carrying off of Lord Saltoun.

I do not know whether he be the same as the Foyers whom Simon, in his letter of 21st March 1740 to Inverallochy, associates with Struy, and calls them two idiots. In a letter the next year he says that Foyers is faithful to him. Our Fraser of Foyers can scarcely be he who, in 1744, seeing, from the gallery of the court-house in Inverness, his chief insulted by Lord Fortrose, jumped into the assemblage, cocked his pistol, and presented it at Lord Fortrose. His Lordship would have been killed had not a gentleman thrown his plaid over the pistol. See Spalding Club *Miscellany*, vol. ii., *Preface and Letters of Lord Lovat*.

Our Foyers was evidently a 'brisk Highlander' in 1689, being the captain of the rearguard out of Lochaber, and trusted with the pursuit of Mackay from Balveny towards the Bogie. He must also have been a soldier of some experience to have had such a charge, and it is probable he was the predecessor of the Foyers mentioned by Lord Lovat, and not the man himself.

His name does not appear in the Proclamations, or in the forfeiture evidence, which may have been due to the danger of meddling with the clan, when the chief was still undecided.

The family of Foyers is said to have sprung, with eighteen others in Strath Errick, from Hutcheon Franchal, an illegimate son of Hugh, third Lord Lovat.

Simon Fraser was the representative of the family in 1825, but who represents it now I do not know.

SCOTI GRAMEIDOS LIB. IV.

Fraseridum domus, atque invito principe gentis
Secum in bella suos vocat alta voce clientes.
Regis amore pii, pulchraque cupidine laudis
Succensus ruit in bellum, quassatque comantem

Fraser wavers in uncertainty as to its future line, and the lord [1] of the clan himself is unwilling to move, he calls his own men with bold voice to follow him to the field. Fired with the love of a pious King, and the honourable thirst for glory, he rushes to the war. He tosses as he goes the streaming hair-plume of his

---

[1] Hugh, Lord Lovat, was the chief of the House of Fraser at this time. He was born 28th Sept. 1666, and succeeded his father, Hugh, tenth Lord, in 1688. From a large black spot on his lip he was called Mac Shime Bal-dù. John Anderson, in his History of the family, Edinburgh 1825, notes as a curiosity three chiefs of clans named from physical blemishes at this time, besides Lovat, viz., black-eyed Mackenzie, squint-eyed Macintosh, crooked-eyed Chisholm. This historian is not at one with our Poet as to the uncertainty of the line of this Lord. He says, 'the marshalling of his followers under Dundee is the only public scene Lord Lovat seems to have engaged in.' According to him also a Fraser, closer to the head of the house than Foyers or Culduthil, was out with Dundee, viz., Alexander, eldest son of Thomas of Beaufort, and brother of the notorious Simon. Thomas of Beaufort was the natural successor of Hugh on failure of heirs-male. Alexander dying without heirs, Simon succeeded his brother as Master of Lovat, and became Lord Lovat. This Alexander, the heir of the house, says Anderson, raised the standard for James with Dundee, and was one of the first to join him. The Acts of Parliament bear out our author as to the hesitation of Hugh, eleventh Lord Lovat. He would seem to have been present at the meeting of Parliament in 1689, and was appointed with Seaforth to raise 500 horse. He was present also in 1690, but fined for non-attendance in 1693, and took the oath on May 22d, 1695. He married Amelia Murray, only daughter of the Marquis of Atholl. He had two sons who died before him, Hugh, born 1690, and John, 1695, and four daughters. The husband (or father-in-law, for it is not clear which is meant, but both father and son were of the same character) of Amelia, the eldest daughter, was Alexander Mackenzie of Prestonhall, of whom it was said

> 'Some do compare him to an eel—
> Should mortal man be made of steel?'

His dying without surviving male issue made room for the Beaufort family, and brought about the efforts of Tullibardine to change the succession, and the extraordinary conduct of Simon, resulting in the condemnation for high-treason, etc. etc., of himself and nineteen other persons. He was afterwards pardoned, but came to the block eventually. See *Historical Account of the Family of Fraser*, by John Anderson, Edinburgh, 1825; *Culloden Papers*, London, 1815, and papers referred to there, p. 24; *Miscellany of Spalding Club*, vol. ii., letters of Lord Lovat.

Incessu galeam, et clypeo septemplice septus,
Telum immane manu, atque humeris gravia arma ferebat,
Ingentesque animos ingenti in corpore versans,
Ingreditur magno castra exultantia motu.
Inde locum juxtaque tenens Kilduthlius ibat,
Bellantum cinctus juvenum florente caterva,
Totus et aere rigens, ferroque auroque renidens.
Cinxerat ense latus, valida thorace lacertos,
Loricaque humeros, taurino tegmine suras,
Fertque super galeam viridantis vimina taxi.
Undique ferratis et nunc circumdatus armis
Castra petit magni signis fulgentia Grami.
His quoque se comitem Morisina ex valle ferebat
Grantius egregius bello, non degener ille

helmet, and fenced with a sevenfold shield he bears a mighty weapon in his hand, and heavy armour on his shoulder. His was a great mind in a great body, and he moved into the exulting camp with grand stride. Holding the place next him came Culduthil,[1] surrounded by the flower of his warriors. All stiff with brass, and shining with steel and gold, his sword girt his side, the mail coat his body, while the bull's hide clothed his legs. He bore upon his helm a sprig of the green yew. Now armed at every point he seeks with his standards the brilliant camp of the great Graham. With them also, from Glenmoriston, came as their companion in the war, the valiant Grant;[2]

---

[1] Fraser of Culduthil. I have not come on any details concerning this Cavalier.

The family is descended from John Fresall of Farlyne, who married Katharine Rose of Kilravock in 1529. He fell at the battle of Loch Lochy 1544, leaving three sons, the youngest a posthumous child, called James. From James descended the Frasers of Culduthill. The property was in their hands till lately.

[2] This is John Grant, younger of Glenmoriston, called Ian-a-Chragain. He was still a minor at Killiecrankie. The family traditions speak of his path in the battle as to be traced in after years on the field by the greenness of the sod, but Glengarry and the Chamberlain of Glenmoriston—a famous man in the family—get a share in the credit of this enriching of the soil. His mother was a Fraser, and his joining with Foyers and Culduthil would be natural both from locality and from family connection. His father, who lived till 1703, was also a John Grant, but surnamed Donn, *i.e.* the brown-haired. I find him parting with some land to the laird of Grant a few years after this date, the necessity doubtless arising from the expense and failure of this expedition of his son. He probably gained the aid of his powerful kinsman, the despised owner of Belcastle, for his escape from the list of attainted persons. It would seem that the Laird of

Grantiades Balli dictus de nomine castri,
Qui Batavi partes praedonis, et arma secutus

not that degenerate Grant who takes his name from Bala

Grant got a recommendation from the Estates for the making good of his losses in Urquhart as well as in Strathspey, and he claims the return of rents of Urquhart, of which he had been deprived from 1689 to 1693. The castle of Urquhart, too, had been much injured by King William's soldiers, and he claims for that. Whether the Laird of Grant had thrown his plaid round Glenmoriston, and saved him from the fate of the other gentlemen out in 1689, and at the same time gathered some of the lands under his own name, I do not know. Balhaldy says the enemy were so enraged against Glenmoriston that they burnt his own seat to the ground, plundered his people, and made such horrible devastations that the poor gentleman was obliged to offer some proposals of submission. He got a safe-conduct to Edinburgh to plead his cause. Glenmoriston is said to have taken out 150 men with him.

Ian Donn would seem to be the same man who, in 1664, carried off the Laird of Inches bodily into the Highlands, that he might effect by violence 'what friends,' says John Forbes of Culloden, 'could easily have persuaded Inches to have given.' See *Thanes of Cawdor*, pp. 317-18. He got remission for this deed, but was afterwards charged with instigating the mutilation of a Robert Anderson in 1683, who sought the intervention of David Forbes and the Laird of Calder, 'in order to the getting some small acknowledgment for his little finger.' —*Thanes of Cawdor*, pp. 364-5. The following reference,—somewhat involved —appears also at p. 403, in a letter of Colin Campbell of Boghole to Sir Hugh of Cawdor, dated 1705 : 'Only one thing that ye omitted that I see nothing to discourage you from adjudging Glenmoriston's whole estate, etc., which I think may utterly defeat all former ones ; if it is not yet that Glenmoriston might cancel Inches' disposition to him, and take a new disposition in a trustee's name, and, considering the temper of that two-footed, limping animal, it's to be feared a tempting bait would make him yield.'

Ian-a-Chragain took part in the skirmish of Cromdale, and fought alongside of Glengarry at Sheriffmuir, whom he materially assisted, if the family tale be true, under the very embarrassing circumstance of the giving way of the belt which held up his trews. One can fancy even a great Highland chief tried, in the presence of an active and numerous enemy, by the entanglement resulting from such an accident. However, Ian-a-Chragain was at hand, and by ridding Glengarry of his foes by a few well-directed blows, gained time for the important adjustment of the garment of the aged chieftain.

The estates were sequestrated and remained crown property till 1732, when they were sold by auction, and purchased by Sir Ludovic Colquhoun of Luss, afterwards Sir Ludovic Grant of Grant, for £1200, through whose good offices they were eventually restored to the family.

Ian-a-Chragain was twice married, his second wife being one of the eleven daughters of Sir Ewen Cameron of Lochiel. She survived her husband, and died in 1759 at the age of eighty, leaving behind her no fewer than 200 descendants. The following obituary notice is from the *Scots Magazine* of that year: 'Died at Invermoriston, in the eightieth year of her age, Janet Cameron, daughter of Sir

Sustulit Auriaci vexilla nefanda tyranni.
Ille sed incoctum[1] fido qui gestat honestum
Pectore, Caesareos Urquhartius acer in hostes.
Magnorum usque adeo mores imitatus avorum
Corripit arma manu, Regi inconcussus acerbis
Temporibus laturus opem, perque invia montes
Scandit inaccessos, magnoque in bella paratu
Arduus agmen agens graditur, quem Grantia pubes
Ordine servato ductorem in castra secuta est.

Castle,[2] and who was following the party and the army of the Batavian robber, and was upholding the nefarious standard of the Dutch tyrant; but the bold Grant of Urquhart, bearing unstained honour in a faithful breast, and keen against the foes of the Caesar. He, following the ways of his great ancestors, took arms, and, undeterred by the misfortunes of the time, he contributed his help to his King. Through pathless tracts he climbs precipitous mountains with great equipment for the war. Tall in stature, he advances, leading his line, and there follows him, into the camp, as their chief, the children of the Grant, all in good order.

Ewan Cameron of Lochiel, and relict of John Grant of Glenmoriston, Esquire, to whom she bore ten sons and five daughters. By these, who were all married, there were about 200 persons descended of her own body, most of whom were present at her funeral. Her corpse was carried to the churchyard by her children, grandchildren, great-grandchildren, and great-great-grandchildren.'

The family is now, I believe, represented by the fourteenth Laird, Ian Robert James Murray Grant, born 1860, and succeeding his grandfather in 1868.

The shield and sword with which Ian-a-Chragain fought at Killiecrankie are still preserved at Invermoriston House. See *The Grants of Glenmoriston*, by Rev. A. Sinclair.

The outlawed Glenmoriston men in Prince Charlie's time, resisting in their poverty a bribe of £30,000, and faithfully discharging their trust in protecting the Prince, have contributed much to the true glory of their name. See in *Bishop Robert Forbes' Journal*, edited by Rev. J. B. Craven, p. 314·5, a touching account of one of these men, of whom a gentleman remarks that he was 'as damned a thief as ever was in the Highlands, but since he had the honour to have a hand in preserving his master in his greatest distress and dangers, no man dare say he has ever been guilty of a dirty or ungentlemanny action.'

[1] Cf. Persius, ii. 74: 'Incoctum generoso pectus honesto.'

[2] In the original it is difficult to say whether the word is Belli or Balli. I have ventured to print it Balli, because Castle Grant, which is the castrum alluded to, was formerly called Ballach Castle, or Bala Castle. Sometimes, however, the spelling is Bel Castle. The Grants of Ballach Castle, *i.e.* of Castle Grant, were thoroughgoing supporters of King William, and the mainstay of Mackay at this period; hence the disparaging remark 'non degener ille.'

Hos super Argadiae de rupibus advolat altis
Flos juvenum fidi Nauchtani filius audax.
Dundarous rutilis pariter conspectus in armis,
Egregiusque animi, tanto nec degener ortu,

Besides these, from the high rocks of Argyll, there hastens the flower of young men, Dunderaw,[1] the bold son of the faithful Macnachtan. As he is conspicuous in shining armour, so is he noble

---

[1] This young chief hailed from that interesting and picturesque castle, now in ruins, on Loch Fyne, a little above Inveraray, Dunderaw. His father, to whom allusion is made as in some way triumphing over his neighbour Argyll, was Sir Alexander Macnachtan, who distinguished himself very much in the civil wars, and was rewarded with a large pension and knighthood by Charles II. at the Restoration. He was a relative and great ally of Lochiel's, and a joint adventure of theirs is recorded in the Memoirs. Three English colonels, having been commissioned by General Monck to survey the state of garrisons in the Highlands, after inspecting Inveraray, were lodging for the night at a small inn in the neighbourhood. The colonels were very watchful, and there was no chance of approaching them by the door, as sentries were posted there. The weak point of their shelter was the roof, and the confederates, drawing their men secretly to the back of the house, where the ground rose nearly to the thatch, by a simultaneous effort, dislodged sufficient of the timbers to admit their party. In a moment they made prisoners of every person in the house, another moment saw them into a boat and off to Dunderaw with the three English colonels, and other persons of distinction, among whom was Lieut.-Colonel Duncan Campbell, a gentleman of their own acquaintance. The 'glory' alluded to, of in some way 'reducing the Campbell to the laws,' was evanescent, for the Macnachtan was soon obliged to join the ranks of the dependants of Argyll, and the loss of their estate some time afterwards through the operation of legal diligence, says Skene, reduced them still lower, until there was little left to them but the recollection of former greatness, which the ruins of various of their strongholds, and the general tradition of the country, would show not to be visionary.—Skene, *Highland Clans*, p. 204.

The clan would seem to have been originally of Moray descent, and to have been transported by Malcolm IV. to Strathtay. They had possessions very early, between Loch Fyne and Loch Awe, in the glens of Ara, Shira, and Glenfyne.

The laird described by our author is frequently referred to in the evidence of forfeiture, vol. ix., *Acts of Parl. Scot.*, and in the decreet he is condemned to death when apprehended, his name, fame, memory, and honours to be extinct, his blood tainted, etc. In the bond he undertakes to bring 50 men for the mutual defence of the Jacobite chiefs.

The last lineal descendant of the house would seem to have been the person noted on page 354 of the Abbotsford edition of the *Memoirs of Lochiel*, from which we have quoted. He filled the situation of Collector of Customs at Crail, about the middle of last century. Dr. James Macknight, the commentator, was understood to be of the clan, and the editor of the *Memoirs* is of the same family.

Nec genitore minor, fracti quem legibus olim
Gloria Campbelli famae late evehit alis.
Nec magnis minor ille atavis, nunc impiger ibat,
Subsidio Regi, pubemque in bella trahebat,
Servorumque globos, cognatorumque maniplos,
Quos piscosa palus nutrit, quosque arida misit
Dundaroae rupes, vicinaque rupibus ora.
Ipse etiam patriis ingens ciet agmen ab arvis
Natus Alexandri, nulli Mavorte secundus
Inter et Argadiae genuit quos terra rebellis
Lowpius heroes, Regi fidissimus unus,

in spirit, and worthy of his great origin. Nor is he inferior to his father, whom the glory of reducing the Campbell to the laws, raised high on the wings of fame. He, not less than his great ancestors, now readily brings his aid to the King, and leads to the war his clansmen, retainers, and kinsmen, those whom the finny lake[1] nourishes, and whom the bare rock of Dunderaw and its neighbouring shores sent forth. The hero, Loupe, was one most faithful to the King, among those whom the rebel land of Argyll begat. The mighty M'Alister,[2] second to none in warlike spirit, summons his clan from the paternal fields. He speeds

---

[1] The reference to the wealth of Loch Fyne in fish, at this date, is to be noted.

[2] Alexander M'Alister of Loupe was a faithful supporter of King James to the last. He was at Killiecrankie, and at Cromdale, and though losing faith in Buchan, yet with the remnant of his followers who escaped the slaughter in the latter fight, he passed over to Ireland, and took part in the battle of the Boyne. A painting of him is preserved at Kennox House, by the present representative of the family, Charles Somerville M'Alester of Kennox, Esquire, who tells me that he appears from the picture to have been a strong man, of a somewhat stern countenance. His expression is firm and determined, eyes dark brown, hair auburn, in ringlets. He wears a coat of mail, with necktie of old point lace. There is no helmet, sword, battle-axe, or target in the picture, which is considered a good specimen of the Dutch style. Mr. M'Alester informs me that his is the correct spelling of the name, and that Loupe should be Loup. It is now too late to change our spelling. He married Grace, daughter of Sir James Campbell of Auchinbreck, and had issue. The family is a very ancient one, branching off from the lordly family of the isles, in Alexander, the son of Angus Mor, the ally of Haco in his efforts to retain the Isles as a possession of the Northmen. The M'Alisters became an independent clan after the breaking up of the power of the Lords of the Isles, and held extensive possessions in the south of Knapdale and north of Kintyre. They soon became exposed to the encroachments of the Campbells, and, as Skene says, their principal properties found their way into different branches of that widespread race. Loupe, the last of the M'Alister estates in the district, has now passed into other hands.

Accelerat per saxa viam per stagna profunda
Tetheos, et montes agili pede transilit altos.
Quin et Lauchlanidum princeps fortissimus una
It comes, et fidos sub signa coegit amicos.
Necnon ille animi insignis florente juventa
Stipatus patriis Lawmonthius ibat alumnis
Arduus, et tyrio scapulas circumdatus ostro,
Regia fulmineis jam castra subibat in armis.

his course over rocks and sea, and with agile step crosses the mountains. There comes with him, as a comrade, the brave chief of the M'Lachlans,[1] bringing his faithful friends to the standard. The illustrious Lamont,[2] too, in the flower of youth, his shoulders girt with Tyrian purple, tall amid his clan, enters the royal camp

---

[1] A manuscript quoted by Skene, supposed to have been the work of a Maclachlan in 1450, traces this family to Gilchrist, the son of Dedaalan, who was the son of an Anradan, from whom descend M'Neils, M'Gillevrays, M'Ewens. Anradan was of the family of the Isles. The Maclachlans seem to have acquired their lands in Cowal by a marriage with an heiress of the Lamonts, the daughter of Lachlan M'Rory, who is exactly contemporary with Angus M'Rory, lord of Cowal, chief of the Lamonts. Their original seat seems to have been Lochaber, where a very old branch of the family has been settled from the earliest time. The Maclachlans in Cowal were reduced in their possessions by the Campbells, but they never hesitated to assert their independence in action, as on this occasion, when opportunity arose. In 1745 they were estimated at 300 fighting men. The chief is Maclachlan of Maclachlan, Castle Lachlan, in Strathlachlan, and Skene gives the oldest cadet as Maclachlan of Coruanan in Lochaber.

[2] Lamont or Lamond. Though the Lamont who was out with Montrose has left clear traces of himself, I have not been able to get hold of any information concerning the Lamont who went out with Dundee. The clan is a very old one in Argyllshire. They were the most ancient proprietors in Cowal, the Stewarts, M'Lachlans, and Campbells obtaining their possessions in that district by marriage with daughters of that family. The genealogy of the Lamonts, Skene remarks, can be proved by charters, at a time when most other Highland families are obliged to have recourse to the uncertain lights of tradition and the genealogies of their ancient sennachies. Their great antiquity could not protect them from the Campbells, by whom their possessions were soon reduced to their present dimensions. The notice by our author of Lamont bringing the Dougals with him is interesting, as it shows these two clans still sticking to each other under reversed circumstances. In former times, before the Lamonts changed their name from M'Earachar, they were wont to stand side by side. When the Dougals of Craignish were of great power, a part of the clan, *i.e.* clan Earachar, followed that family as their natural chief, although hey had no feudal right to their services.

Ibat et antiqui proles generosa Doualli
Promptus ad arma manu ; secumque in castra nivosae
Trans juga Knapdaliae, perque aspera frigora Lornae,
Ducit amicorum praestanti robore turmam
Armatam rigidis patrio de more sarissis.
Spicula pars duro gestant stridentia ferro,
Tela alii, teretique gerunt mucrone dolones.
His quoque sica fuit, simul omnibus aereus ensis,
Et succincta chlamys ; quibus et solenne supremi
Per domini jurare manum, manesque parentum.
Ipse Doualiades clypeo munitus et ense,
Terribilis vultu, et saevis metuendus in armis
Incedit, totaque latus stipante corona
Carpit iter, quassansque gravem violentior hastam
Castra petit, magnoque subit tentoria plausu.

in flashing arms. The noble offspring of the ancient Dougals,[1] prompt to strike, came with him, and leads a troop of followers, men of mettle, over the snowy heights of Knapdale and the frozen wilds of Lorne, armed, according to ancestral use, with the long lance. Some carry the javelin headed with iron, and others bear iron-tipped stakes with keen point. Theirs, too, was the dirk, and they all carry the brazen-hilted sword, and wear the girded plaid. Among these men it was the custom solemnly to swear by the Hand of the Supreme Lord,[2] and the spirits of their ancestors. Dougal himself, in shield and sword, terrible in aspect, and to be dreaded in the battle, advanced, a complete company of men allied to him. He leads the way, shaking a heavy spear with increasing violence. He seeks the camp, and enters it amid vast applause.

---

[1] The Dougals of Craignish are here meant, who, although compelled to adopt the name Campbell, ever preserved their own, and showed their independence on every fitting occasion. The old name was M'Eachern, and they were of the same race as the M'Donalds. The MS. of 1450, referred to in note on the M'Lachlans, derives their descent from Nicol, son of Murdoch, in the twelfth century. Murdoch was the father of Gillebride, the ancestor of the Siol Gillevray, and from this Skene gathers that the Siol Eachern and the M'Gillevrays and the M'Inneses were of the same clan. The home of the clan would seem to have been Morven and Ardgour; and Craignish, a later possession of a branch of the family, gave its name to that branch which was called the Clan Dougal Craignish. I understand the family is represented now by two gentlewomen in Edinburgh. Arrows, pikes, Lochaber axes, claymores, all appear in this passage.

[2] This may indicate a special clan oath, which may, perhaps, in the hands of those learned in such matters, throw some light on the family and its connections. See note on Highland Oaths, Book III. p. 103.

Grampiadum jam tota ducum chlamydata caterva
Atque equites, peditesque, omnisque[1] exercitus uno
Consedere loco ; celsis in collibus alae
Stant peditum, junctisque simul pro Caesare turmis
Sparsa ducum mediis volitant insignia castris.
Planitiem possedit eques, fraenataque totis
Agmina densantur campis ; hinc Dundius, illinc
Fermelodunus agit niveas in praelia turmas.
Ductoresque ruunt alii ; Halburtonius ingens
Agmen anhelantum campo ductabat equorum,
Et qui Pannoniis meruit stipendia castris,
Ille Caledoniae dictus de nomine villae ;

And now the whole plaided forces of the Highland chiefs, both horse and foot, the entire body, take post. The wings of infantry rest on the high hills, their clans united together for the King. The ensigns of their chiefs float out in the midst of the camp. The cavalry holds the level ground, and are massed in companies over the whole plain. Here Dundee, there Dunfermline,[2] moves out his snowy squadrons for the war. Other leaders too, are scouring over the ground. The huge Hallyburton[3] was leading a troop of panting horse, and he who had earned a soldier's reward in the Hungarian camp—he who took his name from the Caledonian city (*Lord Dunkeld*),[4] and

---

[1] The 'que' is added in one copy to make the line scan. It is not in the original.

[2] See note, Book II., for notice of Lord Dunfermline. The connection of some of the troopers who followed Claverhouse with the dragoons who became the Scots Greys may account for the adjective 'niveas,' and suggest inquiry as to date of the grey mounts of this distinguished regiment. 'Niveas turmas' is an expression which the historians of the regiment may consider. The Captain Bruce, who addresses the two troops of Scots Greys later on in this Book, does so as having been one of them, and there were others with Dundee who were officers in the Scots Dragoons.

[3] See note on Hallyburton of Pitcur, Book II. p. 64. The adjective 'ingens' I have given to himself in this passage, as he was a man of great stature.

[4] James, Lord Dunkeld, third Baron. Beyond the facts of his sharing in this rising for King James, his fighting at Killiecrankie, his forfeiture and retiring to the Court of St. Germains, I have not become acquainted with much concerning this nobleman. He is mentioned by Dundee in his despatches as bearing the privations of Lochaber. He became a colonel in the French service, and was killed in battle. He left a son, James, who assumed the title in France, and in the service of that country rose to be a general. A daughter of the third Baron, the Honourable Mary Galloway, entered the nunnery of Val de Grace in France. See Sir Robert Sibbald's *History of Fife*, and *Scottish Nation* by

Brussius et Batavis fama memorandus in oris
Sudantes quatiunt ferrata calce caballos.
Inde alii coiere duces, quos enthea virtus
Extulit, et sêclis sacravit fama futuris.
Fullertonus, et ipse animi Ventonus honesti,

Bruce,[1] who had gained his fame in the wars of Holland, with iron heel urge on their smoking steeds. Then gather the other captains, whom a lofty spirit has brought to the field, and whom fame has made sacred for future years. Fullerton,[2] and

---

William Anderson. The title is now extinct. It was conferred in 1645 on Sir James Galloway of Carnbie, in Fife, Master of Requests to Charles I. and II., whose father was Mr. Patrick Galloway, a minister in Perth, and afterwards in Edinburgh. The mother of Sir James was the daughter of Mr. James Lawson, also a minister in Edinburgh. The second Baron was Thomas, and by his wife, Margaret, daughter of Sir Thomas Thomson of Duddingston, he had three sons and five daughters. The eldest son, James, succeeded him, and he is the subject of this notice in the *Gramiad*. He is said to have served in the army, and our author would indicate that part of the service had been in the pay of Hungary. The Caledonian City is an old name for Dunkeld. The Primacy of the Scottish Church had its seat there under that name before St. Andrews obtained the dignity.

[1] Captain Andrew Bruce, son of Sir Andrew Bruce of Earlshall in Fife, may have been the officer here named. He was a colleague and lieutenant to Claverhouse in dealing with the west-country rebels (or martyrs). He commanded the party at Airds Moss where Cameron was killed, and Hackston of Rathillet, the assassin of Sharp, was captured. His letter to Lord Linlithgow, dated Dumfries, 17th March 1679, is preserved in *Letters of Viscount Dundee*, Bannatyne Club, p. 16. See also Napier's *Memoirs of Dundee*, Index.

There was a Lieut. W. Bruce, one of Dundee's officers, who went to France, and died in Perpignan Hospital. Officers of rank became Lieutenants and private soldiers in the Scottish Regiment, serving the king of France, and it is possible that our Captain Bruce was Lieut. Bruce of Perpignan. I find a Lieut. Alexander Bruce in the Royal Regiment of Dragoons, now Scots Greys, in 1686, under Captain Lord Charles Murray. In Claverhouse's own Regiment, besides Captain Andrew Bruce in 1683, there was a Lieut. David Bruce of Clackmannan, in the troop commanded by Colin, Lord Balcarres. See *Old Scottish Regimental Colours*, by Andrew Ross, a most valuable work, and see also *Memoirs of Dundee* by an officer of the army.

[2] Fullerton of Fullerton is the cavalier named here. There is little I have been able to gather concerning him. The family was an old one in the neighbourhood of Meigle, where a farm still bears the name. The site of the old castle of Fullerton is still remembered in the district. Many distinguished families in Scotland claim connection with it. Its chief representative, I understand, is H. A. F. Lindsay Carnegie of Kinblethmont, Esq., who informs me that most of the Fullerton papers were taken to France and lost there in the last century, and that a clean sweep of all the others was made last year, when his house was burnt to the ground. 'This time last year,' he says, 'I could have given you no end of Fullerton papers, but not a scrap remains now.'

Bandalochusque, acerque etiam Cockstonus in armis,
Et praeceps animi Newtonus, et indolis altae

Venton[1] himself of honest mind, and Bandalach,[2] and Coxton[3]

---

[1] Venton of the honourable or honest mind I have not been able to identify. Mr. Napier calls him Renton of Renton, but on what grounds I know not. He is not named, nor do I discover any similar name, in the lists of summoned, proclaimed, or forfeited gentlemen of the time, nor is he mentioned in the long lists of Claverhouse's officers. I am inclined to think he may have been a Fenton of Ogil, a property not far from Fullerton's near Kirriemuir. Pitcur, Fullerton, and Fenton were all near neighbours, and the three named by our Poet joined Claverhouse at the same time, and are mentioned together. He was probably a little lower down than Fullerton, and the farmer of his own acres. In Book II. the Poet introduces him as *ipse acerrimus armis Ventonus*, which would mean that he was a keen soldier, and there may be a touch of humour about the *ipse*.

[2] John Grant of Ballindalloch joined Claverhouse before the descent on Perth. He there got a fresh mount, having obtained Pollock's best horse, a good bay. The horse is borne witness to by Colt, and by James Osbourne, a trooper from Coupar-Angus, who took part with Claverhouse in the raid. He signs the Bond of Association at Tomintoul, and the letter from Birse, dated 17th August 1689, addressed to Mackay. His name appears in the proclamation of July, but not in the summons of May. He was probably not well known at the time to the informants of the committee.

[3] Sir Alexander Innes of Coxton, Knight-Baronet. He and the family of Coxton are spoken of by Duncan Forbes of Culloden as being held in the greatest respect in Morayshire, and coming next the chief of the name of Innes, *i.e.* Innes of Innes, in importance. Sir Alexander was the son of John Innes of Culdrain, and succeeded to Coxton on the death of his uncle, another Sir Alexander. In the notes to *Ane Account of the Familie of Innes* by Duncan Forbes, edited for the Spalding Club by the late Mr. Cosmo Innes, p. 257, I find the following :—

'This Sir Alexander Innes of Coxtoun was esteemed by all that knew him to be one of the first gentlemen in Scotland, being a graceful person and of fine naturall parts, and a man of remarkable honour and undaunted courage. His eldest son was Sir George, who succeeded him, and dyed in the 1715, leaving his eldest son Sir Alexander Innes to succeed to the title of Knight-Baronet, but not to the estate of Coxtoun, that being now sunk with debts.'

He seems to have joined Claverhouse very early in the rising, and to have taken part in the raid upon Perth and Dundee, as he is included in the summons by the Estates, dated 14th May 1689, to appear before them for treasonable rising in arms, and joining the Viscount Dundee, a declared rebel. His name, curiously enough, does not occur in the process or decree of forfeiture which followed the rising, and he seems to have escaped scatheless, through some friend at Court. He returned to Morayshire, and earned or maintained the estimate of him given by Duncan Forbes. The exhaustive terms of a disposition by him to George Innes of Dunkinty (the Episcopalian nonjuring provost of Elgin) of some property, shows a man of business—somewhere in the Innes family. 'The town and lands, maynes, *etc.*, with all and sundry their manor places, houses,

Kinnardus, promptusque manu Clelandius, audax
Frater et ipse ducis consanguineique sequuntur;

the brave in arms, and hasty Newton,[1] and Kinnaird of lofty

biggings, yards, orchards, dovecotts, milns, mill lands, multures, kilns, barns, byres, office-houses, tofts, crofts, outsetts, insetts, mosses, mures, graisings, commonties, pasturages, parts, pendicles, with teinds, with the salmond fishing upon the water of Lossie . . . and sicklyke the great stone lodging and tenements of lands, high and laigh, back and fore, with their houses, biggings, yeards, and pertinents, lying within the burgh of Elgin, 3d March 1704.'—*Family of Innes*, Spalding Club, p. 251.

Sir Alexander would seem to have died about the year 1707, and to have been succeeded by his son Sir George, who died in 'the 1715,' as it is expressed. Whether the expression means that he took part in the rising of that year, and died in battle does not appear. At his death the property was hopelessly sunk in debt, and had to be parted with. His son, Sir Alexander, had provision through his mother, who was the heiress of Towie-Barclay.

The family still survives in the person of Sir George Innes of Cockstoune, Bart.

The old tower visible from the road between Fochabers and Elgin is a most perfect specimen of its class, and is fire-proof outside and in. It is given in Billings' *Baronial Remains*.

[1] James Edmonstone of Newton of Doune is here meant. Lieutenant Colt depones that he saw him in arms with the Viscount of Dundee in Badenoch, and that he continued so until deponent went to Mull. Lieutenant Nesbit saw him at Blair on horseback after the affair at Dunkeld. Charles Stewart, younger of Ballechin, depones that he saw James Edmonstone of Newton of Doune in arms with the rebels marching all alongst with them after Dundee's death. He stands high up in the decreet of forfeiture, next to the name of Pitcur. He probably joined in Badenoch or Lochaber, as his name does not occur in the early summons of May 14th. Lieut. John Hay, son of the laird of Nauchton in Fife, was well acquainted with Newton, and saw him during three days at Blair, and depones that he was in arms, and left Blair to follow the army of the rebels.

The house of the Newton of Doune still stands, though much reduced, an object of interest on the banks of the water of Ardoch, just outside the village of Doune, and almost beneath the shadow of the Castle. It is still the dwelling of gentlefolks. The Newton is mentioned in a deed of 1562, by which David, Commendator of Dryburgh, with consent of the convent of Inchmahomok, granted a lease of the teinds to their servitor, Allan Oliphant and his heirs, when Newton was rated at 18 bolls meal, and 2 bolls bear, and the neighbouring property of Wester Row at 16 bolls meal, and 5 bolls 1 firlot bear.—*Red Book of Menteith* by W. Fraser, vol. i. p. 531. In the contentions between Margaret, widow of James IV., and William Edmonstone of Duntreath as to her reception within the castle of Doune with her servants, the Newton appears in the various documents. The Edmonstones were stewards of Menteith for a time, and keepers of the castle of Doune. The Newton remained in the hands of a cadet of the family of Duntreath, of which cadet family our cavalier was the representative.

Regia et ipse meis portabam signa lacertis.
Adamsonus et hinc, et Scotus lumine laesus,

genius,[1] and Clelland[2] ready of hand, and the bold brother of the commander himself, and those of his own blood,

---

Later on John James Edmonstone, the friend of Walter Scott, represented the family. Lockhart speaks of a visit of Scott to Newton, 'a beautiful seat, close to the ruins of the once magnificent Castle of Doune.' I understand the family is now extinct, and their house seems to stand within the policies of Inverardoch. See *Red Book of Menteith*, vol. ii. 392-36.

[1] This may be Kinnaird of Culbyn, who figures last in the Proclamation of July 18, 1689, or Mr. Charles Kinnaird, brother to Lord Kinnaird, named in the Remit to the Justice Court to prosecute the rebels in France, given in Appendix to *Acts of Parl. Scot.* vol. ix. p. 114. If the former, the fate of his manor-house, buried beneath its own sands through the folly of its owners, symbolises the house of Stuart for which he fought, overthrown by its own people through the folly of the later kings. On the 16th July 1695 the Parliament of Scotland, 'considering that many lands, meadows, etc., lying on the sea-coasts, have been ruined and overspread in many places of this kingdom by sand driven from adjacent sandhills, the which has been mainly occasioned by the pulling up by the root of bent, juniper, and broom bushes, which did loose and break the surface and scroof of the said hills, and particularly considering that the Barony of Culbin and house and yards thereof is quite ruined and overspread with sand—the which was occasioned by the foresaid bad practice of pulling bent and juniper—it therefore prohibits the bad practice either by proprietors themselves or any other, the same being the natural fences of the adjacent countries to the said hills.' On the 17th of July we find the laird himself petitioning for a reduction of cess on his property, as the greater part of it was under sand.—*Acts of Parl. Scot.*, p. 452.

The family was an old one in Morayshire. On Feb. 25th, 1478, there is an instrument of seisin under the great seal in favour of Alan Kinnaird of that ilk and of Culbin and Joneta Keith, his spouse, in the lands of Culbin. In 1492 the young Baron of Kilravock signs a protest taken at the Capitale Messuagium de Culbyn, 'which,' says the editor of the *Thanes of Cawdor*, p. 79, 'now lies hid under the sandhills of Culbyn.'

Besides the Charles Kinnaird mentioned above in this note, there was united with Claverhouse as his Quartermaster, in 1684, a James Kinnaird, another brother of Lord Kinnaird, see Ross's *Regimental Colours*, p. 70.

[2] John Clelland of Faskin, ready of hand, was early in the field, and took part in the raid on Perth and Dundee. Colt saw him at Perth when he was taken prisoner, and when Lieut. Nesbit was made prisoner at Killiecrankie by Major Grahame of Balwhapple, Clelland and Duncan Menzies were at his elbow. Colt saw him after the failure at Dunkeld, conversing with the laird of M'Nachtan, at Duart, and he was wearing his sword. He had seen him constantly with Dundee while in Lochaber. His name occurs in the Proclamation by William and Mary, 18th July 1689, and comes next to General Cannon's in the decreet of forfeiture.

A Lieutenant William Cleland served with Claverhouse in the west, and rose

Raedus uterque illinc simul et Johnstonia pubes,
Et Ramisaeus, equis vecti sublimibus omnes

follow.[1] And I[2] myself was bearing in my arms the royal standard.
And here Adamson,[3] and Scott,[4] blind of an eye, and there the

---

to the rank of Captain. He is frequently mentioned in the despatches of the time. I do not know whether he was of the family of Faskine or not. A William Cleland appears as Captain of the 6th troop of Scots Greys in 1683. Many of the Clelands were on the other side in politics, and one was killed at Dunkeld serving against the Highlanders in the Cameronian Regiment, now the 26th.

[1] David Graham, brother of Dundee. The two brothers matriculated at St. Andrews together, and through life were most faithful to each other. On the appointment of Claverhouse as Sheriff of Wigtown, David was made Sheriff-Depute, and was one of the judges who tried the Wigtown martyrs in 1685. Whether they were martyrs indeed is not yet proven, but the only connection of Claverhouse with the matter is that one of the judges on their trial was his brother the Deputy-Sheriff, one of the Lord Justices of Wigtownshire. As to this post, see *Acts of Scot. Parl.*, vol. ix. p. 65, restoring Sir Andrew Agnew to it, who, according to the narrative, had been 'wrongously and summarily and without order of law removed from being Sheriff of that shire, and John Graham of Claverhouse nominated in his place, and hereafter commission renewed in favour of David Graham his brother.' His name appears on the July proclamation of the rebels; and he had previously been summoned to Edinburgh on 14th May as joining in arms with the Viscount. He appears frequently in the evidence of forfeiture, and shares the doom of the decreet. After the death of the infant Viscount, who died within three months of his father, David assumed the style of 3d Viscount Dundee. A David Graham is entered as Quartermaster in his brother's Regiment, August 1st, 1683, and in 1684 there is an entry of a David Graham as Cornet in the same regiment.

Among those of his own blood was Graham, younger of Duntroon, who is summoned in May to appear for joining with Dundee. No doubt he joined him at Dudhope, with the other gay youths mentioned in Book II. He had taken the benefit of the indemnity by 12th May 1690, but was named in 1695 as one of those in France to be prosecuted. Many relics of Dundee are preserved at Duntroon—his marriage-contract, patent of nobility, several letters, his chair, the pistol which was on him when he fell. The family claimed the peerage after David Graham. Another Graham was Major William of Balwhapple, who appears frequently in the evidence of forfeiture, and shares in the common doom. I presume he is the Lieut. in the regiment under Captain the Earl of Airlie in 1685. A Robert Graham was Aid-Major in 1684.

A Captain P. Graham and a Lieut. P. Graham appear on the lists of exiled officers, and on the prosecution list of 1695.

[2] The author himself, it seems, on this occasion at any rate, held the Royal standard. Macaulay exhibits Glengarry as holding it, but he had too much to do for such work. See Preface on Life of the Author.

[3] Adamson I cannot trace, unless he be Captain M'Adams, who is on the list of those in France ordered to be prosecuted. I also find David M'Adam as Lieut. under Lord James Murray in the Royal Scots, 1686.

[4] Scott, though so marked, I have not been able to trace. A John Scott

Cornipedum rigidis urgent calcaribus armos.
Ipse inter medios fulget ceu sidereus sol
Dundius, aut stellas velut inter luna minores

two Reids,[1] and the Johnstone youth,[2] and Ramsay,[3] all well mounted, drive the spur into their horses' flanks. Dundee himself as a bright sun, glows in their midst, or shines as the moon at

---

appears as lieutenant in the Mar regiment in 1684, under Captain John Bruce; and I notice an Andrew Scott in the Royal Scots in 1687. Colonel Andrew Scott in France was appointed Lieut. in the Company of Scottish Gentlemen joining the French Army. A Walter Scott of Tushielaw had been laid hold of by the committee on the 1st of May 1689, and submitted to be bound on his faith and honour to live peaceably and in obedience to the Government, and either to serve in Holland under Sir David Colliers, or to appear from time to time before the committee of Estates. Should this be he, the physical defect in his eye would not be his only shortcoming, but doubtless Walter Scott was true to his word.

[1] I have not been able to identify either of the Reids. There was a loyal family of Robertsons of Straloch, who for centuries, in common usage, called themselves, and were called, Red, Rua, or Roy. Baron Red or Reid was their style. The first of the family had red hair, and the name Rua went on, though the signature was always Robertson. The younger children did not take Rua, but only the representative of the family. General Reid, the founder of the Music Chair in Edinburgh, and of the delightful Reid concerts, and the composer of 'The Garb of old Gaul,' was the representative of the house, and assumed Reid as his surname permanently. See *Sketches of the Highlanders*, by General Stewart of Garth, p. 118. It is suggested that the Reids may belong to the family of Straloch. If the possible reading 'ater' instead of 'uter' be adopted, the combination of colours in the name would be striking, and the scanning impossible.

[2] Who the 'Johnstonia pubes' is I do not know, unless it be 'Mr. John Johnston, brother to the Earl of Annandale,' who is named for prosecution in France. See Appendix to *Acts of Parl. Scot.*, p. 114. In the evidence of Lieut. Nisbet we have the following reference to one Johnston—he depones that when he was prisoner at the castle of Blair after Killiecrankie, several persons came to the room where he was and said that the said Viscount's body was interred, and remembers particularly that one named Johnston told the deponent that he had catched the Viscount as he fell from his horse after his being shot. The Viscount then asking the said Johnston how the day went, and that he answered, 'the day went weel for the King' (meaning King James), but that he was sorry for his Lordship, and that the Viscount replied, 'it was less matter for him seeing the day went weel for his master.'—*Ib.* p. 56.

[3] Ramsay I take to be Gilbert Ramsay, who was killed at Killiecrankie. His remarkable dream the night before the battle is given in Lochiel's Memoirs, p. 280-81, where see other details about him. He passed, according to Balhaldy, his trials, and was admitted advocate with great applause about the time the king fled. He joined Dundee as a volunteer, throwing up his career at the bar, and stuck faithfully to him. He, with Major William Graham, were

Plena nitet; turmas volat atque ante arduus omnes.
Jamque in precinctu steterant, abitumque parabant.
Sed nox atra ruit, suadentque orientia somnos
Sidera, defessos gravis et sopor occupat artus.
   Jamque invectus equis bijugo petit aethera curru
Phoebus, et instantis radiatum insigne diei
Extulit, et vitreis aurora rubebat in undis.
Dundius insomnem traducens pectore noctem
Volvebat curas animo, secumque volutans
Fortunae casus dubios, jam luce propinqua
Duris membra levat stratis, simul excutit ipsos
Castrorum vigiles, et totis agmina castris.
Ecce ad surgentis radios, et primula solis
Lumina, jucundo strepuerunt castra tumultu;
Ductor ut in medio posuit vestigia campo
Sublimi subvectus equo, fragor aethera pulsat
Grampiadum, laetique ducem clamore secundo
Excipiunt; gaudet florentes aere catervas

the full among the lesser stars, and proudly gallops along the front of his lines. And now they stood ready for the advance, and prepared to march, but night comes on, and the rising stars woo to rest, and deep sleep claims the wearied limbs.

And now Phœbus, borne along in his chariot by his steeds, seeks the upper sky, and Aurora has shot forth the first rays of the coming day, and was casting a glow upon the glassy waves. Dundee, passing a sleepless night, revolved his cares in his anxious breast, turning over in his mind the doubtful chances of fortune. On the approach of light he rises from his hard couch, and at once rouses the sentinels of the camp, and the whole host. Lo! at the first rays of the rising sun the camp resounded with joyous tumult, and a great shout went up when the commander, mounted on his noble charger, took his place in the midst of the army. With encouraging cheer they welcome their leader. He exults as he beholds the bands gleaming with brass, and admires

---

charged by Dundee with his letter to Lord Murray, July 25th, 1689, and to wait on his Lordship and receive his positive answer. Lord Murray refused to see them, and thus undeceived the men of Athole, who then ceased to follow him. He was one of the sixteen who followed Dundee in the battle, and he fell where he was posted, by Mr. Drummond's side. Our author is supposed to have written a panegyric on him. I find a Mr. Gilbert Ramsay, a minister in Aberdeen, who repudiated the General Assembly and its acts. By 1695, however, he passed from his repudiation. Was he the father of the above-named cavalier?

Aspicere, et pictas radiato murice turmas
  Miratur, sonituque tubae recreatur acuto.
  Tandem Grampiaci sublimis ab aggere castri
  Verba dedit, talesque emisit pectore voces.
  ' O Fergusiadae bello gens inclyta Scoti !
  Fidaque sceptrigero per tot modo sêcla Stuarto !
  Gratulor unanimes in proelia surgere gentes,
  Atque acres spectare viros, qui fortibus armis
  Dedecus ulturi possint sarcire ruinas
  Caesaris, et patriis haeredem assistere [1] sceptris.
  Vos O fida cohors detrudite fortiter hostem
  Finibus arctois, transque alta cacumina Grampi
  Pellite praedonem patriae, rabidique tyranni
  Prodigiale caput stygiis damnate tenebris.
  Gloria virtuti, scelerique infamia turpis
  It comes, et manes sequitur post busta sepultos.
  Jam neque me ambitio, nec gloria nominis urit,
  Nec belli civilis amor, sed Caesaris alti
  Majestas calcata [2] jugo praedonis iniquo

the companies in their brilliant colours, and is refreshed by the sharp note of the pipe. Then from the rampart [3] of the high Grampian camp he thus addresses the clans, and from his heart gave utterance to these words: 'O sons of Fergus, Scots, illustrious in war, faithful ever, through so many ages, to the royal race of Stuart, I rejoice that the clans rise unanimous in this war, and am happy to look upon brave men, who, with strong arms to revenge dishonour, may also retrieve our ruin, and bring back the heir of the Caesar to his country's sceptre ! O faithful band ! bravely expel the enemy from the northern border, and drive him, the robber of his country, across the Grampians, and quickly condemn to Stygian darkness the monstrous head of the tyrant. Glory goes as companion to virtue, vile infamy to guilt, each following the spirit beyond the grave. Neither ambition nor the glory of a name holds me loyal, nor the love of civil war, but the majesty of the lofty Caesar, ground under the evil yoke of the robber, has impelled me to demand the aid of your race.

---

[1] *Var. lect.* asussere. 'Assistere' here should mean to *assist* to his ancestral sceptre; but this is not Latin. 'Asciscere' may have been the intention.

[2] 'calcanda' in original.

[3] The use of 'castri' here for 'castrorum' is accounted for, if we suppose that the little army had entrenched itself, or was occupying a site which had from its frequent service as a camp become a castrum. Dalmacommer was such.

Impulit auxilium vestrae deposcere gentis.
At prece nec pretio venales quaerere dextras
Est animus ; Batavi petat impia castra tyranni
Qui metuit mea signa sequi, discedite segnes
Imbellesque animi, quorum nec pectora pulsat
Regis honos, decorisque nec urget honesta cupido.
Jam neque me clausis ignavum vivere castris,
Nec patitur vano tempus trepidare tumultu ;
Arma sed adversum metuenda feramus in hostem.
Tuque adeo arctoi gens o fidissima mundi
Vosque duces, proceresque, securigeraeque catervae
Vadite,[1] terribiles hostique ostendite vultus ;
Illius et stricto jugulum distringite ferro.
Jam[2] dictis mora nulla meis, nunc ipsa vocat res.
Arma viri validis ultricia sumite dextris,
Signifer et fulvum castris attolle leonem.[3]
Me duce si qua potest arctoo surgere caelo
Gloria gestarum successu splendida rerum
Experiar, junctasque acies in praelia mittam
Primus ego, effundamque ferox hostilia castra.'

Yet in this request I have no purpose of seeking by pay the right hand of mercenaries. Let him who fears to follow my standard seek the impious camp of the Dutch tyrant. Let the sluggard and the coward depart, and all whose hearts throb not for the honour of the king, and all whom true love of honour impels not. My spirit will not suffer me to lead an ignoble life in the close camp, or to waste time in vain tumult. Let us turn our dreaded arms against the enemy. And you, O northern race, most faithful ! you, O chieftains and nobles and axe-bearing clans ! advance ! show your faces, terrible to the enemy, and have at his throat with the drawn sword ! Let not my words delay you ; action itself demands us. Men, seize the avenging arms in your strong right hands ! Standard-bearer, raise aloft the tawny lion in the camp ! While I am your leader, I will prove by the success of our campaign whether any splendid glory may be found in the north, and I myself will be in the van when I hurl your united bands against the foe, and fiercely scatter the host of the enemy.

---

[1] *Var. lect.* vadito.   [2] 'Jamque' in original.
[3] The reference is, of course, to the 'ruddy lion ramping in gold' of the Scottish standard.

Haec effatus; et interea sol aureus axem
Jam medium rapidis superârat paene quadrigis.
Ecce ingens castris post alta silentia clamor
Exoritur, caelum hinc resonat, Balnavius illinc,
Et juga terribilem ingeminant concussa fragorem.
Mox martem strepuere tubae, tunc classica belli
Rauca dedere sonum, atque horrendo cornua cantu;
Jam cunei, turmaeque parant discedere castris,
Abriadum variisque ardens exercitus armis
Signa movet clangente tuba, castrisque relictis
Grampicus hinc campo graditur globus omnis aperto. ·
Agminis it primi ductor Glengarius audax
Ante aciem, certo praecedit et ordine turmas
Ter denis comitatus equis, tum cetera turba
Heroumque ducumque subit statione locoque
Quisque suo, sequiturque ducem sua quemque juventus.
Quos celer instructa jam pone cohorte secutus
Foyrius extremum non segniter intulit agmen.
Jamque adeo totis sese diffuderat arvis
Picta cohors, stravitque viam per saxa per amnes,
Transieratque procul vallis confinia Roae,
Aereasqué Alpes, et magnae moenia Garvae.
Jam vada transmittit Spejae, campumque tenebat

Thus he spoke. Meanwhile the golden sun in rapid car had nearly passed meridian. Lo! after the deep silence a mighty shout arose from the camp, and here the heavens, and there Ben Nevis, resounded, and the stricken mountain-tops re-echo the terrible thunder. At once the pipes struck up the pibroch, and the clarion and bugle sounded from hoarse throat the dreadful note and chant of war. Already squadron and battalion prepare to leave the camp. The army, brilliant with the varied weapons of Lochaber, moves the standard, while the pipe sounds, and the whole force in marching order advances into the open country. The bold Glengarry, as leader of the first line, marched in the van, accompanied by thirty horse in due order. Then the rest of the chiefs advanced each in his own station, and followed by his own people. Swift Foyers, following with his marshalled clan, brought up smartly the rear. And now the tartaned host had poured itself out upon the fields, and forced its way through rocks and rivers, and had left behind the confines of Glen Roy, and the lofty mountains and walls of Garviemore. Now it is over the fords of Spey, and is holding the open country. With mighty

Ingenti clamore fremens, caelumque fatigat,
Et terram jam mole gravat, solem aere lacessit
Ignivomisque armis, et territat aethera pilis ;
Grampica fulmineis et turba coruscat in armis.
Utque tuos tandem tetigit, Badinothia, fines,
Sparsa per acclives extendit cornua colles ;
Sole repercussae procul effulgere catervae,
Mille micant galeae, totidem sonuere pharetrae ;[1]
Et mille auratis radiant mucronibus hastae;
Atque securigeris pulsantur rura maniplis ;
. Grampius et signis volitantibus horruit ingens.
      Extemplo terrore quatit[2] vicinia tota,
Deserit inde lares, et pendula stramine tecta,
Et magni quisquis Grami non castra subibat
Antra petit, cursuque vagus[3] et rupibus abdit.
Ipse animi fidens spes pectore concipit alto

cheer they assail the skies, with heavy tramp they oppress the earth. The Highland army, with its glitter of brass and flash of bright musket, braves the sun, and with bristling spears affrights the air, as it moves forward. When at length it touched thy borders, O Badenoch! its wings were extended widely over the declivities of the hills. Far off the clans were seen shining in the light of the sun. A thousand helmets glitter, as many quivers resound; a thousand spears, from their points bright with golden light, reflect the rays, and the fields feel the tread of the axe-bearing Gael, and the Grampians are terrible with the flaunting banners.

Forthwith in terror the whole district trembles, and every one who joins not the camp of the great Graham, deserts[4] his household

---

[1] Punctuation here, and at the end of the two following lines, that of the author.

[2] 'quatit,' intransitive for 'quatitur'; not Latin as it stands, probably due to the English 'shake' being transitive and intransitive.

[3] 'vagus' is two shorts. The line does not scan. It is suggested that the line might read '. . . cursuque vago se rupibus abdit.' The alteration is slight and gives to 'abdit' an object.

[4] A remarkable testimony to the accuracy of our author is afforded by the following extract from the letter of Lord Murray to the Duke of Hamilton, dated 'Blair, June 4th, 1689, 12 o'clock at night. I am certainly informed that our neighbours, the Badenoch men, would never rise with Dundee though he has been all this while in their country, for fear of the Athole men, who, if they should not join too, would destroy their country when they were away, so that Dundee

Dundius ingentes, momentaque maxima rerum
Mente revolvit ovans ; et nunc tendebat in hostem
Alta pruinosi cunctantem ad flumina Spejae.
Ventum erat ad patulos viridanti gramine campos,
Clunia frugiferis terram qua vestit aristis ;
Inde sacerdotis dictam de nomine gentem
Gramus ad arma vocat; toto mox agmine cinctus
Rhaetia castra petit volitantibus undique signis.
Jamque inclinato Titan temone petebat
Littoris Hesperii metas, cursuque peracto,
Nunc Hypercanium[1] demersit in aequore currum :

gods, and cottage with its overhanging thatch, and seeks some cave, hiding as a fugitive among the rocks. Dundee himself, full of confidence, conceived great hopes in his breast, and in exultation revolved the weighty questions of the war in his mind. He led his force towards the enemy awaiting him beside the deep waters of the chilly Spey. He reached the green fields of Cluny, where the earth is clothed with fruitful corn. There the Graham calls to arms the race[2] deriving its name from the priest. Presently, surrounded by his whole force with flying colours he seeks the Castle of Raitts.[3] Already was Titan, with descending team, seeking the bounds of the Hesperian shore, and, his long course

---

has been forced to burn their houses, and take their goods ; to save which some are gone to him, but the most part have not, but are now lying in the mountains with wives and children, in a most pitiable condition, and that country is quite ruined.' See Mackay's *Memoirs*, pp. 224, 225.

[1] 'Hyp': false quantity.

[2] *i.e.* The Macphersons, sons of the Parson, the Clan Vuirich. According to Skene there can be no doubt that Macpherson of Cluny is the true chief of the Clan Chattan, though the Mackintosh, the oldest cadet of the clan, was captain of Clan Chattan for two centuries. The two families are descended from Gilliechattan Mor, who, on the breakdown of the Celtic Earldom of Moray, possessed the whole of Lochaber and Badenoch, with Strathnairn and Strathdearn, holding them direct from the Crown. His two sons, Neachtan and Neill, founded the two powerful families now called Macpherson and Macintosh. Neachtan was the elder, and from him descended the Macphersons. For discussion of the whole matter, and the identifying of the clans who fought on the Inch of Perth in 1396 with these two families, see Skene, *Highlanders of Scotland*, vol. II. p. 171. Muirich, Mureach, or Murdach, from whom the clan gets the name Vuirich, was great-grandson of Neachtan. The Macphersons took no decided steps in this campaign. See note in Book II.

[3] The old castle of Raitts, on the north side of the Spey. Belleville, and the monument to the translator of Ossian, I believe, are near the site. The burn of Raitts falls into the Spey a little above Belleville. This castle is to be distinguished from the MacIntosh Castle of Rait in Nairn.

Noxque secuta tegit terram pallentibus umbris.
  Crastina forte dies Maii vicesima nona
Lampade nocturnas exorta dispulit umbras.
Dundius Abriaci rectores agminis unum
Convocat in coetum, et viridi stans cespite fatur,
' O Fergusiadum gens Grampica gloria regum,
Festa dies reduci Carlo celebranda quotannis
Hactenus auricomam diffudit ab aethere lucem.
Hanc ego si Batavis essem[1] vagus hospes in oris,
Exul et Hadriacas fugerem si vilis ad undas,
Officiis et honore colam, quocunque sub axe
Annua pacifero solvam solennia Carlo,
Civica qui positis certamina sustulit armis,
Saeclaque sopitis qui rettulit aurea bellis.
Ergo diem laetis ad sidera plausibus omnes,

ended, was plunging his wearied chariot in the sea; and night coming on covers the earth with gloomy shadows.

The morrow[2]—it was the 29th of May—arose, and with its light dispelled the shades. Dundee gathered together the leaders of the host, and, standing on a grassy knoll, he thus addressed them: 'O Grampian race! the glory of the Fergus-descended kings, the annual festal day of the restored Charles has at length shone out in golden light. This day, were I a wanderer on Batavian shore, were I flying as a wretched exile to the Adriatic[3] waves, would I observe with its due offices and honours, and wherever under the heavens I may be, I will perform this annual solemnity in honour of the peace-bringing Charles. He, arms being laid down, put an end to the civil war, and peace restored, brought round the Golden Age.[4] Therefore, with glad plaudits sent up to the skies, let us all celebrate the birthday and the

---

[1] 'essem ... fugerem ... colam': irregular sequence, not uncommon with our author.

[2] The 29th of May was the birthday of Charles II. as well as the day of his entry into London on his Restoration. 'The fond imaginations of men,' says Hume, 'interpreted as a happy omen the concurrence of two such joyful periods.'

[3] The point as to the Adriatic is not very apparent; the Batavian shore one can imagine an objection to, on the part of Dundee and his audience, and Adriatic may mean Turkish territory.

[4] Our author, in so often alluding to the reign of Charles II. as the Golden Age, is using a phrase of the time, quoted in the *Vicar of Bray*, and revived in the novel by Edna Lyall, *In the Golden Days*. The first chapter is styled 'Good King Charles's Golden Days.' See *Parody of Virg.* Ecl. iv. at end.

Et natalitium Carli celebremus honorem.'
Haec ait ; unanimique omnes eadem ore fremebant.
Castrorum in medio silvestribus asper ericis
Campus erat, surgens parvoque¹ cacumine collis.
Huc sese multis medium cum millibus Heros
Contulit, et longa proceres utrinque corona
Stare jubet, vulgique procul consistere turbam.
Ingentemque pyram sylvis, et² abiete secta,
Lignorumque struem taedis, pinguique resina³
Ocyus incendi mandat, primusque favillas
Addidit, accensos et sulphure suscitat ignes.
Jam tuba solennem cantu intulit horrida pompam.
Ipse tenens dextra cyathum spumantis Iacchi,
Tempora felici fulgebat cinctus oliva,
Atque in Sidonio solito conspectior ostro
Constitit ante pyram, tum jussa silentia linguis ;
' En ' ait ' in meritum defuncti regis honorem,
Natalemque diem Carli, reditumque secundum,
Successum inque pii fratris Regisque salutem,

honour of Charles.' This he said, and with one heart and mouth they all sent up the cheer. In the midst of the camp there was a plain, rough with wild heather, and on it rose a little hill. Thither the hero, amid his thousands, betook himself, and bidding his officers stand around in wide circle, and the rank and file to form behind, he orders a huge pyre of brushwood, branches, and logs steeped in resin, to be raised and fired. He first applied the lighted sparks, and aroused them into flame with sulphur. Then the dread pipes with their music inaugurate the solemnity. The Graham,⁴ olive-crowned and in his wonted scarlet, and holding a cup of foaming wine, stood before the pile, and silence being commanded, thus he speaks : ' To the due honour of the late King, to his natal day, and the day of the happy restoration of Charles, to the success of his pious brother, to the health of the King and

---

¹ 'parvoque surgens' in original.
² 'et': false quantity. 'atque' would scan.
³ 're': false quantity.
⁴ It might be unfair to ask where he got the olive leaves in Strathspey, but is the Poet right, from a classical point of view, in thus crowning him? The scarlet coat is to be noted as the wont of Claverhouse. In the evidence of forfeiture, James Malcolm, who is particular as to what the personages wear to whom he bears evidence, remarks upon the red coat of Sir Donald M'Donald of Sleat.

Atque exoptatum proavita ad sceptra regressum,
Haurio jucundis haec pocula plena labellis.'
Dixit; et ante omnem nudato vertice turbam
Stabat, et ingenti crateram combibit haustu.
Haec eadem dixere omnes proceresque ducesque,
Atque avido plenos exsiccant gutture scyphos.[1]
Tollitur in coelum stridorque fragorque tubarum;
Collucent per castra faces, ignescere credas
Arva procul, totosque accendi lampade montes.
Et jam sol rapide devexior[2] ibat Olympo.
Gramus ait; 'non haec tempus solennia poscit
Ludicra, nec levibus vacat indulgere choreis.
Tollite signa, duces, pars quantulacunque diei
Jam superest, positis Bellonam[3] intendite ludis.'
  Haud procul hinc saxis olim constructa vetustis
Arx Ruthvena ducis Batavi statione recepta

his restoration to his sceptre, with glad lips I drink this full cup.' He spoke, and with uncovered head he stood before the whole throng, and quaffed the bowl at a mighty draught. These words all his captains repeated, and with eager throats they drained their full goblets. The crash and clang of the pipes rose to the skies, and the flaming fagots lighten up the whole camp, so that one might believe that the distant fields and all the mountains were enkindled by the blaze. Already the sun was going down in rapid course from Olympus, and said the Graham, 'This is no time for the games[4] of the day, nor may we indulge in the light dance. Generals, raise your standards; give the little that remains of the day to Bellona, and dispense with the games.'

  Near at hand the lofty castle of Ruthven,[5] built in bygone

---

[1] 'scy': false quantity.

[2] Participles rarely compared. A critic says 'devexior dies' is late (Claudian, end of fourth century A.D.). Had our author read Claudian? 'rapide' looks like 'rapido' in original.

[3] The treatment of Bellona here is scarcely Latin. She should be the agent or instigator, but is here used, like 'Martem,' as a synonym for war.

[4] See *Old Mortality*, chap. ii., and note as to cultivation of games under the Stuarts. The Highland games, now so popular, had doubtless an important place in a Highland army in the seventeenth century, camping at any rate within the Highland line. The dance too, would be apt to tempt Highlanders away from the side of Bellona.

[5] Ruthven Castle, the ruins of which attract the eye and the interest of the traveller as he nears Kingussie, has seen something of Highland wars. Standing at a crossing point of tracks north, south, east, and west, on the great valley of

Alta tenebatur, munita hostilibus armis ;
Hanc jubet eversis prosternere turribus arcem
Dundius, et rapidis exurere moenia flammis.
Audacemque virum qui jussa referret ad arcis
Custodem, toto selectum ex agmine mittit.
Haec ait alta petens ad propugnacula turris,
' Scote, meo juveni huic dic nomine moenia linquat,

days of stones of an older building, is held and fortified as a post of the Dutch General. Dundee commands the castle to be destroyed, its towers thrown down, and the place given to the flames. He despatched a man of courage, chosen from his host, to carry his orders to the commander of the castle. As he seeks (with him) the outworks of the stronghold, he says: ' O Scot, tell that youth, in my name, to leave these walls, or I will level

---

the Spey, it saw and felt every raid westward by Gordons, Grants, MacIntoshes; eastwards by M'Donalds, Camerons, M'Leans, and Campbells; southwards by them all, with additions of Macphersons, Mackenzies, and many more; and northwards by the regular forces of the kingdom. The Poet seems to allude to the old stones which had had their places in many succeeding buildings. Huntly in fighting the bonny Earl of Moray repaired it; Argyll besieged it in vain when held by Macphersons; Montrose, Monck, Lilburn, and now Mackay garrisoned it, each successive occupant having to make it habitable for himself; and next Dundee burns it. It again figures in the '45, when the relics of Prince Charles's force, several thousand strong, under Macpherson, rallied round the old walls. It was commonly known as Ruthven Barracks. It was made a garrison for 40 'musketters' in 1664, and in 1668 it is ranked as one of the strongholds of the kingdom appointed for the incarceration of prisoners. Its condition in 1693 is spoken to by Colonel John Hill, and his words apply equally, he says, to Blair Athole. He says it is 'almost ruinous, being neither wind nor water tight, so that many of the soldiers there posted, through the incessant rains in the night-time, have contracted fluxes, scurveys, and other diseases, and others of the soldiers do frequently desert because of the bad accommodation,' ' there not being habitable space for 40 men, though there were 4 score centinells beside officers in the garrison.'—*Treasury Register*, September 8, 1693, quoted by Ross in *Old Scottish Colours*, p. 27. Mackay had stationed Captain John Forbes, with some of Grant's men, in the castle as an advanced post, and in order to make easy the junction of Ramsay, who was trying to force his way through Athole with the reinforcements sent from the south. Mackay, having advanced about half way to Ruthven from Inverness, got a message from Forbes, that Ramsay was retreating southward, and that Dundee was only twelve miles from Ruthven up the Spey. Mackay moved to Culnakyle and Belcastle, *i.e.* Castle Grant, and from that base moved up the Spey to within a short distance of Dundee's camp at Raitts. Finding him strongly posted he fell back upon the kirk of Alvie, where we shall next find him, Ruthven being left to its fate.

Aut ego plana solo sublimia culmina sternam.'
Ille refert magni fidus mandata magistri ;
Et primum clangente tuba discedere mandat
Praesidium, reddique sibi jubet ocyus arcem.
At contra excelsi responsum ex aggere castri,
'Hanc ego pro Batavo teneo Forbesius arcem
Principe, proque illo (si Dii voluere) tenebo.'
Nec mora ; responso cuncti fremuere superbo,
Mittitur ingenti circumdatus agmine ductor
Kapochus extemplo ad turrem, murisque propinquat
Cornicinum clangore gravi, sonituque tubarum,
Undique Ruthvenos et cinxit milite muros.

their lofty turrets to the ground.' He faithfully bears the message of his great master, and first sounding his bugle, he bids the garrison depart, and orders the castle to be quickly rendered. But from the high rampart came the reply, 'I, a Forbes,[1] hold this castle for the Prince of Orange, and for him will I hold it, if the gods permit.' There was no delay, all were roused at the proud response. Keppoch, as the commander, was sent at once with a strong force. He approached the walls with sound of horn and pipe, and encircled Ruthven Castle with his men. Thrice

---

[1] Captain John Forbes, brother of the Laird of Culloden, Duncan Forbes. He was employed by his brother to convey his address to the Prince of Orange, and by his influence was made Major in Grant's regiment, I presume, in 1690, over the nominees of Melville and Mackay. He became lieutenant-colonel, and was employed (as he was at any rate going north) to carry the order respecting the Glencoe massacre to Sir John Hill. He expressed his horror at the order when the letter was opened. He afterwards commanded at Fort-William. Dundee treated him with great leniency on this occasion, and let him depart free, with his garrison. He passed through Dundee's camp, and noticed the horses all saddled and bridled, and concluded that this was for immediate action. As he passed down the Spey towards Mackay, he met two troopers from Mackay's force, about a mile from Raitts, one in red, the other in blue, 'whereof,' to quote Mackay's words, 'he in blue challenged Captain Forbes in French with a " *Qui vive*," who returning " *Vive le Roy Guilleaume*," the other said he had presently been commanded out of our post to get news of the enemy, and notwithstanding Forbes told him he would run great hazard of being caught by Dundee's men, he nevertheless pursued on his way.' These were the messengers of Lieut.-Col. Livingstone (afterwards Lord Kilsyth), and the Scots Dragoons, who were negotiating the transference of their service to Dundee. Forbes having informed Mackay of this event, inquiry was set on foot, which ended in Mackay becoming assured of the projected desertion, and thus being forced to retire towards the south, keeping his eye on the two troops of dragoons, till his strength should be increased. See notes, pp. 178, 179.

Terque palam magna custodem voce vocavit ;
Grampiacosque instare duces, Gramumque sub armis
Nunciat, obsessum qui funditus eruat arcem ;
Ni sese et victum dedat cum milite castrum.
Sed frustra ; sese pars apparat utraque pugnae.
Hic sibi commissam statuit defendere turrem ;
Kapochus in tenues hanc voverat ire favillas.
Continuo tormenta, Jovis quae fulmina vincunt,
Explodit, plumbique volant jam grandinis instar
Flammiferae glandes ; positisque ad moenia scalis,
Aggere lignorum fossas trabibusque repleri
Imperat, et rapidum submittere moenibus ignem.
Ipse dato tandem signo Forbesius inquit,
' Hoc mihi qui castrum ductor dedit ille tenendum
Haud procul est, qui si non inter solis eoi
Exortus aderit ternos, haec Gramus habebit
Moenia, et exutis discedam inglorius armis.'
Ter Tartesiacis Phoebus se immersit in undis,
Terque caput nigris rutilum referebat ab Indis.
Cum promissa dies tradendae advenerat arcis,
Nulla acies campo, nusquam M'Kaius instat,
Subsidiumve tulit ; captam Forbesius arcem,
Et sese, et totum victori dedidit agmen.

with loud voice, he summoned the commander to conference. He told him that the Highland clans had taken the field, and that the Graham was in arms, and that unless he yielded up his post, himself, and his force, the castle would be levelled to its foundations. It is in vain. Both parties prepare for the fray : this one determines to defend the stronghold committed to him, and Keppoch vows that he will give the place to the flames. Forthwith he discharges his guns, surpassing the weapons of Jove, and like hail fly the bullets of lead. Ladders are fixed to the walls, and he bids the ditch be filled with piles of wood and beams, and to apply the rapid flame to the fortress. At length, the signal being given, Forbes himself spoke : ' That general, who gave me this castle to hold, is near. If he come not within three risings of the sun in the east, the Graham shall have these walls, and I will depart inglorious, laying down my arms.' Thrice sank the sun in Tartessian waters, and thrice he raised his rosy head from the dark Indies. When the day appointed for the surrender of the castle arrived, there was no host on the plain, Mackay pressed not forward, nor brought relief. Forbes yielded the captured

Ille autem mediis projecit lampada tectis
Primus, et ardentes prosternit culmine muros.
Inde trahit captam victor longo ordine turbam ;
Et petit antiqui tentoria more triumphi.
  Interea gelidae ductor M'Kaius Alvae
Ad delubra loco jam castra tenebat iniquo.
Sublicius trabibus vastis a fronte jacet pons,
A tergo atque altae fluctabant gurgite fossae,
Cinxit et amne latus dextrum, silvaque sinistrum.
Temporaque ignavo perdens hic lenta veterno.
Conscia sollicitis exolvit pectora curis.
Grampiadum medio sublimis in agmine Gramus
Rhaetia sublatis linquens munimina signis,
Per campos patefecit iter, gravibusque gementem
Tellurem pulsabat equis ; cum nuntius hostes

castle, and himself, and his whole force, to the victor, who at once applied the torch to the roofs, and threw down the burning walls. Then, as a conqueror, he leads the captured throng in long line, and in the manner of an ancient triumph he sought the camp.

  Meanwhile, General Mackay was now encamped at the Kirk of chilly Alvie, in a position difficult to attack. In his front lay a wooden bridge of vast timbers; in his rear was a ditch of deep rolling water; a burn [1] protected his right, and the woods his left. Here, passing away his time in sluggish lethargy, he relieves his breast, conscious of anxious care. The Graham, mounted, in the midst of his array of Highlanders, leaving with raised standards the Castle of Raitts, made his way through the open country. The earth was trembling under the heavy tramp of his cavalry, when a messenger with a lying rumour [2] reported that the enemy was

---

[1] It is difficult, without study on the spot, to identify this camp. If the bridge was over the Spey, which is not probable, we may suppose the camp at the north end of it, the rear covered by the Loch of Alvie, the right by a local stream, and the left by the woods. If he were facing up the Spey, he might have his rear towards the west side of the loch, with a bridge over a considerable stream in his front, the winding of the burn would protect his right, and the woods between him and the Spey, the left. Perhaps Bruce addressed him from the Waterloo Cairn Rocks, or from the Tor of Alvie, or from where the Duke of Gordon's monument now stands.

[2] I suppose that this movement was caused by a rumour of Mackay's presence, and that Mackay had not shown himself in his reconnoitring at Raitts. The rumour may have been late intelligence of Ramsay's former effort to get through Athole into Badenoch, or early news of his return.

Mendaci rumore refert denso agmine montes
Scandere, Nassiacas et pone instare cohortes.
Flectit signa, viam retro monstrante Loyello,
Dundius, atque aciem mittit duce fratre pedestrem
Surgentem ad tumulum, denso qui vimine silvae
Cingitur hinc atque hinc, et Spejae clauditur alveo.
Ipse celer turmam supra ardua ducit equestrem
Saxa per et scopulos, totoque ex agmine lectos
Mittit in arma viros; nusquam tamen agmina contra,
Et nullae hostiles apparent rupibus alae.
Brussius ad celsae fanum praemittitur Alvae
Bis senis instructus equis, atque appulit hostem.
Intra castra videt tuta statione teneri.
Constitit adversi sublimis vertice saxi,
Increpuitque ducem, dictisque instigat acerbis.
'Tune ille arctois M'Kaius ortus in oris,
Perfidus in patriam, qui pro praedone nefanda

crossing the mountains in strength, and that the Orange troopers were pressing on in his rear. He wheels about, and Loyell[1] leads the way. Dundee also despatched a body of foot under his brother, to a rising ground, which, with a dense girdle of wood surrounding it, was also fenced by the current of the Spey. He himself leads some horse over the rocky heights, and through the rugged defiles he sends out chosen scouts. Nowhere was there an enemy to be seen, and nowhere could any wing of the alleged army be descried.[2] Bruce, who was sent forward towards the Kirk of Alvie with a dozen horse, and approached the enemy, discovered him holding his safe post within his camp. Stationing himself on the top of a high rock, he assails the general, and lashes him with bitter words: 'Art thou then that Mackay from the North, faithless to your country, who, on behalf of the robber,

---

[1] Napier translates 'Loyello,' Lochiel, and he may be right; but I was inclined to look upon this as a mere movement of videttes, and to suppose that it was led by the laird of Loyal. No Ogilvy has appeared in the *Grameid*, but Sir David Ogilvy of Clova was certainly out with Dundee at this time. I do not know whether there was an Ogilvy of Loyal in those days, but it is now an Airlie property. Dundee's despatch compared with Mackay's account supports Napier's view. Lochiel led the force which went much farther than Dundee intended.

[2] Captain Bruce; see former note on him, p. 158. In a note in Book V. on Mackay at Edinglassie he is referred to again as having been with the dragoons. The construction here is involved, and only a suggestion as to the rendering of the passage is given above.

Bella geris, patriae patrem civilibus armis
Opprimis, O Stygii poenis digne omnibus Orci!
Et malefide Deo, et patriae, Regique rebellis,
Non impune diu laetabere crimine tali.
Castra, miser, Batavi scelerata relinque tyranni,
Et sua redde suis; et Caesaris arma capesse.
Aut si rem dubiae mavis committere pugnae
Hoc te siste loco, et campo te crede patenti.'
Mox equitum celeres elata voce cohortes
Affatur, notosque vocat blaeso ore sodales
Atque ait; 'O Socii, quondam pia signa secuti
Caesaris, at Domino nunc transfuga turba relicto
Arma quid attonitam praedonis fertis in arcton?
Inque Caledonium convertitis impia Regem
Agmina? degeneres quae tanta ignavia mentes
Possidet? O servum pecus ingens dedecus aevi!
Quaerite nunc latebras, aut praepete fidite[1] cursu,
Non erit huic sceleri murus satis iste tuendo.

wages this ill-starred war, and oppressest the father of the country? O wretch! worthy of all the penalties of Stygian darkness, faithless to God, and to your country and your king a rebel! Not with impunity shall you long rejoice in such crime. Leave the defiled camp of the Orange tyrant, give him back his own, and take up the arms of the Caesar; or, if you prefer it, leave your stronghold, and trust to the issue of a battle on the open plain.' Presently, with uplifted voice, he addressed the dragoons,[2] and calls his former comrades in agitated tones. 'O comrades, do you who once followed the sacred standards of the King, your master deserted, do you now, a pack of turncoats, bear the arms of the robber against the astonished North? Do you against the Scottish King turn your impious force? Does such villainy possess your degenerate souls? O pack of slaves, disgrace of your age, seek now the darkness, and trust to your heels, for the strength of

---

[1] 'fidite' should have the dative.

[2] These were the two troops, which had all along, through Lord Dunmore's influence, and the action of Lieutenant-Colonel Livingstone, and other officers, been keeping up communication with Dundee, and awaiting a suitable opportunity for joining him. Lady Dundee had been an instrument in the communication, while the dragoons lay near Dudhope. 'Blaeso ore' I have translated 'agitated tones' by perhaps a stretch. 'Blaesus' is applied to the shaking condition of a man in drink, and may mean here shaking or agitated speech.

Dundius, haec ferro qui crimina vindicet, instat
Agmine, meque olim ductorem agnoscite vestrum.
Si quis in ore pudor, virtusve in corde residit,[1]
Flectite signa, viri, nostrisque accedite castris.'
  Sic fatus : responsa viro fumantia reddit
Scaurius, horrendis accenso pulvere bombis.
Brussius ignivomis contra tonat impiger armis
Inde pedem rigidae muris referebat ab Alvae,
Et procul hostiles speculatus ab aggere turmas
Lora dabat levibus salebrosa per arva caballis,
Atque in castra redux ignavum nuntiat hostem
Carpere securos inter tentoria somnos.
Protinus ad famam vicini laetior hostis
Dundius instructis denso advolat agmine turmis.
Nauchtanique procul Dunum post terga relinquens,

your position will not avail you in such crime. Dundee, with the sword of vengeance for your guilt, is near you in force. Look at me, your commander in former times. If in your face any shame, and in your heart any virtue, remains, men! turn your standards and come to our camp.' Thus he spoke, and for answer Scourie sent a smoking reply, the powder being fired in the terrible guns. Bruce quickly fired back, and withdrew from the walls of Alvie. Giving rein to his light horse through woods and fields, he returned to the camp, having reconnoitred from his post the strength of the enemy, and made his report, that they in sloth were taking safe rest within their camp. At once Dundee, rejoicing at the tidings of the nearness of the foe, advances with a compact body of troops in good order. Having left Dun Nachtan[2] some way behind, he marvelled

---

[1] Dog-Latin for English 'resides.'

[2] Dunachton, the old castle of the Mackintosh on Loch Inch. It was never rebuilt after this destruction by the hand of Keppoch. It is probable that it received its name from Nectan, a monarch of the Picts, who exercised important influences on his country, and gave his name to more than one place in it. He defeated the Southern king Ecgfrid in the great battle of Dunnichen, in 685, and drove the Saxon power south of the Forth. He yielded, however, to Saxon influence in the hands of the Church, and bowed to the teaching of Ceolfrid, from his monastery of Jarrow, as to the Roman rites. A mysterious Boniface also had to do with this change. In 717 he expelled the Columban clergy from Pictish territory, and himself became a cleric. After various commotions both within the Scottish kingdom of Dalriada, and the Pictish, whose seat was at Scone, Nectan returned to claim his crown. He was eventually defeated by Aengus, on the banks of a lake formed by the river Spey, called

Surgere miratur glomerantem ad nubila fumum.
Kapochus haec magna rediens ad moenia pompa,
Postquam Ruthvenas a culmine straverat arces,
Vindictae stimulis, praedaeque accensus amore,
In cinerem, et rapidis commiscuit ignibus aedes.
Hinc pecora, et ruptis populata magalia[1] tectis,
Abductique boves, crebraeque per arva rapinae,
Nec cohibere valet saevi dux militis iras,
Quin ruat, et rapidis permisceat omnia flammis.
Hinc volat acer equo peditemque equitemque fatigat,
Et pernice gradu Dalradia transilit arva,
Saxa, amnesque secans, et muris imminet Alvae.
Scaurius ut sensit venientem cominus hostem

to see there clouds of smoke rising to the skies. Keppoch after he had destroyed Ruthven Castle, having returned with great pomp to this house, fired it, urged by the spur of revenge, and the love of plunder, and reduced it to ashes. The flocks, the ravished wealth of the harried houses, oxen, and the common booty of the fields, were carried off. Nor was our general able to restrain the violence of this savage soldier from breaking out, and wrapping the whole district in flames. Dundee, on horseback, moved swiftly forward both horse and foot, and at quick step passed through the fields of Dalraddy, crossing rocks and streams, till he threatens the camp at Alvie. Scourie,[2] when he perceived the

---

Loogdeae, but now, according to Skene, Loch Inch, and his name probably stuck to the Dun where the defeat occurred. He died the following year, the date being probably 729 A.D. See Skene's *Celtic Scotland*, vol. i. chaps. v. and vi. Also for very interesting matter connecting the site with St. Columba and St. Adamnan, see Life of St. Columba, vol. vi. of *Historians of Scotland*, p. 328, and *Early Christian Times*, Rhind Lectures for 1879, by Joseph Anderson, pp. 195-8. Why, however, should it not be named after Neachton, the founder of the house of Macpherson?

Claverhouse had moved down the north bank of the Spey from Raitts, had passed Dunachton, leaving it unharmed, and was pressing forward towards Alvie, by Boat of Inch, Kincraig, and Dalraddy, when he beheld Dunachton in flames, and the country around in a blaze, through the personal vengeance of Keppoch. See note on Keppoch in this Book, pp. 127-8.

[1] False quantity.

[2] To account for this sudden departure of Mackay, it must be remembered, 1st, that his strength lay in horse, and though Grant supplied some oats and forage, yet the horses were finding nothing in the fields, and were losing their bellies, as Mackay phrases it, and while many died, many more became useless; 2d, having received two fresh troops of dragoons from the south, his suspicions

Praecipiti sua castra fuga sub nocte reliquit
Clam media, silvasque metu, montesque tenebat.
Formidanda velut cervo duce turma leonum
Agmina cervorum metuit ductore leone.
Clara viri sic fama valet pro mille maniplis,

enemy upon him, with precipitate flight left his camp secretly at midnight, and in fear took to the hills and the woods. Thus does the formidable army of lions,[1] when led by a stag, fear the army of stags, when led by a lion. Thus the bright fame of a hero is worth a thousand swords. The name of the Graham was

---

were aroused about them, and they could not be trusted. Two days after they arrived at Culnakyle, which was his headquarters, two deserters came in from Dundee's camp, instigated, it would seem, by Blair and Pollock, who told the general that the dragoons were negotiating with Claverhouse to desert to him. Mackay did not trust these deserters, though they named Lieut.-Col. Livingstone, Captains Murray, Livingstone, and Creighton, as ringleaders in the matter. Balfour and the Majors were not inculpated. He sent them—the deserters—to Bala Castle, till he should learn more. On comparing notes with Colonel Thomas Livingstone, suspicion was increased, and the arrival of Forbes, with his story of the two dragoons, one in red and the other in blue, and the fact coming out that they had not been sent out for news, all made clear that his two fresh troops were worse than useless, and a positive danger. The appearance of Dundee the day after receiving Forbes' account in the neighbourhood of the camp at Alvie, to which he had moved a portion of his force from Culnakyle, settled his determination to retire swiftly at night, thinking that Dundee would not know where he was gone, as he might have gone by either of three ways. He showed no suspicion of his dragoons, but put them in the front as usual, near himself, while Balfour and the Majors, with part of the dragoons, brought up the rear. He placed 200 of his Dutch grenadiers in rear of the leading horse, then 70 English horse, and 200 brisk Highlanders, and, setting out from Culnakyle at night, he took his way down the river, to use his own words, 'with hungry horse and men, and marching by a gentleman's house called Grant of Ballindalloch, who was with Dundee, made no halt till he came to a place called Balvany, where he was forced to settle himself, till he should get some bread for his men and oats for his horses.' He stayed at Balveny till near sunset.—*Memoirs*, p. 32. There can be no doubt that, in the circumstances, Mackay showed himself a wise and vigorous commander. It should be added that he obtained little or no supplies till five o'clock in the afternoon, and he was kept on the stretch all day, owing to the disappearance of a reconnoitring party, sent out in the morning to gain intelligence as to Dundee's approach. Our author would seem to indicate that Mackay's flight was from Alvie. Comparing the other accounts, I am convinced that Mackay's headquarters were at Culnakyle, and that his camp at Alvie was only an outpost from the camp, or perhaps a resting-place, as Mackay fell back from his expedition up the river.

[1] I think the above is the sense, though it may not sound complimentary to the Highland army. It is the fame of the hero that gives point to the proverb.

Et Grami sat nomen erat quo terreat hostem,
Urgeat atque loco dare terga inhonesta relicto.
Inde rapit gressus, atque Alvae praeterit aedem,
Et silvas, Rothemurce, tuas, et flumina Spejae
Transmeat ad Coili dictum de nomine campum.
Et nemora, et vastos solerti indagine saltus
Lustrat Abrenethios, et Cromdala rura secabat,
Subsequiturque ducem fugientem, atque agmine toto
Instat, et hostiles ceu turbine dissipat alas ;
Bellisonoque procul terram clangore tubarum
Concutit, ignivomis et sidera territat armis.
  Ecce repens totis rumor penna alite castris
Discurrit magno chlamydata per agmina plausu,

enough to affright the enemy, and to compel him to desert his post in disgraceful flight. Dundee hurries on, and passes the house of Alvie,[1] and thy woods, O Rothiemurchus,[2] and at the fields named from Coilus,[3] he fords the Spey. With wary skill he traverses the woods, and vast forest paths of Abernethy,[4] and onward marches through the haughs of Cromdale,[5] pursuing the flying general. He presses after him with his whole force, and, as a whirlwind, disperses the hostile squadrons. He shakes the earth with the clang of the trumpet, and affrights the stars with the fire flashing muskets.
  Quickly, on flying wing, amid the applause of the plaided host,

---

[1] I do not know anything of the house of Alvie. The kirk has long been famous, with its manse and lochs, and lovely scenery around. Kinrara may have replaced the house of Alvie.

[2] With the Doune of Rothiemurchus, and its great forests of pine, travellers are very familiar.

[3] This, I think, is Kinakyle, the head of the strait or pass, as Culnakyle is the foot, or back of it. Here upper Craigellachie—the rock of alarm—guards the Grant country, and here there was a ford over the Spey. Dundee passes to the south, or rather east side of the river here. Our author, for his derivation, still falls back upon King Coilus. See note in Book III. p. 112.

[4] The great forests of Abernethy are still the chief features of the place, with the magnificent Cairngorm towering over them. Ballindalloch and Glenmoriston would recall stirring scenes in their family history as they rode through this forest. See *Memorialls of the Trubles*, Spalding Club, vol. i. p. 2. James-an-Tuim, the famous freebooter, was related to them both, and had caused much ill-blood among the Grants for which Abernethy saw mutual vengeance.

[5] Cromdale and these localities were soon to see Dundee on his march back with his Highlanders in safety, and the next year, to see them, under Buchan, routed and slaughtered, 1st May 1690.

Jam Batavum cessisse ducem, turpique dedisse
Terga fugae, camposque metu liquisse patentes,
Et petere australem pede praepete littoris oram.
Dundius urget iter, curvaque in valle Liveti,
Ut procul ad riguos contorsit lumina campos,
Prospicit hostiles latitantes aggere turmas.
Grampiadum subito surgens ferit aethera clamor.
Adventasse diem gaudent quo contigit hostem
Cernere, et egregiis virtutem ostendere factis.
Arma manu expediunt alacres, fusique per omnem
Planitiem aequales[1] inter se passibus ibant;
Taurea nudatis subducunt tegmina plantis,
Et chlamydum jacta strue nudi in bella parant se.

the word passes that the Dutch general is giving way, and has indeed taken to base flight, that he was leaving the glens, and with swift foot was seeking the South. Dundee pushes on, and in the winding Glenlivet,[2] as he turned his eyes on the distant watered plains, he beheld the hostile force passing into concealment behind a hill. At once to the heavens rose the shout of the clans. They rejoice that the day has come when they see their enemy, and when they may display their valour in brave deeds. With alacrity they draw their swords, and extended on the plain, they move in ordered ranks; they cast their brogues of bull's hide, and make a pile of their plaids, and thus stripped, prepare

---

[1] Perhaps 'aequatis.'

[2] It would seem that Dundee was doubting whether he should strike up Glen Livet, and into Strath Deveron, when, catching sight of the rearguard of the enemy, probably between Ballandalloch and Balveny, he prepared to attack. Mackay feared the Strath Deveron movement, and had sent out a party, both on the way he was going, and the way he had come. He hardly gave his men any rest, or time for food after he had procured it, and his party not returning from the side towards the Highlanders, he marched them off in the same order as the day before. About a couple of miles on, he, looking back, saw the Highlanders gathering in their stragglers, and forming into clans; presently their cavalry, about 150 strong, passed over a stream, and 'embattled themselves, to favourise the passage of the infantry, who also crossed, and embattled,' and then followed their baggage. Mackay, judging his men by this time to be two miles ahead of him, turned to follow them, but his nephew stayed on where he was, and got a fright, from the return of the morning party, who seemed to be taking matters very easily. It seems they were commanded by the man in blue, who was Lieutenant-Colonel Livingstone's sergeant. By this time, Gordon of Edinglassie had appeared with the country foot, and the Master of Forbes with some horse. Mackay continued his march all night, till he crossed the Bogie at four o'clock in the morning, dead tired.

Gramus ab excelsi speculatus vertice montis,
Cernit ut hostiles raptim dare terga cohortes,
Et cessisse loco, jubet incentiva sonari
Classica, Grampiacas marte impulsura catervas.
Ergo ruit, Batavumque tubae clangore lacessit
Buccinus, ingentemque procul dedit aere recurvo
Ipsa ante ora sonum, 'Gramo duce, et auspice Gramo,
Rex Jacobe iterum regnis potiere Britannis.'
Ut tuba terribilem sonuit mavortia pugnam,
Pulverulenta citis M'Kaius ocyor euris
Terga dedit, cursuque ad littora tendit anhelus.
Ut jejuna petens plenas vulpecula caulas
Nocte sub obscura duris latrata molossis
Vertit terga fuga, silvis tectura pudorem,
Demisitque jubas, et caudam subjicit alvo.
　　　Dundius in patulo pugnam poscentia campo
Signa movet, praecepsque fugacem fertur in hostem.
Atque animo exultans humeros thorace fatigat,
Et galea effusos pressit rutilante capillos ;

for the battle. The Graham, looking from a hill-top, perceived that the enemy's squadrons were stealing away from their position. He bids the trumpet sound the set on,[1] to incite the Highland host to the pursuit. Then rushed out the trumpeters, and affrighted the Dutchman with the blare of the clarions, pouring out from the curved brazen throats in his very face, the grand notes of 'The King shall enjoy his own again.'[2] As the war trumpets sounded to the fray, Mackay, swifter than the east wind, turns his dusty back, and panting, hurries towards the coast. Thus the hungry fox, seeking in the darkness of night the full sheepfold, turns when he hears the barking of the fierce dogs, and with drooping neck and brush trailing in the mire, he hides his shame under the cover of the woods.

Dundee moves his standards waving on to battle into the open plain, and speeds headlong after the flying enemy. In exultation he weights his shoulders with his corslet, and presses back his flowing locks within his gleaming helmet. He calls for his

---

[1] I have translated *incentiva* 'the set on,' in compliment to Lord Dunfermline, whose war-cry as a Seton was 'Set on.'

[2] The author has, no doubt, in his mind the old Cavalier song, 'The King shall enjoy his own again,' very popular with the Royalists during the Commonwealth.

Bellantemque poposcit equum, cumque omnibus armis
Praecipiti insiluit saltu, sonipesque superbum
Sessorem dorso impositum sentire videtur,
Et cursu superat boream, non Castoris ibat,
Sic nec Achillis equus, nec praepete Pegasus ala,
Bellerophonque leves non acrior impulit auras.
Jamque ruit variis chlamydata per agmina gyris
Hortaturque duces: fidumque ad jussa clientem
Fraserium vocat, et paucis affatur euntem.
'Ite O sceptrigero nunquam adversata Stuarto
Beulea progenies, hostemque urgete fugacem
A tergo, et subitae praeludia sumite pugnae.
Ite citi, cursuque leves praevertite nimbos.'
Ille volat, cervoque omni velocior ibat,
Tergaque flammivomis Batavi ducis atterit armis,
Atque lacessitum dictis mordacibus hostem
Stare loco jubet, atque aequo se credere campo.
Hoc magis ille citos urgens ad littora gressus,
Praecipiti tepidum cursu properabat ad austrum.
Illum fulmineus toto premit agmine Gramus
Turbinis in morem, profugumque per arva secutus

charger, and in complete armour he leapt into the lofty saddle. The war-horse seemed to feel the pride of his rider, and flew faster than the north wind. Not the horse of Castor, nor of Achilles, went thus; nor Pegasus on fleet wing. Bellerophon ne'er cleft the light air more fleetly. Now the Graham gallops circling amid the plaided host, and exhorts the leaders. He calls the cadet of the Frasers,[1] faithful to his commands, and addresses him as he goes, in few words: 'Go! O son of Beauly, never found opposed to the Royal Stuart, press on the rear of the flying enemy, and begin the battle. Swift must be your course, pass the light clouds in your speed.' He flies, fleeter than any stag, and attacks the rear of the Dutch force with musket fire, and bids, in cutting words, the harassed enemy to stand, and trust himself on the level ground. But he, urging his steps all the more rapidly towards the coast, hastened his precipitate course southwards. The lightning-like Graham presses him with his whole line, and, like a whirlwind, follows the fugitives through the fields. In one

---

[1] Fraser of Foyers. See previous note on him. Beauly, of course, refers to the chief seat of the Frasers. The picture of Dundee arming, and mounting his charger, and such a charger, is very fine, and full of life.

Uno[1] eodemque die ter castris exuit hostem.
Jam juga transierat Balrynnidis alta nivosi,
Et post terga procul Balvenia rura relinquit.
Sol ruit interea et vesper processit Olympo.
Assurgit fremitusque virum, flatusque sequentum
Fervet equûm ; resonatque ingens clamoribus aether,
Antra gemunt, tellusque gravi tremit icta pedum vi.
Hinc peditum legio ruit, hinc ferrata trementem
Ungula cornipedum saltu secat alite campum.
Nec requies donec nox abstulit atra colorem
Rebus, et effusae terram texere tenebrae.

LIBRI QUARTI FINIS.

day, he thrice drove the enemy from his position. Already he had crossed the high declivities of snowy Balrynnis,[2] and left the fields of Balveny[3] far behind. The sun, meanwhile, is setting, and the evening star coming forth on the heavens. Still rise the shouts of men, still comes the panting of the pursuing horses; the air resounds with loud clamour, the hollows groan, the earth trembles, stricken with the force of their heavy tramp; here, at the double, comes a regiment of foot, there the iron hoof of the cavalry cuts the quivering turf at the gallop. There is no rest till black night steals colour from the scene, and outspread darkness covers the earth.

END OF BOOK IV.

[1] Scan 'un' êodēmqŭe.'

[2] Balrynnis, or Belrynnis, is the common pronunciation of this hill or mountain. I find Ben Rinnes is the spelling in the maps. Mackay's account and the Poet's square on the whole, but the three halts of Mackay do not appear in his Memoirs. Mackay notices the setting of the sun, and that the Highlanders were preparing to pursue him.

[3] The household at Balveny suffered much during these wars. Alexander Duff of Braco, to whom Balveny belonged in 1695, presented a doleful petition to the Committee for Security of the Kingdom, showing that Mackay had put a garrison of two companies of foot, under Captain Gordon, into the house, and because it was a convenient post between the Highlands and the Lowlands, he had made it a magazine of victual. The petitioner had 500 bolls of meal in the house of his own, which seem to have been made free with. After Killiecrankie, the rebels, he says, entered the house an hour after the garrison left, and seized on the whole meal, extending to 430 bolls. He claims repayment from the county poll, more especially as he himself was attending the Meeting of Estates. His father, too, an old man of seventy, was taken out of his own house, which was plundered, and destroyed by them, and 'he himself keeped in a starving condition, until he was necessitate to pay a ransom.' The Committee considered the meal a debt due by the country, and recommended the petitioner himself to his Majesty. See *Acts of Parl. Scot.*, vol. ix. p. 447.

LIBER QUINTUS.

FAMA levis tota Gramum diffuderat arcto
  Terribilem Batavo formidandumque tyranno ;
Atque accincta vagis nigrae formidinis alis
Terruit attonitum diro rumore senatum ;
Terga dedisse fuga Batavum, celeresque cohortes
Deficere ad dominum, converso marte, priorem ;
Ipsumque innumero stipatum milite Gramum
Ferre triumphatam victricia signa per arcton.[1]

LIGHT fame had carried through the whole North the name of the Graham, terrible and to be dreaded by the Dutch tyrant, and on airy wing had affrighted the astounded senate with the dread rumour of a darksome terror ; that the Dutch general [2] had turned in flight, and that the swift cavalry had deserted to their former commander, changing sides, and that the Graham himself, with a numberless host, was carrying conquering standards through

---

[1] *Var. lect.* At 'arcton' a line is drawn to margin, where a verse is inserted (or parts of two verses). It reads, 'Evolat alt—petens, et turgida gutture solvent ferriitque.' Parts are illegible.

[2] The Poet here has taken some licence as to time. Mackay did not begin to retreat till after Ramsay had begun his retreat from Athole, so that Ramsay's appointment could not have been made in consequence of Mackay's defeat. Ramsay was despatched soon after the 6th May, additional forces were hurried up in consequence of a letter from Mackay, dated 16th May, and Hamilton, in a letter of 24th May, hopes that Ramsay's detachment had found him safely. There is an evident intention on the part of the Poet to exalt the importance of the *Dalhousia proles*, perhaps in compliment to the rising importance of the Dalhousie family in Forfarshire, through the marriage of Lord Ramsay with Lady Jane Maule. A George Ramsay appears as a class-fellow of Philp at St. Andrews, which may account for the special favour, should he be the same.

The consternation which the Poet pictures in Edinburgh at this stage is evidently transferred from the commotions occurring after Killiecrankie. Balcarres tells us, p. 48 : 'Never were men in such a consternation as Duke Hamilton and the rest of the Parliament in Edinburgh. Some were for retiring to England, others to the western shires of Scotland ; they considered whether to set at liberty all the prisoners or make them more close. The last was resolved on, and we were all locked up and debarred from seeing our friends, but never had so many visits from our enemies, all making apologies for what had passed, protesting they always wished us well, as we should see when they had opportunity.'

Ilicet insano turbata Comitia[1] motu
Sede[2] parant alia tectis migrare relictis.
Hinc fremuere viri, saevi quos criminis horror
Exagitat stimulis, et conscia corda flagellis.
Et conjuratus plorat sua damna senatus ;
Proditor ultrices scelerum sibi conscius enses
Horret, et instantem credit jam calcibus hostem.
Illum et cyanea cui crura nitentia vitta,
Cuique humeri rutilo sublimes sidere fulgent,
Arripuit furor, et mentem dolor obruit ingens.
Ergo coit pleno sua conciliabula coetu
Ille opifex diri sceleris, cui plurima dictis
Consiliisque fides ; et voce silentia rumpens,
Postquam conceptum sedasset mente dolorem,
Attonitique graves animi compescuit aestus :
' En ' ait, ' haud alios inducunt fata tumultus,
Quam cum Saxonidum civilibus obrutus armis
Carolus undantes rerum amisisset habenas.

the subdued North. Forthwith the troubled Committee, in wild commotion, leaving their place, prepare to change it for another seat.
Then rage the men whom fear of punishment, and hearts conscious of guilt, urge on as with whip and spur. The conspiring council bewails its losses. The guilty-minded traitor shrinks from the avenging sword, and believes the enemy to be pressing on his heels. He,[3] on whose decorated limb the blue fillet shines, and whose lofty shoulders are adorned with the radiant star, is now carried away with fury, and now oppressed with woe. Then he, the author of the dire deed, having great faith in words and counsels, gathers in full assembly his whole committee, and pressing down his fear, and quieting his stricken soul, he breaks silence : ' Lo,' he says, ' the Fates bring on us convulsions, like to those which they sent us when Charles, o'erwhelmed in the English civil wars, lost the flowing reins of power. Under his auspices

---

[1] 'Comitia': false quantity.   [2] *Sic* in original.

[3] See note, p. 30, on Hamilton and the Garter. Balcarres notes the manner of the Duke in the Convention, saying, that he and his Jacobite friends had nothing to do but to sit still and hear Hamilton bawl and bluster after his usual manner, and Sir James Montgomery and Sir John Dalrymple scold like watermen.

Rothes, in a letter which Queensberry labels as a 'pleasant story of Duke Hamilton,' speaks of his 'scoulding and rage.' See Napier, *Memoirs*, vol. i. p. 387. The Poet does justice to his verbosity in giving him these 50 hexameters.

Illius auspiciis Montis ferus ille Rosarum
Marchio juratos solenni foedere Scotos,
Agminaque infestis stravit socialia signis.
Quot dedit ille virum violento millia Letho ?
Quot lanianda feris, terraeque inhumata reliquit
Corpora ? quot crudo cumulavit funera ferro ?
Quot miseras caesis nudavit civibus urbes ?
Innocuoque altos quot sanguine tinxerat amnes ?
Ille pios patrio conjunctos foedere fratres
Efferus ad Veterem prostravit caedibus Ernam,
Tibberis et campum caesorum oneravit acervis.

that fierce Marquis of Montrose overthrew, by his hateful arms, the Scots, covenanted together under the solemn league,[1] and their allied forces. How many thousands did he send to Lethe ? How many bodies did he leave unburied on the ground to be torn by wild beasts ? With the cruel sword what destructions did he multiply ? How many miserable cities did he depopulate by slaughter ? How many deep rivers did he tinge with innocent blood ? At Auldearn[2] that fierce Captain

---

[1] 'Marchio juratos,' etc. Marchio, late Latin for Marquis. I at first translated it as 'Martio,' pertaining to the month of March, and concluded that it had reference to the National Covenant, signed in that month in 1638. The Solemn League and Covenant is probably that bond referred to here. It was the product of the Assembly of 1643 and the English commissioners, headed by Sir Harry Vane, came out in August, was accepted at Westminster in September, and sworn to in Scotland in October of that year.

[2] The victories of Montrose alluded to in this speech of Hamilton are—

1*st*, Tippermuir near Perth (spelt Tibber by our author and by Spalding), where he defeated Lord Elcho and the Covenanters, Sept. 1st, 1644.

2*d*, Inverlochy, where Argyll and the Campbells were defeated, 2d Feb. 1645.

3*d*, Auldearn in Nairn, where General Hurry was routed, 5th May 1645.

4*th*, Alford in Aberdeenshire, a victory over General Baillie, 2d July 1645.

5*th*, Kilsyth, where Baillie was again defeated, 15th August 1645.

The battle of Aberdeen on 13th September 1644 is not noticed, but the allusion to the defeat of Montrose is of course to Philiphaugh, received on the same day in the following year, September 13th, 1645. The reference to the unburied dead is no doubt true enough owing to the haste of the marches, and the following extract from Spalding, *Trubles*, vol. ii. p. 407, bears out the statement : 'It is lamentabill to heir how thir Irishis who had gottin the spoyll of the toune did abuse the samen. The men that thay killit thay wold not suffer to be bureit, bot tirrit (*i.e.* stripped) thame of thair clothis, syne left thair naikit bodeis lying aboue the ground.' At p. 410 vol. ii. we are told, however, that this conduct of the Irish was contrary to the order of Montrose, who had directed the people to bury their dead, which they did only in fear and trembling.

Illum magnificis etiam concurrere signis
Abria, et insignem vidit victricibus armis,
Kilsythum pulsoque superbum fecerat hoste,
Extulit inque suis victorem Alfordia campis.
Et quocunque acies, ultriciaque impulit arma,
Nominis ille omnem terrore repleverat arcton.
Ausurus majora, ducum nisi provida cura
Gnaviter incoeptis obsisteret undique tantis,
Saxonidum turmas et ad arma vocasset equestres,
Ipsumque in mediis fudisset marte trophaeis.

 Dundius ex illo jam surgit germine germen
Nobile militiae, et Martis generosa propago,
Unica depulsi Gramus tutela Stuarti,
Atque reformati[1] spes praesulis omnis, et omne
Praesidium, Cathari terrorque stuporque Britanni.
Heu quanto arctoas excivit turbine gentes,
Auriacique ducis victricia repulit arma;
Impulit et versis hostem dare terga maniplis.
Et nunc Caesareis multum metuendus in armis,

overwhelmed the pious brethren, leagued together under the native Covenant, and he loaded Tipper Muir with heaps of slain. Him Lochaber too beheld in the battle, under triumphant standards, and illustrious in conquering arms, and he made Kilsyth proud over a beaten foe, and Alford showed him as a victor on its plains. Whithersoever he led his lines and avenging arms he filled the whole north with the terror of his name. He would have dared greater things had not the provident care of the commanders vigorously opposed on every hand these beginnings, and called up English cavalry to the war, and in the midst of his triumphs brought upon him defeat.

 'Now rises for the contest Dundee, a noble plant of the same stock, the gallant son of Mars, a Graham, the only protector of the exiled Stuart, the only hope and stay of the reformed prelates, the terror and confusion of the British Puritan. Alas! with what a commotion has he brought together the northern clans, and driven back the forces of the Dutch general, unused to defeat. He has compelled him to retreat with routed troops. Now he—

---

[1] The word is found frequently in the Pasquils of the time as a nickname for the stricter sect. See Preface.

Fulminat ad rapide currentia flumina Spejae.
Successu rerum tumidus, victorque secundo
Marte ruit, profugumque ad sceptra paterna Stuartum
Jam revocare parat, nostrumque ultricibus armis
Rumpere concessum, finemque imponere regni
Auriaci, et Batavas maria ultra arcere cohortes.
Hanc si vestra sinat crescentem ignavia pestem
Serpere, et ulterius gliscendo acquirere vires,
Sedibus his alio cuncti migrate relictis
Nudumque Abriaco jugulum submittite ferro.
Ergo agite, O nostri clarissima lumina regni,
Magnanimi heroes, victori occurrite Gramo,
Mittite in arma viros Batavorum ex agmine lectos;
Praestantemque ducem virtute, et fortibus armis
Eligite, et tantae rectorem imponite turbae;
Ilicet occiduae socialiaque agmina gentis
Addite in auxilium, et lapsis succurrite rebus.'
His dictis sedet, et finem dedit ore loquendi.
Assensere omnes nutu; fit plausus, et omnis
Aula strepit, magnoque tonat domus alta tumultu.
Garrula ceu densa sub nube caterva volantum

much to be dreaded—thunders with the royal army, by the swift waters of the Spey. As a victor elated with success under the favour of Mars he presses on, and already prepares to recall the Stuart to the ancestral sceptre, to annul by vengeful force what has been conceded to us, to put an end to the Orange reign, and to hurl the Dutch beyond the sea. If your sluggishness permits this growing evil to spread, and to acquire strength by further growth, then prepare to depart elsewhere from these seats, and submit your naked throats to the Lochaber claymore. Therefore act, chief lights of the kingdom! great-souled heroes! meet the conquering Graham, send men chosen from the Dutch force to the war, select a general eminent in virtue and valour, and make him chief of a great host. Forthwith, for our protection, bring up the covenanting levies of the west, and succour our afflicted state.' They all nod assent; then comes applause, and the whole chamber resounds, and the lofty roof thunders, with the sound of the great uproar. Thus the garrulous flock of crows,[1] when flying under a thick cloud, keeps deep silence, but as soon

---

[1] The translation is a suggestion of the meaning of a confused passage.

Corvorum strepere¹ tenet alta silentia linguae ;
Ut primum motis nigri dux agminis alis
Suscitat,² atque atram increpuit clamore catervam,
Tota cohors eadem modulamina gutture rauco
Perstrepit, et resono quatit ora loquacia cantu.
　Ductor erat Batavis acer Ramisaeus in armis
Celsi animi juvenis, clarisque parentibus ortus.

as the leader of the dusky crowd, with flapping and cawing, rouses up the black company, the whole body, then, with hoarse throat, utters the same cadence, and sings the same tune.
　There was a commander in the Dutch force, the courageous Ramsay,³ a youth of lofty soul, sprung from noble parentage. He,

---

　¹ What is 'strepere'? Perhaps 'strepitu' is meant, which will give the sense of keeping from noise.
　² *Var. lect.* 'Suscitat' seems to be written over 'agitat.'
　³ This was the Honourable George Ramsay, second son of George, second Earl of Dalhousie. He is described as colonel of dragoons. Colt, who gives such full evidence in the forfeiture proceedings, was lieutenant in Erskine's troop of Ramsay's regiment. He had served in Holland. Besides the notice of him in the *Grameid*, on which I give some remarks below in this note, I find he commanded the second party of the advanced guard which penetrated Killiecrankie Pass, in front of Mackay, and that, with the same party, he was posted on the left in the battle. The left began to flee before they were really attacked, and when Mackay was leading off the shattered remains of his force along the hills towards the castle of Weem, 'in the obscurity about two miles off the field, he came upon Colonel Ramsay, who had kept up the matter of 150 runaways without arms, and knew not in the world how he should best get them off.'—Mackay's *Memoirs*, pp. 58-61. In 1690, after the battle of Valcour, Ramsay was made a Brigadier-General, and Colonel of Scots Regiment of Guards. In 1702 he was appointed Commander-in-chief of all the forces in Scotland. The editor of Dundee's *Letters* has the following note, p. 58: 'I find the following notice respecting him in one of Robert Milne's MS. collections, which is now in the possession of my friend, Mr. Dundas of Arniston: *Nota*, The Earl of March and Major-General Ramsay were killed by too much drink, given them by the Marquis of Annandale, at ane entertainment in yᵉ Cannongate, 9th September 1705, occassioned upon the Court having defeat yᵉ country in a vote. Chanʳ Ogilvie and several others was with them.'
　An effort had been made to get for him the forfeited lands and title of Dundee, on account of his connection with the older family Scrymgeour, Earls of Dundee. He was a nephew of Margaret Ramsay, second daughter of the first Earl of Dalhousie, who had married John, first Earl of Dundee, and so he seemed to claim through his aunt. See also note, p. 187.
　The following statement as to the movements of Ramsay, and those of Mackay and Dundee, may help to harmonise the various accounts, or at any rate to reach the truth :—

Militis hic magni clarum sibi nomen adeptus,
Inclytus et gestis Belgarum ad littora rebus,

having made for himself the distinguished name of a great soldier,
and having become noted in affairs on the Belgian coast, gave hope

---

1st, An order by the Committee of Estates to Collectors of Customs to expedite Ramsay's baggage, without searching it, is dated 6th May 1689.

2d, His departure from Edinburgh was delayed two or three days, through the fright caused there by the appearing in the Firth of Forth of a fleet of 'Holland's herring bushes,' which were thought to be a French invasion.

3d, The next date I notice is the 18th May, when the Committee order all magistrates of boroughs to furnish Ramsay with horses and carts for his baggage as he may require. His march, after crossing from Leith to Burntisland, was through Fife to Perth.

4th, Hamilton, writing to Mackay, May 24th, says that Ramsay left Perth on the Wednesday preceding, which, as the 24th was a Friday, must have been the 22d. In this letter he assumes that Ramsay and Mackay would have effected a junction by the date of his letter.

5th, Having marched from Perth to Athole, he experienced hindrances, more or less serious, from Ballechan, which came to a head near Loch Garry, when, expecting an attack from Dundee in force, and the Athole men being very hostile, he blew up his ammunition, left his heavy baggage to be plundered, and retreated. On the morning of the 24th he had written from near Loch Garry that he would be at Ruthven that night, but instead of that he was beginning his retreat.

6th, His letter reached Mackay at Inverness on Saturday night, the 25th, who immediately prepared to march towards Ruthven to join him. He marched out of Inverness on Sunday morning, the 26th. When half-way to Ruthven—say, early on Monday morning—he received a message from the commander there that Ramsay had retreated, and that Dundee was only twelve miles above Ruthven, on the Spey. Mackay hesitated, but at last marched all the rest of the day and all night to Castle Grant and Culnakyle, far down the Spey.

7th, Dundee left Lochaber late on Saturday night by Glen Roy, reaching Garva on Sunday morning the 26th, and by the time the messenger left Ruthven for Mackay, his advanced party, at any rate, was within twelve miles of that castle. It is clear, then, that Ramsay fled on the strength of false intelligence, for he could have been in Ruthven Castle on Friday night before Dundee had left Lochaber. He was at a great disadvantage, owing to his not knowing the country, and not being able to trust those who did, while the minute directions sent to him by Mackay were intercepted by Ballechan and forwarded to Dundee. Our author's account of Ramsay's march by Cairn-a-month and Suy Hill is a mistake. It was Barclay's and Lesly's regiments from Forfar and Coupar-Angus which joined Mackay at Suy Hill on Wednesday the 5th June. Ramsay really returned from Perth by Athole and Badenoch, and Lord Murray, writing from Blair at twelve o'clock at night on the 4th June, speaks as if Ramsay had passed that place, and might be meeting Dundee, who, he understood, was still in Badenoch. Dundee was at Edinglassie by twelve o'clock at night on the 4th June, and Ramsay passed Ruthven and went on to Inverness, seeing nothing of the enemy, and hearing nothing of Mackay.

Spem dedit acceptam reparandi Marte ruinam.
Hunc placuit summo ductorem in bella Senatu
Mittere florentem aetate, et Mavorte superbum;
Milite Grampiacas armato ut rumperet Alpes,
Utque duci profugo rebus solamen in arctis
Ferret, et Auriacis nova jungeret agmina castris.
Ille audax animi nimium calidusque juventa
Rumpere inaccessas terrae super ardua rupes
Nititur, et scopulos boreae parat ire per altos.
Bis conatus erat nimbosa cacumina Grampi
Scandere, et Atholios cursu transcendere montes.

of retrieving the present ruin by his military skill. It pleased the supreme Council to send this general, in the prime of life, and proud of his soldiership, to the war, to burst through the Grampian Alps with an armed force, to carry support to the flying general in his straits, and to unite his fresh troops to the Orange strength. He, bold in spirit, and with the fire of youth, strives to force his way through the difficult passes of the lofty mountains, and over the high crags of the north. Twice he attempted to climb the cloudy summits of the Grampians, and to cross in his course the Athole hills. Twice the elder Ballechan,[1] taking up arms with

---

[1] Patrick Stewart of Ballechan, Baillie of Athole. He is named in the proclamation calling together the militia, dated 30th March 1689, and nominated a commissioner for the shire of Perth, April 27th, that year. When Dundee was returning from the raid into Angus, on his march to Loch Rannoch, he passed the house of Ballechan, and Colt bears witness that he gave the Viscount some bread and ale, and young Stewart says he himself walked two miles with them on foot as they rode away. It would seem that the Laird of Pitcur had been sent up to the house of Ballechan to desire Stewart to come and speak with Dundee. No doubt the hospitable elder Ballechan came down to the road-side with his servants, and the bread and ale, and an arrangement would be come to as to dealing with Ramsay's force, and other antagonistic movements through Athole. This, at any rate, was the first service that Ballechan rendered to Dundee in the campaign. When Lord Murray, the heir of Athole, had assembled his clan under Ballechan, and refused to declare for King James, they filled their bonnets with water, and drank a health to that King. Ballechan excluded Murray from the castle of Blair, and held it for King James, under a commission from Dundee, dated at Struan, July 21, 1689, and he is appointed 'Colonel of all men of Athole, vassals, or tenants, or neighbours, who have been in use to serve the Marquis of Athole.' A witness describes him as an old man standing at the gate of Blair with a gun in his hand. Mackay's movement, for the capture of Blair from Ballechan, resulted in Killiecrankie. Patrick Stewart signs the Bond of Association, with the other Highland chiefs, on the 24th August 1689. His name does not appear in the Decree of Forfeiture,

Olli bis sumptis senior Balachnius armis
Nobilis Atholii comitatus stirpe Stuarti,
Atque Robertiadum tota stipante caterva,
Inter preruptas ad conflua flumina cautes
Occurrit ; retroque pedem et dare terga coegit.
Bisque illum versis rapto secum agmine signis
Repulit ad Geream magno terrore paludem.
Consulit ergo fugae, et turpi formidine praeceps
Linquit nubiferos proles Dalhousia montes,
Acceleratque citos ad proxima littora gressus.
Arripit inde viam, et tuti legit aequoris oram
Agmine confecto, turmaque instructus equestri

the race of the noble Stuart of Athole, and the Robertson[1] clan, encountered him at the meeting of the waters among the rugged rocks, and forced him to give way. And twice again, at Loch Garry, he repulsed him, the force with him being plundered. Therefore the scion of the house of Dalhousie, seeking safety in flight, leaves the misty hills in base fear, and speeds towards the nearest shore. Then he takes his way with a recruited force by the safe coast road,[2] and furnished with a troop of English horse

---

and his son Charles, younger of Ballechan, aged 29, married, gave evidence in the proceedings, and took the benefit of the indemnity. A touching letter from King James 'to our trusty cousin the Laird of Ballechan' is preserved in the family, and quoted by Napier, p. 654. See *Acts of Parl.*, vol. ix.; Dundee's *Letters*, etc.

[1] The Robertson clan was very loyal to the Stuarts, serving under Montrose and Glencairn in the civil wars, and now uniting with the other Athole men under Ballechan. The chief, Alexander Robertson, is not mentioned in the *Gramiad*, though doubtless he would have been, had its narrative embraced Killiecrankie. He was, at the beginning of our story, at the University of St. Andrews, and hurried home to join Dundee, when Struan became the Viscount's headquarters immediately before Killiecrankie. He was present at the battle, and is witnessed to in the evidence, and suffered attainder. He signs the Bond of Association. He was out again in 1715, and in 1745 almost the only leader who was out in all these three times of trouble. After Prestonpans he is said to have returned to Rannoch in Johnnie Cope's carriage. He died at Carie in Rannoch in 1749, aged about seventy-nine. His portrait and knife and fork are preserved at Croiscrag in Rannoch, to the lady of which mansion I am indebted for most of these details.

[2] See conclusion of note on Ramsay, a little way back, for correction of this mistake of our author. Ramsay retreated to Perth, received fresh instructions from the Council, was recruited by 100 dragoons of Barclay's regiment, 200 men of Leven's, and 100 of Hastings' regiments, and marched to Inverness by Athole and Badenoch, at the very nick of time, to find the coast clear, for Dundee was down the Spey after Mackay. When he joined Mackay from Inverness, Dundee, in Lochaber, was dismissing his Highlanders to their homes for a time.

Saxonidum, celeri transit juga Carnia cursu,
Transmeat et Dejae, violentaque flumina Donae.
Dumque petit Suii sublimia culmina montis,
Ecce redit prisci fugiens picta agmina Scoti
Scaurius, et patuli properabat ad aequora campi,
Maestior. Ut sociae jam cognita signa catervae,
Et vigil Auriaci tonuisset nomen amici;
Protinus attonitam permulcent gaudia mentem.
Tandem utrinque data, simul acceptaque salute,
Sic prior ore ducem Batavum Dalhousia proles
Increpat, irato conversus ad agmina vultu.

he climbs with quick step the heights of the Cairn,[1] and crosses the Dee, and the strong current of the Don. While he is making his way up the steep sides of Suy Hill,[2] behold Scourie flying from the tartaned hosts of old Scotland, and sadly hurrying to the Lowlands! When now the standards of the friendly force were recognised, and the advanced guard of the Orange troops had shouted out the pass-word, 'A friend,' at once joy soothed his affrighted mind. Salutes having been exchanged, Ramsay, looking to the troops with angry countenance, first upbraids the Dutch general: 'Whither dost thou flee, and why dread an enemy not

---

[1] The well-known north road over the Cairn-a-Month is referred to.
[2] Suy Hill, a well-known mark on the north road, at the watershed between the Don and the Bogie. Mackay arrived here about eight o'clock in the morning of Wednesday, 5th June, as I calculate. He left Balveny on Tuesday evening, marched all night by Edinglassie to the Bogie, which he crossed at four o'clock in the morning, 'neither horse nor foot being able to march further.' There the oats and oatmeal, which had come to Balveny the previous evening, were distributed, and the horse were allowed to feed on a spot of corn, the men holding their bridles. Having rested two hours, and got news of the approach of Barclay's and Lesly's force, 'he marched three miles towards his succours, putting a very ill pass betwixt him and Dundee, and rested at Suy Hill, upon the common road from the south to the north, over which he expected the foresaid two regiments, and from whence he could discover two miles to all hands and ways by which the enemy could approach him.' At the foot of Suy he allowed his troops to rest, and sent on to the house of Lord Forbes (*i.e.* Druminnor), 'two miles off, to see if any bread could be had, or quickly baked of oatmeal, to supply his hungry soldiers, the horse getting something now in the fields to pick at.' At twelve o'clock, on this Wednesday as I suppose, Barclay arrived with his dragoons, and Lesly with his foot at six o'clock in the afternoon, having had a long march that day. Between ten and eleven o'clock at night he was beginning his march back upon Dundee at Edinglassie, putting his 200 Dutch fusiliers first, because of the straightness of the ways.—Mackay's *Memoirs*, pp. 34-37.

Quo fugitive ruis? quidve hostem horrescis inertem?
Praedonumne ducem, praedatricemque catervam
Jam fugis? ab tantis frustra circumdate turmis
Saxonis et Scoti? Batavorumque agmine toto
Deseris infando cur credita castra tumultu?
Siste fugam; junctisque sequamur viribus hostem.
Dixerat; et spumantis equi M'Kaius armos
Calce premit, rursusque ad bella nefanda redibat;
Versaque Grampiacos jam signa ferebat in hostes.
  Cynthius inverso tandem declivis Olympo
Tinxerat immersos alto sub gurgite currus.
Gramus Edineae turrita ad moenia Glassae

pursuing you? Are you not now fleeing from a leader of robbers and a robber band? Are you surrounded to no purpose by such a troop of English and Scots? Why, in this sorry rout, with a whole army of Dutchmen on your side, do you desert your safe position? Stop this flight, and let us with our united strength turn upon the enemy.' He spake, and Mackay, pressing the flanks of his foaming steed with his spur, faced about towards the ill-starred combat, and once more turned his standards to front his Highland foe.

Cynthius, in the western heavens, at length had bathed his chariot deep in the waves. The Graham, having pursued the fugitive Mackay o'er hill and dale, as far as the turreted walls of Edinglassie,[1] fearing that there was an evil purpose in the flight,

---

[1] Edinglassie. The house of Sir George Gordon, who was made Sheriff of Banff, and was very much trusted by the Committee of Estates. He and Lord Findlater, with the Master of Forbes, seem to have been the chief upholders of William and Mary in Aberdeen and Banff. In an account of the parish of Glass, dated 1726, given in *Antiquities of Aberdeen and Banff*, vol. ii. (Spalding Club), the house is described as ruinous, doubtless the ruin caused by this visit of Claverhouse. 'By the river side standeth the ruinous house of Edinglassie, once belonging to the late Sir George Gordon, father to the present Carnousie, but is now in the possession of Braco. About a quarter of a mile below this house runneth a considerable burn, over which the said Sir George built a stone bridge of one arch, upon which is engraved his name and arms. Near to this bridge standeth ane miln, with a little village and tolbooth, which he designed for a burgh of barronie.' It was here that the great tragedy in the family of Innes was avenged by the death of 'its perpetrator, Innes of Innermarky, at the hands of Alexander Innes, called Craig-in-perill.' 'There was no mercy for him,' says the historian, 'for slain he was, and his hoar head cut off, and taken by the widow of him he had slain, and carried to Edinburgh, and casten at the King's feet—a thing too masculine to be commended in a woman.'—*Account of the Family of Innes*, Spalding Club, p. 38.

Jam profugum per saxa ducem perque arva secutus,
Crimen inesse fugae metuens, furtivaque bella,
Insidiasque timens, dubiaeque crepuscula noctis,
Substitit, et rauco signum intonat aere morandi;
Conciliumque vocat belli de rebus agendis,
Atque in concessu procerum sic ora resolvit.
'O mihi non dubia rumoris cognita fama
Grampiadum stirps alta ducum, sed fortibus armis,
Et factis testata fidem, et Mavortia corda,
Macte, duces, vestra pulsus virtute recessit
Scaurius, et castris uno ter sole relictis
Aufugit, et tota cessit jam territus arcto.
Sed fuga ficta ducis, suspectaque bella videntur,
Ni[1] trahat, et patuli deducat ad aequora campi.
Mox rediens equitatu auctus levibusque caballis
Picta securigeri prosterneret agmina Scoti.
Cunctandum est, coeptoque moram licet addere bello,

and a snare, and dreading an ambush in the perplexing darkness of the night, stopped his course, and sounded from the hoarse clarion the signal for a halt. He calls a council of war to consider the question, and, in the assembly of chiefs, thus he speaks: 'O great race of Highland chieftains, known to me not by the doubtful voice of report, but by your prowess in arms, and attesting your fidelity and your warlike hearts by deeds, Scourie, repulsed by your eminent valour, has retreated, and thrice in one day has fled from deserted camps, and, terrified, has forsaken the North. But the flight of the general may be feigned, and his conduct of the war seems to be open to suspicion,[2] lest he be protracting matters for a purpose, and drawing us down to the plains of the Lowlands. Presently returning, strengthened with horse and dragoons, he will overwhelm the tartaned lines of the target-bearing Scot. There must be delay, and though it defer the opened war, it is best, whatever happens, to halt at these lands.'

---

[1] 'Ni,' probably author's mistake for *Ne*. The sequence is careless here—'trahat, prosterneret,' as also below near end of paragraph, 'prius quam surgat, . . . aut proferret, prosterneret,' followed by 'obruet,' future.

[2] The sentence is involved in the original, and the translation aims only at the general sense of the passage. The original and copies have *ni trahat*, and though *ne* gives a better sense, it is possible the author may mean that if Mackay is not protracting things, and leading them downwards to the low country, his conduct at any rate is suspicious.

Quo res cunque cadat, placet his consistere terris.[1]
Haec ait; ecce vagae per amica silentia lunae
Dum redit adjutus Batavorum Scaurius armis,
Nuntius hostili delapsus ab agmine noctu
Advolat, et magni ruit ad tentoria Grami,
Atque equitum celeres Scotorum nuntiat alas
Velle iterum Batavo jam regia castra relicto
Sponte sequi; sic velle duces, sic velle cohortes,
Commoda si rebus bene cesserit[2] ansa gerendis.
Jamque refert Batavum multis legionibus auctum
Raptim instare ducem, rursusque ad bella reversum
Transiliisse cito Bogi vaga flumina cursu.
Et prius a cano quam surgat nata[3] marito
Memnonis, aut roseos proferret Lutea vultus,

Thus he speaks; Lo! while Scourie returns, favoured by the friendly obscurity of the moon, his force increased with the troops of Dutchmen, a messenger,[4] slipping away from the hostile army, flies hither by night, and runs to the tent of the great Graham, and announces that the swift troops of Scotch dragoons desire now again freely to follow the Royal camp, deserting from the Dutchman; that thus the officers willed, thus the troopers, if a convenient opportunity should arise for happily achieving the business. And now he tells of the Orange commander, his strength increased by many companies (or regiments) pressing on secretly, and that, with his face once more to his foe, he had crossed the winding streams of Bogie in rapid course. And he says that before the daughter[5] (*mother*) of Memnon rises from the couch of her aged

---

[1] *Var. lect.* turris; also 'castris.'

[2] 'Cesserit ansa': a singular phrase, but giving good sense metaphorically.

[3] 'Nata,' a mistake of the author for *Mater*. See translation, and note[5].

[4] This messenger was Sergeant Provensal, a confidential servant of Lieutenant-Colonel Livingstone, afterwards Lord Kilsyth. He and another dragoon were found hid in a wood near Edinglassie, along with a servant and a boy belonging to our friend Captain Bruce (see Book IV.). After the discovery of Provensal, and the evidence of his companions, Mackay ordered the arrest of the disaffected officers. Poor Provensal got a good word from nobody. Mackay urges his being put to torture. Sir John Dalrymple, while excusing Livingstone, says: 'There is one Sergeant Provinciall, a Papist, who was the most guilty, he may serve for an example.' See Mackay's letter, urging torture, p. 240 of Appendix to his *Memoir.* Also 'Remits and Orders for torturing dragoons,' quoted from Privy Council Register in Napier's *Dundee,* where also see pp. 684, 685, interesting correspondence on the subject.

[5] Our author here makes a slip as to the relationship of Aurora to Memnon. She was his mother, not his daughter, his father being the aged spouse Tithonus.

Regia furtivo prosterneret agmina bello,
Obruet inque ipsis chlamydata examina castris.
Dixit, et obversis sua castra petivit habenis.
  Dundius ad subitae vitanda pericula pugnae,
Cum Batavum tantis geminato robore turmis
Sciret adesse ducem, castrisque instare propinquum,
Ocyus adstantes equitum, peditumque tribunos
Demittit,[1] sparsosque jubet per rura maniplos
Ad sonitum revocare tubae, cunctique parent[2] se
Candida purpureos nectat quam Aurora jugales
Ante referre pedem, aut stricto decernere ferro.
Ipse animi dubius quo vergat pondere bellum,
Fessa negat dulci membra inclinare quieti,

spouse, or Aurora lifts her rosy face, he (Mackay) will attack the royal lines in a movement of surprise, and will destroy the plaided bands in their very camp.' He spoke, and with turned rein he sought his own quarters.[3]

Dundee, to avoid the danger of sudden encounter, when he knew that the Batavian general was advancing in a strength increased by so many troops, and that he was already approaching closely on his camp, sends out quickly the members of his cavalry staff, and the officers of the infantry, and commands to recall, with sound of trumpet, the bands straggling through the fields,[4] and that they all prepare before that fair Aurora yoke her purple team, to retreat, or to try the issue with the drawn sword. He himself, in doubt as to where the blow may fall in its weight, denies his wearied limbs the sweet repose of the couch, and turns in his

---

—Virgil, *Aen.* iv. 585 and vii. 26 were on the mind of the author, though he may not be quoting these passages :

'Tithoni croceum linquens Aurora cubile,'

and

'Aurora in roseis fulgebat lutea bigis.'

I have left *Lutea* with a capital because it is so in original, and in the copies, and I am inclined to think the author considered Lutea a name for Aurora.

[1] Author's mistake, I suppose, for *Dimittit*.   [2] *Var. lect.* parant.

[3] He did not reach these quarters, but with another dragoon was found in a wood near Edinglassie along with Captain Bruce's servants, and some Highlanders. See note above.

[4] Mackay was counting much on cutting off the numerous stragglers whom the love of plunder—a great motive in these Highland raids—drew far from their camp. He says 'the Highlanders cannot be kept from straggling over the face of the country, as well as in their marches as camping—they serving more for plunder than affection for the service.'—Mackay's *Memoirs*, p. 37.

Multa sed insomnem per noctem mente revolvens.[1]
Huc atque huc vario curarum fluctuat aestu,
Incertus teneatne [2] fugam, Martemve lacessat.
Ira dolorque simul mentem in contraria versant,
Impelluntque animum : tandem indignatus apertae
Se dare terga fugae, profugumque excedere castris,
Vocibus his tristes emisit ad astra querelas.
'Mene,' ait, 'ingenti victum desistere coepto
Fas erit ? heu Superos nunquam ante expertus iniquos.
Nunc [3] et perniciem,[4] et coepti infortunia belli,
Adversosque Deos agnosco, inimicaque fata
Praevideo ; nobis iter est per mille labores
Quaerendum, fortique animo toleranda Deorum
Invidia, et saevi superanda injuria fati.
Tu vero arctoae gentis praedo improbe, tanti
Fons et origo mali, Nassovi, ingrate virorum,
Immeritum quid me nunc Caesaris arma secutum
Prosequeris, toties et iniquo Marte fatigas ?

mind many things through a sleepless night. Hither and thither in varying tide of cares, he fluctuates, uncertain whether he shall betake himself to retreat or engage in battle. Anger and sorrow at once move his mind in differing directions, and urge his spirit ; at length, enraged that he should be reduced to turn his back in open flight, and as a fugitive to desert his camp, he sent up to the stars with his voice these sad words : ' Is it for me, alas !' he says, ' as vanquished, to desert this great undertaking—for me who never before experienced hostile fates! Now I foresee disaster, and an unfortunate beginning of the campaign and gods hostile and opposing fates. Our progress lies through a thousand labours, and the envy of the gods with bold breast must be borne, and hostilities of a cruel fate must be endured. But O thou infamous robber of the northern race, fount and origin of so great an injustice ! thou of Nassau, the most ingrate of men ! why dost thou undeservedly pursue me now as I follow the arms of the Caesar, and so harass me in unequal strife ? Did not I,[5] when thou fleddest on wearied steed

---

[1] ? revolvit.
[2] *Var. lect.* tentetne. The conclusion of this line is in the original apparently, and in copies certainly, *Martemne lacessit.*
[3] This line has no real caesura.   [4] *Var. lect.* pernitiem.
[5] The allusion is to the story, which here gets weighty support, that Claverhouse at the battle of Seneff, August 11th, 1674, rescued William when he was about to fall into the hands of the French. Macaulay dismisses the story

Nonne ego cum lasso per Belgica stagna caballo
Agmina liligeri fugeres victricia Galli,
Ipse mei impositum dorso salientis equi te
Hostibus eripui, salvumque in castra reduxi?
Haecne mihi meriti persolvis praemia tanti?
Proh scelus! O soceri raptor nequissime sceptri!
Vir scelerate vagum quid nunc me hostilibus armis
Obruis? et castris exutum cedere cogis?
Cedo equidem, tristem patriae quando omnia casum
Portendunt. At tu stellantis Rector Olympi,
Alme Caledonium serva inter bella Stuartum.
Quod si adversa premant arctoum fata Britannum,

through Belgic marsh from the conquering troops of lily-bearing France—did not I myself snatch thee from the enemy, and mount thee on the back of my fresh steed, and restore thee safe to the camp? And dost thou thus pay me these rewards for so great a desert? O shame! O vile ravisher of thy father's sceptre! O man of wickedness, why dost thou crush me, now a wanderer, with these hostile arms? Why dost thou drive me from my camp? I yield indeed when all things portend a sad lot to my country. But thou, ruler of starry Olympus, benignly preserve the Scottish Stuart in these wars. But if adverse fates oppress the northern Britain, I pray that the Orange Prince may expiate it all with his

---

as resting alone on the authority of the officer, who wrote the short memoir in 1714. In 'The Muse's New Year's Gift, and Hansell, to the right honoured Captain John Graham of Claverhouse, January 1683,' printed from the MS. in the *Fugitive Scottish Poetry of the 17th Century*, edited by David Laing, Esq., 1825, and quoted by Napier, vol. i. p. 325, etc., we have the following—

> 'Unto the allies' camp he does resort,
> And is advanced to the great Orange Court.
>   .   .   .   .
> I saw the man who at St. Neff did see
> His conduct, prowess, martial gallantry;
> He wore a white plumach that day; not one
> Of Belgians, wore a white, but him alone;
> And though that day was fatal, yet he fought,
> And for his part, fair triumphs with him brought.'

Taking this account of Claverhouse's prowess and gallantry at Seneff, along with the 1714 story, and adding our author to these authorities, there is fair evidence of the general trustworthiness of the tale. See discussion of the question in Napier's *Memoirs of Dundee*, under Seneff, Index; and in a little book on Claverhouse by Mowbray Morris in Longman's series of English (*sic*) *Worthies*.

Auriacus cervice precor luat omnia princeps,
Impius in socerum qui sustulit arma verendum;
Qualia terrigenas sumpsisse et fama gigantes
In superos, celsi peterent dum culmina coeli.
Hos pater omnipotens injecto fulmine fratres
Aethere Phlegraeos Stygias detrusit ad umbras.
Sic cadat in Batavi caput exitiale tyranni
Caelestum gravis ira deum, telisque petitum
Obruat, et Stygio damnatum mittat Averno.'
Haec secum, et surdas suspiria misit in auras.

   Texerat umbra polum gravis, et jam nocte silenti
Tarda Lycaonius volvebat plaustra Bootes.
Scaurius optatis rerum successibus usus
Flectere cornipedes in praelia mandat anhelos,
Ocyus atque acies una jubet ire pedestres.
Ipse praeit laeto testatus gaudia vultu,
Acceleratque gradum, sub tegmine noctis opacae
Hostica furtivis ut castra lacesseret armis.
Urget et acer iter, rapidoque simillimus euro

neck, he who raised his hand against his venerated father-in-law; a deed like that, as goes the tale, which the earthly giants essayed against the gods, when they assailed the heights of heaven. These brethren the Almighty father, with lightning hurled, drove from the air of heaven into the shades of Stygian Phlegethon. So may the punishment of the heavenly gods fall on the execrable head of the Batavian tyrant, and stricken with their bolts may he be crushed and sent to Stygian Avernus.' These things with himself he uttered, and sent forth his breath to the deaf air.

   The deep shades had covered the poles, and already the Lycaonian[1] Bootes was driving his tardy wagon through the silent night. Scourie, availing himself of his wished-for succours, bids his panting cavalry turn again for the fight, and with them, commands his foot to advance at speed. He himself goes before them, witnessing to his satisfaction with glad countenance, and he hastens their pace, that under the cover of a dark night he might attack the hostile camp by surprise.[2] Swiftly he presses on his way, and, like the east wind, he crosses the lofty heights of cloud-

---

[1] See article 'Arctos' in Smith's *Clas. Dict.*

[2] Mackay hardly hoped to surprise the Highland army in a body because of the shortness of the night, and the good service in daylight done by the Highland sentries upon the tops of the hills. He, however, hoped that if he could not get them in a body, he might catch some of them and discourage the whole.

Ardua nimbiferi juga transilit Achindori.
Tandem frugiferam Bogi de nomine vallem
Praeterit, et dictis socios affatus amicis:
'Praecipitate, viri, celeresque attollite gressus.
Tuque O belligeros inter dilecte sodales
Duc Ramisaee acies in castra inimica pedestres.
Ipse ego Saxonidum turma stipatus equorum,
Agmina nocturno sternam chlamydata tumultu.'
Haec ait; et totis in praelia viribus ibat.
Nec mora longa viae, per saxa amnesque citato
Fertur anhelus equo, atque instar torrentis inundans
Terruit attonitos tota regione colonos.
Qualis ubi incubuit caelo nimbosus Orion,
Nigrantes nebulas, tempestatesque sonoras
Inducit subito terris, caelumque videbis
In pluvias ruere, et rapidis fervescere nimbis,
Diffugere agricolas, pecudesque absistere campis,
Pastorem et patulae recubare sub ilicis umbra.

capped Auchindoir.[1] . At length he passes the fruitful Strath of the Bogie, and addresses his allies in friendly words : ' Forward, my men, step out at speed! and thou, O Ramsay,[2] beloved among my comrades, lead up your lines of infantry against the enemy's camp! I myself, with a troop of English horse, will overthrow the plaided lines in a nocturnal assault.' Thus he speaks, and goes forward to the fight with his full strength. Nor did he dally on the way; he is borne panting on swift steed, o'er rocks and rivers, and, like an overflowing torrent, he affrights the astounded peasants, throughout the whole district. Thus, when the stormy Orion has settled himself in the sky, and has suddenly brought up over the earth the black clouds and sonorous tempests, you will see the heavens rush down in rain and burst into violent storm; you will see the husbandman flee, the flocks desert the fields, and the shepherd crouch in the shelter of the wide-spreading

---

[1] Auchindoir, a mountainous parish at the head of the Bogie. Rhynie is the post-town of the district. The route lay, I fancy, by Rhynie, Cabrach, the Deveron (or Doveran), and Baldornie to Edinglassie, a very rough road. Mackay was afraid of a too hasty advance in such rough country in the presence of an enemy. As no mention is made of Lismore, and the roughness of the way and the bad pass are mentioned, I conclude it was the higher track that was followed.

[2] Ramsay is here a poetic introduction from a different field. At this time he was nearing Inverness, if he had not arrived there. See previous notes on Ramsay, p. 192.

Jam matutinas surgens Aurora quadrigas
Extulit, atque diem cecinit cassita[1] propinquum,
Scaurius ut lati descendit ad aequora campi,
Divrona gramineas qua lambit gurgite ripas;
Utque in conspectu jam Grampica castra tenebat,
Excubitorum equitum rapidum praemiserat agmen,
Ut cursu quaterent campos; ipse imminet altis
Pulverulentus equis, se sequi[2] bella parabat.
 Ecce autem ad primos Phoebeae lampadis ignes
Exploratores aderant, hostemque reportant
Esse in conspectu, et rapido ruere obvia cursu.
Dundius Abriacas extemplo ad signa cohortes
Convocat, et cunctis edicit castra relinquant.
Nulla mora, imperio parent, et jussa capessunt.
Grampiadumque manus cuneum coit omnis in unum,
Sublimesque in equis considunt ilicet omnes,
Atque omnis castris chlamydata caterva relictis

oak. Already rising Aurora has brought forth her morning team, and the crested lark has sung the approach of day, when Scourie descends to the level ground of the open plain, where Deveron[3] laves the grassy banks with its waters. As he came in sight of the Highland camp, he sent a light body of horse to reconnoitre and to scour the fields. He himself, covered with dust, towers over his cavalry, and prepares himself to follow the fight.

But lo! on the first rays of the lamp of Phoebus,[4] when the videttes of Dundee had approached the enemy, and had reported him in sight, and advancing in rapid course, Dundee immediately assembled his Highland companies on a signal, and commanded them all to leave the camp. There is no delay; they obey the order, and carry out the command. The whole body of the Highlanders is formed into column, and forthwith the cavalry mount their horses, and the whole plaided army, with floating banners,

---

[1] 'Cassita': very rare word, used by Pliny and Gellius. 'Whence did our author learn it?' Perhaps from Holyoke's *Dict*.

[2] *Var. lect.* 'seseque' instead of 'se sequi.' Neither text nor *var. lect.* is right. Read 'seseque in bella.' These slips suggest that the poet is writing from a copy.

[3] The point where he would touch the Deveron would be near Invercarrach, where several streams unite. Crossing there, the route lay down the banks of the river to Edinglassie.

[4] The connection here is not very clear, but the new paragraph and the context show that it is Dundee's outposts who are meant by the 'exploratores.'

Jam signis campo volitantibus ibat aperto.
Fit fragor, ingenti concussa est pondere tellus
Castra relinquentum cursu, fremituque sequentum
Intremuit tellus, glomerantur in aethere nubes
Pulveris, et densa tegitur caligine campus.
Dundius elusum jam pone reliquerat hostem,
Atque e conspectu exierat, montesque tenebat,
Et subito aereum praetervolat Auchinadunum,

went forth from the deserted camp into the open plain. There was a crash; the earth shook under the mighty weight of those leaving the camp in their course, and reeled at the shout of those who followed; clouds of dust were thrown into the air, and the plain was covered with a misty gloom. Dundee had now left the eluded enemy behind, and had passed from his sight. He kept to the mountains, and quickly passes the lofty castle of Auchindoune.[1]

---

[1] Auchindoune Castle. Dundee took his way up the Fiddich, past this castle. The ruins of it still stand, crowning a high green mound. Gordon, in his *History of Scots Affairs*, speaks of it as standing seven miles from Strathbogie Castle, near Balveny, and 'built as is affirmed by Cochrain, who was minion to king James the Third.' A Sir Adam Gordon possessed it in 1581, and a Sir Patrick Gordon of Auchindoune was killed at the battle of Glen Livet. It was bought by that remarkable man George, 1st Marquis of Huntly, the first of the family who bought lands. In November and December 1643, he was busy at the Bog of Gight, making preparation for the marriage of his daughter Lady Mary, with Alexander Irvine, the young laird of Drum, 'and in the meintyme was furneshing the place of Auchindoun with all necessares.' On March 14th of the following year, the young bridegroom with his brother Robert, and some of the Gordons, about 100 strong carried off from Aberdeen as prisoners, Patrick Leslie the provost, Alexander Jaffray late provost, John Jaffray Dean of Guild, and Mr. Robert Farquhar; and after taking them to the Bog carried them to Auchindoune. There they had to pay for their own maintenance, and to keep also the Captain of the castle with sixteen men, besides cooks, etc. On their remonstrating they were told that the Marquis had to pay for his keep in Edinburgh Castle, when he was a prisoner there. The castle was frequently the shelter of the Gordons in times of trouble, and their chief valuables were always conveyed there in such times. Argyll took possession of it, and quartered an Irish regiment in it. General Cannon had his headquarters there for a short time. In an account of the parish of Murthlac, 1730, it is called the decayed castle of Auchindoune, and it is said to stand on a rising ground a mile southward from the church. In 1742 an account by James Ferguson says, 'An old castle called Auchindown, now ruinous, lies three miles south from the church.' There must have been some movement in the castle, the church, or the miles during these twelve years, if both tales are true. The burning of the castle is commemorated in a ballad bearing its name. Dundee and his Highlanders passed it on the morning of Thursday the 7th, if I am right in my dates.

Transit et Oweni campum, vallemque Liveti,
Castraque Cromdalias nocturna locavit ad aedes;
Languida ubi placidae concessit membra quieti.
Ecce vigil tremulae deceptus imagine lunae
Excubitor, madidas cernens armenta per umbras,
Clamitat instantem repetitis [1] vocibus hostem.
Grampica fulmineus jubet ocyus agmina Gramus
Signa sequi, adversos et pergere mandat in hostes.
Continuo strepuere tubae, atque effusa virum vis
Tota ruit densis ad compita nota catervis.
Ille autem vigiles, et ludicra praelia ridens,
'Sistite,' ait, 'gressum, coeptumque inhibete furorem;
O nunc Caesareis gens Grampica fortis in armis,
Hactenus ingentes animos, et martia corda
Expertus, didici quantum in certamine virtus
Vestra valet; Batavus si in praelia ductor adesset

He crosses the plain of Owen,[2] and the valley of the Livet,[3] and fixes his camp for the night, by the houses of Cromdale. There he yielded his weary limbs to peaceful rest. Lo! the alert sentinel, deceived by the shadows of the trembling moon, perceiving a flock of sheep through the mist, shouts with repeated warning that the enemy is upon them. The lightning-like Graham bids the Highland host at once gather round their standards, and prepare to meet the foe. The trumpets sound and the whole force of men rush in compact bodies to their rendezvous. But he, laughing at the sentinels and the absurd battle array, says, 'Stay your pace; stop this rising rage. O now, ye Highlanders, brave in the royal cause, having so far tried your great minds and martial hearts, I have learned how much your valour will avail in the battle. Were the Dutch general

---

[1] 'repetitis,' or some such word, is inserted on margin—the word in the line has a *g* in it, but it is nearly all obliterated.

[2] The plain or field of Owen, or Glen of Owen, I do not recognise, unless it be Glen Avon, which is pronounced Glen Aàn in the district, and sometimes the sound is not unlike Glenoen. An old spelling was Awine. Dundee would have to cross the Avon before reaching Cromdale. His route was doubtless on the track now represented by the road from Dufftown to Tomintoul, as far as the Livet, down which he would go towards the point of its junction with the Avon, crossing which again, a few miles' march would bring him to Cromdale.

[3] Glen Livet, the scene of the battle between Huntly and Errol on one side, and Argyll on the other, when Argyll was defeated. There are few Scottish Glens whose names have attained such wide recognition as Glen Livet, and there are few glens that are so little known.

Haud impune diu nobis illuderet hostis
Caesaris, et versis plorasset Cromdala fatis.
Jam quia nocturnis Dictynna invecta quadrigis,
Et vaga pallidulo consurgunt sidera caelo,
Figite disjectis laeti tentoria ramis,
Lassaque jucundo demittite corpora somno.

here for the contest, not with impunity would the enemy of the Caesar longer elude us, and Cromdale[1] bewail a reverse. Since now the moon is carried on nocturnal car, and the wandering stars are coming out on the pale sky, cheerily frame your tents of the cut-down[2] branches, and yield your bodies to pleasant sleep. But as

---

[1] The author seems to make Dundee's speech prophetic of the defeat of the Highlanders in the following year, on the Haughs of Cromdale, but the *versis fatis* may mean in the leader's mouth only that he was now in retreat, whereas Cromdale last saw him in pursuit. The catastrophe of Cromdale in the following year arose just from the want of that alertness which is the feature of the amusing incident of these lines. The following is the short account of the fight, in the *Memoirs of Dundee*, by an officer, 1714: 'On May 1st Major General Buchan had about 1500 men at Cromdale, lodged in villages round the country, and his advanced guards advantageously posted, when the want of intelligence, and the negligence of two captains, Brodie and Grant, each of them commanding a hundred men at the church on the river Spey, suffered Sir Thomas Livingstone, with 17 troops of dragoons, 900 of Grant's men, and three regiments of foot, to pass the river and church without opposition, who fell upon Buchan and his Highlanders sleeping in their tents and houses, and killed several of them, but to their expence, for the Highlanders fought in their shirts, with swords and targets, and killed so many of the dragoons and their horses, that Sir Thomas never attempted any pursuit.'

I think the author in giving this scene at Cromdale meant to contrast the alert attitude of the Highlanders under Dundee with the surprise which the unpopular Buchan suffered them to fall into on the same ground.

[2] The following extracts, first, from Gordon's *Scots Affairs*, and, second, from Spalding's *Memorialls*, illustrate the custom of forming sleeping-places with branches of trees, even in armies better provided than Dundee's. Monro in 1640, in coming to Strathbogie, which had all been planted and laid out with taste by the Marquis of Huntly, 'took a course to lodge his soldiers, by cutting down the woods or rather bushes of trees next adjacent to the castle, which he caused his soldiers build up in huts and lodges.' Spalding says, 'coming after this manner to Strathbogie, the first thing they entered to do, was hewing down the pleasant planting about Strathbogie, to be huts for the soldiers to sleep within, upon the night; whereby the haill camp was weill provided of huts to the destroying of goodlie countrie policie.' See Gordon's *Scots Affairs*, vol. iii. p. 211, and Spalding, *History of Troub.*, vol. i. p. 222. The passage is touching too, as to the 'meddling with the meal girnells, the beiff, mutton, hen, capon, and such like, out of Glenfiddich and Auchindoune, where the country people had transported their bestiall.'

At vero ut sudo lux crastina reddita coelo
Arma parate viri, et signum sperate duelli.'
   Ortus erat Titan, volucremque per aetheris axem
Incipiebat equos stridenti urgere flagello,
Rursus pulchra suos belli in certamina Gramus
Suscitat, et pictas strepero[1] ciet aere catervas.
Utque dedit dirum procul horrida buccina cantum,
Et raucae strepuere tubae, dicto ocyus omnes
Arripuere viam, peditumque equitumque catervae
Pulvere fumantem pulsant pede praepete campum.
Nec[2] mora nigrantes donec nox humida campos
Abstulit ex oculis, et coelum condidit umbra.
Gramus Abernetheis figit tentoria silvis.
Signabant mediam noctis jam sidera metam,[3]
Primaque in excubias vigiles ciet hora secundas.
Ecce autem fidi generosa ex gente Cleani
Jam Gramo laturus opem Lochbowius ibat,

soon as the morrow's light returns to the clear sky, prepare your arms, and look for the summons to the battle.'

Titan had risen, and was beginning to urge on his horses with swishing lash, over the swift pole of the heavens, when the Graham again rouses his troops to the noble contests of war, and summons his painted host with the noisy clarion. And as the horrid trumpet uttered its dread note, and the harsh pipes sounded, quicker than word they were all on the way, companies of horse and infantry tread with swift foot the plain, clouded with dust. Nor was there a halt, till a damp night hid the darkening plains from our eyes, and covered the heavens with shade. The Graham fixed his tents in the woods of Abernethy.[4] Already the stars were indicating the middle of the night, and the first hour calls the second watch to their posts. But lo! Lochbuy, of the noble race of faithful Maclean, bringing aid to the Graham, was

---

[1] No good authority for this adjective. Holyoke gives it with doubtful mark.

[2] *Var. lect.* 'nec' or 'ne' is inserted on margin in different hand.

[3] In the last four lines of the column several words are illegible in original, and are supplied now from old copies.

[4] The march from Edinglassie to Cromdale on the 7th June was a long one, and would itself account for the shortness of the distance covered on the next day. It is accounted for besides by Dundee's illness. In the detailed account sent by M'Swine we have the following, 'The Viscount fell sick, which gave boldness to the disorderly, and disheartened others. The first day he marched back, he made a long march. Mackay sent a party of horse, who seized some

Tercentum egregiis patriae stipatus alumnis,
Usque a belligerae saxoso littore Mullae
Venerat, et rapidi nunc alta ad flumina Spejae
Nocte securigeram per rura tacentia pubem
Quaerebat magni castris conjungere Grami.
Forte errore viae sublustri noctis in umbra,
Dum placidum[1] pertentat iter, socia agmina credens,
Incidit in celeres Batavorum nescius alas.

advancing, and had come from the rocky shores of warlike Mull, accompanied by 300 gallant youths.[2] Beside the deep waters of the Spey, through the quiet fields, he was seeking in the night to bring his shield-bearing clansmen to the camp of the great Graham. While he pursues his course by a mistaken path in the glimmering shades of the night, he fell ignorantly among the outpost squadrons of the Orange horse, thinking they were friends.

---

of the Duke of Gordon's gentlemen that went off, and some of the plundering stragglers, but never came in sight of the rear-guard. The next two days, the Viscount did not march six miles in all, and Mackay's foot came not within ten miles of his, but in the evening of the last day, he sent up a party of 200 horse and dragoons, who, led on by Grant, were brought upon a party of Macleans.' Here follows some account of the Lochbuy incident, on which see below. If this account is right, he stayed about the Abernethy woods on the nights of the 8th and 9th, and the Lochbuy incident transpired about 3 or 4 o'clock on the morning of the 10th.

[1] *Var. lect.* 'tacitum' for 'placidum.'

[2] This is Hector Maclean, younger of Lochbuy. His father, Hector Maclean, was an old man at this time, bnt quite capable of going frequently from Lochbuy to Dowart, and mingling among the Jacobite leaders as they went and came about that stronghold. When young Hector escorted the Perth prisoners from Lochaber to Duart, old Lochbuy met them, and when the officers came from Ireland he managed to sell a horse to Lieut.-Col. Douglas. He was engaged on the Jacobite side, in the earlier part of the century, and Auchinbreck denounces him as one of the ravagers of his houses and lands. Young Hector, the hero of Knockbrecht, was bringing up a contingent of Macleans to join Dundee, and was keeping by mistake on the Alvie side of the Spey, while Dundee was on the Rothiemurchus side. Among other acquisitions of the skirmish, young Lochbuy gained a dun horse which had belonged to the dragoons, no doubt Owenstone's own horse, as James Malcolm of Balbadie testifies. He signs the letter to Mackay from Birse, Aug. 1689, and was much engaged in all the Jacobite enterprises of the time. He had a son Murdoch, who is called younger of Lochbuy (or possibly he may be a younger brother), who fell into the hands of the laird of Cawdor, and was carried to Edinburgh by order of the Committee.

Lockhart's *Dr. Johnson* and the *Tour in the Hebrides* supply an interesting link with the later history of the family and house of Lochbuy, which is now represented by the hospitable chief, Murdoch Gillean Maclaine of Lochbuy.

'State viri,' rauco excubitor procul increpat ore
Belgicus, instantes jaculumque emisit in hostes.
Mox sublimis equis, vigilantum turbine turma
Ingruit, ignivomisque horrendum intonat armis.
Et contra accensas nitrato pulvere glandes
Torsit, et in cuneum Lochbowius agmine facto
Ipse pedes, ferroque viam molitus et igne,
Jam juga vicini properabat scandere collis.
Ardua rupes[1] erat de nomine dicta cruoris,

'Stand, men!' shouts the Belgic sentinel with hoarse voice at a distance, and hurled his javelin[2] at the advancing foe. Like a whirlwind came on the whole troop of outpost cavalry, and thunder out a dread discharge from their fire-vomiting weapons. Against them Lochbuy sent a shower of bullets fired from his guns, and forming his men into a wedge-shaped column, himself on foot, forced his way by fire and sword towards a neighbouring hill, which he hastened to climb. It was a lofty rock, taking its name from marks of blood,[3] rearing its great mass to the clouds, its sides

---

[1] 'rupes': false quantity. 'Ardua erat rupes' suggested.

[2] 'Jaculum emisit.' Does this mean that he actually hurled a javelin or sped an arrow, or merely that he fired a shot?

[3] The hill is called Knockbrecht by all authorities who name it; but I have not sufficient acquaintance with the locality to be able to identify it. The author's identifying *brecht* with blood—the Speckled Hill, speckled, *i.e.* with blood,—suggests an explanation of the Speckled Kirk, *i.e.* Falkirk, not to say Edinburgh, Cathbregion, and other names signifying painted or speckled. See Skene's *Four Books of Wales*, p. 93, vol. i., and our note on Falkirk, Book II.

The skirmish of Knockbrecht is referred to with variations by the different authorities. Our author's account is that of an eye-witness, and though it be given in heroics, seems to me to tally with the best-authenticated facts. It would seem that on the night of the 9th June, when Dundee had moved up the Spey as far as Rothiemurchus, or to some point between it and Abernethy, Mackay was at Culnakyle. He had ordered Sir Thomas Livingstone with 200 dragoons to cross the Spey to support the Laird of Grant's men, who had not been able to protect themselves from Dundee's foragers. Sir Thomas took a much stronger force with him, and having advanced on the night of the 9th two miles from the river, his advanced party came on the Macleans looking for Dundee on that side, whereas he was posted on the other. Happily for the Macleans, the advanced party of the dragoons were very far in advance, and without connecting files, and the Highlanders, having got some 'advertisement,' fired their muskets, and, bursting through the surrounding cavalry, ran for half a mile towards this hill, where they fought as described. The attacking party was composed of some Scots dragoons (now the Scots Greys) and Berkley's horse (now the 4th Hussars). In a paper of Macpherson's, the commanding officer of the detachment, who was killed, is called Captain Wane; but doubtless our author is right in calling him Owenstone.

Ingentem attollens celsa inter nubila molem,
Et latera exesis obtendens invia saxis;
Belliger hac tandem insedit Lochbowius arce,
Et sese tutis sepsit velut aggere castris.
Ocyus insequitur vigilantum exercitus omnis,
Et Teuto, et Batavus, Scotusque et Cimber et Anglus
Conantur validum detrudere colle Cleanum.
Ille urget jaculo, et ferientibus eminus hastis,

covered with weather-worn boulders. The martial Lochbuy at length established himself on the summit, and as in a sure camp, fenced himself in with a rampart. Quickly comes up the whole force of the cavalry detachment, and German and Dutch, Scots, Welsh,[1] and English, strive to expel the strongly posted Maclean from his hill. He wages his war from above, with javelin and iron

The details of the uniform are interesting, and correspond in the main with the description given in the Historical Records of the British Army, more especially in the account of the uniform of the 4th Dragoon Guards of the period. I have not seen the Records of the 4th Hussars.

The historian of the regiment may find some contribution in our author's narrative as to uniform (which I have translated livery, because such was the word for uniform in use at the time; the nobleman or gentleman raising a troop, giving its members his own livery, or settling what it was to be).

The following is Balhaldy's English versification of this passage descriptive of the hill, which emphasises the speckled hill, and supposed origin of the name—

'Nor halted they untill
They gained a neighbouring eminence, a rock
Whose frowning top among the clouds concealed
Show'd all its battered sides, with ragged stones
And fragments huge perplex'd and tooke its name
From blood which their impervious surface stained.'

Our author gives 300 (Balcarres gives 200) as the full strength of the Lochbuy contingent, and Claverhouse says in his despatch that 'they lost not more than four men with their baggage, and two old men and boys that were with it.' Mackay says the Macleans were 500 strong, and lost 80 or 100 men, and would all have perished but for the adjutant riding a quarter of a mile in advance, and so giving time to the Highlanders to reach the great steep hill. He admits the death of an officer, a captain of Berkley's horse, with six dragoons of both regiments and some wounded. Hearing that Sir Thomas Livingstone was engaged with Dundee, Mackay passed the river, which really put the river between him and Dundee, and met Sir Thomas returning, and they all recrossed to Culnakyle together. Dundee moved in the morning towards Ruthven Castle.

[1] The poet, and not the historian, was asserting himself here. The detachment attacking Maclean was composed of some men of the Scots Dragoons, the very same men, who had been through Lieut.-Col. Livingstone coquetting with Dundee, and a portion of Berkley's horse.

Et contis, sudibusque, altaque a rupe superbum
Egit praecipitem saxis ingentibus hostem.
Acer erat bello dux Owinstonus in illo,
Natus ad aequoreas Rhutupini littoris oras,
Saxonidumque regebat equos, pugnamque ciebat
Arduus, et Batavis immane fremebat in armis.
Colla viri fulvo radiantia torque nitebant,
Et cramosina humero pendebat laena sinistro,
Totus et in Tyrio procul emicat aureus ostro.
Ille ubi depulsas conspexit colle cohortes,
Atque virum toto confossa cadavera campo,
Infrendens graviter, tumidaque accensus ab ira
Turbidus exclamat : ' descendite rupe, latrones
Semiviri, et stricto mecum decernite ferro.'
Jamque morae impatiens, mentem impellente furore,

spear, and dart and pointed stake, and from his high rock he drives the proud enemy headlong with great stones. The active leader in that fight was Owinstone,[1] born by the watery shores of the Richborough[2] coasts. As captain of the English horse, he, towering aloft, led on the charge, and in Batavian arms, fierce was the sound of his oncoming. His neck brightly gleaming with a gorget of golden hue, and a crimson jacket[3] hung from his left shoulder, all in gold and Tyrian scarlet, he shone from afar. When he had seen his squadrons repulsed from the hill, and the dead bodies of his men lying pierced over the plain, grinding his teeth fiercely and fired with rising wrath, he shouts wildly ' Descend from your rock, ye barbarous robbers, and settle the matter with me with the drawn sword.' Impatient of delay, rage impelling his mind, he madly assays to climb to the high summit of the hill,

---

[1] Our author gives with warmth the gallantry of this brave Englishman, but his mood is uncertain, and indicates a mind at once respecting the English captain, contemning the rebel, and expressing a coarse sympathy with the Highland barbarities of which he was the victim. The gallant captain deserves to be remembered, and Richborough may still know something of him.

[2] Rhutupini. The point on the British coast, whence, in Roman times, passage was made to Gesorlacum, now Boulogne, was Rutupiae, and answers to Richborough. Probably the Poet did not mean to be more definite than Kent or the south coast.

[3] The ' laena ' was a lined cloak, and the word is very fittingly used by our Poet here, for the lined cloak or jacket of a horse-soldier. The cloak, when not in actual use, was hung over the left shoulder, where it was serviceable against sword cuts. It survived till lately in Hussar regiments ; and still survives in foreign

Sudanti fremebundus equo fastigia montis
Scandere celsa parat, toto comitante suorum
Agmine, magnanimi natumque ex stirpe Cleani
Bellantem petit ense virum, atque extrema minatur.
Isque ubi ductorem cristis sublimibus Anglum
Aspicit, atque armis fulgentem, et vana tumentem,
Haud jam dicta dabat, nec inania verba retorquet,
Sed parat ignivomo responsa remittere bombo.
Desuper arma tonant, vastoque impulsa fragore
Machina liventis displosit pondera plumbi.
Ipsa per ora viri, perque ilia labitur Angli
Plumbea glans, patulique foramina transiit ani.
Ille excussus equo ceu diri fulminis ictu
Procubuit moriens, et languida lumina somno
Composuit, tenuesque animam diffudit in auras.
O sors digna viro, nec mors indigna rebelli!

on his sweating steed, his whole force accompanying him. He seeks with the sword the warlike son of the great-souled Maclean, and threatens him with destruction. He, as he beheld the English captain with his lofty plumes and shining armour, boasting vain things, answered nothing, and returned no empty words, but prepares to send his answer by a shot. From above the muskets thunder, and discharge with mighty crash their balls of livid lead. A leaden bullet entering by the very mouth of the Englishman passed through his bowels, and went out at his back. He, thrown from his horse, as by the stroke of dread lightning, lay dying, closed his languid eyes in the sleep of death, and breathed forth his spirit to the thin air. O fate worthy of a man, and a death not unworthy of a rebel! He, who but a little before, was shining

---

armies. Red cloaks, lined for the horse-soldiers, costing £2, 5s., appear in the estimates of the period.

The following extract, from the Historical Records of the British Army—4th Dragoon Guards—giving the sums paid for the clothing of the horse at this time, is of interest:—

Scarlet coats,	£3 10 0	Cloth waistcoats,	£0 1 5
Corporal's coats,	4 10 0	Buff gloves,	0 7 6
Red cloaks lined,	2 5 0	Horse furniture, viz. housing	
Hats edged with lace,	0 15 0	and holster caps embroidered,	1 5 0
Sword and belts,	1 0 0	Jacked boots,	1 6 0
Carbine belts,	0 7 0	Cartouch-boxes,	0 2 6

Each captain clothed his own trumpeter, and the colonel the kettle-drummer.

Qui modo sarrano fulgebat comptus in ostro,
Quique coruscabat fulgentibus aureus armis,
Nunc sine veste jacet media revolutus arena,
Et sua fata gemens concessit inermis ad umbras.
Cogitur et Stygias nudus remeare paludes.
At vigilum tremefacta cohors, ductore perempto,
Aufugit, effusis campumque reliquit habenis.
   Dundius interea, per muta silentia noctis
Fulminat ignivomo dum machina[1] utrinque boatu,
Excitus, velut ad pugnam vocat agmina cantu.
Mox gliscente vago vallavit castra tumultu,
Et locat excubias ad Spejae fluminis undas,
Hinc atque hinc vigilesque, locis incinctus iniquis
Hostem expectat equis venientem in castra citatis.
Verum ubi nocturnis caput eluctaverat umbris,
Et radios Aurora suos donaverat orbi,
Victor ovans alto descendit colle Cleanus,

arrayed in Sarrian[2] purple, and gleaming in golden arms, is lying, now without garment, rolled in the sand, and lamenting and unarmed, has yielded his lot to the shades. Naked he is forced to ferry the Stygian lake. But the outpost squadrons, their captain being slain, fled, and with loosened rein quitted the field.

Dundee, aroused meanwhile when the musketry fire maintained on both sides was resounding through the silence of the night, calls out his force by the war-note,[3] as if to battle. Presently, as the remote tumult increased, he strengthened his camp, and placed outposts by the waters of the Spey, and on each side sentries, and being girt in by ground difficult for the enemy, he awaited his coming against his camp with his swift cavalry. But when Aurora had raised her head above the shades of night, the victorious Maclean descends triumphantly from his high hill rejoicing in

---

[1] See Preface as to weapons.

[2] 'Sarrano.' The following extract from Holyoke's *Dict. of Names*, 1677—new in our author's time, and perhaps used by him—accounts for the employment of this strange word: 'Sarra, dict. a Sarra pisce ex cujus sanguine tingebatur sericum in purpuram. A city in Phoenicia whence we have our scarlet dyed. Unde "vestes Sarranae." This city was called Tyre.' See Holyoke under *Sarra*. He gives a reference to Martial.

[3] I have supplied an epithet to *cantu*, and taken liberties with the sequence of the tenses.

Gaudens hesternos sic sustinuisse labores.
Nunc et per dumos juvat ire cruore natantes,
Et spolia exanimis caesorum haerentia membris
Carpere laetatur, rapidique ad flumina Spejae
Alba procul vacuos attollens signa per agros,
Tendebat celeres dumeta per invia gressus.
Atque ego tum vigilum rector praemissus equorum,
Ut vada cum lectis servarem tuta maniplis,
Grampica belligerum deduxi in castra Cleanum.
Adventu strepuere tubae, per agmina plausus
Tollitur, et magna victorem voce salutant.
Exuviasque ducis gaudent spectare perempti,
Armaque rapta humeris, et vulsas vertice cristas,
Aureaque obtorto detracta monilia collo.
Mirantur fulvi jam tot talenta [1] metalli,
Diversosque habitus; hic cocco [2] insignis et auro,
Alter cyaneo, rutilo ille refulget amictu;

having come through the labours of the night. Now through the thickets wet with blood he delights to go, and eagerly strips [3] off from the dead bodies of the slain the spoils adhering to their members, and raising white standards through the empty fields by the waters of rapid Spey, he hastened his quick steps through the pathless woods.

And I, having been sent forward in charge of a party of cavalry outposts to keep the fords safe with a detachment,[4] led the warlike Maclean into the Highland camp. At his coming the pipes resounded, applause is raised throughout the host, and they salute the victor with a great hurrah. They welcome the sight of the dead officer's spoils, his armour torn from his shoulders, and his crested plume from his head, and golden gorget from his twisted neck. They marvel at so great a weight of golden metal and the various vestures; this one arrayed in scarlet and gold, another in blue, and a third in red livery;[5] and when they beheld so many

---

[1] 'talenta': the scanning of talenta is bad, but there is no meaning in 'labenta,' the apparent reading of the original.

[2] *Var. lect.* 'cocio'; also 'croco.'

[3] The stripping of the slain was at once proceeded with in these Highland victories over Lowlanders. In one account of the death of Claverhouse his body is spoken of as stripped on the field. See note on the *unburied* at beginning of Book v.

[4] Another personal allusion which gives greater security as to the trustworthiness of the account.

[5] See preceding note on uniforms.

Totque ut parta manu videre ex hoste trophaea,
Et tot opima virum spolia ornamentaque caesis
Rapta cadaveribus, laetas ad sidera voces
Attollunt, coelum atque solum clamore resultant.[1]
Jam Titan summos spargebat lampade montes.
It campis chlamydata cohors, et utrinque ruebant
Lata per arva viri, volat hinc dux Grampius, illinc
Belgicus instabat ductor, patulaeque tenebant
Aequora convallis Spejae, geminasque sub armis
Ostentant acies, hic cis, trans fluminis undas
Alter Grampiacas raptabat ad ardua turmas.
Scaurius ambustam Ruthveni sistit ad arcem.
Hinc petit australes Forthae ultra flumina tractus
Ut referat summo coram sua facta senatu.
Verum tardigrado procedens agmine Gramus

trophies wrested from the enemy by their hands, and so many rich spoils and decorations stripped from the dead bodies of the men, they lift their exulting voices to the stars, and heaven and earth re-echo the clamour. Already Titan was suffusing the highest hills with his light. The plaided companies were moving in the plains, and on either side the men were in motion all over the wide fields. Here flies forward the Highland leader, there presses on the Belgic general, and they were holding the level ground of the wide Strathspey, presenting two armies,[2] here one on this side, there the other on that side the river, hurrying on the Highland troops towards the mountains. Scourie stopped by the blackened walls of Ruthven Castle. Then he seeks the southern lands beyond the Forth, and tells his tale before the Supreme Convention. But

---

[1] The original and copies have 'resultat.'

[2] Dundee was marching towards Ruthven and Mackay was keeping a day behind him, maintaining a position at Culnakyle. Dundee proceeded onwards through Badenoch towards Lochaber. He had thought of taking up a strong position in Rannoch, but 'finding the Lochaber men going away every night by forties and fifties with droves of cattle, and finding all the rest loaden with plunder of Grant's land and others, would needs go home, gave way to it and came into Lochaber with them, dispersed them all to their respective houses with orders to be ready within a few days, if the enemy pursued, if not, to lay still till further orders.'—*Letters of Dundee*, p. 62. Mackay followed as far as Ruthven, and found that Dundee was passed into Lochaber, where he resolved to leave him because 'there were no good wayes to be fournished over all with provisions, and without them no regular body of forces can subsist together.'—Mackay's Letter from Head of Strathspey, June 13, 1689.

Ut Batavum Abriacas intra praecluderet Alpes,
Cunctanti similis Fabio se ostendit in armis;
Utque abiisse ducem, et castris cessisse relictis
Cognovit, rapidis Badenothea passibus arva
Transit, et Abriacos scandit trans ardua montes.
Jamque virum coetu procul hic semotus ab omni
Dum sedet undantem Roae taciturnus ad amnem,
Lecta manus procerum coit, et sibi juncta propinquo
Sanguine turba latus spissa cinxere corona.
Quos ubi gramineo compostos aggere vidit,
Incipit, et mentis permulcet taedia curis.
Atque ait; 'Arctoi regnator maxime mundi
Inter et Hectoreos O Septime magne Stuartos
Quid jam labentes cunctando perdimus horas?
Dum tonat arctois gener, heu! crudelis in oris,
Exagitatque feris me presbyter impius armis
Arma nefanda ducis Batavi et res sponte secutus
Me petit insidiis, et iniquo marte lacessit.
Presbyteri ante oculos hostilis oberrat imago

the Graham, proceeding leisurely with his force towards the Lochaber mountains, that he might by them as a barrier shut out the Dutch general, now showed himself in this strategy an imitator of Fabius Cunctator. When he was aware that Mackay had departed, and forsaken his deserted camp, he passed through the fields of Badenoch and crossed over the summits of the Lochaber hills. Here, while now he silently sat remote, by the flowing Roy, there gathered to him his favoured company of chiefs and that great number of blood relations who followed him, and in a close circle surrounded him. When he beholds them seated on the grassy bank, to ease the tedium of his mind under its cares, he begins, and thus speaks:[1] 'O chief ruler of the Northern kingdom, the great seventh James of the heroic Stuarts, why do we lose in delay these gliding hours? Why does thy cruel son-in-law, alas! dominate in the North, and the impious presbyter harass me with fierce arms? Why does he, following the execrable standard of the Dutch general, and supporting his cause, assail me with these plots, and wage against me an unequal war? The hostile image of the

---

[1] As to this concluding portion of Book v. I think the author had it by him for some other purpose and puts it into the mouth of Claverhouse to fill up the book. Its extraordinary abusiveness constitutes the passage a curiosity in its way, and its composition is very careless.

Insomnemque premit, noctesque diesque fatigat.
O mihi fatalis cunctisque infestior hostis
Hostibus! O dirum caput, execrabile nomen
Presbyter et patriae furialis Enyo ruendae;
Perfida sceptrigeris et gens inimica Stuartis.
Odi ego presbyterum cane pejus et angue rebellem.
Propterea egregii proceres, et lecta juventus,
Dum vacat, et siccos exurit Syrius agros,
Presbyteri ingenium, facta atque immania pandam,
Ipsumque ingenuo pinxisse colore juvabit.
   Turba sacerdotum mala bestia, bellua Lernae,
Multorum capitum monstrum, Scyllaeque biformis
Progenies, veterum dura de stirpe gigantum,
Centimanusque[1] viri, Lapithumque horrenda propago,
Saevior atque Getis, dirisque rapacior Hunnis,
Quaeque adeo majora olim damna intulit orbi
Terrarum, quam Turca ferus, quam Tartarus ingens,
Pontificum ante alios scelerata superbia Romae
Infandos toto permiscuit orbe tumultus,
Et bruto attonitos tremefecit fulmine reges.

presbyterian hovers before my eyes and oppresses me in my sleepless hours, weighing on me night and day. O enemy fatal to me, and more hostile than all others! O dread head, execrable name, presbyter, furious Enyo of your ruined fatherland. O race disloyal and hostile to the royal Stuart. Worse than dog or snake do I hate the rebel presbyterian. Wherefore, noble leaders and chosen youths, while we have nothing else to do, and the Dog-star blazes over the dry fields, I will unfold to you the temper of the presbyterian and his savage deeds, and I will paint him in his true colours.

'That tribe of Priests—*mala bestia*—a monster like that of Lerna of many heads, and like the progeny of the bi-formed Scylla, sprung from the rugged race of giants, men of the hundred hands, and dread offspring of the Lapithes, more savage than the Getae, more rapacious than the dread Huns, a tribe of men which has brought in past time upon the world misfortunes as great as e'er fierce Turk or mighty Tartar wrought—the accursed pride of Roman pontiffs has raised up convulsions in the world more disastrous than all others, and by its noisy fulminations has made stricken kings to quake. While the successor of the fisherman

---

[1] Thus in original and copies. Did he think the adjective was declined as *Manus-ūs*, the noun?

Dum piscatoris successor quaerit haberi
Primus in orbe deus; quas o non[1] struxerit olim
Regibus insidias triplicem dum Papa tiaram
Gemmiferam praeclara super diademata regum
Extulit, augustosque super caput extulit[2] omnes.
Verum ut Romuleae varia inter dogmata turbae
Nequior est falso mentitus nomen Jesu,
Ipse reformatos inter nequissimus omnes
Presbyter, et similes eructat uterque furores.
Presbyter infelix patriae fatalis Erynnis,
Invisus superis, turbator pacis, in iram
Pronus, avaritiae cultor, luxusque magister
Impiger, obscaeno necnon petulantior haedo,
Et scelere infamis, praeclarus et arte Pelasga,
Fraude Caledoniis Graia et bene notus in oris,
Insignisque dolo, et simulati numinis arte,
Aequorei similis cancri, et testudinis instar
Dirigit huc gressus, obliquum lumina torquet;
Improbus impostor, qui religione deorum
Territat attonitas vana et formidine mentes,
Obfuscat veneranda patrum monumenta profanis
Commentis, alioque loqui sermone facessit

made his claim to be regarded as the first deity in the world, what plots did not the popes of old frame against kings, as they sought to rear the jewelled tiara above illustrious crowns, and to uplift their own heads above all the great. But as among the various schools of the Roman multitude there is none worse than that which falsely assumes the name of Jesus, so among the reformed the presbyter is the vilest, and they each raise like storms. The miserable presbyterian, the fatal fury of his country, hated by the gods, the disturber of peace, prone to wrath, the student of avarice, earnest master of lust, wanton as a goat, infamous in guilt, a very Greek in deceit, and well known on Scottish shore for Grecian fraud, distinguished in artifice and in the arts of hypocrisy, like the crab of the sea or the tortoise, he directs his steps hither while he looks the other way; vile impostor who in name of the religion of the gods, and by vain fear terrifies the weak minds, confounds by his profane comments the venerable monuments of the fathers, and attempts to preach in other words the

---

[1] *Var. lect.* quas o non : *non* omitted in original.

[2] I have here given a reading from an old copy, as 'exterit' is not sense. He may have meant 'erigit' or perhaps 'extruit.'

Biblia[1] sacra suo sensu ; sanctum sed in sua verba
Torquet Evangelium, et Christi mandata refellit,
Atque e suggestu cerdonum oracula fundit.
Dum studet insipido fallax imponere vulgo,
Spem vultu simulat, pansisque ad sidera palmis
Ore, oculis, gestuque loqui divina videtur,
Atque inter lachrimas, et singultantia verba
Instruit arte dolos, et fraude resuscitat iras.
Mox vultum videas distortum, atque oris hiatum
Ingentem, inque modum raucorum ululare luporum,
Cumque preces longas fundit, ciet horrida bella
In patriam, patriaeque patrem ; sic relligionis
Ludificat stolidam mentito nomine plebem.
   Presbyter et Scotus toto notissimus orbe
Exhibet indomiti specimen fatale tyranni,
Cujus triste sonat nunquam laetabile nomen.
Invidus, insidiosus, iners, malefidus amicus,
Impius, ingenio vafer, et Pharisaeus oliva
Unctus, nequitiae genuinus Machiavelli
Discipulus, tam fraudis amans, quam litis alumnus.

sacred Scriptures under a sense (not their own). He turns the Gospel to suit his own discourse, makes light of the commands of Christ, and from the pulpit pours out the oracular utterances of the mere cobbler. While the deceiver seeks to impose upon the foolish common people, he assumes an expression of hope, and with palms spread open to the heavens he seems by mouth, eyes, and gestures to be uttering divine things, yet amid tears and sobbing words he skilfully lays his plots, and by his arts kindles strife. Presently you may see his face distorted, and his vast gaping mouth howling after the manner of hoarse wolves, and while he pours out long prayers, he raises up horrible wars upon his country and against his country's father. Thus in the feigned name of religion he plays upon the stupid people.

'And the Scotch presbyter, the most notorious in the world, presents the fatal specimen of the incorrigible tyrant whose sad name never comes with any note of joy—envious, cunning, lazy, faithless in friendship, unfilial, subtle, anointed Pharisee, a true disciple of Machiavellian guile, loving lies as a lawyer loves a lawsuit. He is a plague inflicted as a punishment by the angry gods

---

[1] The verse will not scan as given in original. 'Sub' has been replaced by 'suo,' and the epithet 'sanctum' supplied: it was an evident slip.

Iratis olim in poenam mortalibus aegris [1]
A superis illata lues, nec turpius ullum
Jupiter immisit terris per saecula monstrum.
Regibus infandum portentum, omenque sinistrum
Triste stupendum ingens. Non tot se vertit in ora
Proteus, aut plures dedit uno in corpore formas.
Nunc leo, nunc aries, nunc curva in cornua taurus,
Nunc Harpeia nocens, torvo nunc ore chimaera.
Miles, et ante aras Tyriaque in veste sacerdos;
Mortalisque deus, regnansque in saecula daemon.
Presbyter infidus, scelerati foederis author,
Ira deum, sentina mali, pietatis alastor,
Pestis acerba soli, infensi gravis iraque coeli,
Fexque hominum prognata Erebo, nutrita Genevae
Perfidiae, horrendis atque educatus [2] in armis,
Adversisque ortus fatis, et sidere laevo
Editus, et primis huc usque rebellis ab annis.
Impia in arma furens, sumptisque inglorius armis,
Et patriae praedo, et mundi turbator in aevum,
Osor et optati toties mortalibus aequi.
Proditione, dolo, scelere, atque libidine et ira

upon miserable mortals, and never did Jupiter in all the ages send a worse monster on the earth. To kings he is a portent unspeakable, an omen evil, sad, stupendous and powerful. Not to so many forms does Proteus turn himself, or present more shapes in one body—now a lion, now a ram, now a bull with curving horn, then a noxious Harpy, then a Chimaera with grim jaw. A soldier now, and before the altars a priest in Tyrian vestment; a god, yet mortal, a demon ruling in the world. The faithless presbyter, the author of the accursed Covenant, the scourge of the gods, the sink of evil, the plague of piety, the bitter pest of the earth, the heavy scourge of outraged heaven, the dregs of men, begotten in Erebus, suckled in faithless Geneva, and brought up mid the horrors of war, conceived by hostile fates, born under an evil star, and from earliest years till now a rebel. Raging in impious arms, and inglorious in them when they are assumed, both a robber of his country and the everlasting disturber of the world, and the hater of the equity so desired by mortals. Infamous for treachery, guile, wickedness, lust and anger; to whom his will alone serves for

---

[1] 'Aegri mortales'—Virg. *Aen.* ii. 268.
[2] False quantity here.

Infamis ; cui sola placet pro lege voluntas,
Cui fera bella, doli, cui dira rebellio cordi ;
Subdola lingua, rapax manus, et concordia discors ;
Ingenium et Catharo semper mutabile Scoto.
Seditione potens, populum stimulatque rebellem
Principis in damnum, largisque indulget habenis.
　　Presbyter ille exlex, subversor Caesaris, hostis
Imperii, nisi forte choro praesultet, et omne
Agmen agat, socii sceleris sua signa sequuntur,
Arbitrio nisi forte suo stet summa potestas ;
Et nisi curva suos moduletur tibia cantus
Cujus triste jugum comitatur tota malorum
Congeries, animi fastus, scelerata cupido,
Ingluvies ventris, rabies vesana cruoris,
Ferrum, flamma, fames, bellona, incendia, caedes ;
Cujus et indomitum fastum, pectusque superbum,
Elatumque animum, vultumque et turgida verba
Aequavit regum nemo, nec atrocibus ausis
Ullus adhuc toto praeclarior orbe tyrannus.
Fercula sola placent magno cui parta labore
Nulla nec arrident Catharo nisi vina taberna.

law, to whom fierce war, plots, and dread rebellion give keen delight. A deceitful tongue, a greedy hand, broken peace, and a changeful temper, ever characterise the Scottish Puritan. Powerful in sedition, he stirs up a rebellious people to the destruction of their Prince, and casts loose the reins.

'The presbyter is lawless, the overthrower of the Caesar, the enemy of the empire, unless perchance he may dance before the whole choir, and lead the whole line ; unless supreme power stands at his will his companions in crime are quickly up after his standards ; and unless the crooked pipe be tuned to his notes, a whole mass of miseries accompany his miserable domination— arrogance, covetousness, gluttony, blood-thirstiness, sword, fire, famine, war, flames, and destruction ; whose unconquerable pride, haughty mien, elated vanity ; whose aspect and swelling words no king ever equalled, and whose atrocities no tyrant in the whole world, however notorious, ever rivalled. To him no dishes are pleasing save those obtained at great cost, no wines smile upon the Puritan save the tavern cups.[1]   Him, too, an insatiable avarice

---

[1] Tavern wines—these were reputed the best at this time, and were of a higher class than could be found in private houses. In 1692, the Lords of Council and Session ordaine the wynes to be sold within the town of Edinburgh,

Illum etiam misere tenet insatiabile crimen
Tristis avaritiae, quo non deformius ullum,
Namque hominem in tygres mutat, rapidosque[1] leones ;
Et terram pelagusque, profundaque Tartara miscet.
Sed pelagus nec terra satis, non sufficit orbis
India, nec dives Pactolus, nec Tagus uni
Sufficiunt Catharo ; tanta est flagrantia nummi,
Prodidit ille auro patriam, regemque deumque
Vendidit, et sese venalem mancipat Orco.
Presbyter et plures pridem dedit astus alumnos
Christo, sancta fides fidos quam fecit amicos.
Contemptor legum, fax seditionis, et irae
Flagitiique faber, civilis buccina belli,
Ut trahat ad sese imperium, fascesque tyranni
Induat, et tota solus dominetur in arcto.
Impia bella fovet, litesque et jurgia nutrit,
Et summos solio Augustos detrudit[2] avito.

binds, than which there is no crime more destructive, for it changes men into tigers and rabid lions ; and it mingles sea and land and the depths beneath. But sea and land suffice not, nor the world, nor India, the rich Pactolus nor Tagus rolling together, content the Puritan ; so burning is his love of money that he sold his Country for gold, and his King,[3] and his God, and for money binds himself as a servant to hell. And the crafty presbyterian has given more alumni[4] to Christ than holy faith has made true friends. Despiser of the laws, torch of sedition, fabricator of malice and crime, trumpet of civil war, all this is he, that he may draw empire to himself, that he may sway the fasces of the tyrant, and rule alone throughout the North. He fosters impious wars, nourishes quarrels and complaints, and hurls the supreme rulers from the

---

and suburbs thereof, at the rates following, viz., that the pint of the best French wines do not exceed 28 shillings Scots, and the pint of the best Spanish wines 40 shillings Scots, and that the Magistrates of Edinburgh forthwith make proclamation of these rates by tuck of drum. In 1736, the retailers of wines and spirits in bottles are required to bring with them a stoup of the denomination of the bottle, and an extra bottle, called an oullage bottle, for making up what the bottle may be deficient of the just measure.—*Acts of Sederunt*, 1553-1790, pages 201 and 311.

[1] Did he mean 'rabidosque'?
[2] *Var. lect.* 'deturbat' for 'detrudit.'
[3] Referring to the selling of King Charles I. by the Scots.
[4] The meaning here is obscure, and the passage may be corrupt. See note in Preface.

Magnanimosque duces, raptatque in funera reges,
Mutua sanctiloquos truditque in vulnera fratres,
Et miseram revocat dura in certamina plebem,
Horridaque attonitam succendit bella per arcton.
Ista [1] trucis Cathari scelerata licentia vocis
Complet caede domos ; toties et terruit orbem
Arctoum gladiis flammasque vomentibus armis.
   Quanta Caledoniis excivit praelia campis
Presbyter, et tragicos per barbara bella tumultus ! [2]
Quot patriae armatas in propria viscera turmas
Truserit, et fratres in mutua vulnera [3] fratrum !
Provocat et quantas diris rumoribus iras ! [2]
Quot martem sonuere tubae ! [2] quot classica belli
Rauca dedere sonum ! [2] tenuit cum presbyter aras
Perfidus, et fortem premeret [4] ditione Britannum.
Intulit hic patrio majora incommoda Scoto
Quam quondam infestus regni pro finibus Anglus,
Centum continuos deducens bella per annos.
Et majora dedit septenis [5] tempore lustri

ancestral throne. Great generals and kings he hurries to destruction, and forces the brethren, teachers of sacred things, to mutual hurt, and calls back the unhappy people to the hardships of strife, kindling throughout the stricken North the horrors of civil war. That accursed licence of the truculent voice of the Puritan fills homes with slaughter, and affrights the northern land with sword and flame-vomiting weapons.

'What contests has the presbyterian not provoked on Scottish fields, and what barbarous wars through his deadly rebellions ! What bands of armed men has he not forced out against his country's life, brother to the mutual injury of brother ! and what strife has he not provoked by his horrid slanders ! How many pipes, how many hoarse clarions have given the signal of war, all since the false presbyterian has held the Altars, and oppressed the bold Briton beneath his sway ! He has brought more evils upon the Scottish fatherland than ever did the English enemy fighting for the borders of the kingdom, though he prolonged his wars for a hundred years at a time. In the forty years he has given worse wounds than did Danes united with

---

[1] *Var. lect.* ' Ira' for 'Ista.'   [2] Original has marks of interrogation here.
[3] *Var. lect.* 'funera' for 'vulnera.'   [4] 'premeret': careless sequence.
[5] ? septeno.

Vulnera, quam valido Cimber cum Saxone, vel quam
Romulidae rerum domini, Dacive feroces,
Hibernive truces potuere ab origine mundi.
Scilicet invicto stigma indelebile Scoto
Indidit, et dirum posuit per saecula probrum ;
Perjuriique[1] notam, dedit atque ignobile nomen,
Et patriae fatale malum, gentique Britannae
Attulit infandam maculam, tristemque ruinam.
Finibus in patriis per barbara bella cruentum
Tale dedit genii specimen, tot stragis acervos
Edidit, et rigido tot fortia pectora ferro
Sustulit, et tristi demisit caede sub umbras.
Quaeque fidem superant hominum tot facta nefanda
Gesserit, assumpta pietatis imagine ficta
Quae nec Scriba vafer, nunquam Pharisaeus iniquus,
Nec qui Mosaico docuit praeputia ritu ;
Neve sacrificulus quisquam tumidusve sacerdos,
Nec qui gemmifera circundat[2] tempora mitra
Pontificum quisquam nunquam ausus talia Romae.
Ut vel posteritas dictis male credula nostris
Haec trahat in dubium, aut vana insomnia dicat,

stout Saxons, than did the Romans, the rulers of the world, Dacians or Irish, from the beginning of time. Without doubt he has fixed a stain indelible on the unconquered Scot, and has brought upon him, for ages to come, a foul disgrace. He has imposed upon him the mark and dishonouring name of perjury, and on the country he has raised a curse, and on the British race unspeakable contempt and miserable ruin. On the borders, by the barbarity of war he gave a true specimen of his temper, piling up heaps of carnage, piercing brave breasts with cruel sword, and sending souls to the shades by a miserable butchery. His deeds are beyond belief, the false form of piety being assumed with an hypocrisy. beyond that of subtle Scribe, unjust Pharisee, or any teacher of the Mosaic rite of circumcision. Nor did any sacrificing proud priest, nor any one of the pontiffs of Rome who surrounds his brow with jewelled mitre, ever dare such things. So is it that incredulous posterity may either hold these words in distrust, or declare them vain dreams or deny them, and our children repute

---

[1] 'Perjurii': false quantity. In a copy the *u* is marked short.
[2] The spelling of the original.

Aut neget, et nostri reputent ea falsa nepotes
Nostra, sequensque omnis mundi mirabitur aetas.
  Ista tamen nostras aeternum vulnera mentes
Laedunt, et tristi tundunt praecordia planctu,
Incenditque animum miseranda memoria¹ rerum,
Atque iterum lachrimas, moestosque effundere fletus,
Damnum ingens patriae, gentisque infamia nostrae
Sollicitant veterum nimium meminisse malorum.
Insidiosa cohors Catharûm atque ab origine sectae
Pestiferae furibunda suae bacchatur, et armis
Impia sceptrigeris accendit bella Stuartis.
Clara Caledonii Regina Maria Britanni
Presbyterûm infandos primum perpessa labores,
Improba vaniloquae subiitque opprobria linguae.
O quantas, invicta animo, vultuque sereno
Pertulit aerumnas, terraque marique procellas !²
Quotque tulit tragicos generosa mente tumultus !²
Insectata odiis procerum, vulgique furore
Pulsa tribus regnis, totidemque exuta coronis,
Atque agitata malis ; bis carcere clausa nefando

these our words as false, and every succeeding age of the world will wonder.

'These wounds nevertheless make sore our minds with a lasting hurt, and affect our breasts with a melancholy woe; and the miserable memory of these things fires our minds, and anon compels tears and mournful wailing, as the great loss of our country, the infamy of our race, and our old misfortunes, are recalled to mind too vividly. The treacherous band of Puritans, mad from the very beginning of the pestiferous sect, revels like drunken Bacchanal, and in arms raises impious wars against the royal Stuarts. The illustrious Mary, Queen of Scots, first patiently bore the miserable work of the presbyterian, and underwent the impudent abuse of his boastful tongue. O what great miseries did she endure, what storms by land and sea! unconquered in spirit, and with countenance serene. How many tragic tumults did she go through with noble mind! pursued by the hatred of the nobles, driven from three kingdoms³ by the fury of the people, deprived of as many crowns, and overwhelmed with misfortunes;

---

¹ False quantity here.   ² In original these are marks of interrogation.
³ While Queen of France and Scotland, she claimed also England, and her title to England and Ireland was upheld by the Roman party.

Presbyteri ingenio, patriisque penatibus exul
Submisit rigidae tandem pia colla catastae.
　Filius imperium tenet inde Jacobus avorum
Gloria, pacifici gaudens cognomine Regis.
Magnum Fergusi decus est,[1] quique evehit altum
Nomen ad usque polum, famamque ad sidera caeli.
Hic quoque presbyteri stimulis agitatus acerbis
Impiaque horrendae perpessus jurgia linguae,
Ingentesque iras teneris expertus ab annis;
Quem nisi firma fides pacisque intensa cupido,
Altaque vis animi, et virtus contermina caelo
Aemula majorum, et triplicis nova gloria sceptri,
Imperii et moles, aeternaque numina caeli
Incolumem voluere suis salvumque Britannis
Esse diu, tristi jamdudum vulnere victum,
Presbyter ingenti rapuisset caede sub umbras.

twice by the accursed genius of the presbyterian shut up in prison, she at length, as an exile from her country's hearths, laid her sacred neck on the cruel block.

'Then James, her son, possesses the throne, the glory of his ancestors, rejoicing in the name of the peaceful king.[2] He is the great ornament of the house of Fergus, and the one who raised his name even to the Pole, and his fame to the stars. He also, moved by the sharp stings of the presbyterian, having undergone the impious abuse of his horrid tongue, and experienced from his tender years his great rage; whom, stricken ere long by cruel wound, the presbyterian would have hurried to his end by a tragedy, had not a steadfastness to his religion, an intense love of peace, a lofty force of character, and a virtue rivalling that of his ancestors and reaching the heavens, and had not the new glory of the triple sceptre and the might of the great empire, and had not the gods willed him to be safe, and to escape his people.

---

[1] In original there is *et* after 'decus' instead of *est*.

[2] Hume says, 'While James was vaunting his divine vicegerency, and boasting of his high prerogative, he possessed not so much as a single regiment of guards to maintain his extensive claims; a sufficient proof that he sincerely believed them to be well grounded.' He also says, 'With peace so successfully cultivated and so passionately loved by this monarch, his life also terminated.' My attention has been called to the following mottoes on the James I. coinage: 'Faciam eos in gentem unam,' 'Tueatur unita Deus,' 'Quae Deus conjunxit, nemo separet,'—all illustrating the desire of James to be considered the peace-loving King.

Carolus inde nepos solium conscendit avitum
Vatidicus, Christi praeco Rex, martyr et heros,
Vera Jovis proles, subolesque uberrima divum,
Quo pietate viro major, nec pulchrior armis
Ullus erat, meliorve fuit nec justior alter.
Hunc tamen arma manent, galeaeque, ensesque, cruenti,
Tibicinumque [1] gravis sonitus, clangore [2] tubarum
Aere, Regum sceptris, pictisque tapetibus aulae
Ilicet expectant; ipsoque in limine regni
Presbyter horrendo saevit temerarius aestu,
Turbidus irarum totasque effundit habenas.
Aggrediturque nefas dirum, facinusque nefandum,
Consiliumque horrendum iniit, foedusque cruentum
Contrahit, atque dolos Regi struit impius almo;
Subdolus et fictae pietatis imagine falsa
Horrida degenerem trahit in certamina plebem.

'Charles then, the grandson (of Mary), ascended the ancestral throne, a prophet,[3] a king, and preacher of Christ, a martyr and hero, the very child of Jove, the rich offspring of the gods, greater than any man in piety; nor was there any of fairer fame in arms, nor any man more just or better than he. Him, however, arms at once await, and helmet and cruel sword, and doleful sound of pipes,[4] with clash of brazen clarion, instead of royal sceptre and tapestried hangings of the court. On the very threshold of his reign, the audacious presbyter works with horrid ferment, and sets himself free, in the storm of his wrath, from all restraint. He advances to his dreadful deed, to his unspeakable crime; he enters on his horrid purpose; he forms his bloody covenant, and for the benign monarch lays snares, and plotting under the mask of religion, he draws on the common people to war. Hence the

---

[1] False quantity. [2] *Var. lect.* clangoreque.
[3] Vatidicus. The Poet is seeking to bring out the prophetic, priestly—in the way of preaching—and royal character of Charles. The prophetic claim is probably to be based on the *Sortes Virgilianæ*, in which Charles prophesied his own fate and coming events. The *Icon Basilike* gives a title (in the eyes of all Jacobites at any rate, believing it to be the work of the King) to Charles to be considered a preacher of Christ. It passed through fifty editions in a twelvemonth, and, as Hume says, 'it is not easy to conceive the general compassion excited towards the King by the publishing at so critical a juncture a work so full of piety, meekness, and humanity.' See additional note in Preface.
[4] I think this is the meaning of the passage, though other interpretations may be possible.

Hinc rapidae caedes, atque horrida bella per arcton
Ingeminant, tortoque fremit Bellona flagello.
Centum acies valido cinctae[1] munimine belli
Arripuere locum pugnae, Martemque dedere ;
Et toties toto certatum corpore regni.
Regis in exitium validae bis mille carinae
Mille rates vasti subeunt freta spumea ponti.
Presbytero ducente chorum, Rex optimus orbis
Fluctibus innumeris et tempestatibus actus,
Et toties tanta fusus cum caede suorum,
Et profugus, Martem totiesque expertus iniquum,
Innocuus patrio statuit se tradere Scoto.
Presbyter at Scotus, funesto stigmate dignus,
Hostibus exiguo Regem divendidit auro.
Artibus his rabidi praeclaro Rege potiti
Presbyteri, tragico subvertunt cuncta tumultu.
Colluviem coeunt hominum, conflantque cruentum
Judiciale forum, coram spectante popello,
Judicio Regem sistunt, damnantque stupendo
Nec prius audito titulo, quin denique cogunt
Innocuum rigido jugulum submittere ferro.
Illa dies nigro semper signanda lapillo.

frequent slaughter, wars renewed, and Bellona raging in the North with twisted lash. A hundred regiments in full panoply of war take the field and give battle, and a hundred times, with the whole strength of the kingdom, the struggle is made. Two thousand powerful ships, a thousand barks, cover the foaming surface of the great sea for the destruction of the King. By the presbyterian's leading in the plot, the best of Kings in the world, driven by numberless waves and tempests, and so often overthrown with great slaughter of his men, guilelessly determines to trust himself as a fugitive to his kindred Scots. But for a little gold the Scottish presbyterian, worthy of damning stigma, sold his King to his enemies. Possessed of the King by these means, the wild presbyterians turn everything to tragic tumult. They gather together the off-scourings of men, they create a bloodthirsty tribunal, before the eyes of the gazing people, they summon the King to judgment, and by a monstrous title, hitherto unknown, they pronounce doom, nay, at length force him to submit his innocent neck to the sharp

---

[1] *Var. lect.* 'auctore' and 'auctae.'

Tempore et ex illo pereat male presbyter oro
Degener, aeternum atque inglorius exigat aevum.
Aurea stelliferi current dum lumina caeli,
Dumque jubar solis radiis fulgebit Eois,
Presbyteri infaustum execretur Scotia nomen.
   Carolus et pronepos proavorum gloria Regum
Prisca Caledonii soboles, stirpsque inclyta Scoti,
Atque sagittiferi decus immortale Britanni,
Jam genitore pio crudeli funere caeso,
Turbida presbyteri primaevo in flore juventae
Ingenia, ingentesque iras, moresque superbos
Pertulit, et rigidae conamina bellica turbae.
Sceptra per innumeros proavos dum missa capescat
Protinus armorum durus circumstrepit horror
Bellicus, et rauco clangunt cava classica cantu,
Rursus in arma vocant, saevique in proelia Martis
Tympana, magnanimum sternuntque inimica rebellis
Agmina presbyteri Regem, profugumque sequuntur,
Et magna insontem vitam mercede requirunt.
Carolus interea patula latet ilice tutus,

axe. That was a day to be marked with a black stone [1] for ever. From that day I say my prayer, 'May the vile presbyterian come to a bad end, and to all time carry his shame! While the lights of the starry heavens shall run their course, while the sun shall continue to cover the east with his rising rays, may the ill-omened name of *presbyterian* be execrated in Scotland.'

'Charles, also the great-grandson (of Mary), the glory of the kingly race, primitive stock of Caledonia, illustrious stem of the Scots, unfading ornament of the arrow-bearing Briton—his father having now met his cruel fate, he underwent, in the flower of his youth, the moody temper of the presbyterian and his bursts of rage, his haughty manner and the hostility of the rigid sect. While he is holding the sceptre inherited from numberless ancestors, without delay the harsh clang of arms resounds and the trumpets sound their hoarse notes. Again the drums call to arms to the contests of cruel Mars. The hostile forces of the rebel presbyterians overcome the magnanimous King, pursue him as a fugitive; and by the offer of a great reward they seek his innocent life. Charles, meanwhile, lies safely concealed in the wide-spreading oak, and seeking

---

[1] Cf. Persius ii. : 'Hunc diem numera meliore lapillo.' Lucky days were marked with white, and unlucky days with black, stones.

Suffugiumque petens pelago dare vela coactus,
Et profugus patriis abiit projectus ab oris.
Illum autem aeterno superi regnator Olympi
Sustentat fato, scutoque obnubit amoris.
Post varios belli casus sine sanguine tandem
Ipsa suum reducem videt alma Britannia Regem.
Jamque redux patria rursusque in sede locatus,
Presbyter antiquum premit alto corde dolorem,
Infandos stimulat motus, rabidosque tumultus
Suscitat, et diris fera praelia provocat armis,
Et fremitu ingenti campo se sistit aperto
Impius, et stricto causam mucrone tuetur ;
Terga tamen trepido dat per juga Pictica cursu
Degener, et tristi procumbit vulnere victus.
  Ipse ego presbyterum, magna stipante caterva,
Horrida ter patrio minitantem bella Stuarto
Conspexi, et rabido turbantem cuncta tumultu.

a refuge he is compelled to spread sail on the deep, and as an exile he departs, driven from his country's shores. But according to his eternal purpose, the ruler of high Olympus upheld him, and covered him with the shield of his love. After various hazards of war, Britain, once more benign, sees the King, without blood, restored. The King returned, and again sitting on his throne, the presbyter presses back into his heart his ancient grudge, but stimulates rebel movements, creating outbursts of riot, and provokes the fierce battle in terrible arms, and takes impiously the field with great commotion, preparing with the drawn sword to maintain his cause. In confusion and flight over the Pentland Hills,[1] however, he ignobly turns his back, and sinks stricken with a grievous wound.

  'I myself have thrice seen the presbyterians with great following making war against the native Stuart, convulsing all things in wild confusion. Having, however, adventured himself

---

[1] 'Pictica juga,' the Pentland Hills. Pentland is a Saxon word, corrupted from Pectland according to Skene, *Books of Wales*, vol. i. p. 150. Its common derivation is Pict's land, and this was no doubt the derivation in our author's day, as he renders it by Pictica.

The battle of Pentland, or Rullion Green, was fought on November 28, 1666, when the Covenanters under Colonel Wallace (as he was termed) were defeated by General Dalyell. About 50 were killed and 150 taken prisoners. The gentlemen sent in pursuit had pity on the countrymen, or the slaughter would have been greater. See Buchanan's *History of Scotland*, continued by Aikman, vol. iv. p. 526; Glasgow edit. 1827.

Hunc tamen in bello, campoque aggressus aperto,
Inque fugam versum vidi, victumque fugavi;
Atque alacri sequor usque animo pro Caesare primum
Bothvelium ad pontem, cinctus fulgentibus armis
Bella gero, et patriae fugientem prosequor hostem.
Rursus et horrendi vocor in certamina belli,
Cum ferus illicitis Comes Argathelius armis

into the open plain in his generalship, I saw him turned to flight, and routed I pursued him. And first at Bothwell Brig,[1] I with eager spirit serve the Caesar, girt with bright arms I wage the war and pursue the flying enemy of my country. Again I am called to the war when the fierce Earl of Argyll[2] — the stinking lees and offscourings of the wicked presbyterians — in rebellious arms

---

[1] The Battle of Bothwell Brig was fought June 22d, 1679, exactly ten years almost to a day before the telling of this tale by Claverhouse. He had no important command in the battle, but shared in it with his troop of horse, as also in the pursuit and in carrying out the proceedings which followed the battle. 'The fiery and vindictive part assigned to him by Scott rests on the authority of the most amazing tissue of absurdities ever woven out of the inventive fancy of a balladmonger.'—*Claverhouse*, by Mowbray Morris, p. 85.

[2] Archibald, ninth Earl of Argyll, son of the famous Marquis, having escaped from Edinburgh Castle as a page, holding the train of Lady Sophia Lindsay, went to Holland, where he became a leader in the Dutch plot, resulting in a feeble invasion of Scotland in concert with Monmouth's rebellion. He set sail with his force in the *Anna, Sophia, and David*, on the 2d May, and was off Kirkwall in three days. He eventually landed at Campbeltown. At Tarbet his whole force was only 1800 horse and foot, but was increased by the junction of Sir Duncan Campbell of Auchinbreck to 2500. His little fleet cruised about Bute and put into Greenock for supplies, getting only a little oatmeal. He fortified Eileangreg, where he placed his stores, which soon fell into the hands of Sir Thomas Hamilton, along with a standard bearing the inscription, '*Against Popery, Prelacy, and Erastianism.*' His lieutenant, Rumbold, took Ardkinglass, and Argyll moved by Glendaruel to Loch Long, which he crossed 'troublesomely in boats and lay all night on the rocky side of it.' On the 16th of June at night he crossed the Leven three miles above Dumbarton, and next day reached the village of Kilmaronock. Before night the royal forces appeared, and Argyll escaped with the remains of his force through the stratagem of leaving good campfires burning on his deserted post. He then kept up towards the hills, and the Water of Blane seems to have been the limit of his march in that direction. At Kilpatrick he gathered together the relics of his force, now amounting to only 500 hungry and dejected men. Here the force was scattered, and Argyll, failing to get shelter in the house of an old servant, crossed the Clyde, and making his way through Renfrewshire, at the ford of Inchinnan he was challenged and captured by a few militiamen. He was carried to Glasgow and then to Edinburgh, where, undergoing the same indignities which with approbation he had

(Rancida presbyteri faex eluviesque nefandi)
Ingrueret patriam, Blanum fremebundus ad amnem.
Nunc demum Auriacus multo quando agmine princeps
Artibus Arctoum Cathari submissus in orbem,
O scelus! in socerum grassantia sustulit arma,
Et patriae insontem pepulit ditione parentem,
Saeva iterum pulso pro Caesare bella secutus
Cingor in arma lubens, dubiique in pulvere belli
Arma ducis contra Batavi Catharique rebellis
Agmina, tam diros quantumvis solus in hostes.
Quo patriae me raptat amor, quo laesa potestas
Caesaris, ultro armis animisque ingentibus ibo.
Non me Belga rapax, nec Saxonis arma superbi,
Non conjurati conjuncta potentia mundi,
Terreat incepto.   Verum si segnis ad arma
Grampicus infausto Mavorte peribit alumnus,
Armatae venient acies regione remota,
Me pulsante solum, novus ibit in agmine miles,
Atque armis foetae exsurgent tellure cohortes.

invades his country, storming beside the river Blane. Now, at length, when with strong force the Orange prince, brought into the North by Puritan plots, has uplifted, O wickedness! arms against his father-in-law, and driven the good father of the land from his sovereignty, gladly am I ready for war, in the dust of doubtful battle, against the arms of the Dutch general, against the bands of the rebel Puritans, alone against so many and such dread enemies. Whither love of country carries me, where the wounded majesty of the Caesar, there briskly will I go with good sword and spirit. Not me the rapacious Belgian, nor the arms of the proud Englishman, nor the allied power of united Europe, shall affright from my undertaking. But if through slowness in rising to arms the Highland youth perish in a fatal field, armed regiments from remote lands shall come if I stamp on the earth, a new soldiery

---

watched Montrose suffering thirty-five years before, he was carried to execution and beheaded June 26th. His two sons, Lord Lorn and Lord Neill Campbell, were banished.—See Browne's *History of Highlands*. Fountainhall gives the following picture of the Earl: 'Though Argyll was very witty in knacks, yet it has been observed he has never been very solid since the trepanning of his skull in 1653. He was so conceitty he had near twenty several pockets, some of them very secret, in his coat and breeches; and brought a printing press with him and artificial bullets and pistols.'— See Napier's *Dundee*, p. 463, vol. iii.

Quae nunc causa morae ? patiarne impune Sicambri
Insultare equitem, et peditem volitare per Alpes
Grampiacas ? Nunquam, me vivo, a stirpe Stuarto
Ad Batavum Hectorei transibunt sceptra Britanni.'
Tunc gemitum de corde ciens, 'O Jupiter,' inquit
'Maxime caelicolum rector, me exaudi[1] precantem,
Tollentemque manus ad lati lumina caeli.
Cernere da pulsi victricia Caesaris ora,
Et reducem patriis gnatum consistere terris
Ante meum nigris quam mors caput occulet umbris.
Da, precor, et nostris infandum dedecus armis
Fortiter ulcisci, atque abolere ignobile nomen.
Victricique manu, et valido da sternere ferro
Auriaci praedonis opes, inimicaque castra
Armaque presbyteri da rumpere saeva nefandi,
Et conjuratas Orco detrudere turmas.'
Dixerat, atque polo nox roscida labitur alto,
Invitantque leves surgentia sidera somnos,
Languida tum placidae cesserunt membra quieti.

LIBRI QUINTI FINIS.

shall move in battle array, and troops of horse sprung from the soil shall arise in arms. What now is the cause of delay ? Shall I suffer with impunity the German horse to prance, the German infantry to speed over the Grampian Hills ? Never, while I live, shall the sceptre of heroic Britain pass from the Stuart race to the Dutchman.' Then drawing a groan from his heart he says, 'O Jupiter, highest ruler of heaven, hear me as I pray and lift my hands to the lights of the wide sky. Grant me to behold the face of the exiled Caesar bringing victory, and to place his son restored upon his native land, before death cover my head with his black shadow. Grant too, I pray, that we may avenge by our arms the foul disgrace and clear off the name of dishonour. Grant that with conquering hand and strong sword I may scatter the strength of the Dutch robber, and make me the destroyer of the hostile camp and the savage arms of the vile presbyter, and may I hurl his covenanting squadrons to Orcus !' He spoke, and now the dewy night is gliding over the pole, and the rising stars are inviting to light slumber. Then wearied limbs yielded themselves to peaceful repose.

END OF BOOK V.

---

[1] 'di' in 'exaudi' false quantity.

LIBER SEXTUS.

AURORA optatam mortalibus aethere lucem
Extulit, et summos perfudit lampade montes.
Exciti per rura viri, perque arva manipli
Gnaviter assuetos repetunt cum luce labores.
Dundius Abriacis otî pertaesus in arvis
Tot transisse dies sine Marte dolebat inertes,
Totque una resides cunctando currere soles
Maerebat, querulis incusans sidera dictis.
Jamque dies votis, et nox absumpta querelis,
Cynthia dum plenos radians collegerat ignes.
Sceptriger interea non aequo Marte Stuartus
Pulsus, et adverso fati prostratus ab ictu,
Moenibus obsessae subduxerat agmina Derrae.

AURORA raised her light, dear to men, above the horizon, and suffused the mountain-tops with her rays. The awakened peasants betake themselves diligently, in their little bands, to their wonted labours in the fields. Dundee, wearied by delay in these regions, grieves that so many days pass in idleness without a contest; he laments that so many suns rise and set in such long succession while he waits, and he raises his complaints to the stars. Now the day is spent in prayerful longings, the night in murmurings, till radiant Cynthia has gathered the fulness of her light. Meanwhile the royal Stuart, defeated in no equal contest, prostrated by an adverse stroke of fate, has withdrawn his forces from the walls of besieged Derry.[1] Now accusing himself and his

---

[1] Our author is a little out in his dates here. James had returned to Dublin for the sitting of the Parliament, leaving General Rosene to carry on the siege of Derry. No doubt the holding out of Derry was a practical defeat so far, but the besiegers were still hoping for success. The following is King James's letter to Dundee, probably conveyed by Cannon with the detachment of troops :—

'To our right trusty and well-beloved cosen and councellor, John,
    Viscounte of Dundee.

'JAMES R.—Right trusty and well beloved, we greet you well. The good

Nunc sese, summosque duces modo prava suorum
Consilia increpitans, Dublinia tecta petebat
Tristis, et ingenti turbatus pectora cura.
' Nos,' inquit, ' fusi pugna, retroque ruentes

generals, and anon the misleading counsels of his trusted friends, he was seeking sadly the walls of Dublin, oppressed in breast with weighty care. 'We,' he says, 'routed in battle, in full retreat,

and acceptable services you have done to us at this time doe confirme in us the good opinion we always had of your worth and loyalty; for which we at present return you our most hearty and royall thanks, and shall, by the assistance of God, hereafter, make you and your family an instance of our royal bounty and favour to such as serve well. Wee doubt not of the continouance of your zeal, and we have sent you one regiment to your assistance, and all the Scotts officers, excepting Buchan and Walcob (Wauchope), whom we could not dispence till the siege of Derry was over, which is now near done, and so soon as that is over, we shall send them to you with all speed; and shall with all care send, from time to time, to your assistance, tho ther is great difficulty in the passage. But by our Mint, which we are speedily to send to you, you shall be mor fully informed of all things; in the mean time, what commissions we have sent, or what others we shall send, we leav to you to cancell or suspend as you shall think fitt, having reposed in you the trust of that affair; and so we bid you heartily farewell.

'Given at our Court in Dublin Castle, 7th July, 1689, and of our reign the 5th year.—By His Majesty's command,   MELFORT.'

Colonel Cannon and the Scotch officers, with a regiment of Irish 500 strong, embarked at Carrickfergus on the 10th July, in three frigates, commanded by Monsieur de Quesne. On the same day the little fleet fell in with the two Scotch privateers called the Glasgow frigates. 'The fight continued for about an hour very obstinate, and some of our Scotch officers were killed, but the two captains of the privateers, Hamilton and Brown, being killed, Monsieur de Quesne became master of them, and putting some of his equipage on board, sent them to Dublin, and pursued his course for Scotland, where he safely landed the forces he had on board.'—*Life of James II., written by himself*, in *Macpherson's Original Papers*, vol. i. p. 214, quoted in *Letters of Viscount Dundee*. The small force arrived safely in Mull, and were conveyed to Inverlochy, but the ships which carried their provisions being delayed, were captured by some English frigates, and a half-starved, half-naked company of undisciplined, insufficiently armed Irishmen, numbering about 500, was all that Dundee received in place of the expected five or six thousand soldiers. By the 15th July Claverhouse was at Struan, whence he writes to Lord Strathnaver, and mentions that he had been to Inverlochy to give orders anent the forces, arms, and ammunition sent from Ireland. Cannon had rank as a Lieut.-General, and the regiment was commanded by Colonel Pursell. There were several Scotch and English officers. We meet in the evidence of forfeiture with several of the Scotch officers who accompanied Cannon and the Irish regiment. The Earl of Buchan, Viscount Frendraught, Sir William Wallace of Craigie (who, by an unfortunate job of his brother-in-law Melfort, pro-

Terga damus, camposque, urbesque relinquimus hosti,
Dum meus ille duces inter fidissimus omnes
Dundius arctois magnum molitur in oris,
Et pro me auspiciis victricia signa secundis
Extulit, et patriis victor quatit agmina campis.
Hos O fulmineus si Dundius isset in hostes,
Castrorum summas et si rexisset habenas,
Non ita me victum dare terga rebellibus armis
Derrea, nec profugum vidisset Iernia regem.
O consultorum manus insidiosa meorum!
O scelerata cohors palponum, et inutilis armis,
Aulica colluvies, quae facta ingentia Grami
Obliqua invidia, atque odio suppressit iniquo.
Credulus heu nimium qui detractoribus aures
Concessi faciles, et demens ante negavi
Subsidium Gramo, qui me nunc omnibus unum
Prosequitur votis, me Gramus amatque colitque.

turn our backs, and leave to the enemy, cities and plains, while that most trusty among all my generals, my Dundee, effects great things in the North, and has raised his conquering standards for me under favouring auspices, and as a conqueror moves his lines on his native plains. O if dashing Dundee had been opposed to these enemies, and if he had held the supreme command in my camp, not thus would Derry see me retreating overcome by rebel arms; not thus would Ireland look upon her King a fugitive! O deceitful band of counsellors![1] O evil company of flatterers, and useless in battle! O sweepings of the Court, who by covert envy and hostility have suppressed the great deeds of the Graham! Alas! too credulous, I have yielded my ears easily to detractors, and madly have refused in the past help to the Graham, who still me alone follows with all his prayers; me the Graham loves and

---

duced a commission to command the cavalry at Killiecrankie, and superseded Lord Dunfermline, by far the better man), Sir Archibald Kennedy of Culzean, Lieut.-Colonel Douglas, formerly Major of Dragoons, Lieut. Murray, and others, all came from Ireland at this time. Macdonald of Auchteraw and Major Farquharson arrived from Ireland about 28th June. The former is spoken to in the evidence by James Malcolm, as 'a grosse man with a blewe coat carrying arms.' In Mull they were kindly entertained by the people at Duart, though Sir John Maclean had already set out with his company to join Dundee. The Irish took their post next the Macleans at Killiecrankie.

[1] See Preface on influences at Court hostile to Dundee.

Nunc vero invitis quamquam monitoribus istis,
Arma virosque dabo, atque instructam remige classem.'
Talia commemorans (nec jam sedaverat iras
Dicendo) vocat ingenti clamore cohortes,
Ingeminans, ' ferte arma meo ferte agmina Gramo ;
Tuque adeo lectos inter selecte tribunos,
O Buchane, meis decus et tutamen in armis,
Cannonio medias socio comitante per undas,

honours. But now, though these my advisers be unwilling, I will send him arms and men and a fleet well equipped.' Thus speaking (nor yet had he calmed his wrath by such utterance), he calls with loud voice his troops, reiterating ' Carry arms, carry troops to my Graham; and do thou, O Buchan,[1] ornament and strength of my army, choose from among the best of my captains, Cannon[2]

---

[1] Buchan here mentioned is no doubt Major-General Thomas Buchan (though the Earl of Buchan accompanied the expedition), who received his commission for succouring Dundee at this time, though he did not take the field in Scotland till April in the following year. He had served King James in happier circumstances as colonel of Mar's regiment, which, according to the custom, became, and was called, Buchan's Regiment, and is now the Royal Scots Fusiliers, or 21st Regiment. With a considerable number of his men he joined the King in Ireland, and 'several sergeants, corporalls, drummers, and sentinells (besides those accompanying him) having deserted the regiment and run away from their collours without liberty or passes under their officers' hands, and come down to Scotland,' the filling up of the empty ranks involved a petition to Parliament for aid both in catching the deserters and finding new recruits. The regiment was then styled from its new commander O'Farrel's Fusiliers. He had received his military training in the Douglas Regiment (now the Royal Scots), and is one of the 16 officers specified in the Privy Council Warrant of June 1671, as authorised to recruit in Scotland for that regiment. He is occasionally referred to in the Register of Privy Council during, and after, the year 1684, as next to Claverhouse in command of the troops in south and west of Scotland, being then Lieut.-Colonel of the regiment which he afterwards commanded.—*Old Scottish Regimental Colours*, by Andrew Ross, p. 19. General Buchan took command in Scotland in April 1690, Cannon having lost all the fruits of Killiecrankie by that time. The new commander by the beginning of May ruined all the Highland hopes in the haughs of Cromdale. He brought with him from Ireland Lord Seaforth and Colonel Brown. On March 23d, 1692, Buchan and Cannon applied for permission to transport themselves abroad, and obtained a pass for the ship that was to carry them from Leith to Havre de Grace. With many other officers they sought the Court of St. Germains. In 1695 they both appear on the long list of Jacobites in France to be prosecuted.—*Acts of Scot. Parl.*

[2] Colonel Alexander Cannon. See as to his command of the Irish Regiment, etc., previous notes. He assumed the command of the Jacobite army on the death of Dundee, and proved himself unequal to the post. After a more or less

Et tu me in dubiis Purselle secute procellis
Ite,' ait, ' O crudis exercita pectora bellis ;
Signa Caledoniis haec nostra impellite campis,
Castraque Grampiacis Gramo duce jungite castris ;
Et quicunque velit mea signa relinquere, laetis
Ille eat auspiciis, et Gramum sponte sequatur.'
Sic fatus ; tectis se turbidus intulit altis.

    Haec ubi dicta duces Buchanus et asper in armis
Cannonius belli socius consorsque laborum
Et lecti proceres, et Marti assueta juventus
Circumstant propere, et prompti mandata facessunt.
Continuo motis ad proxima littora castris
Expediunt laeti classem, portumque relinquunt.

LIBRI SEXTI FINIS.

accompanying you over the sea, and do thou Pursell,[1] my follower in stormy dangers, go with them.' He says again, 'Go, hearts inured to the hardships of war, speed these our standards to the Highland camp ; Graham being commander, unite your strength to the Grampian army ; and whoever desires to leave my host, let him go under happy auspices, and as a volunteer follow the Graham !' Thus he spake, and, much moved, retired within his lofty dwelling.

    When these words were spoken, the generals, Buchan, and his consort and ally in the labours of war, Cannon, fierce in arms, and the selected captains, and the young men inured to war, quickly gather together and promptly obey the command. Forthwith the camp is moved to the nearest shore, gladly they unmoor the fleet and leave the port.[2]

END OF BOOK VI.

---

skilful defensive campaign he was superseded by Buchan's arrival, and in 1692 retired with him to France, they having made the best terms they could for their force and the clans they were leaving.

  [1] Pursell. See previous notes in this Book. I have not been able to obtain any further information concerning this officer than his connection with the Irish Regiment, and his appearing in Mull.

  [2] Here ends the *Grameid* as it appears in the neat little volume in the Advocates' Library, written 'in manu auctoris.' Several blank leaves remain, one paged and headed, awaiting, as I fancy, the correcting of the rough MS. from which the author entered his corrected lines. The rough MS. may yet remain hidden somewhere, and tell to the end the tale of the dashing Dundee and Killiecrankie.

POEMATA.

Q

PANURGI PHILO-CABALLI SCOTI
POEMATA.[1]

BRITTANIARUM ET VALLIAE PRINCIPIS

NATALIS

JUNII DECIMO ANNO 1688

PARAPHRASIS VIRGILIANA.

PIERIDES, magni proles Jovis aurea, vatum
Pectora quae sacro succenditis Enthea[2] motu,
Vos mihi jam dignum tanti date Principis ortu
Carmen, et altisono[3] modulemur magna cothurno:
Non semper dicenda levi sunt rura cicuta,
Nec juvat exiles nimium cecinisse genistas:
Si tamen aereas calamo tentabimus ulmos,
Fraxineasque trabes, et adultae robora sylvae,
Forsitan haec magnis dignentur carmina Divis.

---

[1] This is the title-page of the original MS., and these pieces which follow are at the beginning of the book instead of at the end, as they appear here. Over the words 'Panurgi Philo-caballi' there is inserted in a much later hand 'Jacobi Philp sub nomine,' and under the words 'Paraphrasis Virgiliana' there appears in the same modern hand 'auctore Jacobo Philp.' Napier takes the writing of the inserted words to be that of Goodall, one of the keepers of the Advocates' Library under the learned Ruddiman, who assisted him in the preparation of the Catalogue of 1742. Goodall was the author of a defence of Queen Mary. The spelling, capitals, and punctuation of the original are strictly followed in these lesser pieces, except where noted. The first piece is, of course, a parody of Virgil, *Ec.* iv.,—the Prince of Wales, Graham, Wallace, Bruce, Merlin, etc., taking the places in dull manner of the personages of the beautiful original.

[2] Thus in original, and so spelt as an adjective in later dictionaries, such as Ainsworth.

[3] Mixed metaphor, pronounced frigid by our critic.

Mystica Merlini[1] fulgent oracla Britanni
Et vatum manifesta fides, quorum igneus ardor
Saecla Stuartaeis promiserat aurea sceptris.
Quatuor exactis jam magni aetatibus orbis
Surgit ab integro seclorum maximus ordo
Atque humiles caelo terras Astrea relicto
Virgo[2] colit, virtusque viris invisa revisit.
Magnarum et series longe pulcherrima rerum
Nascitur, atque alto stirps aurea manat Olympo.
Scilicet hoc tanto Divini Principis ortu
Prisca securigero succrescit adorea Scoto.
Jam quoque mutato redeunt Saturnia ferro
Saecula, nec qui jam fulsere ab origine soles
Incipiunt, capiuntque novi primordia menses,
Et nova decursos reparant jam sidera motus.
    Pulchra Diana veni: mundum regit alter Apollo,
Tuque Stuarte puer, Superi nunc munus Olympi
Magna Patris, major Matris, sed maxima Regni
Gloria tergemini, coelestia tempora lauro
Cinge triumphali, Duce te jam laeta resurgunt
Saecula, et aeternos tibi Cynthia colligit ignes.
Teque auctore truces, per barbara bella, tumultus
Alta pace jacent, et inania murmura vulgi
Fessa cadunt, longumque orbis sine lite quiescat.[3]
Jamque Dei in terris traducas nectare vitam
Ambrosiisque epulis vives, Divosque remistos
Semideis cernes, atque alto sanguine Reges:
Invictosque regas magna ditione Britannos.
    Jam tibi, chare puer, tellus donaria templis
Prima tuis, male-culta licet, fragrantia finxit
Balsama, thura, apium mirham, nardumque, crocumque,
Victricemque hederam,[4] et ramum faelicis olivae,
Sertaque purpureis mittit permista corollis
Aemula cinnameis et odoribus inficit auras.
Nunc ultro laetae venient ad mulctra capellae,

---

[1] See note on Merlin, p. 20.
[2] Note alliteration of this line.
[3] The other verbs are in present indicative.
[4] I fear the original has 'haederam' here.

Arrida jamque ipsis lactescant ubera vaccis ;
Lactea nectareis, et inundent flumina rivis
Jam neque nocturnus circumfremat ursus[1] ovile,
Nec lupus ad caulas lactantes terreat agnos,
Sed canibus mistae repetent jam pabula damae,
Ipsae etiam e cunis surgent violaeque rosaeque
Mollia luteolos fundentque cubilia flores.
Jamque malus coluber cadit, et perit anguis, et omnis
Herba nocens, pereunt medicataque pocula Circes,
Atque venenatae cecidit vis alta cicutae,
Inque vicem mediis erumpunt lilia sylvis,
Et longe incultis amaranthus surgit in arvis.
    Attamen ingentis quae sint praeconia famae,
Et quae magnorum sint Martia facta parentum,
Virtutes, viresque altasque in pectore dotes
Jam sequere, et studiis coelestibus imbue mentem.
Alma Ceres gravidis passim flavescet aristis,
Paulatim et steriles linquent jejunîa campos:
Nunc tibi maturis nutabit pampinus uvis.
Flumina et electro manabunt purius omui,
Et tibi mella fluent duri de vulnere saxi,
Et tibi jam soles lucebunt clarius auro.
Nulla dehinc suberunt tragici vestigia belli
Quae jubeant positas iterum tractare secures,
Atque armare natos,[2] aut cingere milite muros.
Gramus et alter erit, Vallasque erit alter in armis,
Rursus et ad Banocum pugnabit Brussius amnem.
Victaque Cressiacas metuet jam Gallia pugnas,
Alter et Ausoniis Aubignius[3] ibit in oris.
    Hinc ubi maturis quamprimum adoleveris annis
Ignavus medio requiescat navita ponto,

---

[1] A wolf would have seemed more appropriate here.

[2] False quantity. Mixed subjunctives and futures only partially sorted on this page.

[3] The reference is, I think, to the Sire d'Aubigny who commanded for Louis XII. the army which crossed the Alps for the invasion of Italy in 1501. By a victory at Terranova, December 25th, 1502, he reduced all Calabria, and at the head of his French and Scottish gendarmerie rode from one extremity to another of the province without opposition.—Prescott, *Ferd. and Isa.*, vol. ii. p. 247. The prominence of the Scottish contingent will account for the notice here.

Littora nec patriae linquet mercator arenae
Vivet at ipsa suis instructa Britannia rebus.
Ubertimque ferax effundet terra racemos :
Omnis et humanis dabit usibus omnia tellus,
Semina nec sulcis committet laeta colonus,
Sed juga suspenso taurorum solvet aratro.
Candida coccineos capiet nec lana colores,
Ipsa sed in silvis sua vellera tinget in ostro
Haedulus, in Tyrio vervex ardebit amictu :
Vestiet hirsutas et Sandyx[1] sponte capellas.

    Aurea jam laeto ducebant pollice pensa
Unanimes stabili Divorum munere Parcae
Et junctim teretes hortatae in stamina fusos
Currite continuo cecinerunt secula filo.
Ingredere O magnos celsae virtutis honores
Clara poli soboles, novus alti splendor Olympi,
Quae te aeterna manet venturis gloria seclis
Tempora jam rebus dat Jupiter aequa gerendis,
Aspice cunctarum nutantia culmina rerum,
Et maria, et montes, atque alti moenia coeli,
Cerne procul seclis laetantur cuncta futuris.

    O mihi jam seros si vita supersit in annos
Inclyta et immensum referam tua facta per orbem
Non me Maeonidae vincat vena aurea vatis,
Carmine quin dubiam faciam tibi Mantua palmam.
Ergo age, magne Puer, major sed deinde futurus
Incipe Divinis stillans exugere in annis
Nectar et aeternis Divorum pascier escis,
Et pulchram blando Matrem mulcere susurro
Cornua cui decimae dederant fastidia Lunae.
Eja age, magne Puer, tibi jam risere Parentes,
Jupiter et mensâ, Juno et dignata cubili est,
Te Deus et sacras jam primum sanxit ad aras.

                                                          Finis.

---

[1] In old editions of Virgil a capital is used here as by our author. See Ainsworth.

In Annum Mirabilem
1. 6. 8. 8.
Poësis Extemporanea.

Fata pharetratis dudum largita Britannis
Secula fulcigeri non infoelicia Divi;
Quêis passim se quisque sua sub vite recumbens
Carpebat placidam securus ab hoste quietem.
Nunc tamen in refugos iterum conversa recessus
Jurgia succensis serpunt civilia bellis:
Et fera discordes agitat discordia cives.
Jam gladii streperaeque tubae, lituique sonoro
Murmure perstringunt aures, tonitruque tremendo
Aerea sulphureas tormenta vomentia glandes
Iam reboant raucos clangunt et classica cantus:
Sistra sonant, equitumque procul peditumque per agros
Grassantur turmae, tanti sed causa furoris
Nulla fuit, tantos potuit quae accendere motus,
Aut purpuratos[1] armare in proelia Patres
Atque indignantem stimulare in vulnera clerum:
At regni Proceres, audax et Episcopus una
Regis in exitium et patriae irreparabile damnum
Conspirant, strictumque conduntque per ilia ferrum:
Externumque vocant ultro jam in moenibus hostem.
O populi furor! o Procerum male sana libido!
O secli impietas! O degener Anglia diris
Cladibus exposta, et civilibus obruta bellis!
In ferrum flammasque ruunt tria Regna nefandis
Motibus, insanis Mavors nunc ardet in armis
Improbus. O quantos potuit suadere tumultus
Relligio in varias ut tempora versa figuras.
Huc gener, oppositis illuc stat avunculus armis,
Et socer innumeris instructus uterque maniplis
Utraque sanguineos et habebant signa Leones:

---

[1] False quantity here.

At malefida cohors mentito nomine pridem
Militis indomiti,[1] bellatorisque superbi
Deseruere fugâ Regem, mox Principis ultro
Auriaci versis sine sanguine cominus armis
Castra petunt signis post terga inhonesta relictis.
Sic victor sine victo, hostisque sine hoste triumphum
Rettulit, et facilem sine caede aut sanguine palmam.
O infidum, atrox, genus et mercedibus emptum
Bellatorum hominum! O soboles ignava Gradivi!
Quae fictae insignem pietatis imagine Regem
Prodidit infaustae Sarum prope moenia villae:
Et misere abjectis dare terga coegerat armis:
Atque alio positas sub Sole exquirere sedes.
Quis sciat an mediis vitam positurus in undis;
An cadat insidiis? hoc O Deus omen in hostem
Convertat, faxitque precor non irrita vota.
    Alme Pater vasti torques qui sidera coeli,
Et rerum dubias nutu qui flectis habenas:
Fac precor incolumem per mille pericula Regem,
Et reducem patriis tandem consistere terris
Da Pater, et laetum post tristia nubila Phoebum.

FINIS.

---

[1] This suggests the question as to whether there was a regiment at the time which assumed the name of 'Invincibles.'

PANURGI PHILO-CABALLI, SCOTI:

EPIGRAMMATA.

JACOBO SEPTIMO BRITANNIARUM REGI
PARAENESIS.

MAGNE[1] Jacobe pater patriae qui legibus aequis
    Jam regis Arctoi sceptra superba soli.
Haec tria nec mentem mutant, animumve remittunt
    Ingenium genio sed docuere suo.
Hyrcano de rure lupus provectus ad urbem
    Non facile innocuas creditur inter oves.
Et qui Mosaicis descripta sacraria libris
    Deserit, et Christi transfuga castra petit.
Gente Caledonius patriae qui Sacra relinquens
    Hic sequitur Latiae dogmata dira lupae.
Haec fuge ceu scopulos, et naufraga saxa sub undis,
    Et tribus his minimam noli adhibere fidem.

GULIELMO PRINCIPI AURIACO
POST CLADEM ANGUIENSEM.[2]

AURIACE auspiciis olim infaelicibus orte,
    Pestis atrox populi, proditor et Soceri.

---

[1] The points are the suspicions attaching—1st, to the tame wolf among sheep; 2d, to the Jew turned Christian; 3d, the Scot becoming a Roman Catholic. There may be an allusion to the efforts of James to dispense from the Tests Act in *legibus aequis.*

[2] Is this the battle of Landen, in which the allies lost 7000 men, 69 pieces of cannon, and so many standards and colours that the Duke of Luxembourg was nicknamed the Upholsterer of Notre Dame, because he furnished the church with so many trophies?

Improbe quid coelum, terramque atque aequora misces?
  Ut Soceri per vim sceptra verenda feras.
Jamque exute armis, Sociisque relicte peremptis,
  Dic quibus in terris nunc nova regna paras?
Aethera si scandas Coelo te Juppiter alto
  Obruet injecto fulmine ut Enceladum.
Gallus te terris arcebit, et aequore Delphin;
  Sic potes haud ullo tutus inesse loco.
Sed tibi Styx superest post versum a cardine mundum
  Et mersa innumeris post tria Regna malis.
Ergo age cum sociis culpae Cromvello[1] et Juda
  I furiis totum nunc Acheronta move.
Tristia semper erunt scelerati gaudia facti,
  Et conjuratos mors inopina manet.

Absolonis,
In Patrem Conjurati,
Mors.[2]

Absolon ingenti dum tendit ad arma tumultu
  Praetendit Summo solvere vota Deo.
Impius infando Patrem dumque opprimit ausu
  Et gerit hostili bella cruenta manu,
Vincitur, et densae fugiens per vimina silvae
  Arboris a ramo triste pependit onus.
Furca fuit quercus, funem tribuere capilli,
  Prestitit et promptam furcifer hinnus opem.
Sic Deus ipse hostes Regum vult pendere poenas,
  Et merita ante suum morte perire diem.

In
Ducem Luxenburgensem.

Qui lucem in burgo tituli pro nomine gestat
  Fax est Francigenae Luxque corusca Soli.

---

[1] Passage scans thus: Crōmvēll' ĕt Īūdā.

[2] A comparison of William and Absalom in their end is suggested.

[3] François de Montmorenci, who routed William at Steenkerke, and at Landen, and generally put the allies into the shade. See note, p. 248.

Lucida lux totum radios sparsura per orbem
　Jam micat in medio Phoebus ut ipse polo.
Lumen habet, luxque haec lucem dat fulgida Franco,
　Auram quae obfuscat Principis Auriaci.
Qui rutuli Luxenburgi cum haud viderat umbram
　Terga dedit trepida non sat honesta fuga.
Nec mirum (male qui fecit lucem odit et astra)
　Ferre nequit tanti lumina Clara Ducis.
Luceat aeternum lux haec, et fulguret hostem,
　Fulgeat et tanto Gallia Clara viro.

Jacobi Regi,
Votum.

Nemo Jacobe magis reducem te optaverit unquam,
　Nemo tamen reducem sentiet esse minus.

Vitae Privatae
Laus.

A Jove qui procul est, procul ille a fulmine distat,
　Et bene qui latuit vixerit ille bene.

Ex Anglico[1]
Francisci Quarrellii.

Alme Pater corvos tune es qui pascis hiantes?
Lillia tune amicis nec me dignabere veste
Nunquam ego diffidam Domino pro veste nec esu
Lillia dum florent, dum corvi guttura pascunt.
　　　　　　　　　　　　　　　　Finis.

---

[1] This piece, from the obliterations on the other side of the page showing through, and from chemical treatment, is scarcely to be read. The passage is given from an old copy, probably taken before the treatment referred to. It is however not to be relied on for accuracy. It is a translation of one of Quarles's happy paraphrases of Scripture. Francis Quarles had need of the trust he here expresses, and doubtless our author got support in trouble from the same source. Quarles's *Emblems* were extremely popular in England before he took the side of King Charles, but Jacobites in Scotland would hold on to them after the taste had changed in England.

In
Jacobum Carnegium de Balnamoone.[1]

Mene caballino perfusum flumine vatem,
Et studiis taciti gaudentem mollibus oti,
Impius usque fori rauco clamore lacessit
Carnegius Bellae[2] dictus de nomine Lunae?
Inque meum ferus ille forensia sustulit arma
Pro mucrone caput, quem regia castra secutus
Nicolas[3] ipse meo mutaverat ense sacerdos.
Hunc sibi ceu proprium reddi jam postulat ensem
Carnegius lucro incumbens, et dira minatur,
Dum movet ambiguam sub iniquo judice litem.
Ille autem pulchri quamvis sibi nomina Solis
Asserit, haud unquam mucronem impune feribit[4]
Nec gladium hunc fuso sine sanguine victor habebit
Si modo supremus faveat mea jussa senatus.
Sed quid nunc opus est ferro, quid bellicus ensis
Conferet iste senis, cum jam nodosa podagra
Crura premat tumeatque ingenti abdomine venter
Quod si consortis thalami (prius ille maritam
Tartareas Bromio madidantem[5] misit ad umbras)

---

[1] All except the heading, and the word 'armatus' at the foot of the page, being the catchword for the first line of the following page, has been obliterated carefully with a heavy pen, probably the pen which transcribed the Balnamoon copy now in the Library of the University of Edinburgh. It is possible to make out sufficient to prove the general accuracy of the text here given, which is taken from a copy earlier than the Balnamoon transcript. See remarks on MSS. in Preface. Cf. first line of *Persius*: 'fonte caballino.'

[2] Observe the maintenance of the spelling *Bal*, with the sense of the common pronunciation *Bonny*, indicating the pronunciation in seventeenth century of Bonnymoon.

[3] Priests, Clerks, or Knights of St. Nicholas—thieves so called because St. Nicholas was their patron; not that he aided them in their wrongdoing, but because on one occasion he induced some thieves to restore their plunder. 'I think yonder come prancing down the hills from Kingston a couple of St. Nicholas' Clerks.'—Rowley, *Match at Midnight*, 1633. Query; Does Nick's Clerks, meaning the Devil's Clerks, originate the name Nick for the Devil.

[4] Thus the word stands, explain it who can.

[5] See Ainsworth's Dictionary, the collection of 'voces carbone dignae': 'Madidans, tis. part. [qu. à madido] *Wringing wet, dripping*.' 'Madidatus, *Soaked*.'

Jam jugulum mucrone petat, ferroque secabit
Ceu[1] femur uxoris transmiserat ense prioris,
Ille habeat ferrum, et meretrix si barda nefandos
Hoc premat ense nothos quos merserat ante profundo,
Canabe cum fauces elisaque guttura fregit.
I nunc et tali victor mucrone petito
Armatus, contende foro, vadimonia quaere,
Et litem viduis orbisque intende pupillis,
Atque senes patrios jam linquere coge penates;
Sed cave Castaliis sic litem inducere Musis,
Aut mea te tragico jugulabit carmine Clio.

FINIS.

---

[1] 'Ceu' for 'ut.'

[The following Epitaph in the Author's hand is written on the last of the blank pages provided for the continuation of the *Grameid*. It is very much rubbed in some places, and difficult to decipher with accuracy. For the subject of the Epitaph see Note below.[1]]

SISTE VIATOR

Hoc monumentum tibi referet memoriam viri admodum colendi, Guilielmi Aikman de Carnie. In supremo foro Juridico causarum Patroni conspicui, pariter et facundi, Qui dum in agitandis et tuendis clientium et amicorum suorum causis voce et calamo totus incumbit, tandem deficiente, proh dolor! habitu semetipsum perdidit. Spiritus itaque ex corporis hoc ergastulo elapsus ad Elysias beatorum sedes nec tam abiit quam avolavit. Corpusculi vivus sui exuvias hic recondi voluit. Demum post actum vitae suae heu nimis brevis curriculum in humanis esse desiit mense   Anno Dom   aetatis suae   Itaque hominem ex humo in humum revertentem intuere serius et disce sincerius hic vivere, et mori.

---

[1] William Aikman, the subject of the above epitaph, prepared before it was wanted in a half-playful half-serious spirit, was a contemporary and neighbour of our author. In the Catalogue of the Faculty of Advocates from the Institution of the College of Justice to the Revolution in 1688, by Sir David Dalrymple of Hailes, Baronet, he is given under the date 16th Jan. 1672, and is entered as Carnie's son. He married the daughter of Sir John Clerk of Penicuik, by whom he had a son, William, who succeeded him. The son sold the property on his father's death about 1707, and after studying in Rome rose to eminence as a portrait-painter, enjoying the patronage of the Duke of Argyll and Sir Godfrey Kneller, and the friendship of Somerville, Allan Ramsay, Thomson, and Mallet the poets, all of whom mourned him in verse, the work of the last-named being

inscribed on his tomb in Greyfriars Churchyard, where was buried, but six months before, the son of the artist, a lad of seventeen.

The epitaph begins :—

> 'Dear to the good and wise, disprais'd by none,
> Here sleep in peace the father and the son.'

One monumental reference more to the Aikman family I find in Jervise's collection of papers in the Antiquaries' Library. On a flat red sandstone in the Abbey Churchyard, Arbroath, the family burying-place, is thus marked : Hic est tumulus antiqua Aikmanorum famil. de Lordburne 1560, and another having the date 1591 seems to be indicated. In 1638, and for some time previously, the lands of Lordburne, Dishland, and I think Keptie, were in possession of the Aikmans. They are eventually found in possession of Susannah Philp, the grand-daughter, as I suppose, of our author, these lands having passed into the hands of the Philp family some time before. The names still survive in Arbroath streets, and Carnie is well known in the neighbourhood. See Hay's *History of Arbroath*, p. 430. Also on p. 195 of same book, see claim of John Aikman, the father of the lawyer, for too much room in the parish church.

INDEX.

INDEX.

ABERDEEN, battle of, 189.
Aberlemno, traces of ancient sepulture in, 23.
Abernethy, 182 and *note*, 209 and *note*.
Aboyne, 51, 52.
Abria, 118, 120, 130.
Adamson, 162 and *note*.
Adriatic, 170 and *note*.
Aengus defeats Nectan, 179.
Agathyrsi, 83 and *note*.
Agnew, Sir Andrew, sheriff of Wigtown, 162.
Aidan crowned by St. Columba, 86.
Aikman, William, epitaph on, 254.
—— family, 254, 255.
Airlie, Earl of, 162.
Alford, Aberdeenshire, 189, 190.
Alvie, house of, 182 and *note*.
—— kirk of, 173, 176, 180.
Anderson, Robert, mutilation of, 151.
Angus, 17, 63, 69.
Annandale, Earl of, 163, 192.
Annat, 75.
Antrim, Earls of, 119.
Appin, 74.
—— Stewarts. *See* Stewarts of Appin.
Arbroath, 255.
Ardersier parish, 54.
Ardgour. *See* Maclean of Ardgour.
Ardincaple, property of the Cowals, 136.
Ardkinglass, 233.
Ardoch water, 160.
Argyll, Duke of, receives estates of Maclean of Duart, 137.
—— Archibald, 9th Earl of, 233 and *note*.
—— Marquis of, 129.
Arran, Earl of, 43.
Athole, 20, 41, 193.
Aubigny, the Sire d', reduces Calabria, 245.
Auchinbreck. *See* Campbell, Sir Duncan.
Auchindoir, 204 and *note*.
Auchindoune, 206, 208.
—— Castle, 206 and *note*.

Auchteraw. *See* Macdonald.
Auldearn, 53, 189.

BADENOCH, 57, 61, 112, 119, 168, 169, 193, 218.
Bagpipes, 120 and *note*.
Baillie, General, 189.
Bala Castle, 151, 181.
Balbadie. *See* Malcolm, James.
Balcarres, Earl of, 46.
Balfour, Captain, 69 and *note*, 181.
Balhaldy. *See* Drummond, Alexander.
Ballachulish, 142-144.
Ballechin. *See* Stewart, Patrick.
Ballindalloch. *See* Grant, John.
Balmuir, 49.
Balrynnis, 186 and *note*.
Balvany, 181, 186 and *note*.
Balwhapple. *See* Graham, William.
Banquo, 131.
Barclay, Robert, of Ury, 131.
Barclay's regiment, 195, 196.
Barnacle goose, 84 and *note*.
Barra, 23, 119, 145.
See also Macneill of Barra.
Beaufort family, 149.
Beauly, 185 and *note*.
Belcastle, 173.
Belgium, 42.
Belleville, 169.
Benbecula. *See* Macdonald, Donald.
Ben Nevis, 79.
Ben Rinnes, 186.
Berchan, St., 86.
Berkley's regiment, 67.
Birse, 51, 52.
Births, customs at, 82.
Black Isle, 126 and *note*.
Blair, William, of Blair, 60 and *note*, 145, 181.
Blair Castle, 59 and *note*, 65, 138, 163, 194.
Blane, the, 233, 234.
Blood from heaven, 20.
Boat of Bog, 51.
Bog of Gight, 51, 206.
Boghole. *See* Campbell, Colin.
Bogie, the, 52, 199, 204.

INDEX.

Bo'ness, 67.
Bonnet Hill, 66.
Bothwell Brig, battle of, 233.
Boulogne, 100, 213.
Bowain in Glendochart, property of the Macnabs, 136.
Braco. *See* Duff, Alexander.
Breacan, or plaid, 123.
Brodie, Captain, 208.
Brown, Colonel, 239.
Bruce, Captain, 177-179, 199-200.
—— Lieutenant Alexander, 158.
—— Captain Andrew, 158 and *note*.
—— Sir Andrew, of Earlshall, 158.
—— Lieutenant David, of Clackmannan, 158.
—— Captain John, 163.
—— Lieutenant W., 158.
Brude, Pictish king, 86.
Brutus, first king of Britain, 2.
Buchan, Major-General, 208, 237, 339 and *note*.
Buchan's regiment, 239.
Buntine, Major Hugh, of Kilbryde, 44.
Burntisland, 193.

CAIRNBURG ISLAND, 61.
Cairngorm mountain, 182.
Cairn o' Mount, 51 and *note*, 193, 196.
Calabria, 245.
Calder. *See* Campbell.
Caledonian canal, 120.
—— city or Dunkeld, 158.
Cameron of Glendessary, 135 and *note*, 137.
—— Sir Ewen, of Lochiel, 123, 129, 131, 177.
—— Ewen M'Connell, 134.
—— Janet, 151.
—— John, father of Lochiel, 129.
—— John, eldest son of Lochiel, 133.
Camerons, origin of the, 134.
Campbell of Calder, 118.
—— of Glenorchy, 129.
—— of Lochnell, 143.
—— Alexander, of Strondour, 144.
—— Archibald, of Octomor, 118.
—— Colin, of Boghole, 151.
—— Lieutenant-Colonel Duncan, 153.
—— Sir Duncan, of Auchinbreck, 139, 144, 233.
—— Grace, 154.
—— Sir Hugh, of Cawdor, 57, 121, 140, 210.
—— Lord Neill, 234.
Campbeltown, 233.
Camus, leader of Northmen at the battle of Barra, 23.
Cannon, Colonel, 131, 133, 161, 206, 237, 239 and *note*, 240.

Carbridge, 112.
Cargill, kirk of, 62.
Carnasarie, 144.
Carnbie, Fife, 158.
Carnburg, isle of, 145.
Carnegie, H. A. F. Lindsay, of Kinblethmont, 158.
—— James, of Balnamoon, 252.
Carrickfergus, 237.
Cassilis, Earl of, 47.
Castle Menzies, 74.
—— Stuart, 54.
—— Swen, 145.
—— Terrim, stronghold of the Clanranalds, 118.
Cathbregion, 211.
Cawdor. *See* Campbell, Sir Hugh.
Ceolfrid, 179.
Cess taxes collected by Graham, 63 and *note*.
Charles I., death of, 8-9; persecuted by the Presbyterians, 229 and *note*; sold by the Scots, 230.
Charles II., reduces Ireland to obedience, 10; his sufferings at the hands of the Presbyterians, 231, 232.
Churchill, General, treachery of, 33.
Cimbri, the, 121 and *note*.
Clan Chattan, 127.
Clan Ranald, the, 118, 125. *See also* Macdonald, Allan.
Clan Vuirich, 169.
Clans, gathering of the, 118-164.
Claverhouse. *See* Graham, John.
Cleland, Lieut. William, 161.
Clelland, John, of Faskin, 161 and *note*.
Clerk, Sir John, of Penicuik, 254.
Clova, 177.
Cluny. *See* Macpherson, Duncan.
Cochrane, Lady Jean. *See* Dundee, Lady.
—— William Lord, 47.
Coile, 112 and *note*.
Coilus, King, 112, 182 and *note*.
Colchester's Dragoons, 49.
Coll. *See* Maclean, Lauchlane.
Collessie, 64 and *note*.
Colliers, Sir David, 163.
Colquhoun, Sir Ludovic, of Luss, afterwards Sir Ludovic Grant of Grant, 151.
Colt, Lieutenant, evidence in the process of forfeiture, 60; regarding the taking of Ruthven Castle, 61; Hallyburton of Pitcur, 64; Macneill of Gallachallie, 144; Edmonstone of Newton, 160; Clelland of Faskin, 161; Col. Ramsay, 192; Stewart of Ballechin, 194.

INDEX. 261

Columba, St., 86.
Comets, 19, 22.
Compton, Bishop of London, 11, 16.
Comrie Castle, 74.
Constantine the Great, 13.
Constantine II., of Scotland, 13.
Cope's carriage, 195.
Cornbury, Lord, deserts from the King's army, 33.
Coronation stone, 87.
Corpach, 79.
Corryarrick Pass, 57.
Coupar-Angus, 193.
Cowal, 155.
Cowals, the, 136 and *note*.
Coxton. *See* Innes, Sir Alex.
Craigellachie, 128, 182.
Craigievar, 52.
Craignish. *See* Dougals of Craignish.
Creighton, Captain, 181.
Crinan Moss, 86.
Croiscrag in Rannoch, 195.
Cromar mountains, 52.
Cromdale, 128, 151, 182, 207, 208 and *note*, 239.
Culbyn, 161 and *note*.
Culduthil. *See* Fraser.
Culnakyle, 112, 173, 181, 193, 211, 212, 217.
Cupar, 64, 74.

DALCOMERA, meeting of Highland chiefs at, 120 and *note*, 165.
Dalhousie family, 187. *See also* Ramsay.
Dalnacardoch, 75.
Dalnaspidal, 75.
Dalraddy, 180.
Dalriada, kingdom of, 179.
Dalriadic Irish, 86.
—— Scots, 86.
Dalrymple, Sir John, 188, 199.
Dalwhinnie, 57.
Dalzell, General, defeats Covenanters at Rullion Green, 232.
Danby, Earl of, 11.
Danes, traces of battles with, 23.
Danubian provinces, 2.
Dark Isle, 126.
Darnaway Castle, 53 and *note*.
Dead, the, rise from their graves, 20.
Dee, the, 51, 196.
Derry, siege of, 94, 236, 238.
Deveron, the, 204, 205.
Devonshire, Earl of, 11.
Dishland, 255.
Don, the, 50, 196.
Donald of Gallachallie, 144, 145.
Donovald, St., 49.
Dougals of Craignish, 155, 156.

Douglas, Lieut.-Col., 210, 238.
—— William. *See* Hamilton, Duke of.
Douglas regiment, 239.
Doune Castle, 160.
Drumcairn, 62.
Drummond, Alexander, of Balhaldy, Lochiel's son-in-law, 45, 80, 106, 131 and *note*, 136, 137.
—— William, son of Drummond of Balhaldy, 132.
Duart Castle, 60, 61, 137, 145, 210, 238.
Dublin, 236, 237.
Dudhope Castle, 44, 45 and *note*, 46, 48, 162, 178.
Duff, Alexander, of Braco, 186.
Dufftown, 207.
Duffus, Lord and Lady, 24.
Dumbarton, Earl of, 43.
Dumbarton's regiment, or Royal Scots, 98.
Dun, Laird of. *See* Erskine of Dun.
Dunachton Castle, 127 and *note*, 179; burnt by Keppoch, 180.
Dunadd, capital of Dalriada, 86.
Dunardarie, 144.
Dunblane, 45.
Duncan, Bailie, of Lundie, 67.
Duncrub, 70.
Dundas of Arniston, 192.
Dundee, 45, 49, 63, 65 and *note*, 66 and *note*, 66-73, 106.
—— John, 1st Earl of, 192.
—— Lady, 47 and *note*, 48, 70, 178.
—— Viscount. *See* Graham, John, of Claverhouse.
—— 2d Viscount, 48.
Dunderaw. *See* Macnachtan.
Dundonald, Lord, 70.
Dunfermline, James Seton, 4th Earl of, 53 and *note*, 62, 157, 184, 238.
Dunkeld, 59 and *note*, 61, 63, 74, 158.
—— James, Lord, 157 and *note*.
Dunmore, Lord, 178.
Dunmore's regiment, 70.
Dunnichen, battle of, 179.
Duntroon. *See* Graham.
Dunvegan, Skye, 146.

EARLSHALL, Fife, 158.
Eassie, kirk of, 64.
Ecgfrid, defeated by Nectan at Dunnichen, 179.
Eclipses, 19.
Edinburgh, 44, 46, 64, 187, 193, 211, 223.
—— Castle, surrender of, 47; escape of Argyll from, 233.
Edinglassie, 138, 140, 193, 196, 197 and *note*, 205, 209.
See also Gordon, Sir George.

Edmonstone, James, of Newton of Doune, 160 and *note*.
—— John James, 161.
—— William, of Duntreath, 160.
Eileangreg, fortified by Argyll, 233.
Elcho, Lord, defeated by Montrose at Tippermuir, 189.
Elgin, 51, 53.
Erc, father of Fergus I., 86.
Erskine of Dun's baggage seized by Dundee, 50.
Esk, North, 50.

FALKIRK, 41, 211.
Farquhar, Robert, 206.
Farquharson, Major, 238.
Faskin. *See* Clelland, John.
Fasnacloich family, 143.
Fasselane, Duncan, 136.
Fenwick, Sir John, 35.
Fergus the First, 86 and *note*.
Ferguson, James, his account of Auchindoune Castle, 206.
Fettercairn, 51.
Fiery Cross, 111, 118.
Fife, 193.
Finbar, St., of Cork, 145.
Firth of Arthur, 54 and *note*.
Firth of Forth, 193.
Flanders, 36.
Forbes, house of, 52.
—— Capt. John, 109, 173, 174 and *note*.
—— Master of, 51, 52, 69, 183, 196, 197.
Forfarshire, 69.
Forres, 51, 53.
Fortrose, Lord, 148.
Fraser of Culduthil, 150 and *note*.
—— Hugh. *See* Lovat, Lord.
—— Simon. *See* Lovat, Lord.
—— William, of Foyers, 148 and *note*, 167, 185.
Frendraught, Viscount, 237.
Fresall, John, of Farlyne, 150.
Fullerton of Fullerton, 65 and *note*, 158 and *note*.

GABINIAN TOGA, 141.
Gabran, grandson of Fergus, 86.
Gallachallie. *See* Macneill, Donald.
Galloway, Sir James, of Carnbie, 158.
—— Hon. Mary, 157.
—— Patrick, 158.
Garmoran, Earldom of, 146.
Garolin, 128.
Garry, the, 58.
Garth Castle, 74.
Garviemore, 167.
Geneva, 7.
Gerard's *Herbal*, 84.

Gesoriacum, now Boulogne, 100, 213.
Gibbons, the, 136 and *note*.
Gigha, family of, 145.
Gilchrist of Angus, 49.
Gildas the Briton, 20 and *note*.
Gilliechattan Mor, 169.
Glamis Castle, 64 and *note*.
Glasgow, 233.
Glen Avon, 207.
Glencairn, Earl of, 130.
Glencoe, massacre of, 174.
    See also Macdonald of Glencoe.
Glendaruel, 233.
Glenelg, 146.
Glenfiddich, 208.
Glengarry. *See* Macdonell.
Glenlivet, 183, 206, 207.
Glenmoriston. *See* Grant, John.
Glen Ogilvy, 49, 74.
Genorchy, seat of the clan M'Gregor, 136.
    See also Campbell of Glenorchy.
Glen Roy, 61, 75, 78, 167, 193.
Glenshee, 52.
Gloy, 80.
Goodall, keeper of the Advocates' Library, 243.
Gordon, Sir Adam, 206.
—— Alexander, Earl of Huntly. *See* Huntly.
—— George, Marquess of. *See* Huntly.
—— Duke of, and 4th Marquess of Huntly, 44; surrenders Edinburgh Castle, 47; some of his men taken by Mackay, 209, 210.
—— Captain, 186.
—— Sir George, of Edinglassie, 52, 183, 197 and *note*.
—— Nathaniel, execution of, 130.
—— Sir Patrick, of Auchindoune, 206.
Gordon Castle, 51 and *note*, 53, 106.
Gordon Clan, 53.
Grafton, Duke of, 33.
Graham, David, brother of Viscount Dundee, 162 and *note*.
—— John, of Claverhouse, Viscount Dundee, 1, 35-37, 40; serves under Turenne, 41; has charge of the queen and prince, 43; leaves Edinburgh, 44; his troops disbanding, 46; proclaimed traitor, 46; marches over the Seidlaws, 49; reaches Kirriemuir, 50; Elgin, 51; retraces steps to the Dee, 51; crosses the Don, and rests in Strathbogie, 52; reaches Gordon Castle, 53; joined by Dunfermline, 53; at the kirk of Auldearn, 53; reaches Inverness, and is joined by Keppoch, 54;

marches to Strath Errick, 56; Badenoch, 57; issues royal letter to the clans, marches over the Grampians to Blair, 58; makes descent on Perth, 59; addresses the army, 62; at Stobhall, 62; collects public dues, 63; at Cupar and Glamis, 64; at Dundee, 65; pursues his way by Cupar and Dunkeld, 74; Loch Rannoch, 75; reaches Lochaber, 78; joined by Glengarry and other chiefs, 96; sends message to the king advising return to Scotland, 105 and *note*; sends the fiery cross through the north, 111; marches to Dalcomera, 121; reprimands Keppoch, 127; made Sheriff of Wigtown, 162; addresses the army, 165; celebrates birthday and restoration of Charles II., 170-171; threatens Mackay's camp at Alvie, 180; pursues him, 182-186; movements from 25th May to 4th June, 193; halts at Edinglassie, 198; hears the Scotch dragoons intend to desert Mackay, 199; refers to his rescue of William at Seneff, 201; retreats on the approach of Mackay, 205; halts in Abernethy woods, 209 and *note*; his illness, 209; at Ruthven Castle, 212; difficulty in keeping the clans together, disperses them at Lochaber, 217; abuses the Presbyterians, 218-235; his relics preserved at Duntroon, 162.
Graham, yr. of Duntroon, 162.
—— Sir John, 41.
—— Capt. P., 162.
—— Lieut. P., 162.
—— Sir Robert, of Strathcarron, 41.
—— Robert, aid-major, 162.
—— Major William, of Balwhapple, 161-163.
—— Sir William, of Kincardine, 41.
Grahams of Morphie, 48.
Grampians, the, 46, 58, 74, 168.
Grant, Captain, 208.
—— of Grant, 109, 211.
—— John, of Ballindalloch, 159 and *note*, 181-182.
—— John, of Glenmoriston, 150 and *note*, 182.
—— John, yr. of Glenmoriston, 151 and *note*.
—— Sir Ludovic, of Grant. *See* Colquhoun, Sir Ludovic.
—— of Urquhart, 152.
Grant Castle, 173, 193.
Grants of Castle Grant, 152.
Greenock, 233.

HACKSTON OF RATHILLET, 158.
Halley's comet of 1682, 19.
Hallowe'en in Forfarshire, 21.
Hallyburton, David, of Pitcur, 64 and *note*, 157.
Hamilton, Lady Margaret, 60.
—— Sir Thomas, 233.
—— William Duke of, 30 and *note*, 44, 46, 66, 69, 168, 187, 188.
Hamstringing, 105 and *note*.
Harlaw, battle of, 140.
Harris, 146.
Hasting's infantry, 67, 195.
Havre de Grace, 239.
Hay, a king's messenger, 106.
—— Lieutenant, gives evidence regarding Hallyburton of Pitcur, 65, Edmonstone of Newton, 160.
Heather, custom of carrying a bunch of, 129 and *note*.
Hebrides, 82.
Herring bushes, 193.
Highland games, 172 and *note*.
—— oaths, 103 and *note*, 156.
Hill, Colonel John, 143, 173, 174.
Hilltown, 66.
Hungary, Turks expelled in 1686, 2.
Huntly, Alex. Gordon, Earl of, founder of Gordon Castle, 51.
—— George Gordon, 1st Marquess of, 206.
—— 4th Marquess. *See* Gordon, Duke of.
Huntly Castle, stronghold of the Gordons, 52.
Hurry, General, defeated at Auldearn, 189.
Hy, island of, 118.

IAN-A-CHRAGAIN. *See* Grant, yr. of Glenmoriston.
Ian Donn. *See* Grant, yr. of Glenmoriston.
Icon Basilike, 229.
Ilanterrim, 118.
Inchcolm, sepulture of Danes on, 23.
Inchinnan, 233.
Innerpeffery, 126.
Innes of Innermarky, 197.
—— of Innes, 159.
—— Alexander, 197.
—— Sir Alexander, of Coxton, 159 and *note*.
—— George, of Dunkinty, 159.
—— Sir John, 51.
—— John, of Culdrain, 159.
Inverardoch, 161.
Invercarrach, 205.
Invergarry Castle, 56 and *note*.
Inverlochy, 138, 142, 143, 189, 237.

INDEX.

Invermoriston, 151.
Invernahyle, 143.
Inverness, 54, 55, 109, 112, 127, 193.
Iona, 86, 118.
Ireland, 10, 18, 36, 238.
Irvine of Drum, killed at Harlaw, 140.
—— Alexander, of Drum, 206.
Isla, the, 64.
Islay, 86, 118.
Italy, invasion of, in 1501, 245.

JAFFRAY, Alexander, 206.
—— John, Dean of Guild, 206.
James VI., persecuted by the Presbyterians, 228.
James VII., 11, 22; sails a fugitive to France, 27; lands with an army in Ireland, 28; banished from his kingdom, 30; betrayed and deserted, 31, 36, 40; retires from Derry to Dublin, 236 and *note*; sends letter to Graham, 236; sends reinforcements to Graham, 237, 239.
James-an-Tuim, a freebooter, 182.
Jarrow monastery, 179.
Johnstone, 163 and *note*.
—— John, 163.
Jura, 118.
Jutland, 121.

KEITH, 50, 53.
Kennedy, Sir Archibald, of Culzean, 238.
Keppoch, 79, 80.
See also Macdonald of Keppoch.
Keptie, 255.
Kilchurn Castle, 129.
Kilcummin, kirk of, 57 and *note*.
Kildrummie Castle, 52.
Killiecrankie, 65, 238.
Kilmarnock, 233.
Kilpatrick, 233.
Kilsyth, battle of, 189, 190.
—— Lord. *See* Livingstone, Lieut.-Col.
Kinakyle, 182.
Kincardine O'Neil, 50 and *note*, 51.
Kincardineshire, 69.
Kinghorn, 1st Earl of, 64 and *note*.
Kingussie, 172.
Kinlochaline, 144.
Kinloch Rannoch, 75.
Kinnaird of Culbyn, 161 and *note*.
—— Lord, 161.
—— Alan, 161
—— Charles, 161.
—— James, 161.
Kintyre, 86.
Kirkwall, 233.
Kirriemuir, 50.

Knapdale, 118, 145, 156.
Knockbrecht skirmish, 140, 210-211 and *note*.
Knoydart. *See* Macdonell.
Kyles, the, 112.

LAMONT CLAN, the, at Lochaber, 155 and *note*.
Lanark, 69.
Landen, battle of, 137, 249, 250.
Lanier, Sir John, 47.
Larch trees, unknown in Scotland, 95.
Largie. *See* Macdonald.
Lawson, James, minister in Edinburgh, 158.
Learmonth the prophet, 20.
Leith, 193, 239.
Lenicroich, or Highland shirt, 123.
Lennox tribe, 136 and *note*.
Leslie, Patrick, Provost of Aberdeen, 206.
Letterfinlay. *See* M'Connochey, and M'Martin.
Leven, the, 233.
Leven, Countess of, 70.
—— Earl of, 46.
Leven's regiment, 195.
Lilburn in Braemar, 130.
Lindsay, Robert, 68.
—— Lady Sophia, 233.
Linlithgow, 45.
—— Earl of, 69.
Livingstone, Captain, 71, 181.
—— George Lord, 44, 64.
—— Sir Thomas, 49, 70, 181, 208, 211, 212.
—— Lieut.-Col. Wm., afterwards Lord Kilsyth, 48, 70 and *note*, 174, 178, 181, 199.
Lochaber, 74, 78, 80, invaded by Fergus I., 87; threatened by Mackay, 98; gathering of the clans, 121-164; the clans dispersed, 217-218.
Lochbuy. *See* Maclean, Hector.
Lochcarron. *See* Stewart, Dugald.
Loch Earn, 144.
—— Eil, 80.
—— Fyne, 154 and *note*.
—— Garry, 58, 193, 195.
Lochiel. *See* Cameron, Sir Ewen.
Loch Inch, 179, 180.
Lochinclan Castle, 128.
Loch Laggan, 80 and *note*.
—— Leven, 144.
—— Linnhe, 86.
—— Lochy, 80, 150.
—— Long, 233.
Lochnell. *See* Campbell.
Loch Ness, 56.
—— Rannoch, 74, 75.

INDEX. 265

Loch Treig, 75, 77.
Lochty, 23.
Loire, the, 41.
Lonoch or Lennox, 136 and *note*.
Loogdeae, 180.
Lordburne, 255.
Lord of the Isles, 124-127.
Lorn, Lord, son of 9th Earl of Argyll, banished, 234.
Lorne, 156. *See also* Macdougal, *and* Stewart.
Lossie, the, 51, 160.
Louis XIV., 18, 27, 28.
Lovat, Hugh Fraser, Lord, 137, 149 and *note*.
―― Simon Fraser, Lord, 149 and *note*.
Loyal, Laird of, 177 and *note*.
Lumley, Lord, 11.
Luxembourg, Duke of, 249, 250.

M'ADAM, LIEUT. DAVID, 162.
M'Adams, Captain, 162.
M'Alester, Charles Somerville, of Kennox, 154.
M'Alister, Alex., of Loupe, 154 and *note*.
MacAlisters from Knapdale, 118.
M'Alpin, Kenneth, 13, 86, 136.
M'Connel, Alan, 136.
M'Connochey, Martin, of Letterfinlay, 134.
Macdonald of Auchteraw, 238.
―― of Keppoch, meets Dundee at Inverness, 54; extorts 4000 merks from the town, 127 and *note*; attacks Ruthven Castle, 174; burns Dunachton Castle, 180.
―― of Largie, 138, 140.
―― Alastair, of Glencoe, 124 and *note*.
―― Alexander, of Glencoe, 143.
―― Allan, Captain of Clanranald, 125 and *note*.
―― Donald, of Benbecula, tutor of Clanranald, 125.
―― Sir Donald, of Sleat, 125 and *note*, 171.
―― Sir James, of Sleat, 131.
Macdonalds of Glencoe, 127.
―― of Islay, 118.
―― of Keppoch, 128, 134.
―― of Sleat, 118, 125.
Macdonell, Alastair Dubh, of Glengarry, joins Dundee, 96 and *note*; his speech, 100-105; raises the fiery cross, 118; at Lochaber camp, 122 and *note*; marches in the van on the army leaving camp, 167; at Sheriffmuir, 151.
―― Allan, of Glengarry, 123 and *note*.

Macdonnells of Glengarry, 123-126.
―― of Knoydart, 118, 123, 126.
―― of Moydart, 118, 126.
―― of Rathlin Island, 119.
M'Dougals of Lorne, 124, 143.
M'Eachern, old name of the Dougals of Craignish, 156.
M'Gibbons of the Lennox, 136.
M'Gillery, Charles, 136.
M'Gregor of Boro, arrives too late for Killiecrankie, 136.
―― Col. Donald, signs the bond of the chiefs, 136.
M'Gregors, 136 and *note*.
―― of Glenstray, 136.
Mackay, General Hugh, of Scourie, besieges Edinburgh Castle, 47 and *note*; marches slowly after Dundee, 49; puzzled by the movements of the enemy, 51; joined by the Master of Forbes, 52; advances by the Ness, 58; lingers in the north, 74; threatens Lochaber, 98 and *note*; retreats to Inverness, 109; leaves Inverness and camps at Culnakyle, 112 and *note*; deserters flock to his camp, 113; backed by the strength of foreign soldiery, 114; prepares for battle, 116; fortifies Ruthven Castle, 173; camped at Kirk of Alvie, 176; on approach of Dundee forsakes his camp, 180-181; continues his retreat, 182-186; his movements from 25th May to 5th June 1689, 193; joined by Ramsay, faces about, and marches to meet Dundee, 197-199; his account of the Knockbreck skirmish, 212; returns unsuccessful from his pursuit of Dundee, 217 and *note*.
Mackenzie, Captain, of Sudry, 127.
―― Col., Governor of Tangiers, 126.
―― Alex., of Prestonhall, 149.
―― Penelope, wife of the chief of Clan Ranald, 126.
Mackintoshes, the, 120, 127, 169.
Macknight, Dr. James, 153.
MacLachlan of MacLachlan, 143.
MacLachlans, the, 155 and *note*.
MacLaren of Ardveich, 143.
Maclean, Bishop, of the Isles, 138.
―― of Ardgour, 140, 144.
―― of Kinlochaline, 144.
―― Sir Alan, of Duart, 131.
―― Sir Alex., of Otter, 138 and *note*.
―― Hector, yr. of Lochbuy, in charge of Blair and other prisoners, 61; defeats Mackay's cavalry at Knockbrecht, 209 and *note*.

INDEX.

Maclean, Sir John, of Duart, escorts Blair and other prisoners to Duart Castle, 61, 145; joins Dundee at Lochaber, 137 and *note*, 238.
—— Lauchlane, of Coll, 144.
—— Lauchlane, of Torloisk, 144.
—— Murdoch, of Lochbuy, 140, 210.
Macleans of Coll, 139 and *note*.
—— of Islay, 118.
—— of Jura, 118.
—— of Lochbuy, 140, 144.
—— of Mull, 118.
—— of Torloisk, 139 and *note*.
Macleod of Macleod, 138, 143.
—— of Raasay, 146 and *note*.
Macleods of Raasay, 119, 146.
M'Martin, younger of Letterfinlay, 133 and *note*.
—— Duncan, of Letterfinlay, 134.
M'Martins of Letterfinlay, 127, 129, 131.
Macmillans, the, 145.
Macnabs, the, 136 and *note*.
Macnachtan of Dunderaw, 153 and *note*.
MacNeill of Barra, 144 and *note*.
—— Donald, of Gallachallie, 144.
—— Gilleonan, 145.
Macneills of Barra, 119.
—— of Jura, 118.
Macomer. *See* Dalcomera.
Macpherson, Colonel, of Glentruim, 57.
—— Duncan, of Cluny, 57, 127.
Macphersons of Badenoch, 119.
—— of Cluny, 169.
M'Rory, Amy, wife of the first Lord of the Isles, 123.
—— Angus, chief of the Lamonts, 155.
—— Lachlan, 155.
M'Swyne, Dennis, carries despatches from Dundee to the king, 60, 105, 209.
M'Tavish, Dugald, fiar of Dunardarie, 144.
Mailchu, a Pictish king, 86.
Malcolm, James, of Balbadie, his evidence regarding Hallyburton of Pitcur, 65; Glencoe, Macdonald of Sleat, and Clanranald, 124-126; the wife of Lochiel, 131; Maclean of Lochbuy, 210; Macdonald of Auchteraw, 238.
March, Earl of, 192.
Margaret, St., feast of, 13.
Martins of Letterfinlay. *See* M'Martin.
Mary, Princess, daughter of Robert III., 41.
—— of Modena, 12.

Mary, Queen of Scots, sufferings of, 227.
—— wife of William III., 34.
Maule, Lady Jane, 187.
Maxwell, Mrs., 66.
Mearns, 69.
Meigle, 64, 65, 158.
Menzies, laird of Weem, 143.
—— Duncan, 161.
Merlin as a prophet, 20, 21.
Middleton, Major, 65.
Monmouth, Duke of, joins Turenne, 42.
Monrimmon Muir, 17 and *note*.
Montgomery, Sir James, 188.
Montmorenci, François de. *See* Luxembourg, Duke of.
Montrose, Marquis of, 42, 189.
Moray, Earldom of, 169.
Moror, family of, 126.
Morven, 156.
Moydart, stronghold of the Clanranalds in, 118.
Mudortach, John, assumes the title of Captain of Clanranald, 126.
Mull, 119, 137, 210, 237.
Mulroy, battle of, 127.
Murray, Captain, 181.
—— Lieutenant, 238.
—— Lord, 50, 59, 164, 168, 193, 194.
—— Lord James, 162.
—— Sir John, of Drumcairn, 62.
—— Sir Patrick, 65.
—— William, execution of, 130.
Murthlac parish, 206.

NEACHTON, founder of the house of Macpherson, 180.
Nectan, king of the Picts, 179.
Newton of Doune. *See* Edmonstone, James.
Nicholas, St., knights of, 252.
Nisbet, Lieutenant, gives evidence regarding the Earl of Dunfermline, 53; Hallyburton of Pitcur, 65; Edmonstone of Newton, 160; Clelland of Faskin, 161; Johnston, 163.
North Water bridge, 50.
Notre Dame, 249.

OAT CAKES, 91.
Octomor. *See* Campbell, Archibald.
O'Farrel's fusiliers, 239.
Og, Angus, a supporter of Robert Bruce, 124, 125.
Ogilvie, Chancellor, 192.
Ogilvy, Captain, 69.
—— Sir David, of Clova, 177.
Oldman's coffee-house, 61.
Oliphant, Allan, 160.

INDEX. 267

Oliphant, William, 70.
Ormond, Duke of, deserts from the army of the King, 33.
Osbourne, James, a trooper with Dundee, 159.
Otter. *See* Maclean, Sir Alexander.
Owen, the plain of, 207 and *note*.
Owenstone, Capt., killed at Knockbrecht, 213-214 and *note*.

PAISLEY, 47.
Patrick, St., 86.
Pentland hills, 232 and *note*.
Perth, 63, 69, 109, 193, 210.
—— Earl of, a prisoner in Stirling Castle, 62.
Philip, James, of Almerieclose, follows the Graham, 45 and *note*; bears the royal standard, 162 and *note*; meets Maclean of Lochbuy after his victory at Knockbrecht, and leads him into the camp, 216.
Philiphaugh, battle of, 189.
Pitcur. *See* Hallyburton, David.
Pitenen, 69.
Pollock of Pollock, 60, 145, 181.
Presbyterians, character given them by Dundee, 218-235.
Presmochora, 57 and *note*.
Prodigies, 20.
Provensal, Sergeant, 199 and *note*.
Pursell, Colonel, 237, 240 and *note*.

QUARLES, FRANCIS, 251.
Quesne, Monsieur de, 237.

RAASAY, 118, 146.
Raitts Castle, 169 and *note*, 176.
Ramsay, Hon. George, 109, 192 and *note*.
—— Gilbert, 163 and *note*.
—— Margaret, 192.
Rannoch, 195, 217.
Rathlin Island, 119.
Ray's *Willughby*, 84.
Reid, 163 and *note*.
—— General, 163.
Religious controversy, 7.
Renfrewshire, 233.
Renton of Renton, 65 and *note*; 159 and *note*.
Richborough, 213 and *note*.
Robertson Clan, 195 and *note*.
Robertsons of Straloch, 163.
Rochester, 43.
Roderick of the Isles, 125.
Rollo, Andrew Lord, 69 and *note*.
Rose, Katharine, of Kilravock, 150.
Rosene, General, 236.
Ross, Lord, 66, 69.

Rothiemurchus, 182 and *note*, 211.
Rottenrow in Dundee, 66.
Roy, the, 80, 82, 91, 94, 218.
Royal Scots, 239.
Royal Scots Fusiliers, 239.
Rullion Green, battle of, 232.
Rumbold, a Lieut. of Archibald, 9th Earl of Argyll, 233.
Russel, Admiral, 11.
Ruthven Castle, 61, 109, 112, 127, 172 and *note*, 174, 176, 193, 212.
Rutupiæ, 213.

SARDINIANS, 97.
Sarrian purple, 215 and *note*.
Scone, 62 and *note*, 86.
Scotch Dragoons, 51, 70, 199, 211.
Scotch Dutch Brigade, 98.
Scotland, antiquity of kingdom of, 86; succession of kings of, 86.
Scots Greys, 157, 211.
Scott, 162 and *note*.
—— of Scotstarvet, 62.
—— Andrew, 163.
—— Colonel Andrew, 163.
—— Lieut. John, 162.
—— Walter, of Tushielaw, 163.
Scotus, Barony of, 124.
Scourie. *See* Mackay, General Hugh.
Scrymgeours, Earls of Dundee, 192.
Seaforth, Lord, 239.
Seidlaws, the, 49, 66.
Seneff, battle of, 201.
Seton, James. *See* Dunfermline, Earl of.
Sheriffmuir, 137, 144, 151.
Skye, 118, 125.
Sleat. *See* Macdonald, Sir Donald.
Solemn League and Covenant, 189.
Sortes Virgilianæ, 229.
Spean, the, 80.
Speckled Hill, the, 211.
Spey, the, 51, 53, 57, 98, 109, 112, 167, 169, 182, 210, 215.
Spottiswood, Sir Robert, 130.
St. Andrews, 162.
St. Coemgen. *See* Kilcummin.
St. Cyrus, 48.
St. Germains, 36, 137, 239.
Stalkair Castle, 143.
Steenkerke, battle of, 250.
Stewart, Provost, of Elgin, 51.
—— Charles, yr. of Ballechin, gives evidence as to Edmonstone of Newton, 160, 195.
—— Dugald, of Lochcarron, 144.
—— Duncan, of Appin, 142.
—— Sir John, Lord of Lorne, 143.
—— John, of Ardsheal, tutor of Appin, 142, 143.

Stewart, Patrick, of Ballechin, 59, 194 and *note*.
—— Robert, of Appin, 142 and *note*.
Stewarts of Appin, 143.
Stirling, 45.
—— Bridge, 44.
—— Castle, 62.
Stobhall Castle, 62 and *note*, 65.
Stormont, Lord, 62.
Straloch, 163.
Stranraer, 65.
Strathbogie, 52, 208.
Strathdearn, 169.
Strath Deveron, 183.
Strathearn, 144.
Strath Errick, 56, 146.
Strathmore, Earl of, 49.
Strathnairn, 169.
Strathnaver, Lord, 237.
Strathspey, 109, 112, 138, 151, 217.
Strickmartin, the laird of, 65.
Strondour. *See* Campbell, Alex.
Struan, 237.
Sulphur in Loch Ness, 56.
Suy Hill, 193, 196 and *note*.
Sweating images, 20.

TANNACHY, 135 and *note*.
Tarbet, 233.
Tarf, vale of, 56.
Tartars expelled from Hungary, 2.
Tavern wines, 223.
Tay, the, 74.
Tealing, 49, 66.
Terranova, battle of, 245.
Thomas the Rhymer, 20.
Thomson, Sir Thomas, of Duddingston, 158.
Tippermuir, battle at, 189.
Tomintoul, 207.
Torbay, 31.
Torloisk. *See* Maclean of Torloisk.
Towie-Barclay, 160.
Tulloch of Tannachy, 135.
Tummel, the, 20, 58 and *note*.
Tummel bridge, 75.

Turenne, General, 41; joined by Duke of Monmouth, 42.
Turks expelled from Hungary, 2.
Tushielaw, 163.
Tyrconnell, General, 28, 29.
Tyre, 215.

UNIFORMS, 213 and *note*, 216.
Urquhart, 151.
Ury. *See* Barclay, Robert.

VALCOUR, battle of, 192.
Vane, Sir Harry, 189.
Venton, 65 and *note*, 159 and *note*.
Vienna, siege of, 1683, 2.

WALLACE, Colonel, defeated at Rullion Green, 232.
—— William, prisoner in Dundee, 70.
—— Sir William, of Craigie, 237.
Wane, Captain, killed at Knockbrecht, 211.
Weem, the laird of. *See* Menzies.
Weem Castle, or Castle Menzies, 74.
Wemyss, Countess of, 70.
Wigtown martyrs, 162.
William the Lion, interview with Gilchrist of Angus, 49.
William the Silent, 14 and *note*.
William III., 11, 14; declared heir, 30; prepares his fleet and army, 31; lands in Torbay, 31; publishes his manifesto, 32; meets James VII. in battle, 33; William and Mary proclaimed King and Queen, 46; raises levies for Flemish wars, 97 and *note*; gives a commission to Maclean of Duart, 137; rescue of William by Claverhouse at Seneff, 201.
Wines, sale of, in Edinburgh, 223-224.
Worcester, battle of, 130.

YORK, DUKE OF, urges Montrose to secure Claverhouse for his troop of horse, 42.

Scottish History Society.

THE EXECUTIVE.

President.
THE EARL OF ROSEBERY, LL.D.

Chairman of Council.
DAVID MASSON, LL.D., Professor of English Literature, Edinburgh University.

Council.
W. F. SKENE, D.C.L., LL.D., Historiographer - Royal for Scotland.
Colonel P. DODS.
J. R. FINDLAY, Esq.
GEORGE BURNETT, LL.D., Lyon-King-of-Arms.
J. T. CLARK, Keeper of the Advocates' Library.
THOMAS DICKSON, LL.D., Curator of the Historical Department, Register House.
Right Rev. JOHN DOWDEN, D.D., Bishop of Edinburgh.
J. KIRKPATRICK, LL.B., Professor of History, Edinburgh University.
ÆNEAS J. G. MACKAY, LL.D., Sheriff of Fife.
Sir ARTHUR MITCHELL, K.C.B., M.D., LL.D.
G. W. T. OMOND, Advocate.
JOHN RUSSELL, Esq.

Corresponding Members of the Council.
OSMUND AIRY, Esq., Birmingham; Very Rev. J. CUNNINGHAM, D.D., Principal of St. Mary's College, St. Andrews; Professor GEORGE GRUB, LL.D., Aberdeen; Rev. A. W. C. HALLEN, Alloa; Rev. W. D. MACRAY, Oxford; Professor A. F. MITCHELL, D.D., St. Andrews; Professor W. ROBERTSON SMITH, Cambridge; Rev. Dr. SPROTT, North Berwick; Professor J. VEITCH, LL.D., Glasgow.

Hon. Treasurer.
J. J. REID, B.A., Advocate, Queen's Remembrancer.

Hon. Secretary.
T. G. LAW, Librarian, Signet Library.

RULES.

1. The object of the Society is the discovery and printing, under selected editorship, of unpublished documents illustrative of the civil, religious, and social history of Scotland. The Society will also undertake, in exceptional cases, to issue translations of printed works of a similar nature, which have not hitherto been accessible in English.

2. The number of Members of the Society shall be limited to 400.

3. The affairs of the Society shall be managed by a Council consisting of a Chairman, Treasurer, Secretary, and twelve elected Members, five to make a quorum. Three of the twelve elected members shall retire annually by ballot, but they shall be eligible for re-election.

4. The Annual Subscription to the Society shall be One Guinea. The publications of the Society shall not be delivered to any Member whose Subscription is in arrear, and no Member shall be permitted to receive more than one copy of the Society's publications.

5. The Society will undertake the issue of its own publications, *i.e.* without the intervention of a publisher or any other paid agent.

6. The Society will issue yearly two octavo volumes of about 320 pages each.

7. An Annual General Meeting of the Society shall be held on the last Tuesday in October.

8. Two stated Meetings of the Council shall be held each year, one on the last Tuesday of May, the other on the Tuesday preceding the day upon which the Annual General Meeting shall be held. The Secretary, on the request of three Members of the Council, shall call a special meeting of the Council.

9. Editors shall receive 20 copies of each volume they edit for the Society.

10. The owners of Manuscripts published by the Society will also be presented with a certain number of copies.

11. The Annual Balance-Sheet, Rules, and List of Members shall be printed.

12. No alteration shall be made in these Rules except at a General Meeting of the Society. A fortnight's notice of any alteration to be proposed shall be given to the Members of the Council.

PUBLICATIONS.

Works already Issued.

1887.

1. BISHOP POCOCKE'S TOURS IN SCOTLAND, 1747-1760. Edited by D. W. KEMP.

2. DIARY OF AND GENERAL EXPENDITURE BOOK OF WILLIAM CUNNINGHAM OF CRAIGENDS, 1673-1680. Edited by the Rev. JAMES DODDS, D.D.

1888.

3. PANURGI PHILO-CABALLI SCOTI GRAMEIDOS LIBRI SEX.—THE GRAMEID: an heroic poem descriptive of the Campaign of Viscount Dundee in 1689, by JAMES PHILIP of Almerieclose. Edited, with Translation and Notes, by the Rev. A. D. MURDOCH.

4. THE REGISTER OF THE KIRK SESSION OF ST. ANDREWS. Part I. 1559-1582. Edited by D. HAY FLEMING.

In Preparation.

DIARY OF THE REV. JOHN MILL, Minister of Dunrossness, Sandwick, and Cunningsburgh, in Shetland, 1742-1805, with original documents, local records, and historical notices relating to the District. Edited by GILBERT GOUDIE, F.S.A. Scot.

A NARRATIVE OF MR. JAMES NIMMO, A COVENANTER. 1654-1708. Edited by W. G. SCOTT MONCRIEFF, Advocate.

THE REGISTER OF THE KIRK SESSION OF ST. ANDREWS. Part II. 1583-1600. Edited by D. HAY FLEMING.

GLAMIS PAPERS; including the 'BOOK OF RECORD,' written by PATRICK, FIRST EARL OF STRATHMORE (1647-95), the DIARY OF LADY HELEN MIDDLETON, his wife, and other documents, illustrating the social life of the seventeenth century. Edited from the original manuscripts at Glamis Castle by A. H. MILLAR.

JOHN MAJOR'S DE GESTIS SCOTORUM (1521). Translated by ARCHIBALD CONSTABLE, with a Memoir of the author by ÆNEAS J. G. MACKAY, Advocate.

THE DIARY OF ANDREW HAY OF STONE, NEAR BIGGAR, AFTERWARDS OF CRAIGNETHAN CASTLE, 1659-60. Edited by A. G. REID, F.S.A. Scot., from a manuscript in his possession.

THE RECORDS OF THE COMMISSION OF THE GENERAL ASSEMBLY, 1646-1662. Edited by the Rev. JAMES CHRISTIE, D.D., with an Introduction by the Rev. Professor MITCHELL, D.D.

In Contemplation.

'THE HISTORY OF MY LIFE, extracted from Journals I kept since I was twenty-six years of age, interspersed with short accounts of the most remarkable public affairs that happened in my time, especially such as I had some immediate concern in,' 1702-1754. By Sir JOHN CLERK OF PENICUIK, Baron of the Exchequer and Commissioner of the Union, etc. Edited from the original manuscript in Penicuik House by J. M. GRAY.

SIR THOMAS CRAIG'S DE UNIONE REGNORUM BRITANNIÆ. Edited with an English Translation from the unpublished manuscript in the Advocates' Library.

THE DIARIES OR ACCOUNT BOOKS OF SIR JOHN FOULIS OF RAVELSTON, (1679-1707), and the ACCOUNT BOOK OF DAME HANNAH ERSKINE (1675-1699). Edited by the Rev. A. W. CORNELIUS HALLEN.

REPORT

OF THE

FIRST ANNUAL MEETING

OF THE

SCOTTISH HISTORY SOCIETY.

The first Annual Meeting of the Scottish History Society was held on Tuesday, October 25, 1887, in the Professional Hall, George Street, under the presidency of Lord Rosebery.

The SECRETARY read the Report of the Council as follows :—

The first financial year of the Scottish History Society began on November 1 of last year. The members, exclusive of public libraries subscribing to the Society's publications, had then reached the number 400, to which it had been agreed to limit the Society ; and there are already numerous applicants who desire to be admitted as vacancies may occur.

The list of members is printed with the second volume of this year's publications, now in the binders' hands. But it must be remembered that no member who has not paid his subscription is entitled to receive these publications, and notice is therefore now given that the names of all who do not remit their subscription for 1886-7 before the end of December will be erased from the roll of members.

The volumes now ready are Bishop Pococke's Tours in Scotland, 1747-1760, and the Diary of Cunningham of Craigends, 1673-1680. Pococke's work is important as the record of an experienced traveller, whose description of Scotland preceded that of Pennant by several years. It has been carefully edited from the hitherto unpublished MS. in the British Museum by Mr. D. W. Kemp, who has spared no pains to gather topographical information in illustration of the text. He has also prefixed to the work a biographical sketch of the author.

Cunningham's Diary has been edited by the Rev. Dr. Dodds of Corstorphine. This journal of the expenditure of a Renfrewshire laird, like all such household books, is interesting as an exhibition of curious details in the social life and habits of a country gentleman of the time. It has, moreover, a statistical value, as a record of prices and wages. The thanks of the Society are due to Mr. Alexander Mackenzie, of Paisley, for the loan of the MS. to Dr. Dodds, and the permission to publish it.

This second volume is comparatively small in size. The two together make up about 640 pages, and it is expected that the volumes in preparation for next year will rather exceed than fall below the promised amount.

The next publication of the Society will be the Grameid, a Latin epic descriptive of Claverhouse's campaigns, by an eyewitness, James Philip or Philips of Almerieclose. The manuscript was made use of by Drummond in his Memoirs of Locheill. The Rev. Canon Murdoch, the editor, has kindly undertaken to add an abridged English prose translation of the poem, as well as illustrative notes. A great portion of the text has already been sent to the printer.

Mr. Hay Fleming has also in the press a portion of the Registers of the Kirk-Session and other Presbytery Records of St. Andrews, now in the University Library of that city. The early date to which these Registers go back, and the prominent ecclesiastical position of St. Andrews at the time, give to this collection an exceptional value. The complete work will form two volumes. The first volume, covering the period 1559 to 1582, will be included in the Society's next year's issue.

Mr. Gilbert Goudie, the treasurer of the Society of Antiquaries, is preparing an edition of the Diary of the Rev. John Mill, Minister of Dunrossness in Shetland, 1742-1805; and

Mr. W. G. Scott-Moncrieff, advocate, promises the Narrative of Mr. James Nimmo, a Covenanter. These two autobiographical memoirs will be bound and issued as separate volumes, but as they are both short pieces, they will be counted together as a single publication for the year 1888-9.

The Council hopes also shortly to publish portions at least of the Records of the Commission of the General Assembly at the time when the General Assembly itself was dissolved by Cromwell. The contents of these volumes have been little made known. They describe the state of the Church at a critical period, and when the history of the Church was the history of the nation.

The main object of the Society will continue to be the editing of unpublished manuscripts illustrating Scottish history. It is, however, proposed to amend Rule 1, by adding to it the words: "The Society will also undertake, in exceptional cases, to issue translations of printed works of a similar nature, which have not hitherto been accessible in English."

If this is approved by the General Meeting, the Council proposes to publish an English version of the *De Gestis Scotorum*, or the History of the Scottish Nation, by John Major or Mair, a Scottish divine and historian, who died in 1550. His History was first printed in Latin at Paris in 1521, and has never appeared in English. Mr. Archibald Constable will translate, and, together with Mr. T. G. Law, will be responsible for the editorship of the work, and Mr. Æneas Mackay will prefix to it a biographical account of the author.

The Council will be grateful for any information or suggestion regarding the existence or publication of historical manuscripts, and is confident that when the aims of the Society become better known, the possessors of such documents will be readily induced to bring them to light under its auspices.

According to Rule 3, three members of the Council retire by rotation, and it was proposed by the Council that Mr. Maitland Thomson, Professor Taylor, and Dr. Skene should retire, that Dr. Skene should be re-elected, and that Colonel Dods and Mr. J. R. Findlay should be elected to fill the places of the other two members.

Lord ROSEBERY in moving the adoption of the Report said :—

I think you will agree with me that this is strictly a business meeting, and is not intended for a display of the graces of oratory. We would rather welcome from any member here present suggestions as to our future work, which is, of course, only in a rudimentary condition at present. The first point in connection with the report I have to call your attention to is the amendment of the rules as regards the translation of printed works which have not yet been accessible in English. That seems to me a clear improvement on the first rule, and I have no doubt the Society will be glad to have it. Then, with regard to the change in the Council, it is quite clear that the Council must have an annual change made in it. All experience tells us that it does not do for a Council to assume an absolutely stagnant form, but that it must have a stream running through it, or else it is likely to be rather dull. We had to make three vacancies by the rule, but we thought we should be obeying the intention and the spirit of the rule by making practically two vacancies and re-electing Dr. Skene, whose authority and name are absolutely, in my opinion, indispensable to the work of the Society. Then, I hope that this meeting will bring before the public the work of our Society. We do not need that, in the sense in which most societies wish their work to be brought before the public—in the sense of inviting additional members to join—because we have already more applications than we can deal with in that respect. But what I am anxious about, and what is really the fundamental idea of the Society, is this—that we should have, from owners of old charter-chests and old family documents, proffers of these documents, which it is the object of the Society to preserve from destruction. A vast amount of the characteristic relics of the past, and of the past century more particularly, are in existence in Scotland beyond a doubt; and if no society takes the pains to collect these together and print them for the sake of permanence, there is great danger that they will be altogether lost. I do not suppose that anybody ever had anything to do with matters of this kind without being aware that owing to the absolute carelessness and recklessness of some people to whom these collections were intrusted they were lost, they were destroyed by rats and mildew, or put into old chests along with paid bills and things of that sort, from whence they are never disinterred; and our great object is to invite proprietors who may care about their records, and who may wish to have them preserved, to offer them for the examination, and, if possible, for printing by the Society. In connection with that, I should be prepared to propose to the Society an amendment on the rules, which, I think, would offer an inducement to the proprietors of such papers to offer them to us. We at present offer twenty copies as the property of the editors of these volumes, and that is, I think, a very fair and adequate arrangement. But I do not think we have made any provision for those to whom the papers belong, and it seems to me that it is well worth the consideration of the Society whether we should not offer to the proprietors of MSS. who are willing to place them at the disposal of the Society twenty or thirty copies, which would be at their sole disposal, and which would make it an object for proprietors to offer them for printing or publication. There are many persons, I do not doubt, who have very interesting diaries and journals and records of the past, and who would be very glad to see them printed, and to be able to have a few copies to give to the members of the family whom they concern. They might not be in a position to print them for themselves, and they might gladly avail themselves of the instrumentality of the Society to secure that family publicity, if I may so say, which they desire. I think that is well worth the attention of the Society; and I trust that those members who know of manuscript journals or collections of letters, or any papers throwing light on the domestic history of Scotland of the past, will not lose any opportunity of impressing on the proprietors of these collections what a chance is offered by this Society of rendering them permanently valuable to the historian of the present and of the future. I think I may congratulate you most warmly on the appearance of your two first volumes. They will vie with the publications of any of the old book-clubs of Scotland, both in appearance and printing. To the future volumes we shall append a short private report of the proceedings of the Society, so that we may not be bothered with those little fly-leaves and those pamphlets which are difficult to preserve. But I think that even in the present we have great reason to be proud of our publications; and I must congratulate the Society upon them. I have nothing more to say about the report, except to move its adoption, and to ask any members present to favour us with any practical suggestions as to developing the further utility of the Society.

Professor MASSON seconded the Motion for the approval of the report. He remarked that it was a good many months ago since he had the opportunity of inspecting a number of folio manuscript volumes kept in the library of the Assembly Hall, in Edinburgh, and he was surprised to find what amount of information was on record appertaining to times respecting which printed documents were very scarce. There was a great deal there in manuscript which, he had no doubt, was already in print; but it seemed to him from the brief inspection he was able to give to this mass of volumes that there was a great deal of matter hitherto not published, especially pertaining to that portion of the history of Scotland during which the General Assembly, which was the centre of ecclesiastical history, was in abeyance. They knew that the last General Assembly, of which there were distinct records, was the Assembly of 1649. From that they had no regular Assembly with records of it until 1690. There could be no records of General Assemblies for a large portion of that interval. But from 1649 onwards—say, to the Restoration—there was a great deal of ecclesiastical activity represented by the Commission of the Assembly. Twice or thrice in 1650, 1651, and 1652 there were attempts to hold an Assembly, and there were many records of these attempts; but in 1652 Scotland was incorporated with the English Commonwealth, and General Assemblies then were impossible. Alluding to the proposed extension of the basis of the Society by publishing translations of rare Latin works, Professor Masson said that a good example of the propriety of the proposal was that old book, the *De Gestis Scotorum* by John Major or Mair referred to in the report—about the most interesting and queer old book existing with regard to Scottish history, and which did not exist in English. Professor Masson added that their friend Mr. Archibald Constable would have a very difficult task in translating the Latin, because it was execrable Latin, although it was capital stuff. There was no direction, "Laugh here," in the margin, but he would have to find out when he is to laugh, and when he is to tell his readers to laugh.

Dr. W. F. SKENE, Historiographer-Royal for Scotland, said he hoped the Society would agree to the suggested amendment to their first rule, so as to enable them to print translations from historical works bearing on Scottish history. This would enable the Society to complete the series of "The Historians of Scotland," which was undertaken by Mr. Douglas, the Publisher, and which was terminated before the scheme was completely carried out. The scheme was to publish the texts, with translations, of all the historians of Scotland prior to the work of Hector Boece; and the only one omitted was this very work of John Major or Mair. To make a simple translation would not, he thought, be altogether satisfactory. It would be necessary to form a correct text before they could translate from it, and the Latin text ought to be printed along with the translation. Dr. Skene further suggested that in the same volume might be included a small chronicle in Norman-French which existed in the Library of St. Geneviève, in Paris. It was a curious work, and contained, in initial letters, portraits of the Scottish kings.

The Report, with the proposed amendments to the Rules, was unanimously adopted.

Messrs. Richardson and Traquair Dickson, W.S., were appointed Auditors, and the proceedings terminated.

ABSTRACT of the TREASURER'S ACCOUNTS for year to 1st November 1887.

CHARGE.

400 Subscribers at £1, 1s.,	£420 0 0	
30 Libraries, at do.	32 11 0	
	£452 11 0	
Interest on Bank Account,	2 8 10	
Sum of Charge,	£454 19 10	

DISCHARGE.

1. *Preliminary Expenses—*
   Printing and posting Circulars, List of
      Members, etc., ... £40 1 2
   Stationery (including Minute-books), 2 16 0
   Postages of Secretary and Treasurer, 5 19 7
   Charges on Cheques, . . . 0 15 6
   Clerical work, ... 2 0 6

                      Carry forward,   £51 12 9

Brought forward,	£51 12 9		
For examining and reporting on MS. collections,	2 3 6		
Designing, engraving, and electrotyping the Society's device for title-page,	6 8 6		
		£60 4 9	

II. *Expenses of 'Pocockc's Tours'—*

Printing and paper per contract,	£86 16 0		
Corrections and extras,	51 0 0		
Printing illustrations,	4 18 0		
Binding,	17 16 3		
Transcript,	17 0 0		
Artist and zincotypes,	26 10 0		
		204 0 3	

III. *Expenses of 'Cunningham's Diary'—*

Printing and paper,	£38 15 0		
Corrections and extras,	17 19 0		
Binding,	17 16 3		
		74 10 3	
	Expenditure,	£338 15 3	
IV. 47 Subscriptions in arrear,		49 7 0	
Balance in Treasurer's hands,	£68 19 7		
Less 2 Subscriptions received in advance for 1887-8,	2 2 0		
		66 17 7	
	Sum of Discharge,	£454 19 10	

EDINBURGH, *7th November* 1887.—The Auditors have examined the Treasurer's Accounts for the year ending 1st November current, and find them correct and properly vouched, with a Balance of Sixty-eight Pounds Nineteen Shillings and Sevenpence, Stg. due by him to the Society.

        RALPH RICHARDSON.
        WM. TRAQUAIR DICKSON.

www.ingramcontent.com/pod-product-compliance
Lightning Source LLC
Chambersburg PA
CBHW030007240426
43672CB00007B/854